Visual Basic
an object oriented approach

We work with leading authors to develop the
strongest educational materials in computer science,
bringing cutting-edge thinking and best learning
practice to a global market.

Under a range of well-known imprints, including
Addison-Wesley, we craft high quality print and
electronic publications which help readers to
understand and apply their content,
whether studying or at work.

To find out more about the complete range of our
publishing please visit us on the World Wide Web at:
www.pearsoneduc.com

Visual Basic
an object oriented approach

Alistair McMonnies

 Addison-Wesley

An imprint of **Pearson Education**

Harlow, England · London · New York · Reading, Massachusetts · San Francisco · Toronto · Don Mills, Ontario · Sydney
Tokyo · Singapore · Hong Kong · Seoul · Taipei · Cape Town · Madrid · Mexico City · Amsterdam · Munich · Paris · Milan

Pearson Education Limited
Edinburgh Gate
Harlow
Essex CM20 2JE
England

and Associated Companies throughout the world

Visit us on the World Wide Web at:
www.pearsoneduc.com

First published 2001

© Pearson Education Limited 2001

ISBN 0 201 64863 6

British Library Cataloguing-in-Publication Data
A catalogue record for this book can be obtained from the British Library

Library of Congress Cataloging-in-Publication Data
McMonnies, Alistair, 1955-
    Visual Basic : an object oriented approach / Alistair McMonnies.
        p. cm.
    ISBN 0-201-64863-6 (pbk.)
    1. Object-oriented programming (Computer science) 2. Microsoft Visual BASIC. I.
Title.
QA76.64.M395 2000
005.265–dc21

                                                                        00-064310

10 9 8 7 6 5 4 3
06 05 04 03 02

Typeset by 43 in 10/12pt Times
Printed in Great Britain by Henry Ling Limited, at the Dorset Press, Dorchester, DT1 1HD

CONTENTS

LIST OF FIGURES

LIST OF TABLES

COMPANION WEB SITE

ACKNOWLEDGEMENTS

The publishers are grateful to Microsoft Corporation for permission to reproduce
copyright material: Visual Basic icons © Microsoft Corporation

PREFACE

Object oriented programming with Visual Basic

During the initial proposal stages for this book, one reviewer (appointed by a less enlightened publisher than Pearson) bluntly stated 'you can not do object oriented programming with Visual Basic'. Object orientation, like programming in general, fires up personal prejudices and divides people into opinionated factions.

I think it is safe to say that that reviewer missed the point completely with his narrow view of object *oriented* programming. Object oriented programming, or OOP, is a way of developing software in which the relationships between the components in the real-world systems being modelled are preserved as much as possible in the software. The idea is to simplify and rationalize software design, not to promote dogma, or a specific language, or even a specific design methodology. James Rumbagh and his collaborators demonstrated this ably in the standard textbook on the object modelling technique, in which they used SQL (a set-oriented database management and query language) to build one example object oriented system.

Visual Basic *does* do object oriented programming – rather well if the results of a great many Visual Basic development efforts are to be taken as evidence. There are a number of specific constructs in the Visual Basic language that are there purely to enable and promote OOP. What Visual Basic does not do is try to emulate C++, or Eiffel, or SmallTalk, or any number of other OOP-capable languages. Microsoft, the developers of Visual Basic, initially produced Visual Basic as a language for developers of Windows programs. As their programming system grew through several versions, they decided that the object oriented core of Visual Basic should be made more accessible to programmers who used the language. Instead of being just a product of OOP, Visual Basic was turned into a major exponent of it.

How to read this book

If you are completely new to programming, I suggest you might get the most from this book by reading through it in the order of the chapters, and working through each of the end of chapter exercises. To work through the exercises, you will of course need a copy of Visual Basic and a Windows-capable PC to run it on, but Microsoft have made limited but free copies of Visual Basic available through a number of channels. All of the free versions are capable enough to support all of the exercises in the book.

If you have done some programming before, then an alternative, more selective approach may be more suitable. There are two possible scenarios. Firstly, you might have programmed in other languages (object oriented or not) and be new to Visual Basic. Secondly, you might have some experience with Visual Basic, but feel the need to learn how to use its OOP capabilities. In either case, there will be chapters you should be able to read through quickly, and others that will contain core material that is essential to your understanding. The list of chapters and descriptions of their contents at the end of this preface should be your guide here.

No matter what your experience of programming and/or Visual Basic is, I do strongly suggest that you work through the end of chapter exercises and, if you have the time and inclination, experiment with the sample fragments of code sprinkled throughout the text. Programming is, above all else, a practical subject. No book, no matter how well written, will be able to teach you to program unless you put the printed theory into practice. Programming is a craft, like crochet or woodturning. You must practise it to gain enough experience to become competent in it. Without practice, you may well retain all of the lessons, but these will be no more than dry facts.

The structure of this book

1. The software development life-cycle

This chapter describes the *process* by which software is developed. It points out that software development is more than just programming and proposes some alternative approaches to the creation of programs. Object orientation and its place in the software development life-cycle is described.

2. Designing software systems

Software design is akin to architecture, or should be. In this chapter, the fundamental features of OOP are described, and these features are then used to show how components in an object oriented system interact.

3. Making objects work

The internal structure of objects is described, and used to illustrate how the concepts of a required software system can be turned into an object oriented design, and from there a program. Simple example classes are developed.

4. Simple programming in Visual Basic

The details of programming – variables, expressions, statements and subroutines – are explained in detail. How and where these constructs would be used in an object oriented program is described. In passing, the constructs and rules of modular programming are covered.

5. Structured programming

The structures common to most forms of programming are at the core of OOP. This chapter covers these necessary features of programming – selection, iteration, data structures and error handling.

6. Object modelling the Visual Basic way

This chapter goes into the details of Visual Basic style OOP. How to create and destroy objects, how to develop object interfaces and how to build *object models* are described.

7. Graphical user-interfaces

No book on Visual Basic would be complete without at least an overview of Visual Basic's GUI-building facilities. In this chapter, we examine the general form of Visual Basic UI elements, controls, and their interface features. We also look at forms (Visual Basic window designs) and how they fit into the object oriented paradigm. An example object oriented system from a previous chapter is given a form-based user-interface, and the end of chapter exercise follows this through for a previous chapter's exercise.

8. Objects as building blocks

In a book on programming that did not espouse the object oriented model, this chapter would have the phrase *Data Structures* in its title. The chapter's purpose is to demonstrate how complex models of information can be constructed using a small number of predefined components for managing groups of objects. Several ways of building structured object models are described and examples developed, with the advantages and disadvantages of each style spelled out.

9. Persistence

Persistence is crucial to any type of programming. It is the facility to save program data to some permanent storage medium so that it can be retrieved when the program is run at a later time. We examine two different forms of persistence – the use of streams (object oriented files) and the use of relational databases. The advantages and disadvantages of each are described, and working examples of each are developed.

10. Polymorphism

Polymorphism is the hallmark of true object oriented programming. While OOP can do much to improve the structure of a program, it is polymorphism, the facility that allows the programmer to create completely interchangeable software components and generalize the code that uses them, that brings the most highly prized benefits. In this chapter, we look at simple changes that can be made to existing code to introduce polymorphism, and then go on to develop a fully polymorphic class hierarchy in a graphical drawing application.

11. Patterns in object oriented programming

Software patterns offer a relatively new approach to program development. The principle is simple enough – look for features that occur in many common programs, and then develop these into abstract forms that can be reused easily. By doing this, we can remove much of the otherwise repetitive design effort required for applications development, and gain the advantage of knowing that the design elements we reuse are correct and more likely to produce bug-free solutions. Visual Basic lends itself easily to the pattern approach to software development.

12. Creating and using ActiveX objects

In this final chapter, we look at how Visual Basic can be used to create Common Object Model components. The Component Object Model, or COM, is Microsoft's mechanism for creating and using objects among different applications programs and the operating system. A COM component is a design for an object that can be accessed via Windows, the operating system. COM allows applications programs to make use of external software components so that their original feature set can be extended.

Finally...

Pearson hosts a web-site to support this book. Find it at www.booksites.net/mcmonnies. All of the example programs are available in a downloadable format. Additional self-assessment questions and answers, slides and lab sheets are available for teachers who wish to use the book and back it up with lectures and labs. By using this site and providing feedback, I hope to maintain a useful resource to newcomers to Visual Basic and object oriented programming.

Every journey starts with a single step – read Chapter 1 now.

Alistair McMonnies, 11 May 2000

CHAPTER 1

The software development life-cycle

This chapter describes the way that computer programs should be developed, by spelling out the different stages in their construction. Software, the code and data that make up computer programs, is described in terms of the requirements it must meet, and alternative construction cycles are proposed.

By the end of this chapter, you should be able to:

- describe the principles governing the use of the software life-cycle,

- describe several forms of software life-cycle,

- develop a simple software requirements specification,

- describe the key features of an algorithm,

- decompose a statement of software requirements into a detailed step-by-step task description.

1.1   Introduction to software

The craft of computer programming has been developing for more than 40 years. This is a small fraction of the time that many other engineering disciplines have had to mature. However, in that brief period there has been an unparalleled amount of progress, so that now, at the beginning of a new millennium, we take for granted that the computer is the enabling tool that will deliver techniques to further every other branch of science and technology.

The reason for this is not difficult to explain. Computer programs allow us to mechanize a process that drives progress – human thought. Before computers, experimental research and development work was continually punctuated by periods in which results had to be worked out in longhand by humans. Every experiment would require a battery of calculations to validate it; in every survey a sea of statistics had to be analyzed. Computers allowed the pace of research and development work to quicken by making the calculation of results almost instantaneous in many cases.

Today, computers are used in business and industry as well as in research and development. They control industrial processes and they automate business processes. More and more, the pace of economic and industrial development is fuelled by the use of computers.

Computers need instructions to do their work. A computer alone is useless. To make it do work, we have to tell it what to do, and how to do it. For this we use software. In many situations, we can buy software off the shelf that will do important work for us. Word processors allow us to create documents, spreadsheets to perform calculations and analyze information, databases to store information and retrieve the parts of it that we need when we need it. There are also software systems to help us with communications, time management, publishing, illustration and design, and a great many other tasks besides.

However, the companies that develop computer software have a harder job providing us with software that will perform highly specialized tasks for us. Every commercial or industrial venture is different, and each would almost certainly make different requirements of a software system that was to be designed to automate it or part of it. While there is a great deal of choice when we wish to buy a word-processor, spreadsheet, or some other tool that can be used by a mass market, there is generally none when we look for a software system that will perform exactly the right job to support our very specific business or other needs. This hole in the market supports thousands of small software development companies who will undertake to develop a piece of bespoke software to fit the needs of their customers.

Software systems and complexity

Small software systems are often created to meet the specifications of a single customer. They are generally simple compared to the sophisticated mass-market products, performing one or a small number of tasks to meet the exact specifications provided by the customer.

The tools used by most developers to create bespoke software systems are known as programming *languages*. These are themselves software systems whose job is to translate written instructions issued by a programmer into instructions that a computer can follow. The instructions issued by a computer programmer take the form of statements that indicate how information is to be represented, and other statements that indicate how the information is to be manipulated. All work that can be done by a computer system must be represented in this way – information (data) and the required operations on that data (see Figure 1.1).

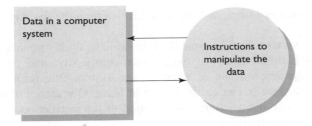

Figure 1.1   *A model of a computer program.*

Over the years computer scientists have realized that the key problem in trying to create *reliable* computer software is in how to organize it. Data and the instructions that manipulate it are separate things. The obvious approach to developing a software system is first to create a data model, describing all of the information needs of a system in terms of standard structures and data representations, and then to devise the instructions that make up the operations to be performed on the data model. In fact, this approach was used successfully for a number of years to develop robust computer software systems.

However, as computers have become more powerful, the tasks expected of them have become more complex, and this simple model for software development has broken down. In a software system of any complexity, there will be a lot of information to represent, and this will require a complex data model. The instructions to manipulate this will have to manage some very complex interactions between different elements of the data model without ever allowing inconsistencies to creep in.

For example, consider a simple computer system that allows an executive in a company to keep track of appointments. Each appointment could be modelled as a combination of several pieces of information – the date and time of the appointment, how long it will last, whom it is with, where it will be, and a description of its purpose. This can be done very simply in a computer program, and while the initial reasoning might be about how to manage the information of a single appointment, we can quite easily arrange for the program to cope with a large number of appointments. The instructions of the program would allow a number of simple operations – add a new appointment, delete an existing one, change the time, date or venue of an existing one, print or display appointments, etc. So far we have described a very tractable computer program that would be fairly easy to create by a skilled programmer.

Now let us assume that the system description is to be expanded somewhat. As well as appointments, the same program is to keep track of the other work-related information for the executive. The names and contact details of people the executive works with are to be stored and made accessible. Records of the sales and purchases that the executive makes with these people are to be managed along with expenses incurred. The tasks that the executive is engaged on must be mapped out in terms of time, contacts, sales, purchases and expenses. No piece of information in the system is to be considered in isolation, so it must be possible to form connections between all of the types of information. This is not an unreasonable expectation for a software system that is to help a busy executive to manage the day-to-day flood of information.

But now the system has become less tractable. With the mass of potential interconnections between pieces of data comes complexity, and the job of coping with two separate descriptions of parts of the system, the information and the allowable operations on it, can easily get out of hand. Our model of a description of the data in the system and a separate description of the instructions that are to work with it seems to be less useful.

Objects in the real world and in software

A key to managing this complexity comes from how we do so in the real world. We think of appointments, personal contacts, purchases and sales to be separate types of things. Each of these is a thing in its own right, and each belongs to a category of similar things. We could deal with all of the different types of thing manually by entering them all into a business diary, where we would differentiate between the types of thing by using different pages that were organized for that type of thing. We could easily cross-reference between diary entries by adding a name to an appointment or a brief description of an expense to an item in a to-do list.

In our paper diary-bound model of the executive's information management system, we would have little difficulty in managing the range of items and the complex interactions between them. The reason for this is that we keep a clear distinction between the various types of thing. The pre-formatted pages of a diary encourage us to list appointments in one set of pages where they are organized in chronological order, contact details in another where they appear alphabetically, and expenses, sales and purchases in balance-sheet pages where they can be tallied up easily. The pre-formatting also simplifies the various operations we might want to perform. Looking up a contact is easier when they appear in alphabetical order. Adding an appointment is simple when we can go directly to the page for the date required.

In the real world, we do not differentiate strongly between information and what we do with it. A diary is both a place to put information and a way of organizing and operating on that information. How we format the information is important to what we are able to do with it. Diary *entries* are individual items, each of which contains some information and each of which has a number of operations associated with it. Operations on individual entries may require the involvement of other entries (for example, an appointment with someone whose details are held in the contacts section). A model of an object oriented computer system is more like that shown in Figure 1.2.

Object oriented programming is a style of software development in which we try to create models of things, or objects, in a holistic way. The information, or data, in an object and the instructions that operate on it are developed and stored together in a way that reinforces how important the interactions between them are. Instead of a software system being created as a lot of data and a separate lot of instructions, it is devised as a lot of objects, each of which is composed of data and the instructions to manipulate it.

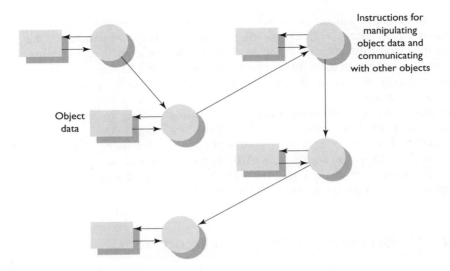

Instructions for manipulating object data and communicating with other objects

Object data

Figure 1.2 *An object oriented model.*

Object oriented programming in Visual Basic

Visual Basic is a software development system developed by Microsoft to support creating programs for the Windows operating systems. The *Visual* part of its name refers to the method in which screens, or forms in Visual Basic terminology, can be designed interactively so that the programmer is able to see the results of changes to them instantly. For a number of years, Visual Basic was the only widely available development system of its type.

In Figure 1.3, you can see a typical *form* (screen design) as developed in Visual Basic. Each of the individual items on the form, the boxes containing text to represent

Figure 1.3 *A form (screen design) from a Visual Basic program.*

time and date, the buttons, the **check-box** (Alarm), the **combo-box** (Priority), and the form itself are objects, available to the programmer. Their availability in the Visual Basic development system makes it very easy to create the parts of a program that a user will interact with (user-interfaces). They also act as a testament to the power of object oriented programming, since without this, Visual Basic would probably never have been created.

In this book, we will be concentrating on the programming aspects of Visual Basic: how data is used to represent information, how instructions can be made to manipulate data, and how data and instructions can be combined to represent objects in the real world are the key features. Although user-interface design is important and will be covered later in the book, our main purpose will be to learn the methods of developing what goes on *behind* the user-interface.

1.2 Undertaking software development

Developing software is more than just programming. Some of the most complex things built by human beings are software systems – suites of programs and data that define an application of computer systems is some way. For example, if we consider a single instruction in a program to be the equivalent of a *part* in any other type of engineered machinery, then a modern operating system or a large computer application program is very likely to be more complex in construction than a jumbo jet or a large building.

Programming, the act of writing computer software to add some function to a computer system, is one part of software development. However, in many cases it may only be a small part. The other things that are done during software development are there to support the act of programming in the same way that architecture, surveying and civil engineering are there to support building. Sometimes, we need this additional support to make the act of programming safe and accurate. At other times we do not.

To understand why this is so, we need only compare the potential range of tasks of software development with that of building (Figure 1.4). If you were to decide to build a wall in your garden, you could probably calculate the amount of bricks and other materials you need on the back of an envelope, go out and buy these and proceed to build the wall. You might finish the whole job in a holiday weekend.

If instead you decided to build a house, you would have to put a bit more effort into calculating the materials needed, planning the construction phases so that the foundations were built before the walls went up, organizing bricklayers and carpenters and so on. Without detailed plans, it is very likely that there would be serious errors – forgetting to lay drains, omitting to provide access for lorries delivering the building materials, and hundreds of other important, but easy to forget, requirements.

If you were building a multi-storey block of flats, there is no doubt that a great deal of effort would have to be put into planning, scheduling, organizing and designing before any building work was done at all.

Figure 1.4   *Three building jobs, each requiring a different level of organization.*

The same principles hold for software development. However, since the effects of the equivalent errors in programming are less visible than they would be in building, many naive software developers are happy to start the building work almost as soon as they have a rough idea of what is expected. For small projects, this approach can work. For larger projects it can seem to work for a time. An ill-defined system development can continue until so much effort has been expended that the only realistic way of putting it right is to start again from the beginning.

In this book on programming, you may consider several chapters on the organization of the software development environment and practices to be superfluous. For the programs you will learn to create while reading the book, the early stages described *will* be superfluous. However, it is as well to realize from the outset that at some point, programming will become only a minor part of the job that you, as a programmer, will have to do. Consider this chapter to be an overview of what you may have to do in the future.

1.3   The software development life-cycle

The software development life-cycle is an idealized model of the processes of software development. It is used to define the various distinct phases of development and the sequence in which these are organized. There are almost as many variations of the software development life-cycle as there are software developers. This is less a feature of the richness of the available knowledge about software development as it is an indication of how immature the field is. As yet, no one has been able to demonstrate unequivocally that one approach to organizing the software development process is any better than the many alternatives. The only real consensus is that software development follows a life-cycle. That is, a software project is born, goes through a number of distinct stages, and finally comes to an end (or dies).

Contrary to what you might expect, the act of programming is only a small portion of the SD life-cycle. Most formal software projects go through a number of phases before programming begins, and then continue through several other phases after programming has been completed. Even in an unstructured environment where undisciplined developers go directly to the programming phase, much of the time will be spent doing things other than programming. The remainder of the life-cycle involves activities that are at least as important as, and often more important than, programming. Most practitioners agree that a life-cycle will involve some or all of the following phases:

- Feasibility study/concept analysis
- Requirements gathering
- Requirements specification
- Software specification
- Structural design/architectural design
- Detailed design
- Implementation/coding and debugging
- Testing
- Maintenance.

Some of these phases will contain sub-phases (e.g. testing will often be implemented as a number of phases: specification testing, unit testing, integration testing, pre-acceptance testing, acceptance testing). Functionally, the list of phases can be broken down into five broad steps:

- finding out what the software is to do,
- designing a system to do it,
- building the system,
- verifying that what has been built does what is required, and finally
- maintaining and supporting the system during its operational life.

Whatever type of software system we develop, and whatever development style we choose to use, we will have to consider all of these stages in some form or other. It is the aim of this book to describe *object oriented programming* in some detail, and to describe enough of an *object oriented design method* to allow you to take a specification and develop software to fulfil it. We should start by putting these activities into a context.

1.4 Software life-cycle models

Left to their own devices, many programmers would develop software in a single phase – programming. During development, errors would be discovered (ideally), and these would be corrected. This life-cycle model is often referred to as *code-and-fix*, since the entire development is based around these two activities. For reasons already discussed, it is not a sensible development model for any but the smallest of software projects. Some more formal process description is necessary.

If in doubt, draw a diagram. This is almost a mantra in computer science, and so when it comes to describing the principles of a particular style of life-cycle, diagrams are used almost exclusively. In our case, we are interested in modelling the life-cycle phases of a system developed in an object oriented style in general, and one suited to the special facilities available to Visual Basic in particular. Different forms of life-cycle are used in different circumstances, the variations being due to a number of factors, including:

- the size of the software project,

- the number of people involved in the project,

- the size of the company employing the developers,

- the level of formality adopted by the company,

- the type of software being developed,

- the expertise and experience of the developers, and

- the knowledge that the customer or end-user has about software and software development.

None of these factors will have any great effect on the projects you will work on as exercises while working through this book, but all have great importance to practising software professionals.

From our perspective, the most useful life-cycle model will have the following features:

- Support for an object oriented development model

- Support for the 'visual' development model espoused by Visual Basic (and several other development systems)

- Scalability – that is, a facility to enable the use of the life-cycle model for projects in a range of sizes

- Ease of use – we have no wish to wrap up an already complex task in layers of bureaucracy

- Best use of the high adaptability and rapid-development features inherent in object oriented programming and visual development.

In fact, a number of different life-cycle models have been proposed that provide some or all of these features. Many of the life-cycle models described in computer science literature are best suited to software development in a corporate environment, where formal standards, accountability and management of teams are of paramount importance. However, a life-cycle model, described later in this chapter, is ideal for small teams or sole developers working in a language such as Visual Basic and developing small and medium-sized projects. Before we look at this, it would be useful to examine the 'grandfather' of all life-cycles – the waterfall model.

Waterfall life-cycle

This is the most fundamental of life-cycle models, and the one most familiar to most practitioners. It provides a way of managing the transition from one phase to the next, and for the need to feed back problems to a previous stage. A project progresses through an ordered sequence of development phases, from the initial concept stage through to maintenance. A review is held at the end of each phase to determine whether the project is ready to advance to the next phase. Members of the software development team conduct the review.

The end result of each phase is a document that presents the work of the phase in a form that makes it a starting point for the next phase: a concept document from the first phase, structured list of requirements from the second, structural diagrams from the third, etc. In this way, the process is document driven: documents act as inputs to a phase, as outputs from a phase and as evidence that the work of a phase has been properly carried out (or not). If anything goes wrong during development, the source of the problem is traced back to the phase in which it arose, and that phase and subsequent ones are reworked (Figure 1.5).

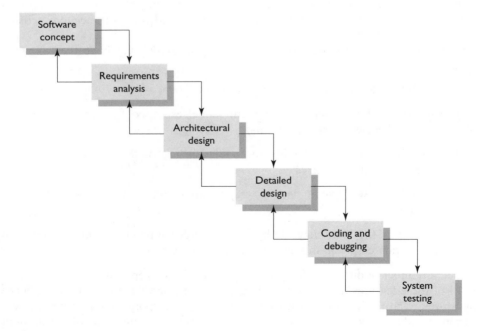

Figure 1.5   *Pure waterfall life-cycle.*

Advantages of the waterfall model are as follows.

- The development process can be planned in advance.

- Complex projects can be tackled with an appropriate allocation of resources at each stage.

- All significant changes to the system requirements can be managed by reworking the phase at which they initially have impact and propagating forward.

There are two disadvantages.

- Few projects are so well specified that their requirements are known at a suitable level of detail at the outset (so change propagation will be likely to be common and time consuming).

- Actual software is not seen until well into the development – often too late to catch significant errors in specification.

In a company used to the staged development of software with teams of developers working together, the waterfall life-cycle can work very well. However, experience is needed to minimize the time spent in transitions from one phase to the next, and any errors that are discovered, especially those that occur early in the life-cycle, can be costly to rework through the phases.

Waterfall life-cycle development has been in use for a long time, since the early 1970s at least, and is therefore based on a number of assumptions about the limitations of the software development process that are not necessarily true today. The computer systems of the time were large and had to be managed by teams of specialists. Development time on a computer was precious, and so actual programming time had to be minimized. Most importantly, neither object oriented programming nor visual development systems were commonly available, and so their benefits could not be factored into the development life-cycle.

A number of alternative life-cycle models have come into common use since the initial development of the waterfall model. Most have elements of waterfall development in them. For newcomers to object oriented programming, it is probably a good idea not to let a formal and complex life-cycle model get in the way of learning the basics of programming in an object oriented style. Because of this, we will use a life-cycle model that, although adequate for the purposes of developing small programs while learning, does not impose the more rigorous constraints of the waterfall model on us. The evolutionary prototyping model will suit our purposes.

Evolutionary prototyping life-cycle

In this life-cycle model (Figure 1.6), the system concept is developed progressively as the project proceeds. As the name suggests, the software system evolves from a very primitive version to the final release version. This will suit the pace that you will adopt as you work through this book.

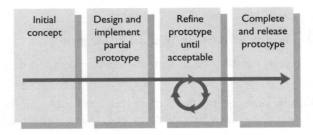

Figure 1.6   *Evolutionary prototyping.*

Development starts with the design and construction of the core of the system, as discovered by analyzing the initial requirements. As development of the prototype progresses, the early versions of the software can be used to answer questions about the true needs of the system, and refinements can be made to its design and implementation.

If a customer was involved, we could use demonstrations of the early prototypes to aid discussions about the true requirements specification. Based on feedback from the customer, the prototype would be developed and demonstrated, and this would continue until the customer agreed that the prototype system was adequate. Any remaining work would be completed and the system handed over to the customer.

In real-life software development, this form of development is most useful for developing systems whose requirements are difficult to capture, for example a transaction management system for a new type of company, where the actual work to be done by the system has not been fully defined. It is also useful when a customer is reluctant to commit to any statements of software requirements, perhaps due to their being unable to envisage how a computer system will be used in their work. Using evolutionary prototyping, the customer can always see the state of progress.

For our purposes, this style of development will suit the small projects we develop while learning object oriented programming. We can quickly get the core of a Visual Basic project up and running, and then refine this as we learn new techniques and gain programming experience.

The main disadvantage of this form of development is that it is impossible for the developer to know how long the development process will take. No price can be put on the software at the outset. A major risk is that the development can degenerate into code-and-fix. Proper evolutionary prototyping requires proper requirements analysis and design, well-organized, maintainable program code, etc. The main difference from the other trusted development life-cycle approaches is that the work progresses in smaller increments.

Life-cycle models in general

Software engineering literature describes many other formal life-cycle models, and even more variations are in use. The product under development and the experience of the developers generally dictate the style of life-cycle model used. Large formal projects benefit from a formalized life-cycle such as waterfall. Safety critical projects (e.g. aerospace, military or nuclear) might require a life-cycle that reduces risk and favours quality assurance.

While it is true to say that a large number of software development houses use a form of code-and-fix with the addition of one or two formal stages for requirements capture and final testing, this should not be treated as an endorsement of code-and-fix. Code-and-fix is used successfully by small developers working on small projects with little risk, but this pattern does not translate to larger projects. Big successful software companies use formal life-cycle models; the bigger and more complex the software is to be, the more important it is to use a formal and well understood development cycle.

Object orientation in the life-cycle

Neither of the life-cycle models described contain features that make them specifically object oriented or not. Object orientation is an organizational principle rather than the use of any specific tools or management methods. Life-cycle models are simply used by developers to organize the various development phases. Any life-cycle model is simply a framework into which we can incorporate any development style we choose.

All of the life-cycle phases will be influenced in some way by the decision to use object oriented design and development techniques. At the requirements specification phase, effort will be concentrated on determining what objects there will be in the system and how these will be expected to interact. At the design phase, how the objects should be connected to each other and the organizational structure will be most under consideration. Implementation will be done in an object oriented style (probably using the specific features of an object oriented language). System verification will be centred on trying to determine whether the objects developed behave as they are supposed to. Finally, system maintenance will involve identifying the objects and services that need to amended or upgraded, and working on these.

All of these tasks could be done using a more established style of development, such as structured system design and development instead of object orientation. The life-cycle model would probably remain the same.

QUESTION 1.1

Why might the waterfall life-cycle model be considered too rigid for small-scale software development?

QUESTION 1.2

How does the evolutionary prototyping model differ from code-and-fix?

1.5   Software requirements specification

The first real stage of development involves identifying what the software has to do. This is generally considered to be the most difficult part of software development. The problem is that programmers and end-users do not speak the same language – even when both speak English. A seemingly simple request, like 'I would like to record a log of all of the communication we have with each customer', is likely to be interpreted differently by each software developer that is asked it. The usual way to overcome this difficulty is to maintain a constant dialogue with the software end-users or customers. In this way ambiguities can be resolved before too much development work is done on wrongly interpreted requirements.

On the face of it, stating software requirements is a simple process; look at the work the software is to do, divide it up into statements of specific functions, list these. In practice, the process is strewn with ambiguities, misconceptions, misunderstandings, variations in the use of jargon and even basic vocabulary, leading to misrepresentation, subterfuge and, in some cases, lawsuits. It is difficult for technical developers to fully understand a customer's description of what may be the basic tasks of their business – every business has its own vocabulary and many business vocabularies reuse common words to mean different things.

In most cases, it is even more difficult for a customer to fully appreciate what a software developer is explaining to them. For a start, their immediate concerns are steeped in their own domain of business, and anything they are told by developers will be interpreted according to this. Storage, for example, means filing cabinets, cupboards and box rooms to most people, and presents a fairly simple set of concepts to comprehend. To a software developer, storage represents a set of software and hardware mechanisms involving a complex set of trade-offs between quantity and speed of access, and in which structure can be paramount. No wonder communication is difficult.

Of course, it is the job of the software developer to understand the customer's requirements – the customer should not have to work too hard to follow the developer's explanations. For a big project, this may mean the developer becoming expert in the customer's subject domain – many software developers are expert in accounting, physics, defence models, etc., simply because they have worked in that area over a long period.

Here is a typical statement of the requirements of a system:

> A new software system for an insurance office is to include a contacts management facility. It should be possible for all of the system's users to look up the details of a customer or contact, and have all of the relevant business and personal details to hand so that telephone contact can be made more personalized.

From the outset, developers will know that this feature will have exacting technical requirements. Storage capacity, storage format, integration with the other systems in use in the company, the style of display screens and several other factors will be concerns that the developers know they will have to face at some point. However, at the requirements specification phase, technical constraints are to be actively ignored; *what is to be done* is the only question that should be pursued. Otherwise, the software design will be locked into a number of assumptions that have little to do with what is required and everything to do with the personal preferences and technical ability of designers and developers.

The first stage of requirements specification is simply to list all of the user interactions that this facility might involve, normally in conference with the customer. For example:

The contacts sub-system will enable the user to...

1. Enter details (name, address, phone, fax, e-mail) of a new contact on to the system, using existing customer information on the main system where possible.
2. Add contact data (reason for contact, queries, disputes, whether resolved).
3. Cross-reference contact details with customer insurance records to allow quick retrieval.
4. Retrieve a customer or contact's data quickly (by entering name, order details or other form of identification).
5. Mark a communication with a contact as *initial, urgent, dispute, for attention of...*, *requires arbitration*, or *resolved*.
6. Retrieve a list of active communications (i.e. those not marked as resolved).
7. Retrieve a personal list of *for attention of...* communications.

This first cut at a requirements specification can be used in discussions with the customer, so that points can be corrected, additional requirements inserted, ambiguities resolved and extraneous features removed. After a few consultations with the customer, the list can be regarded as complete and clear, and at this point, it is usual and desirable to get the customer to sign the list off. Any further additions or changes will then be regarded as extra (with a possible extra cost).

To refine the specification, it is usual to take each point and describe it more fully. This involves adding indications of the source of any data required, the destination of any results and spelling out details of any processing to be done (i.e. what is to be done to the data). By the end of this phase, there should be no doubt *what* the system will do. Indeed it is likely that an experienced developer would now be able to design a first draft of the user-interface of the system, which could go on to drive an evolutionary prototyping life-cycle.

Objects in the requirements phase

Software requirements tend to be expressed as *operations*, since they are descriptions of tasks. In describing the way that an invoice is generated in his or her business, a client will probably set out all of the steps followed in getting the job done. The people doing the job (such as an invoicing clerk), or the items used in getting the job done (such as invoice forms, price catalogues, etc.) may be mentioned, but the emphasis will most likely be on the work done.

If we are to design an object oriented system, our first job will be to express the system requirements in terms of objects and the services that they provide. These will either be the *actors* involved in doing the work (the invoice clerk) or the *items* used (the forms, catalogues, etc.). The translation from a description of processes to an identification of objects can be fairly straightforward or extremely difficult, depending on the system, the client and, most of all, experience of object oriented systems.

One simple method is to go through the requirements descriptions, identifying the actors and items. These will usually appear as nouns or phrases describing specific items in the text. We can start with a rigorous list, taken from each requirement statement:

1. Enter `details` (`name, address, phone, fax, e-mail`) of a new `contact` on to the `system`, using existing `customer information` on the main system where possible.

2. Add `contact data` (reason for contact, queries, disputes, whether resolved).

3. Cross-reference `contact details` with `customer insurance records` to allow quick retrieval.

4. Retrieve a `customer` or `contact`'s data quickly (by entering `name, order details` or other `form of identification`).

5. Mark a `communication` with a `contact` as *initial, urgent, dispute, for attention of . . . , requires arbitration,* or *resolved.*

6. Retrieve a `list of active communications` (i.e. those not marked as resolved).

7. Retrieve a `personal list` of *for attention of . . .* communications.

We would now go through the compiled list of objects, vetting each as candidates for types of objects in the system being developed. For example, we could remove those that did not describe items that had responsibility for specific actions, since these will probably be attributes of some of the other objects rather than objects in their own right. 'Name', 'address', 'phone', 'fax', 'e-mail', 'order details', 'form of identification', 'contact data', 'contact details' and 'customer information' would go on this basis. Vague items, such as 'details', have no place in the final list.

Our final list would therefore be reduced to:

`System`

`Contact`

`Customer`

`Insurance Record`

`Communication`

`List of Active Communications`

`Personal List`

This simple analysis of the initial requirements results in a list of potential objects that we can validate in consultation with the customer or end-user. By returning to the initial requirements statements, we can attach responsibilities to each of these objects. For example, a Contact object must retain details such as Name, Address, etc., in addition to contact data such as Reason For Contact. Using this combination of items and their responsibilities, we can go on to construct scenarios that show how objects will be required to interact in the system (known as **use-cases**) and hopefully add more detail to the requirements statements. Once we have compiled a complete and correct list of objects and their responsibilities, we have a system specification, which is a full description of what the system must do.

A system specification will probably consist of the details of a large number of objects and tasks that they must perform. Normally, these are interrelated, in that an object's task may need to perform some work requiring the information contained in another object. For example, an insurance record object will be related to some customer object and may need to interact with it in order to process an insurance quote.

The system architecture indicates how these objects and tasks are related in terms of the information they must share and the ways in which they affect each other. However, a more fundamental problem is simply how to encode each task so that it can be performed by a computer. We refer to this as **algorithm design**.

QUESTION 1.3

Why do you think it is important to distinguish between what is to be done and how it is to be accomplished in a system's requirements specification?

QUESTION 1.4

It is important to keep the language used in a requirements specification as direct and simple as possible. Give two reasons for this.

1.6 Algorithms

Algorithms are at the core of computer programs and software systems. Before an object can perform a task in a computer program, a designer needs to express the task in terms of statements in a programming language. Described formally, an algorithm is:

> A systematic (mathematical) procedure, which enables a problem to be solved in a finite number of steps

Key points in this description are that it involves a step-by-step procedure, and that the number of steps must be finite. From this, we can see that an algorithm is similar to a recipe; it describes an overall task as a sequence of steps leading to its completion. Since its completion is necessary, the number of steps cannot be infinite. You would be hard pressed to find a food recipe that contained an infinite number of steps, but there is a whole class of mathematical procedures that can be shown to have no definite ending point, making them computationally useless.

Algorithms are related to objects, since objects have responsibilities, or tasks that they must be able to perform. Most object oriented systems are composed of large numbers of objects, and each object can be responsible for several tasks. Therefore, an object oriented program could involve dozens, hundreds or even thousands of algorithms.

Algorithms can be used to describe any number of processes:

Algorithm for making a cup of instant coffee:

1. Add water to kettle and switch on
2. Add required amount of coffee to a cup
3. Add sugar if required
4. Wait till kettle boils
5. Pour water from kettle into cup
6. Add milk to taste if required
7. Look for Hob-Nobs

Algorithm for finding the greatest common divisor of two numbers (m and n):

1. Let quotient = m/n, disregarding any fractional part of quotient
2. Let remainder = m − (quotient ∗ n)
3. Let m = n
4. Let n = quotient
5. If remainder is not zero, go to step 1
6. Greatest common divisor is m

Algorithm to calculate fuel use in miles per litre (MPL):

1. Fill the fuel tank
2. Let initial = milometer reading
3. Run the car for a period
4. Fill the fuel tank – Let F = amount of fuel in litres
5. Let final = new milometer reading
6. MPL = (final − initial)/F

Note that although all three of the algorithms shown above are step-by-step procedures, only two of them start at step 1 and continue to the final step without deviation. The middle algorithm (Euclid's algorithm for finding the greatest common divisor) includes a stage that may involve going back to an earlier step and continuing from there. This *iteration* is a common feature of many algorithms where continued processing depends on some condition being met. It is important in these cases that the algorithm is known to lead to a solution (a finite number of steps); in this case,

Euclid's algorithm is well known and guaranteed to produce a result in a finite number of steps.

Although many algorithms depend on a mathematical process (particularly the more interesting ones), most algorithms that are incorporated into computer programs are ordinary sequences of steps that are followed by humans in clerical, administrative and technical tasks. As such, they are easy to identify and easy to encode as operations performed by objects in computer programs. The vast majority of computer programming involves directing a computer to perform routine humdrum tasks that humans find mind-numbing (the name 'computer' was first used to describe humans who performed repetitive arithmetic calculations for the creation of navigational or ordinance tables). Therefore, most algorithms used in computer programs are easy to develop. The key requirement is to be able to break down a task into a sequence of steps (see the first sample algorithm above).

QUESTION 1.5

Write out a numbered series of instructions that form an algorithm for:

(a) Reading a book.
(b) Setting the timer on a video recorder to record a program.
(c) Looking up a number in the telephone book.

Approaches to task decomposition

Of course, breaking a task into a sequence of steps may not be as innocuous as it sounds. Given a complex problem, it is not always trivial to deconstruct it into a sensible sequence of smaller problems. Sometimes it is difficult to identify specific sub-tasks; at other times, the overall task can be so complex that converting it into a sequence of step-by-step instructions is just too daunting to consider.

To get around this, software designers tend to use well-tried recipes (which are themselves algorithms) for task decomposition. The two most common approaches are often referred to as *top-down decomposition* and *bottom-up composition*.

Top-down task decomposition

Top-down task decomposition proceeds by examining an overall task and dividing it into a few (commonly somewhere between two and eight) smaller sub-tasks. It is also known as *stepwise refinement* and *top-down design*. It is characterized by a move from a general statement of what an operation is to do towards detailed statements describing how information is to be processed.

To perform a top-down decomposition of a task:

■ Start with the overall task description and divide this into the first level decomposition by breaking it into a number of steps.

- Treat each step in the first level decomposition as a whole task, and decompose as for the top level.

- Continue this until each step is computationally trivial.

Using this approach, it is possible to make almost any complex task easier to do. Since programming languages will only allow us to perform relatively simple operations as individual steps, top-down decomposition is a necessary requirement if we are to do useful work with them.

During the top-down decomposition process, it is necessary to follow some simple guidelines to make sure that the task is well defined. Among these are:

- Steer clear of programming language specific details, since it is possible to bias a design towards a particular language simply because of working habits, but this is not a good design trait, since it limits the range of possible implementations.

- Postpone the working out of details until you have reached the lower levels of the task description.

- Formalize each level (keeping to well-understood conventions of notation and design).

- Verify each level (aim to demonstrate that the current level of design is correct, in that its parts are a true description of the task or sub-task they describe, before moving on to the next one).

For example, you might consider the overall task of writing a formal letter as being:

1. Write the recipient's address at the top left of the paper.

2. Write the sender's address at the top right of the paper.

3. Write the body of the letter.

4. Write the closure of the letter (e.g. Yours truly . . .).

Having created the first level of decomposition, we can then consider each sub-task separately, and deal with them in a similar way:

1. Write the recipient's address at the top left of the paper:
    1.1. Write the recipient's name
    1.2. Write the recipient's street address
    1.3. Write the recipient's town
    1.4. Write the recipient's postcode.

2. Write the sender's address at the top right of the paper:
    2.1. Write the sender's name
    2.2. Write the sender's street address
    2.3. Write the sender's town
    2.4. Write the sender's postcode.

3. Write the body of the letter:
    3.1. Write the introductory paragraph
    3.2. Write the main content of the letter
    3.3. Write the concluding paragraph.

4. Write the closure of the letter:
    4.1. If this is a business letter, write 'Yours faithfully'
    4.2. If this is a personal letter, write 'Yours sincerely'
    4.3. If this is a threatening letter, write 'Or else'
    4.4. Write the sender's name.

Note that the notation has been consistent throughout – a feature that will make this easier to understand when you return to it at a later date. Note also that some of the parts of step 4 in the decomposition are *conditional*, in that one of a number of options will be taken depending on a certain condition (the type of letter being written).

Task decomposition continues along these lines until the sub- or sub-sub- (or even sub-sub-sub-) tasks are trivial enough to convert directly into program statements. For example, although we could proceed with much of the letter outlined above, we have not decomposed stage 3 sufficiently to allow us to write the whole letter. To do this, we would probably have to concentrate on decomposing step 3.2 (to 3.2.1, 3.2.2, ..., then possibly 3.2.1.1, 3.2.1.2, etc.) until the actual information required to be in the letter was complete. Note that to do this would involve the introduction of semantic information (meaning) that is not clear from the initial specification. We would have to return to the task of extracting requirements specifications from the customer; no amount of computer programming could add this information. In fact, our inability to complete the letter due to lack of information points to an inadequate requirements specification in the first place.

Figure 1.7 shows pictorially how an overall task (level 1) can be broken down into successive sub-tasks by top-down decomposition.

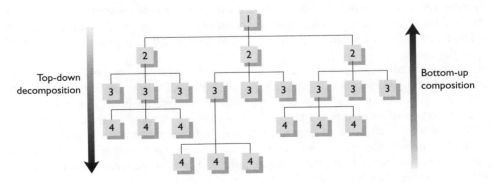

Figure 1.7 *Components of a major task.*

Bottom-up task composition

With top-down decomposition, we worked on an algorithm by breaking it down into a number of steps until each step could be translated into equivalent program statements. Sometimes, this approach is so abstract that it is difficult to get started. Sometimes you need to work with more concrete ideas of what you will be developing. For example, if you are building the communications sub-system of the previously described insurance system, you may be well aware of how communications objects will operate, but need to know how they will fit into the new system.

We could try to use top-down decomposition with the aim of ending up with low-level sub-tasks that fit exactly with the abilities of the communications objects we have available, but this can be difficult. Instead, *bottom-up composition* is a more suitable approach. The general aim is to start from a number of well-understood low-level system capabilities or already defined objects, and work up towards the construction of sub-sub-systems, then sub-systems, etc.

It is unlikely that an entire system design will be done as a bottom-up composition. For one thing, you are very unlikely to have all of the pre-built objects required to do the job. Top-down is still the preferred method of decomposition, since it is ideal for developing new algorithms and designing new solutions. Bottom-up has some specific features that make it fit well into some problem areas, but these tend to be few. Bottom-up composition is best treated as a way to get past the initial hurdle of the top level of design. Normally, once you have identified several low-level objects whose services the system can use, you will be in a more comfortable position to proceed with top-level design, aiming to meet the parts constructed by bottom-up composition somewhere in the middle.

Object oriented design and task decomposition

It is worth stressing that the task decomposition methods described will involve objects in many cases. Object oriented design methods are best used holistically, rather than piecemeal. Although an algorithm, or an individual task, describes a process, the task is likely to be accomplished with the assistance of objects doing some or all of the sub-tasks. This is particularly true when designing for Visual Basic, where a large number of different types of object are used to allow a program to interact with the user.

Object oriented programs are most often designed as assemblies of interacting objects, where each object has its own area of responsibility, and objects request services of other objects to work towards an overall goal. A sub-task in a decomposition of some task is likely to be something that some object can do for us. Objects behave like clients (requesting services) and servers (providing them).

In the simple interaction shown in Figure 1.8, an insurance policy object has access to a database of insurance policy details, and can provide this information as a service to other objects (e.g. the customer object shown).

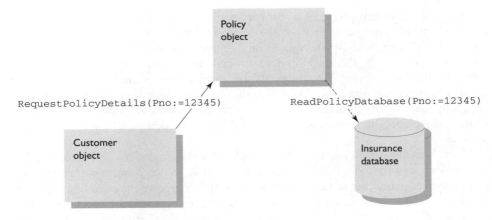

Figure 1.8   *A simple object oriented interaction.*

Object oriented design is normally conducted using the following steps:

- Identify the objects and their attributes.

- Determine what can be done to each object.

- Determine what each object can do to other objects.

- Determine the parts of each object that will be visible to other objects – which parts will be public and which will be private.

- Define each object's public interface (the set of procedures that can be called on by clients of the object).

There is much more to object oriented design and programming than has been described in this brief introduction. When we go on in subsequent chapters to learn the principles of programming, we will work towards an object oriented style.

1.7   Summary

Software development is often approached as a process with a starting point, an ending point, and a number of identifiable phases. The organization of these phases is often referred to as the life-cycle. A number of life-cycle models exist, most of which define how the various phases articulate to, or connect with, each other. The different life-cycle models have different advantages and disadvantages, making them more or less suitable to a project depending on its size, nature, the experience of the development team, the requirements information available at the project's inception, and the available input from the customer or user.

The most important phase of a software project is the requirements specification phase, since this phase defines what the software will do. Requirements statements should be as complete, unambiguous and correct as possible, since changes to requirements later in the development process will require expensive reworking through all of the phases. Requirements are often produced as a structured list of English statements, since in this form the customer can understand them and hopefully identify any anomalies. Requirements can also be depicted in terms of the identifiable objects in a system, and the services or operations these objects can provide.

Algorithms are fundamental building blocks of software designs. An algorithm is a step-by-step description of how to complete a task. Since a software system will comprise a large number of tasks, its development will involve the encoding of a large number of algorithms into a programming language. Fortunately, most algorithms are lists of simple instructions for how to accomplish routine operations. Some algorithms are more mathematical, and it is sometimes necessary to prove that a proposed algorithm will actually produce a solution in a finite number of steps (which is a requirement of any algorithm).

In developing an algorithm or a whole software system, it is often necessary to start with a general description of a task and decompose it into a sequence of sub-tasks. There are a number of approaches to this process. Top-down decomposition involves taking the top-level task description (e.g. a requirements statement or a service) and breaking it down into smaller and smaller parts until it is a trivial matter to code each in a programming language. Bottom-up composition involves taking available designs for specific tasks in a system, and combining these into higher and higher levels of task until the system design is built. In most cases, both approaches will have a role to play in a software system's development.

Object oriented development is a way of building systems by breaking systems down into *objects*. An object is a component that contains data and is associated with specific procedures for manipulating it. Object oriented designs benefit from a tight association between procedures and data; objects form better models of real-world objects because of it. Object oriented design involves creating assemblies and other associations of objects. Since objects provide specific services to other objects, the relationship between two collaborating objects is often referred to as a *client–server* relationship.

1.8 Review questions

1. Indicate which of the following statements about software life-cycles are true and which are false:
   The software life-cycle is a system for describing the life of a computer program.
   Most of the phases in the software life-cycle are interchangeable.

The waterfall life-cycle is based on the creation of documents to ease the transition to the next phase of development.
Code-and-fix is an important life-cycle model.
Life-cycle models are best if suited to the type of software being developed and the experience of the developers.

2. Write a simple requirements specification for a four-function ($+$, $-$, $\times$, $\div$) pocket calculator. Concentrate on what it must do.

3. Write an algorithm for getting cash out of an Automatic Teller Machine (i.e. a hole-in-the-wall bank). You should assume that you are directing someone who has never used one.

4. Write an algorithm for looking up a word in the dictionary.

5. Consider the following tasks, and decide whether you would use top-down decomposition or bottom-up composition or both to describe them in detail. Your answers should take into account your experience of the sub-tasks involved. You need not actually create the detailed task descriptions:
    (a) Making a cup of tea or coffee
    (b) Filling in a tax form
    (c) Writing a report for a small project you are doing for your employer
    (d) Booking a foreign holiday
    (e) Calculating who pays what after a meal in a restaurant.

1.9   Practical exercises

By working through these exercises, you will get a chance to become familiar with the Visual Basic Integrated Development Environment (IDE) before we go on to start programming in subsequent chapters. By the time you have completed them, you should be able to:

- start up Visual Basic,

- save the components of a VB project into a project folder,

- identify the various components and facilities in the IDE,

- write simple code statements in the Immediate window,

- add custom components to the Visual Basic IDE,

- add class modules to a Visual Basic project.

Actions you are to perform in this exercise will be indicated with a ▣ symbol, in a paragraph with a tinted background.

Exercise 1: Starting up Visual Basic

Visual Basic can be started up from the Windows 95, 98 or NT Start button. It will be in a group under the Programs group – either Microsoft Visual Basic 5.0 (or 6.0), or Microsoft Developers Studio.

Find the Visual Basic entry in the Start button and select it to run Visual Basic.

When you run VB, the dialog box shown in Figure 1.9 will be displayed, to allow you to select the type of project to create, or to open an existing project.

Note the tabs near the top of the dialog box (New, Existing, Recent) that allow you to choose whether to start a new project, open an existing one, or select from the list of most recent projects worked on. This last option is very useful if you frequently use the same PC for VB programming.

In all of these exercises, when you create a new project it will be the first option – **Standard EXE**. This simply means a program. Other options allow you to create automatable programs (**ActiveX EXE**), program components (**ActiveX DLL**), etc.

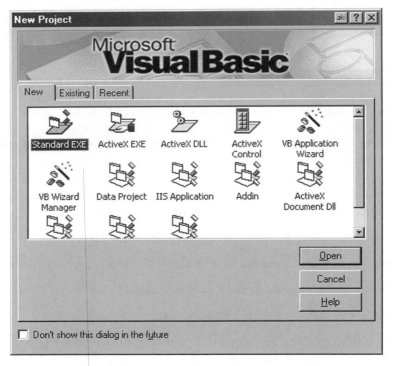

Figure 1.9 *The start-up dialog box.*

Choose the Standard EXE option and press OK to create a new project.

The ***Visual Basic Integrated Development Environment (IDE)*** will now be displayed. It should appear roughly as shown in Figure 1.10 – don't panic if it is a bit different, as may happen if some configuration options have been taken. You can restore any absent components of the IDE using various options on the View menu.

Exercise 2:   Identify VB components and facilities

The IDE shown in Figure 1.10 has been labelled to indicate the name for each component of the VB IDE. Note that several important components are not yet visible – we will come to these later.

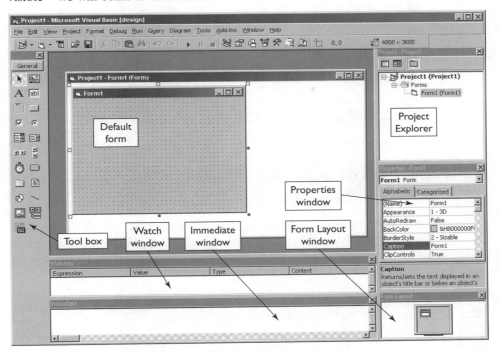

Figure **1.10** *The Visual Basic IDE.*

For each of the components shown, you will be asked to perform a short exercise to give you a better feeling for its purpose.

1. The menu bar

This is the familiar command centre of any Windows program, and gives access to all of the system commands for Visual Basic. The menu titles suggest what each menu list contains, but the best way of learning to use menus is to practise to become familiar with them. You may not entirely agree with the logic used by Microsoft when assigning certain commands to specific menus.

> Select the **File** menu, and choose **Save Project**. The dialog box shown in Figure 1.11 will appear.

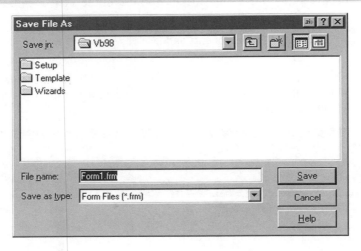

Figure 1.11   *The* **Save Project** *dialog box.*

> Using the combo-box (drop-down list box) at the top, navigate to the disk drive where you intend to store your program files (normally the C: drive).

If this is the first VB project you have created, you should create a folder on your computer for *all* of your VB projects. To do this, press the ⌹ button to create a new folder, and when the folder appears (provisionally entitled **New Folder**), overtype the name to rename it as **VBWork**, and press Enter to confirm.

> Double-click on the new folder to open it. You will now create another new folder to contain this VB project – ideally, you should use a new folder for each project.

> Repeat the process of adding a new folder. This time name it **First**, and once its name has changed, double-click on it to open it.

> Now replace the text in the File Name box with **First** and press the **Save** button. This will save the Form in your project, which is a Window design. The full name will be **First.frm**, but you do not need to type the '**.frm**' part as VB will add this automatically.

> VB will come back with another dialog – this time to save the **Project** file. Again overtype the default name with **First** and press **Save**. The project file will be saved as **First.vbp**.

Note that you have now saved all of the components of the current VB project. If you add anything to the form or project, or alter any settings (including the position and size of the form), you will be prompted to save the changes, and you should always opt to do so *unless* you deliberately want to discard changes you have made. You can quickly save any changes made to the project by pressing the 🖫 button on the toolbar, or using the ***File/Save Project*** menu.

2. The tool bar

The tool bar provides quick access to the most frequently used commands. This can be altered to include the commands you use most frequently if these are different from the standard ones, by selecting ***View/Toolbars/Customize*** ... from the menus. Note that certain tools are *greyed out*. VB only activates tool buttons when it would be valid to use them. Many of the greyed out tools relate to program code that we have not looked at yet.

Check out the standard tool bar:

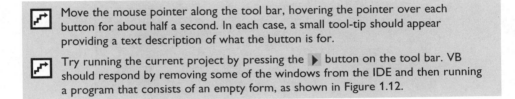

Move the mouse pointer along the tool bar, hovering the pointer over each button for about half a second. In each case, a small tool-tip should appear providing a text description of what the button is for.

Try running the current project by pressing the ▶ button on the tool bar. VB should respond by removing some of the windows from the IDE and then running a program that consists of an empty form, as shown in Figure 1.12.

Stop the project from running by pressing the ■ button on the tool bar or the Close button on the form.

Figure 1.12   *A running project.*

3. The tool box

The purpose of the tool box is to provide a *palette* of components or *controls* that can be placed on the used form. Let's add some controls to the form:

 Add a `Label` control as follows. Start by clicking on the Label tool **A** in the tool box and moving the mouse over to the user form (the grey area with a grid of dots named `Form1`). Now press the left mouse button down, and drag out a size rectangle by moving the mouse down and to the right. Complete the addition of the control by releasing the mouse button. You should end up with the text `Label1` on the surface of the form, as shown in Figure 1.13.

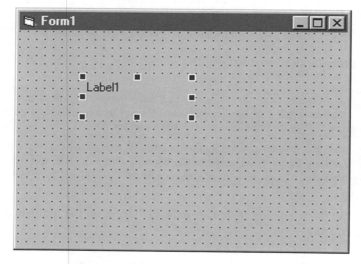

Figure 1.13 *Placing a label on a form.*

 Add a second label to the centre of the form by simply double-clicking on the label tool.

Note that you can select one control on the form by clicking on it, after which you can move it and resize it by dragging on the centre or one of the *drag-handles*, and you can delete it by pressing the `Delete` key on the keyboard.

4. The user form

You have already interacted with this in the previous activity. However, you can resize the form itself by selecting it (if it does not display drag-handles, click on its surface, avoiding any controls on it) and dragging to size. It will always appear at the top left of its design window, but you can change its start-up position from the Form Layout window:

> Move the mouse to the Form Layout window (bottom right on a standard configuration) and right-click on the small picture of a form. When a pop-up menu appears, select the **Start Up Position** item, and choose **Center Screen**.
>
> Start up the program again and note that this time the form appears in the middle of the PC display.

Try some of the alternative start-up positions.

5. The Project window

This window provides access to all of the component files of a project. In our case, the project currently has a single form file, so to provide a realistic picture of this component, we will add a code module to the project.

> Right-click anywhere in the Project window, and select **Add**, then **Module** from the pop-up menu, as shown in Figure 1.14.

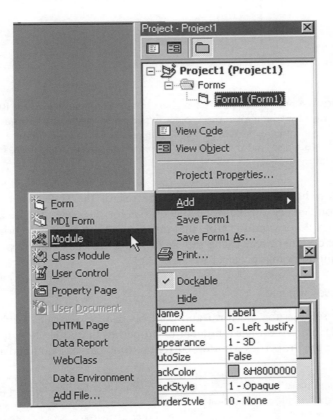

Figure 1.14   *Adding a module to a project.*

When the dialog box appears, choose **Module** and press the **Open** button. A new module is added to the project, and the Project Explorer window changes to reflect this, as shown in Figure 1.15.

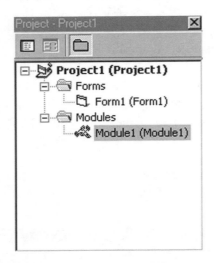

Figure 1.15 *The Project Explorer window, showing an added module.*

 Note that the new module has been given the default name **Module1**. Right-click on the entry for Module1 in the Project Explorer, select **Save** and when the dialog appears, give it the name **First**. VB saves it as **First.bas** (to indicate it is a Basic module). Note also that the module is automatically saved in the same folder as the rest of the project.

A code window has appeared in the design area of the IDE (where the form is displayed). Double-click on the respective entries for the code module and the form in the Project Explorer window. Note that this method can be used to bring an item to the fore in the designer area. Using this facility, the Project Explorer provides quick access to the modules in a project.

6. The Properties window

This is where settings for the form and controls can be asserted. Each visual item (form, control) in a project has a number of properties that affect how it appears and behaves. Using the Properties window, current settings can be examined and changed.

 Change the **Name** property of the form in your project by selecting the form in the designer window (double-click in the Project Explorer). Make sure the form is selected by clicking on its background, and then change the **Name** property in the

Properties window. The Name property is used to refer to the form in program code (i.e. the form's internal name as opposed to its file name), and so is normally set up to make it easy to identify the purpose of this form. For this example, change the name to `frmFirst`, where the 'frm' prefix will indicate that this is a form when we refer to it in program code.

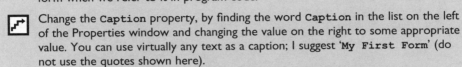

Change the `Caption` property, by finding the word `Caption` in the list on the left of the Properties window and changing the value on the right to some appropriate value. You can use virtually any text as a caption; I suggest '`My First Form`' (do not use the quotes shown here).

Try changing other values in the Properties window to see if there is any immediate effect. Where the effect is not obvious, it is safest to restore these settings to their original value for now. Good ones to try are `BackColor` (click on the little down-arrow to access a colour selection dialog), `Picture` (brings up a file selection dialog – choose any graphics file you find), `Height`, `Width` and `MousePointer` (choose from the drop-down list). Note that the last of these will only become apparent when the program is running.

Select one of the Label controls placed on the form. Note that the Properties window changes to reflect the properties of this component. Try changing some of these properties.

7. Watch/Locals windows

These windows are used for tracking the values of variables in a running program. We will ignore them for now, since they are only useful for examining the effects of program code.

8. Immediate window

This window is used for entering Basic statements at any time. The normal purposes for this are to test syntax, make settings in a running (but paused) program and test code modules. In later exercises, we will make extensive use of this. For now, as a taste of the Basic language:

Click in the Immediate window to get a cursor, and enter *exactly* `MsgBox "Hello World"` followed by `Enter`. A message box should appear showing the message. This form of statement is mostly useless when called from the Immediate window, but very useful to report status in a running program.

Type `3*75+202` and press `Enter`. You should get an error message to the effect that something was missing (a label or end of statement). Try again, this time preceding the expression with the keyword `Print` or the shorthand `?`, as in `? 3*75+202`. The result (427) should be displayed on the next line. The Immediate window works as an expression evaluator.

Exercise 3:	Adding custom components and classes

The final part of this exercise is to demonstrate how to add new components to the Visual Basic project. Firstly, we will add a calendar control to the tool box.

> Select **Project/Components** from the menu (or press **Ctrl + T**).

> Scroll down the alphabetical list until you find the entry for **Microsoft Calendar Control 8.0** and click on the check box to the left of this. Then press the **Apply** button. Note that a new control icon appears in the tool box.

> Add a calendar control to the form (you can delete any label controls on it to make more space if need be). This component is now available as part of the project.

> Run the project and note that you can change the calendar to show any date by selecting from the **Month** and **Year** combo-boxes.

Now we will add a new class to the project.

> Right-click on the Project Explorer, and select **Add/Class Module** from the pop-up menus.

The dialog shown in Figure 1.16 should appear.

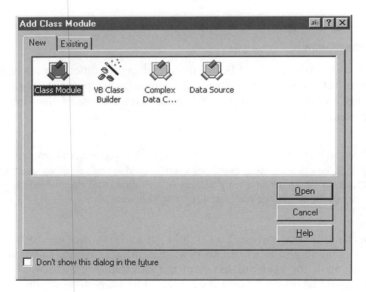

Figure 1.16 *Adding a class module.*

Click on the Open button to add a new class module to the project.

This module will take the form of a new code window, as shown in Figure 1.17.

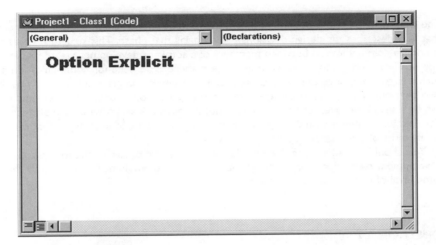

Figure 1.17 *The class module's code window.*

Note that the Properties window now shows the property settings for this class. The list of properties will vary depending on the version of Visual Basic you are using, but in all cases the property at the top of the list will be the class name – initially `Class1`.

 Rename the new class by entering the name `MyClass` in the Properties window.

Note that the caption of the code window changes to reflect the new name applied to the class.

Summary

You should now be more confident in the use of Visual Basic's IDE. Of course, you still have to learn how to write programs, how to develop user-interfaces and how to connect these together, but that is for later chapters. For now, practice in the use of the features covered in this exercise will be profitable in the longer term.

1.10   Answers to questions

QUESTION 1.1

The waterfall life-cycle is document driven, the output of each phase being a document that fully describes the design decisions taken during that phase. This structure exists to maximize communication between members of a software development team that is potentially very large. In a smaller-scale project, there is no need for communication on such a large scale, since the development team is likely to comprise only one or possibly two developers. In such a small-scale project, the generation of detailed documentation can be a significant overhead that is simply not necessary; it will slow up the project development, when it would be more suitable to generate rapid prototypes that can clarify most of the outstanding design issues.

You should consider using the waterfall life-cycle to be similar to the formalized development stages necessary to build a large ship – you would not wish to apply the same level of effort to building a canoe.

QUESTION 1.2

Evolutionary prototyping is significantly different from the code-and-fix approach in a number of respects:

- It always starts with requirements analysis and design phases, which answer many of the questions about the nature of the required software system and its structure. In code-and-fix, it is assumed that these are fully understood at the outset.

- The initial partial prototype is built to implement the requirements. Subsequent prototypes are based on refinements made to the initial requirements, which are updated to stay in line with the evolving prototypes. In code-and-fix, it is unlikely that requirements statements would be well developed and very unlikely that these would be kept up to date with the evolution of the software.

- Code-and-fix is a haphazard process in which refinements are made as deficiencies are discovered. Evolutionary prototyping is always directed towards developing the prototype to meet the latest requirements, as discovered in the previous round of development. Instead of fixing defects as they crop up, evolution is driven by the discovery of new requirements and the refinements they suggest.

QUESTION 1.3

A requirements specification is simply that – a document that states what a system should be capable of doing. If it includes any indication of how the provision of the requirements is to be realized, it becomes a technical specification, and that would render it useless to the non-technical people who are supposed to be able to work with it, such as end-users, marketing personnel, etc. Also, by indicating how the requirements are to be realized, it is possible to lock the system into a technical dead-end. Subsequent technical advances could then lead to the requirements specification becoming redundant, and since it is likely to be the most expensive single stage of development, this would be wasteful.

QUESTION 1.4

1. Direct and simple requirements statements are less likely to be ambiguous or confusing than jargon-laden techno-babble.

2. A requirements document is a statement of the end-user's needs for the software system. This will be very difficult to verify if the end-user, normally a non-technical person, is unable to understand it.

QUESTION 1.5

(a) To read a book...
  1. Hold the book in front of you the right way up
  2. Open the book at the first page
  3. Read the first page
  4. Turn to the next page
  5. Read the left-hand page
  6. Read the right-hand page
  7. If you have not just read the final page, go to step 4
  8. Close the book.

  Note that 'reading a page' has been realized as 'read a left-hand page' or 'read a right-hand page'. This removes any ambiguity brought about by the need to turn pages, since 'read a page' followed by 'turn to the next page' would involve reading only half of the book.

(b) To set a video recorder, obviously there are a wide range of possible solutions, so this one will be as generic as it can be made:
  1. Turn on the video recorder
  2. Insert a blank video tape
  3. Switch the video to 'program' mode
  4. Select the channel to record from
  5. Enter the date of the recording
  6. Enter the start time – hours
  7. Enter the start time – minutes
  8. Enter the end time – hours
  9. Enter the end time – minutes
  10. Switch the VCR to 'timer' mode.

(c) There are a number of possible solutions to this problem, ranging in efficiency from highly inefficient but very simple to very efficient but complex. Two possible approaches are suggested here:

1. Get the phone book
2. Open at the first entry
3. If the required number is the current entry, go to step 6
4. Move to the next entry
5. Go to step 3
6. Note down the number and close the phone book.

Now for a more efficient but more wasteful approach...

1. Get the phone book
2. Open what there is of the book approximately half-way
3. If the names on the open page match the entry you are looking for, go to step 7
4. If the names on the page are before the entry you are looking for, tear the book in half and throw away the right-hand half
5. If the names on the page are after the entry you are looking for, tear the book in half and throw away the left-hand half
6. Go to step 2
7. Examine the first entry in the current open page
8. If the current entry is not the required entry, move to the next entry
9. If the current entry is the required entry, go to step 12
10. Examine the current entry
11. Go to step 9
12. Note the required number and throw away what is left of the phone book.

1.11 Answers to review questions

1. *The software life-cycle is a system for describing the life of a computer program:* False – it describes only part of the life (the construction and maintenance phases) of a computer program. It does not describe its use.

Most of the phases in the software life-cycle are interchangeable: False – the phases of all life-cycle models must be performed in the correct order; it makes no sense to design a system if you have not yet described its requirements.

The waterfall life-cycle is based on the creation of documents to ease the transition to the next phase of development: True.

Code-and-fix is an important life-cycle model: Neither rigidly true nor false. Code-and-fix is not a good method for developing large software systems, but many small utility programs are built this way. Whether sensible or not, the importance of the method cannot be denied. However, there is almost always a better approach.

Life-cycle models are best if suited to the type of software being developed and the experience of the developers: True – some life-cycle models (e.g. waterfall) are best used for large projects in a team development environment. Others favour object orientation, or development of formally certified systems, or minimal risk development.

2. *Write a simple requirements specification for a four-function (+, −, ×, ÷) pocket calculator. Concentrate on what it must do.*

   1. Allow user to enter first operand
      1.1. Reject an invalid entry
   2. Allow user to enter an arithmetic operator
      2.1. Reject an operand that is not +, −, * or /
   3. Allow user to enter second operand
      3.1. Reject an invalid entry
   4. Display result of calculation or error if arithmetic is invalid.

3. *Write an algorithm for getting cash out of an Automatic Teller Machine (i.e. a hole-in-the-wall bank). You should assume that you are directing someone who has never used one.*

   1. Insert card into ATM machine
   2. Enter PIN code when prompted
   3. Select 'Withdraw Cash' option when options are displayed
   4. Enter amount to withdraw
   5. Retrieve card from ATM machine
   6. Retrieve cash from ATM machine.

4. *Write an algorithm for looking up a word in the dictionary.*

   The algorithm for this is very similar to the one for looking up a name in the phone book. Adapt that algorithm.

5. *Consider the following tasks, and decide whether you would use top-down decomposition or bottom-up composition or both to describe them in detail. Your answers should take into account your experience of the sub-tasks involved. You need not actually create the detailed task descriptions:*

   (a) *Making a cup of tea or coffee.* Normally bottom-up, since you can assume the ability to fill a kettle, add coffee, tea, sugar, etc., to a cup and stir the mixture. Each of these is a sub-task in the bottom-up approach.

   (b) *Filling in a tax form.* Probably top-down, breaking down to filling in personal details, employment details, details of income, details of outgoings and details of allowances, then decomposing each of these sections separately.

   (c) *Writing a report for a small project you are doing for your employer.* Almost certainly top-down, breaking the whole report into introduction, various sections and conclusions, and then further decomposing these.

(d) *Booking a foreign holiday.* Bottom-up is likely, since you are likely to be capable of checking passport and visa details, ordering currency and travellers cheques, selecting accommodation and booking flight details – otherwise, top-down.

(e) *Calculating who pays what after a meal in a restaurant.* Either. A top-down approach would be for one person to work through the bill several times, calculating totals for each individual; bottom-up would be for each individual to calculate their own total, count out their cash and hand it to one of the group to make the payment (and just remember I did not have a starter!).

CHAPTER 2

Designing software systems

The major stages in the software development life-cycle are analysis, design and implementation. To design an object oriented system, it is necessary to know what a software object is, how software objects take part in the overall operation of a system, and how the various objects in a system can interact. The major benefit of object orientation in software design is that we can bring our knowledge of how objects in the real world work and inter-operate. Object oriented design is a matter of expressing these capabilities and relationships in software-specific ways.

In this chapter you will learn:

- what classes and objects are and how to describe classes of object,

- how to describe object interactions,

- how different classes of object can be related to each other,

- how to depict these relationships and interactions in simple diagrams.

2.1   Designing objects and classes

In the previous chapter, we described how the process of software development was conducted, and looked at ways in which the requirements of a software system could be stated, decomposed and expressed in a form that made them suitable for rendering in a programming language. We did not consider the actual detailed process of programming or program design. In this section, we will start from the premise that we have fully specified a system and need to develop an object oriented design that describes how to implement it.

Only the most trivial of computer systems are based on a single type of object or algorithm – many of the early programs you write will implement one type of object, but this is purely for the convenience of learning what objects are and how they work. In real software solutions, we need to be able to describe how objects will interact, sometimes in very complex situations. We will learn how to develop an object oriented system, including inter-object interactions, to the point where it can be coded in a programming language.

Previously, we looked at algorithms as a form of description that was entirely separate from the way that a computer program would be required to implement it. The key feature in proposing an algorithm was that it should not be encumbered with details of how a specific programming language would be used to implement it. At some point, we need to reconcile the abstract algorithm with the concrete require-ments of a computer programming language.

We can picture the development phases of the life-cycle as a progression, from very abstract specifications, through the design stages to a concrete implementation, as shown in Figure 2.1.

For our purposes, we can consider these steps in the progression to be as follows:

- Software specification is the identification of the objects required by the system to do its job and the services these objects must provide.

- Software design is the development of a plan of how the various objects will co-operate on the overall job being done.

- Software implementation is the act of realizing a software design as *classes* in an object oriented programming language.

In the previous chapter we saw how a software requirements description could be analyzed so that we could identify the objects required by the system. We can now go on to learn how the objects might be developed to a stage where we could implement them in our chosen language.

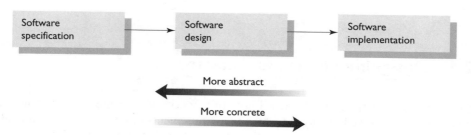

Figure 2.1   *Progression through the life-cycle development phases.*

Class and object

Our first requirement is to be able to describe an object, in terms of what information it contains, and what operations it can perform. Visual Basic comes complete with an entire library of predefined types of object. Most of these are ***controls***, another name for user-interface components. All of them share the key characteristics of any software object:

- They are defined as members of a ***class***, which is simply another way of saying that there are different types of object, and that members of the same class share similar attributes and behavioural capabilities.

- They are ***encapsulated*** – that is, the internal representation of information and operations is protected from users of the objects behind a ***public interface***.

- Their capabilities are defined in two ways – ***properties***, which are the attributes of an object, and ***methods***, which are the operations a particular class of object can perform.

The notion of a ***class*** is one with which you are probably familiar. One very specific use of the word class is to identify a group of students at the same approximate level of learning. However, a more general explanation of the term is that it describes '*a collection or division of people or things sharing a common characteristic, attribute, quality or property*'. In terms of object oriented programming, this description, from Collins' English Dictionary, is ideal.

In object oriented programming, we aim to develop a program by composing it of objects working together to do some job. In the majority of cases, several objects with similar capabilities would be used to divide up the labour and to represent different, but similar, items. For example, a word processor uses a number of documents. All of these can be displayed on the screen, searched for specific words or phrases, printed and stored on a disk.

With this in mind, we can see that it would be very inefficient to develop object oriented programs by creating each individual object as a separate programming task. Objects that share capabilities belong to the same class, and the best approach is therefore to develop *classes* of objects, rather than the objects themselves; see Figure 2.2.

A class is a template for any number of objects that share the same general characteristics and capabilities. When we develop a class, we describe the types of information that an arbitrary object of the class might contain, and the actions or operations that it can perform.

This does not mean, however, that all objects that belong to a class are identical. In the same way that two word-processed documents can be operated on in the same way, even though their text and formatting are completely different, so two objects of a class can contain different information and yet perform the same types of operation. We can make this distinction by saying that two objects of the same class have different *states*. The state of an object is the pattern of data values, or properties, contained in it, so although every object of a class performs exactly the same

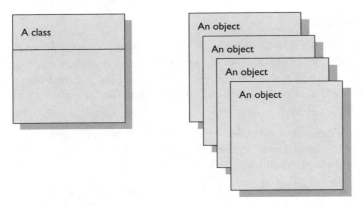

Figure 2.2   *Class and object.*

operations, the operations will have different outcomes because they work with different data.

An example should clarify this. Let's assume that in a given program, we have defined a class of objects that can be displayed on the screen of a computer. All of the objects of the class have the capabilities to display themselves. They all also have a `Colour` property that indicates the colour that an object will display itself in. In the program, we can create two of these objects, one in white and one in grey (Figure 2.3).

It should be easy to see that both objects belong to the same class, since they have the same capabilities and store the same *type* of information, but that both are also different, since the colours specified by their Colour properties are different.

Class notation

If we are to design classes of objects and indicate how they are to be interconnected, we need some form of notation to save having to use text descriptions repetitively. Software developers tend to work with diagrams, since they make very concise shorthand when describing the structure of systems. Figure 2.2 shows a commonly used form of diagram for depicting classes and objects in a system. This can be refined to depict not only the class or object, but also the properties and methods defined for it.

Figure 2.4 shows a general picture of a class, and of an object of that class. The class diagram shows the properties and methods of the class, while the object diagram

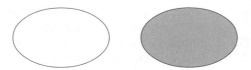

Figure 2.3   *Two objects of the same class with a different Colour property value.*

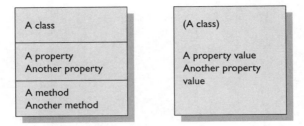

Figure 2.4 *Class and object diagrams, showing properties and methods.*

shows what class the object belongs to and the specific values taken on by each property. There is no need to indicate the methods in the object, since methods are defined for a whole class. Note that in this form of diagram, we show classes in terms of their ***interfaces***. There is nothing in the diagram that indicates *how* information will be stored in an object of the class, or how a particular method actually works.

Figure 2.5 shows a specific class (`Appointment`) and how its interface is defined, and also shows a specific `Appointment` object as an example. Note that there is no need to show the names of the class methods (`AddToSchedule` and `SetAlarm`) on the Appointment instance. Since the object is a member of the Appointment class, we are allowed to assume the availability of these methods.

As object oriented programmers, we take it on trust that an object will behave as its interface suggests, and actively avoid bringing in any indication of how the objects are implemented when we are describing how objects will interact. At another level, we must be able to describe the exact composition and workings of a class. At this *class development* level, we are interested in the specific algorithms used by class methods and the raw information that makes up an object's properties. Class development occurs late in the design phase and in the implementation phase of the life-cycle.

Returning to the example of the objects that can display themselves and have a specific Colour property, if the method that made an object display itself was to be called `Display`, we could depict the class, and objects of it, as shown in Figure 2.6.

Now that we have a notation by which we can depict classes and objects, we can go on to show how specific object relationships and interactions can be described.

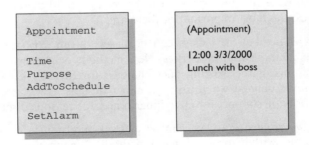

Figure 2.5 *An Appointment class and object.*

Figure 2.6   *The 'ScreenObject' class, with a 'Colour' property and a 'Display' method.*

QUESTION 2.1

Consider a new class that is to be defined for use in a Personal Information Manager program: `DiaryEntry`. Instances of this class will have the following properties:

```
Date
Time
Text
Alarm
```

The class will also have the methods:

```
Display
CheckAlarm
```

Draw a class diagram for this class, and also draw two instances of the class as diagrams with the following instance data:

```
25/12/99, 08:00, "Open Xmas presents", Yes
1/1/00, 09:00, "Start new diary", No
```

2.2   Object relationships

There are several ways in which objects can be related to other objects in programs. For our purposes, the most important of these are:

■ *Code inheritance* – a new class can be based on an existing class so that it inherits its methods and properties. New methods or properties can be added, and definitions of the existing ones changed for the new class. This form of relationship is defined when a programmer designs new classes. Visual Basic does not provide support for code inheritance, for reasons discussed later.

■ *Interface inheritance* – a class can be defined purely in terms of how objects would interact with its properties and methods. It is therefore possible to define 'empty' classes, ones that describe the necessary behaviour that other classes are required to provide – these are interfaces, or interface classes. New classes can be based on these interface classes so that they do provide the required functions. Although interface classes do not take part in any programs, they are often used to define standardized capabilities that may be implemented by a variety of classes. They can therefore be used to enforce compatibility among a number of classes. Visual Basic provides this mechanism, sometimes referred to as *interface inheritance*, to distinguish it from the more usual *code inheritance*.

■ *Composition* – an object is part of another object (a component of it) and is used in such a way that the existing object provides or assists in the provision of some of the new object's properties and methods. The new type of object can *delegate* some or all of its interface behaviour so that the existing component object does the work. This way of delegating some of the responsibilities of an object to another is useful for providing code inheritance-like features in an environment that does not support this form of inheritance (like Visual Basic).

■ *Aggregation* – a member of a class can be composed in part of multiple members of the same or other classes. This is similar to composition, but in aggregation the potential exists for one object to contain or be composed of several existing objects. Methods and properties defined for the new class can delegate some or all of their work to the methods or properties of the objects it contains. Again, the programmer designing a class defines this type of relationship, but the actual aggregation relationships are formed and modified as a program executes. Visual Basic provides good support for this form of relationship.

■ *Message passing* – an object can utilize the abilities of other objects of the same or a different class (a server class) by passing messages to them requesting data or services. This is the main communication method used in object oriented programming, and simply involves accessing the methods and properties defined in the server class.

Using one, two or all of these mechanisms, objects of one class can utilize objects of other classes to distribute the work involved in performing a task. The methods can be used to define all of the interactions that need to be implemented in an object oriented program.

Inheritance

This facility is more generally referred to as ***generalization–specialization***. An existing class, the ***generalized*** class, is used as a starting point when developing a new class, the ***specialized*** class. Specialization can be done by adding new properties or methods to the new class, or by changing the way that existing properties or methods work in the new class, or a mixture of both. The new class becomes a specialized version of the existing one.

This type of relationship is often described as an *is-a* relationship, since the new class is a specialized version of the existing one. In a real-world example, a truck 'is a' vehicle, since truck is a more specialized version of vehicle. A truck has all of the capabilities of a vehicle, plus one or more additional facilities (the ability to carry heavy loads).

Most programming languages that support object oriented development provide a mechanism that allows new classes to be defined in terms of extensions and alterations to existing classes – a feature known as *code inheritance*. This feature allows you to reuse classes you or others have developed by basing a new class on the code of the existing one. If we have the class `ScreenObject`, we can use this as the basis of a new class, say `PrinterObject` that defines much of its behaviour in terms of the existing class. In this case, we would alter the existing method `Display` so that it sent the picture of the object to a printer instead of the display screen. Defining a class with code inheritance is easy, since all of the features of the existing class automatically become features of the new one. The design of the new class is then a matter of adding new properties or methods to it, or changing some of the inherited features.

Code inheritance, the most commonly understood form of inheritance, is a double-edged sword, so much so that some programmers have come to consider it a feature best approached with great care because of the ambiguity that it can introduce into otherwise well-designed classes and systems. There are two particular situations in which the use if inheritance can result in extra difficulties in programming. The first of these is sometimes known as the 'deadly diamond' (Figure 2.7), and refers to an ambiguous inheritance situation.

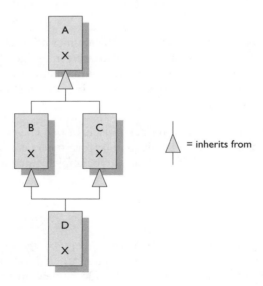

Figure 2.7   *The Deadly Diamond. Classes B and C both inherit from class A. Class D inherits from both classes B and C. If class A has a method 'X', both classes B and C inherit it. Which version of the method 'X' does class D inherit?*

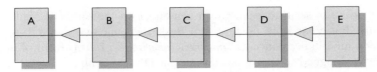

Figure 2.8   *Class E inherits from class D, which inherits from class C, which inherits from class B, which inherits from class A. If a method or property of class A is changed in some way, will classes B to E still behave as expected?*

As Figure 2.7 shows, inheritance from two classes can have certain pitfalls. If classes B and C both redefine a method X that is inherited from class A, it is not possible to say which of these class D will inherit, leading to ambiguous behaviour. Because of this, some object oriented programming languages that do support inheritance only allow a new class to inherit from one existing class. ***Single inheritance*** is considered to be much safer than ***multiple inheritance***.

The second situation is more general, and therefore affects all languages that support inheritance. It happens when a class that has been inherited from is changed when one or more of its properties or methods is altered. This change will propagate through the inheritance chain, affecting all classes that inherit directly or indirectly from it.

Frequently, this propagation is a desirable feature of inheritance, since any fixes applied to a class higher up the inheritance chain will automatically apply to those classes that inherit from it. However, an alteration in the behaviour of a higher class will also apply to classes that inherit from it. If any of the affected classes are deployed in applications, it is possible that the change to their behaviour will have unexpected influences on how these applications work; see Figure 2.8.

This problem is not confined to inheritance relationships since it can also affect an aggregation relationship. Therefore, even languages that do not support inheritance are vulnerable to it. However, since an inheritance relationship is often more subtle, it is more likely that the problem would not be noticed as easily.

Visual Basic up to version 6.0 is considered to have been limited due to its lack of inheritance features, but as we have seen, inheritance does have its pitfalls. The fact remains that Visual Basic programmers do not seem to have been unduly hampered by the lack of inheritance in the language, as evidenced by the range of applications for which those versions of the language were used. The introduction of code inheritance in version 7.0 is a feature that will require a large number of Visual Basic programmers to re-evaluate their design and development methods.

Code inheritance is a facility that is plainly useful in reducing the amount of work required building a complex class hierarchy. However, it is a feature that can make programs more difficult to understand, and it does not provide any capabilities that could not be implemented by other means.

Interface inheritance

To date Visual Basic has had no code inheritance feature. While this can certainly be seen as a limitation, especially when Visual Basic is compared to other languages such as C++, it does not seem to have had much effect on the range of applications for which Visual Basic has been used. Visual Basic has, since version 5.0, supported a more general inheritance concept – ***interface inheritance***. In this form of inheritance, a class can be designed so that it has an interface that is compatible with some more general class. The drawback of this form of inheritance is that all of the inherited interface properties and methods must be re-coded in the new class – no features are added automatically.

Interface inheritance allows a programmer to create families of classes that are compatible with each other, so that you can replace a member of one class with a member of a compatible one without changing any code that uses the object. This facility supports the powerful object oriented facility called ***polymorphism***. This is a feature that allows the creation of programs that can make use of any of a range of compatible classes. Visual Basic is in good company in providing interface inheritance, which is also a key feature of the languages Ada and Java, and the working principle of the Component Object Model (COM), which enables polymorphism between objects from different programs in a Windows environment.

Composition/aggregation

Objects can contain other objects, or references to other objects, and can make use of the capabilities of the objects they contain. Composition is normally used as a way to create a new class of object that extends the behaviour of an existing class without the use of code inheritance. Aggregation is normally used as a way of assembling complex objects by adding together the capabilities of a number of more simple objects.

For example, we might decide to provide our **ScreenObject** class with the ability to display a text caption in a variety of fonts. If we had access to inheritance, we could design **ScreenObject** as a specialist version of a pre-existing **Font** class. However, we do not have inheritance to work with, and, more importantly, it would be wrong to do this since we cannot say that a **ScreenObject** 'is a' **Font**.

We can however make each **ScreenObject** object contain a **Font** object. This type of relationship is referred to as the ***has-a*** relationship – a **ScreenObject** 'has a' font, and is implemented using composition. The relationship is conceptually correct.

A composition relationship is shown diagrammatically as in Figure 2.9. The diamond is drawn at the side of the composed object, and the implicit numerical relationship is that, for example, one **ScreenObject** contains one **Font**.

When one object contains multiple objects of the same or different classes, the relationship is more normally called an aggregation relationship. In such a relationship,

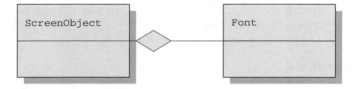

Figure 2.9 *An aggregation (has-a) relationship.*

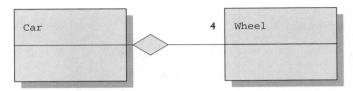

Figure 2.10   *A qualified aggregation relationship.*

we need to show multiplicity. For example, a car has four wheels, and this 'qualified aggregation' relationship can be depicted as in Figure 2.10.

Note that it is normal to show the aggregation as a property of the main class (**Car** in this case), appending an 's' to the end of the property name to indicate that it refers to more than one item. Other qualifications can be used to indicate different quantities in aggregations. For example, many trucks have four wheels, but some types of truck have more than four wheels. This situation can be depicted as in Figure 2.11. Similarly, 0+ is used to mean 0 or more, 1+ as one or more, and so on.

Delegation

We use delegation as an alternative to code inheritance when we wish to extend or in some way alter an existing class – it is used in composition and aggregation relationships as the mechanism for gaining access to the behaviour of the internal object(s). More work is involved, since in a code inheritance relationship, properties and methods in the existing class automatically become properties and methods in the new class. Using delegation in lieu of code inheritance, it is necessary to recreate all of the methods in the new class, delegating their work to the enclosed version of the existing class.

For example, in the earlier illustration of the use of composition, we decided that a **ScreenObject** could be used as the basis of a new **PrintObject** class. Delegation would be used to make the resulting **PrintObject** object make use of its internal **ScreenObject**'s interface. Because we are using delegation, we will need to recreate the **Colour** property and the **Display** method as new methods in the interface of the **PrintObject**.

Since the new class completely redefines the **Display** method, we would treat this no differently than we would in the inheritance situation. However, the **Colour** property will not be automatically available in the new class, and we will have to

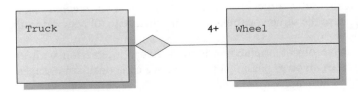

Figure 2.11   *A more general qualification.*

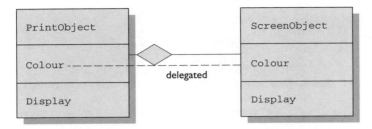

Figure 2.12   *The Colour property, delegated.*

create a new `Colour` property that uses the same property in the class inherited from (see Figure 2.12).

QUESTION 2.2

The `DiaryEntry` class from the previous question is to be used as a component of a new class, `DiaryDay`, where one `DiaryDay` object can contain an unlimited number of `DiaryEntry` objects. The appropriate aggregation symbol for this is the * symbol. Draw a diagram that shows how the two classes are related.

Message passing

The last form of relationship we will consider is where one object accesses the properties or methods of another by 'passing a message' to it. The idea of passing a message is mainly conceptual – we will find it easier to think of objects as collaborating on a task if we can depict this collaboration in a human oriented way. In fact, any program statement in which a property or method of an object is accessed is considered as passing a message to that object.

Continuing the metaphor, we can think of a class as having a vocabulary, which is the range of properties and methods defined for it. For example, the `ScreenObject` class has a vocabulary consisting of the names of its properties and methods – `Colour` and `Display`.

A message is a call to a method in an object of some class. The key distinction between messages and methods is that the same message can be passed to objects from any class that is capable of interpreting it. Each class may well do something different in response to a message; each will have its own *method* of dealing with it. Classes that share the same vocabulary, or interface, can all respond to the same set of messages.

Messages drive object oriented programs. Every interaction with an object as a program executes involves passing a message. We can consider messages as having up to three parts. These are:

■ The *name* part of the message

- The *parameters* carried by the message

- The information returned from, or *result* of the message.

A message is defined for any class of object that has a specific interface. However, a message is always sent to a specific object, and so there is in fact a fourth, implicit part to a message – the *object* to which the message is passed. Not all messages have all of the parts. For example, our `ScreenObject` class has a message, `Display`, which has no parameters and would return no result. Its job is simply to tell the object to display itself on the screen, and no other information is necessary. If we have a `ScreenObject` named `ScrObj` in a program, we can send it the `Display` message with the statement:

```
ScrObj.Display
```

The `Colour` property, on the other hand, defines a message that requires us to pass a parameter. If we wish to change the colour of a `ScreenObject`, we will send it the `Colour` message, stating what the new colour is to be. To change the colour of our object `ScrObj` to red, we use the message:

```
ScrObj.Colour = Red
```

The 'dot' operator used between the name of the object and the message we are sending it is a standard object oriented way of accessing properties and methods.

Note that we could also define the property `Colour` to *return* the current colour of the object. Properties as supported by Visual Basic are flexible in this respect, in that they can normally be defined in two different ways – to retrieve a value and to change a value. A property can pass information into an object, in which case it is referred to as a *Property Let* in Visual Basic. A property can also retrieve information from an object, this type being known as a `Property Get`. Above, we have defined a Property Let: one that passes information into an object in order to change its current setting. Visual Basic allows us to define both Property Let and Property Get versions of a property, so that we can use the same property name to either change a part of an object (using a parameter) or retrieve the current value.

We can show message passing in object diagrams by simply using an arrow to indicate which object sends the message and which receives it. The arrowhead is at the receiver end. If we have an object, say *X*, that sends a message to a `ScreenObject`, `ScrObj`, to change its colour to red, we can depict this as in Figure 2.13.

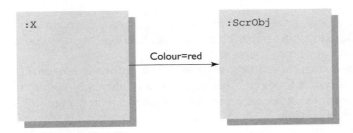

Figure 2.13 *X sending a message to* `ScrObj`.

Note the colon preceding the object's name in this collaboration. The diagram shows a *specific* object sending a message to another, rather than a more general depiction of an object of one class sending a message to an object of another. If the diagram were to involve a number of objects of different classes, the full syntax `ClassName:ObjectName` would be used to clarify matters. If we had wanted the object `X` to *read* the `Colour` property of the `ScrObj` object, rather than setting its `Colour` property to a new value, we would have used the simpler expression `Colour` to annotate the message arrow.

QUESTION 2.3

A `DiaryDay` object needs to determine the `Time` property of a `DiaryEntry`. Draw a diagram to show this interaction message.

2.3 An example class design

It is worthwhile at this stage to look at an example of a useful class, so that we can try out the various mechanisms that make it work. Note that we will only be *designing* the class just now, although we will go on to implement it in the next chapter.

Let's assume we need a class that we will call `BankAccount`. This will model a simplistic bank account and will include facilities for depositing and withdrawing cash from the account and for determining the current balance. The full requirements specification is given below.

1. A `BankAccount` will have an indication of the amount of money currently in the account – the `Balance` of the account.

2. It will be possible to `Deposit` additional cash into the account.

3. It will be possible to `Withdraw` an amount of cash from the account.
   3.1. If the amount to be withdrawn exceeds the current account balance, the withdrawal operation will be aborted.

We can depict this set of requirements in a form known as a use-case diagram (Figure 2.14). This is a simple notation that describes the operations that can be performed on a system by a user of that system.

The use-case diagram can be a good way for a software developer to describe the operation of a system to the end-user or client. It is inherently simple, and text used is normally in the form of very short sentences with a verb and an object, so that it is as unambiguous as possible.

This requirements specification is very simple, and would not be adequate for modelling a real bank account, where each deposit and withdrawal transaction would

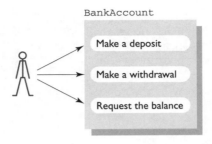

Figure 2.14   *A use-case diagram for a simple* **BankAccount**.

Figure 2.15   *The* **BankAccount** *class.*

need to be recorded so that an account statement could be generated. We will address this more complex requirement in a later chapter. To design the **BankAccount** class we start by drawing a class diagram containing the name of the class (Figure 2.15).

We can now go on by adding a property to indicate the account balance, and methods to allow the deposit and withdrawal of cash. Note that we have distinguished between the actions of requesting information about the internal state of the bank account (the Balance *property*) and applying operations on the bank account (the Deposit and Withdraw *methods*): see Figure 2.16.

Since this is a simple class, there is no need for aggregation. We will, however, expect to be able to operate the class by passing messages to it, and so should define the format of these messages: see Figure 2.17.

Figure 2.16   *The* **BankAccount** *class with properties and methods.*

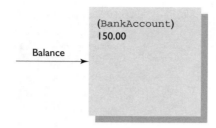

Figure 2.17   *Accessing the Balance property.*

Note the use of brackets around the class name to show we have an ***instance*** of the `BankAccount` class. Note also that the current property value (£150.00) is shown – this is not strictly necessary, and can sometimes cause confusion. The `Balance` message passed to the account will implicitly retrieve the current account balance (i.e. the *value* of that property).

All we have done with these diagrams is to show what messages an object of the class can respond to, and what information (if any) these messages bring with them. In the case of the Deposit and Withdraw operations (Figure 2.18), an additional piece of information is required – an indication of the amount to be deposited or withdrawn. We can always describe the action that the messages will have as a short text paragraph to resolve any possibilities of ambiguity.

In designing a single class as we have done here, it is not possible to show full interactions between objects. At some later stage, we will have to incorporate this and other classes into a design diagram that shows the interactions, and shows which object sends a message and which receives it. Figure 2.19 shows a very simple example of this, using specific object instances rather than classes.

The interactions shown are very simple examples, since there are only two objects involved and all interactions are commands directed from the ATM machine to the `BankAccount` object. Most systems will have to support more complex interactions involving a greater number of objects.

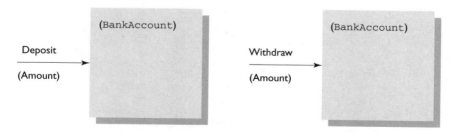

Figure 2.18   *The Deposit and Withdraw methods.*

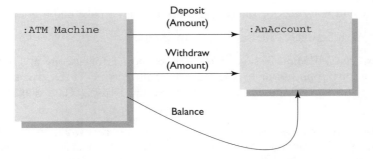

Figure 2.19 *A* **BankAccount** *object and its interactions with an ATM machine.*

QUESTION 2.4

Assume the **BankAccount** class has been extended to include information on transaction operations. As a part of this, it is now necessary for a **BankAccount** to determine the **Date** and **Time** at which a transaction (deposit or withdrawal) is being made. It can do this by sending the **Time** and **Date** messages to the **ATMMachine** object. Show the interactions that happen during a withdrawal operation on a diagram.

2.4 Review questions

1. Insert the missing words in the following sentences:
   Software _____ is the development of a plan of how objects will interact to accomplish a task.
   An _____ is an instance of a class.
   A _____ is a template for all objects that share the same characteristics.
   Classes that have the same names for all of their properties and methods are said to display _____ inheritance.
   A class that inherits the implementation of properties and methods from another is said to exhibit _____ inheritance.
   An inheritance relationship between classes is also often referred to as an _____ relationship.
   Objects of classes that are interface-compatible are interchangeable, and are said to have the facility of _____.
   Objects that interact with others by invoking their methods are said to pass a _____.

2. Distinguish between an attribute and a method.

3. In an inheritance relationship, also referred to as a generalization–specialization relationship, which class (generalized or specialized) inherits from which?

4. How would you describe the relationship between a page and a book?

5. Distinguish between a message and a method.

6. A new class, EMailMessage, has been proposed for use in a desktop communications application. It is to have four properties – **From, To, Subject** and **Body** – and two methods – **Send** and **Display**. Draw a class diagram for this class.

7. The **MailServer** class and the **MailClient** class interact when an e-mail message is sent. The interaction involves the **MailClient** object passing the **MailServer** object a message, which involves the passing of additional information – an **EMailMessage** object. Show this interaction on a diagram.

2.5   Practical exercises

In these practical exercises, you will learn how to:

- create a class which has a simple interface,

- add simple properties and methods to a class,

- make use of the Visual Basic Immediate window to create an object and access its class interface.

The program statements used in this example will be fully explained in the next chapter, so you should concentrate on simply getting the example class working.

Exercise 1:   Create a class in a new project

To start this exercise, you will need to create a new Visual Basic project and add a class module to it (see the exercises at the end of Chapter 1 to remind yourself how to do this). We will develop the simple Bank Account class described in this chapter, so the new class should be named **BankAccount**.

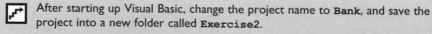
After starting up Visual Basic, change the project name to **Bank**, and save the project into a new folder called **Exercise2**.

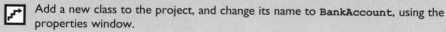
Add a new class to the project, and change its name to **BankAccount**, using the properties window.

The Visual Basic project window should now appear as shown in Figure 2.20.

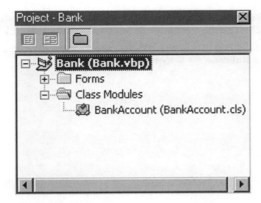

Figure 2.20 *The Project Explorer window for the new Bank project.*

The BankAccount class will have a code window associated with it, and it is here that we will add statements to define class member variables, properties and methods.

Exercise 2:   Adding a simple property

Move to the code window for the bank account class. To do this, you can select the class's entry in the project explorer and then press the view code button at the top of the project explorer window. Alternatively, simply double-click on the class's entry in the project explorer. The code window should come to the fore in the main area of the IDE, with the cursor flashing in it (Figure 2.21).

Note the two drop-down boxes (combo-boxes) at the top of the code window. The left box gives quick access to the general code area or to specially defined class events,

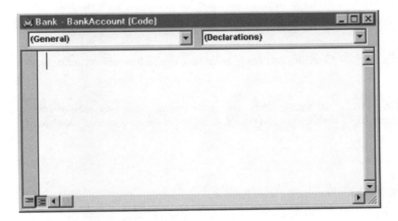

Figure 2.21 *The code window for the **BankAccount** class.*

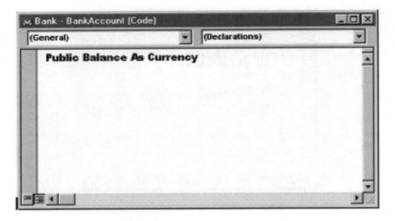

Figure 2.22   *A simple property definition.*

while the right-hand one allows you to look up a specific method in the code. Since the code window will frequently have to deal with long lists of program statements, these controls will provide a quick and convenient method for accessing specific routines.

To add a simple property to the class, we can simply type its definition at the current cursor position in the code window (Figure 2.22).

> Add the **Balance** property to the class, by defining a simple public variable to represent a currency value.

We can think of the **Balance** property as somewhere to keep a note of the current bank account balance – it will remember the value for us. In fact, even at this early stage, we could now create a **BankAccount** object and make use of its **Balance** property. To demonstrate this, we can use Visual Basic's *Immediate* window.

> **Exercise 3:**   Creating and using an object in the Immediate window

> Go to the Immediate window, and enter the following sequence of statements, terminating each by pressing the Enter key on your computer's keyboard.

```
Set A = New BankAccount
A.Balance = 100
Print A.Balance
```

This sequence of statements will create a new **BankAccount** object and apply a value to its **Balance** property. Finally, it will cause the **BankAccount** object (named **A**) to

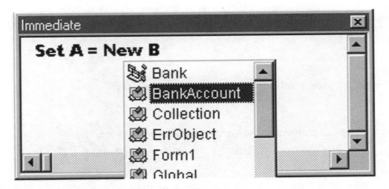

Figure 2.23 *Visual Basic's code completion facility in action.*

retrieve the current value in its `Balance` property, and pass this to the `Print` command, causing the balance to be displayed.

Visual Basic will try to assist you as you enter the statements. As soon as you press the space bar after the keyword **New** in the Immediate window, a pop-up list will appear to offer all of the legal options of types of object you could create with this type of statement. Press the B key, and the first word beginning with the letter B will be highlighted. You can get Visual Basic to complete the keyword from this list by using the up and down cursor keys to scroll to the word you want and pressing the Tab or Enter key; see Figure 2.23.

The second and third statements entered into the Immediate window serve to set the `Balance` property of the newly created bank account object to 100 (dollars, pounds, yen or whatever currency you decide to work with), and then to print this value out. After entering these three statements, the Immediate window should appear something like that shown in Figure 2.24.

Note that the fourth line is the Immediate window's response to the request made in the third statement – to print the `Balance` property of the account object designated by the name **A**.

We could go on to make changes to the `Balance` of the `BankAccount` object, or create other new `BankAccount` objects. However, the current version of the

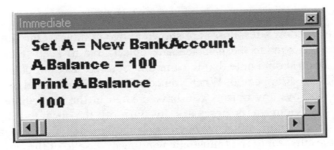

Figure 2.24 *The Immediate window after a sequence of statements has been entered.*

BankAccount class is a little limited, so our next task will be to add some useful functionality to it.

Exercise 4:   Add methods to the **BankAccount** class

 Add a Deposit method to the **BankAccount** class and test it.

Place the cursor on a new line in the **BankAccount** class's code window. If it refuses to leave the first line containing the definition of the **Balance** property, put the cursor at the end of that line and press Enter to add a new blank line. Now type the following sequence of lines:

```
Public Sub Deposit(amount As Currency)
   Balance = Balance + amount
End Sub
```

Note that you will not have to type all of these lines. As soon as you have entered the first line and pressed the Enter key at its end, the last line will be added automatically, and the cursor will be placed at the beginning of the line in the middle, ready for you to enter it. You can indent the middle line as shown above by pressing the **Tab** key once before typing the statement. This will make the body of the method being defined stand out, which will be useful when you go on to create bigger method definitions than this one.

The **Deposit** method as defined will add a specified amount to the current bank account balance. Again this can be tested in the Immediate window:

```
Set A = New BankAccount
A.Deposit 100
Print A.Balance
   100
A.Deposit 50
Print A.Balance
   150
```

The Immediate window's responses are shown above in italics. Our definition of the **Deposit** method has made the **BankAccount** object able to keep track of amounts deposited to it. You should note that the amount set as the account balance in the first test that we did has disappeared. When you edit the definition of a class, Visual Basic automatically destroys any objects you have created in the Immediate window. To test the new behaviour, it is necessary to start off the new test by creating a **BankAccount** object again, either by re-entering the line **Set A = New BankAccount** or by placing the cursor into the Immediate window at the end of the existing line with that command and pressing **Enter**.

Add a `Withdraw` method to the `BankAccount` class and test it.

The `Withdraw` method will be very similar to the `Deposit` method – instead of adding an amount to the current balance you will need to subtract the amount (using a minus sign). *As an exercise, add this method.*

Exercise 5: Making the class more secure

Once our `BankAccount` class has been given its `Balance` property, and its `Deposit` and `Withdraw` methods, it meets the definition devised earlier in this chapter. However, the class as defined can be used inconsistently, since it is possible to change the value of the `Balance` property at any time. Ideally, the amount in a bank account should be a product of the deposits to and withdrawals from the account only. Real banks uphold this rule and we ought to expect our class model of a bank account to behave in the same way.

For example, if I open a new account, deposit $100 to it and then withdraw $50 from it, I would expect it to have a balance if $50. However, since the `Balance` member variable is publicly accessible, any user of the class can contain code that could change the value of the balance without using the deposit or withdraw mechanisms. We need to strengthen the *encapsulation* features of the `BankAccount` class.

Recall that encapsulation is a principle that object oriented programming provides for. In the case of our `BankAccount` class, that principle should make it impossible to change the `Balance` property inconsistently with the deposits and withdrawals. We can provide for this by modifying our definition of the `Balance` property.

 Change the definition of the `Balance` member variable.

Alter the first line of the class definition to appear as shown below:

```
Private mvarBalance As Currency
```

Note that as well as changing the name of the currency variable by adding an **mvar** prefix (standing for *m*ember *var*iable), we have also changed the form of its definition by replacing the `Public` keyword with a `Private` one. This will make it impossible for an external statement to access the **mvarBalance** member variable, although code within the class will still have access to it. We now need to provide an alternative mechanism for retrieving the account balance from an external statement.

Add the following set of statements to the class.

```
Public Property Get Balance() As Currency
   Balance = mvarBalance
End Property
```

 Amend the **Deposit** and **Withdraw** methods to refer to the new name of the member variable.

```
Public Sub Deposit(amount As Currency)
   mvarBalance = mvarBalance + amount
End Sub
```

Repeat this for the **Withdraw** method, and test how the method works in the Immediate window. The full code of the class is reproduced at the end of this section, so you can check whether you have implemented **Withdraw** correctly.

In these alterations, we have changed the operation of the **BankAccount** class quite radically, even though the definition is unchanged. Now, when we access the **Balance** property, we are using a special code routine to retrieve the value, internally held in the member variable **mvarBalance**. When the **Deposit** and **Withdraw** methods change the account balance, they change the value of this same **mvarBalance** member variable. You should be able to rerun the tests tried earlier, and with the exception of the very first test in which the value of the account's balance was modified directly (shown in Figure 2.24) they should all execute as before.

> *You should make sure you save this entire project to disk before you close down Visual Basic. We will return to add to it in later exercises.*

In this exercise, we have developed a simple class and demonstrated how objects of the class respond to simple commands from the Immediate window. In most cases, classes are more complex than this one, and are used in more complex situations in which objects communicate with each other.

In the next chapter, we will go on to examine in detail how to describe the way that more complex objects operate. In its practical exercise, we will extend this example by developing a user-interface class to interact with objects of the **BankAccount** class.

The full **BankAccount** class code

```
Private mvarBalance As Currency

Public Property Get Balance() As Currency
   Balance = mvarBalance
End Property
```

```
Public Sub Deposit(amount As Currency)
   mvarBalance = mvarBalance + amount
End Sub

Public Sub Withdraw(amount As Currency)
   mvarBalance = mvarBalance - amount
End Sub
```

2.6   Answers to questions

QUESTION 2.1

See Figure 2.25.

QUESTION 2.2

The relationship between the **DiaryDay** class and the **DiaryEntry** class is shown in Figure 2.26. Note the use of the multiplicity symbol and the use of * to indicate that a single **DiaryDay** has potentially many **DiaryEntries**, collectively referred to by the **Entries** property.

QUESTION 2.3

The **DiaryDay** class sends the **DiaryEntry** class the Time message (i.e. requesting the value of the **Time** property): see Figure 2.27.

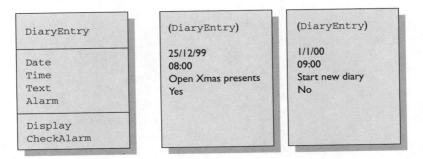

Figure 2.25   *Answer to Question 2.1.*

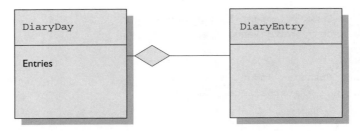

Figure 2.26 *Answer to Question 2.2.*

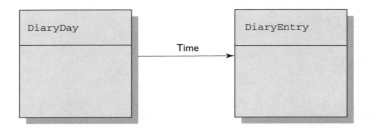

Figure 2.27 *Answer to Question 2.3.*

QUESTION 2.4

An **ATMMachine** object interacts with a **BankAccount** object. The **ATMMachine** sends the **Withdraw** message (passing the amount to be withdrawn), and the **BankAccount** object responds by sending **Date** and **Time** messages to the ATM machine to determine the current values of its **Date** and **Time** properties. See Figure 2.28.

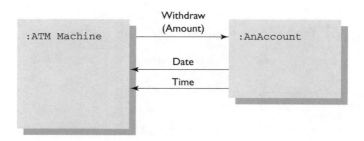

Figure 2.28 *Answer to Question 2.4.*

2.7   Answers to review questions

1.   *Insert the missing words in the following sentences:*

Software design *is the development of a plan of how objects will interact to accomplish a task.*

An object *is an instance of a class.*

A class *is a template for all objects that share the same characteristics.*

Classes that have the same names for all of their properties and methods are said to display interface *inheritance.*

A class that inherits the implementation of properties and methods from another is said to exhibit code *inheritance.*

An inheritance relationship between classes is also often referred to as an is-a *relationship.*

Objects of classes that are interface-compatible are interchangeable, and are said to have the facility of polymorphism.

Objects that interact with others by invoking their methods are said to pass a message.

2.   *Distinguish between an attribute and a method.* An attribute is a setting that all objects of a given class can take on. A method is an operation that objects of a class use to respond to a message.

3.   *In an inheritance relationship, also referred to as a generalization–specialization relationship, which class (generalized or specialized) inherits from which?* A specialized class inherits from a generalized class.

4.   *How would you describe the relationship between a page and a book?* A book is an aggregation of pages.

5.   *Distinguish between a message and a method.* A message is a call to an object. The object responds by executing a method.

6.   *A new class, EMailMessage, has been proposed for use in a desktop communications application. It is to have four properties –* **From**, **To**, **Subject** *and* **Body** *– and two methods –* **Send** *and* **Display**. *Draw a class diagram for this class.* See Figure 2.29.

7.   *The* **MailServer** *class and the* **MailClient** *class interact when an e-mail message is sent. The interaction involves the* **MailClient** *object passing the* **MailServer** *object a message, which involves the passing of additional information – an* **EMailMessage** *object. Show this interaction on a diagram.* See Figure 2.30.

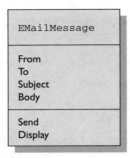

Figure 2.29 *Answer to Review Question 6.*

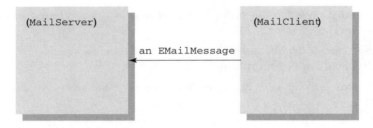

Figure 2.30 *Answer to Review Question 7.*

CHAPTER 3

Making objects work

Objects are combinations of information and operations for manipulating it. Implementing a new type of object involves describing how its information will be represented and defining sequences of instructions to perform the operations. An important feature of objects is the way that certain operations can be defined to provide access to the information they contain.

In this chapter you will learn:

- how the information represented by an object can be modelled,

- how the operations on an object can be described,

- how to decide what parts of a real-world object are worth modelling,

- the distinction between the internal workings and the interface definitions of an object.

As we cover these objectives, we will use just enough Visual Basic keywords and syntax to help explain what is going on. In the next chapter, we will take a more formal and more detailed look at Visual Basic's programming language.

3.1   The internal workings of an object

As we have already seen, an object can be defined in terms of its properties and methods. Properties are expressions of the information or data stored in an object, and are used as mechanisms to access this data. Methods are operations that can be performed on an object, and are able to change the internal data in the object or retrieve information from the object or both. The properties and methods together make up the vocabulary, or interface to an object: see Figure 3.1.

Since an object must have an internal state, made up of the set of values stored in it, we will need to represent this in some way. In the next chapter, we will go on to show in detail how the Visual Basic programming language is used to create classes, and how the internal state of an object and its methods can be defined in Visual Basic. However, no matter what language we use, we need to be able to describe and define the properties and methods of objects. Here we will examine a generic way of doing so.

Algorithms and data

Recall that an algorithm is simply a step-by-step description of how to do a task. The operations supported by objects (i.e. their methods) can be expressed as algorithms. Sometimes these operations are so simple that a description of them would be too trivial to grace with the title 'algorithm'. At other times, an operation can be so complex that we need to be able to spell it out very clearly and in great detail before we try to implement it in a programming language.

It is possible to write algorithms as plain English statements. In most situations, the first cut of an algorithm will be in plain English, since in an English-speaking country that is the language in which the customer is most likely to want to discuss requirements. However, we do not normally continue with this into the detailed design stage of a project simply because the algorithms get too wordy, and wordiness can lead to ambiguities. Therefore, detailed algorithms are best expressed as simple statements that make use of a small set of mathematical symbols.

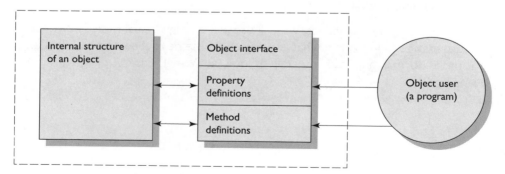

Figure 3.1   *The relationship between an interface, an object and a user.*

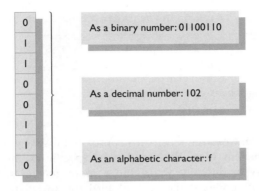

Figure 3.2   *Some representations of a group of binary digits.*

The data or information held in an object must also be represented in some way. In the **BankAccount** class described previously, for example, we need some way to represent the actual cash balance that the **Balance** property accesses for us. Computers use *variables* to store data or information in.

Variables

In computer programs of any type, we need to perform operations on data. All data in computer programs is represented as combinations of binary digits stored in electronic switches – the computer's memory. Groups of binary digits can be used to represent numbers, or letters of the alphabet, punctuation marks, times, dates, currency values or on-off/yes-no states. By combining these simple values, larger groups can represent any form of information we choose to define.

For example, the dots on a colour screen can each be represented as a trio of numbers that indicates the proportion of red, green and blue in their colour. As far as a computer is concerned, all information is simply groups of binary digits, and all of these groups are treated internally as numbers.

Figure 3.2 shows a few ways that a group of binary digits can be interpreted, although this is not exhaustive. In Visual Basic, the same binary pattern represents a dark shade of the colour red, or the date 11/04/1900. We could also choose to make it represent a particular person, a part of a machine in an inventory, or an indication of the gender of eight separate people (male, female, female, male, male, female, female, male, where 0 represents male and 1 represents female).

Operating on a specific number is easy – that is the basis of arithmetic. However, what if we want to operate on a value that might be different at different times or in different circumstances, such as the height of an arbitrary person, the number of goals scored in next Saturday's football match, or the time it takes a uranium sample to decay to a safe level of radioactivity? In cases like that, we use the idea of a *variable*. A variable is simply a placeholder for any value (a number, a name, a date or whatever) that allows us to dispense with specific values and reason about the more general case. We refer to general case values by giving them a symbolic name or ***identifier***.

Figure 3.3 *Manipulating variables.*

For example, we can work out a person's approximate age by subtracting their year of birth from the current year. We could write specific examples for a variety of people and a variety of different years, but a more general solution would be to specify variables that represent the year of birth of an arbitrary person, and the current year (whatever year it is). Using, for example, the identifiers **YearOfBirth** and **CurrentYear** to refer to examples in the range of possible specific values, and the identifier **Age** to refer to the resulting age, we can then express the calculation as:

```
Age = CurrentYear - YearOfBirth
```

Note the use of the = symbol to represent an ***assignment***. We calculate the result of the right-hand side of the expression and assign it to the variable on the left-hand side. If we think of a variable as a box that can hold a specific type of value, then assignment is simply putting a value into the box. If we wish to express a specific case of this example, we can now simply replace the variables **CurrentYear** and **YearOfBirth** with the actual values (e.g. 2000 and 1975): see Figure 3.3. The form of the calculation does not change.

Variables are very important in computer programs, since it is in variables that data, representing information, is stored and operated on. Without variables, it is very difficult to imagine how a computer program could work. In object oriented programming, each object contains its own set of variables, which together make up the *state* of the object.

QUESTION 3.1

The **BankAccount** class described in the previous chapter needs to calculate the new account balance whenever a withdraw or deposit operation happens. Recall that both types of operation require additional information in the form of an **Amount** component to the message. This is either added to or subtracted from the account balance. If the current balance is stored in a variable **curBalance**, and the new balance is to be stored in the variable **newBalance**, write expressions that describe the calculations involved in each type of transaction.

Assignments to variables normally cause the value in the variable to change. In some cases, the change will be due to an operation based on the current value of the variable itself. For example, we might want to add a value to the current value, or subtract a value from it. In this type of assignment, we need to consider how to depict two different values for the same variable: the value before the operation and the value after the operation. To do this, we consider variables on the right-hand side of the assignment operator to contain the values they have *before* the operation. The variable on the left-hand side of the assignment operator will take on the new value. This allows us to write expressions like:

```
Age = Age + 1
```

which indicates that the variable **Age** has its value increased by one, and which we can read as *'Age becomes Age plus 1'*. The assignment operator could also be called the *update* operator for this reason.

QUESTION 3.2

Rewrite the expressions that were the answers to Question 3.1, but this time show how a single variable, **Balance**, will be updated.

Operators

As well as variables, there will be other elements that are required to form the statements that make up algorithms. In the example above, we used the *assignment* operator to assign a value to a variable, and an *arithmetic plus* operator as part of the expression. As you might expect, all of the other arithmetic operators (plus a few extras) can be involved. Statements in algorithms will frequently involve operators, which are just symbols that represent some form of operation on a value. As well as arithmetic operators, we have conditional operators (for making comparisons), string operators (for working on text values) and Boolean operators (for evaluating compound conditions). A useful list of operators is shown in Table 3.1.

Visual Basic provides these operators plus several others. The importance of operators is that they allow us to define fundamental operations clearly and concisely.

Conditional statements

In programs and classes that are required to respond in some way to prevailing conditions, we will need to be able to express *conditions* – statements that have a result that is either **True** or **False**. These are most often based on some form of comparison expressed as an assertion (e.g. $x = 2$) that is true or false – in this case true when **x** is 2, and false for every other value of **x**. Note that this use of the '=' operator is different from the use we make of it when making an assignment: Visual Basic uses the '=' operator for both purposes, and uses the context of the operator in the statement to decide what is to be done.

Table 3.1   *Operators used in our simple algorithm notation.*

Symbol	Meaning	Example
.	The 'dot' operator – object property or method reference	X.Y (refers to method or property Y in object X)
=	Assignment	X = X + 1 (assign a new value to variable X that is one greater than its current value)
+, −, *, /	Standard arithmetic symbols	i.e. Plus, Minus, Times, Divide e.g. x = (y * z)/4 (note that *, not ×, is used for multiplication)
Mod	Modulus – remainder after division	X = 11 Mod 3 (assigns 2 to x – the remainder of 9/3)
<	Less than	X < Y (true if X is less than Y)
>	Greater than	X > Y (true if X is bigger than Y)
=	Equal to	X = Y (true if X and Y are equal: note that the same symbol is used for testing equality and making assignments. Visual Basic manages this apparent ambiguity by examining the context in which the operator appears, as we will see later)
<=	Less than or equal to	X <= Y (true if X is not bigger than Y)
>=	Greater than or equal to	X >= Y (true if X is not less than Y)
And	Logical And	X And Y (true if both X and Y are true)
Or	Logical Or	X Or Y (true if either X or Y is true)
Not	Logical inversion	Not X (true if X is false, false if X is true)
...	Range of values	X : 1 ... 10 (X has a value in the range 1 to 10)

Conditions are used to form decision points in an algorithm – if a certain condition is true, do one thing, if false, do another. For example, to find out how many days there are in February, we need to use the condition of whether it is a leap year. If it is a leap year, February has 29 days, otherwise 28. We might express the condition as:

```
(YearNumber mod 4) = 0 ' True for most leap years
```

Note that we are not saying that **(YearNumber Mod 4)** *is* equal to zero; simply that we are interested in whether it is or not – the assertion can be **True** or **False**. We can use the result of this assertion to decide on which expression to use to set the number of days in a variable called **DaysInFebruary**:

```
If (YearNumber mod 4) = 0 Then
   DaysInFebruary = 29
Else
   DaysInFebruary = 28
End If
```

Note the form that the conditional statement and the statements it controls take. The condition is embedded in an **If...Then** phrase, and is followed by two alternatives. The first is the statement that will be used if the result of the condition is **True**, the second (after the **Else** clause) is that one that will be used if it is **False**. A final **End If** is used to indicate that the influence of the condition ends there.

The condition in the above example is in fact wrongly expressed because of the special conditions for century years – a century year, although always divisible by 4, is only a leap year if it is also divisible by 400. We can define this more complex condition by combining the individual parts with *logical operators*. The resulting expression will be more complex, but that will be true of any complex situation.

```
((YearNumber mod 4) = 0 And (YearNumber mod 100) > 0)
   Or (YearNumber mod 400) = 0
```

Brackets have been used to make sure that the logical expressions are properly connected. For it to be a leap year, we require the year number to be divisible exactly by 4 **((YearNumber mod 4) = 0)**, but not in a century year **((YearNumber mod 100) > 0)**. If it is a century year, then it can only be a leap year if the year number is exactly divisible by 400 **((YearNumber mod 400) = 0)**. We need either the first condition **And** the second condition in combination, **or** the third condition on its own.

Again, we can use the overall condition to control other statements:

```
if ((YearNumber mod 4)=0 And (YearNumber mod 100)=0) _
     Or (YearNumber mod 400)=0 Then
   DaysInFebruary = 29
else
   DaysInFebruary = 28
end if
```

If we were to express this complex set of conditions in English, it would involve more words, take longer to write, and could even contain ambiguities (what do I mean by the word *divisible*, for example?). The more algebraic form used above may initially appear to be more difficult but you can soon get used to that. It is, however, unambiguous.

(a) In the **BankAccount** class, it is important to determine whether a **Withdraw** transaction can be allowed, the criterion being that the current balance in the account must at least cover the amount of the transaction. Write a condition that will be true if a withdrawal can be made, and false otherwise.

(b) Using this condition, write a group of statements in which the condition is used to control a statement that actually makes the withdrawal. Note that it is not necessary to have the **Else** clause and the statement that follows it – in this case, the condition would simply dictate that the controlled statement should be executed or not.

Iteration

Iteration is repetition by another name. A *program loop* is a construct by which one or more statements are repeated a number of times (the word *loop* refers to the order in which the statements are executed, where after the last statement in a sequence, control loops back to the first). If we wish to perform an operation on a number of different values, or on the same values repeatedly, we use iteration to express the general case rather than spelling out each individual operation (there might be thousands of them). For example, refer to Euclid's algorithm for the greatest common divisor of two numbers (described in the previous chapter). This relies on performing the same operation repeatedly until a specific condition is met (a remainder of zero).

Conditions are used to determine whether iteration should continue or not. For example, to work out the value of an investment over a period of 10 years at 5% interest, we can use:

```
Year = 1
Do
   Investment = Investment + (Investment * 5/100)
   Year = Year + 1
Loop Until Year > 10
' N.B The value in the Investment variable is now
' inclusive of compound interest.
```

Note that on each iteration (each time around the loop), 1 is added to the **Year** variable and the value of the **Investment** variable is increased by 5%. Note also the final condition to exit the loop, which is that the value in **Year** must be bigger than 10. The only reason we are using the **Year** variable at all is to count through the 10-year period of the investment. It takes no other part in the calculation.

This is quite a common feature of iteration; we use a specific variable to count through the number of times the loop contents are executed. Of course, it is also possible, and common, to refer to the loop control variable within the repeated statements. We can use its value in the calculations going on inside the loop.

We can use other types of loop where, for example, the condition is tested at the start rather than the end – a *while* loop. In that case, the statements contained within the loop would not be executed if the loop condition were already false.

Objects

We use a combination of variables, operators, conditions and iteration to define what an object is and how it works. In most cases, what goes on inside an object is based on quite simple operations such as assignment, simple arithmetic and conditional tests. Computer programs seem to be powerful because they can perform simple tasks at great speed, and objects are simply a way of organizing these tasks so that they are easy to understand.

3.2   Abstraction

Abstraction is a way of looking at a problem or situation, so that we remove all unnecessary detail and home in on the fundamental features. As you might guess, this is an important requirement when developing an algorithm. When working on a financial problem, for example, it pays to ignore many of the attributes of an item of real money. Its colour, date of issue, weight, molecular density of the ink, country where it is used, root origin of its name, etc., are important features of money, but not in financial calculations. In these cases we need to concentrate on the important issue – its value.

Abstraction is a way of dealing with an object at a variety of levels of detail. A printer may well be concerned about the molecular weight of ink used in a note of a certain denomination, and would use a different abstraction than an accountant would because of this.

The value of abstraction is that it allows us to reduce a real-world problem to a simplified symbolic representation, exactly as we would hope to do in a computer program. In financial circles, abstraction has become a specific form of reality. When we deal with money, we are dealing with an abstraction (the notional value of a certain amount of gold). When we write a cheque, we deal with another abstraction (the written down value represents an amount of money that is itself an abstraction). A financial trader will deal with an even more abstract abstraction (a notional value as represented by electronic impulses received and sent by a computer system).

In computer programming terms, everything is an abstraction. We represent money, time, height, weight, customers, documents, tax returns, forms, etc., as values in variables, and manipulate them using program statements so that we can predict, verify, represent or guess at values in real life.

When we wish to calculate the speed of a car, we need not model a whole car but simply the pertinent attributes: the rotational velocity of the wheels and the circumference of a wheel (Figure 3.4).

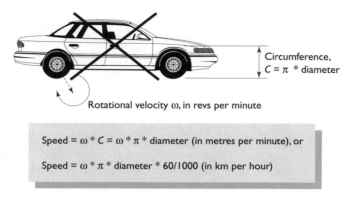

Circumference,
$C = \pi * \text{diameter}$

Rotational velocity ω, in revs per minute

Speed = $\omega * C = \omega * \pi * \text{diameter}$ (in metres per minute), or

Speed = $\omega * \pi * \text{diameter} * 60/1000$ (in km per hour)

Figure 3.4 *An abstraction for calculating the velocity of a car.*

The power of abstraction is that it simplifies otherwise complex circumstances, objects and events. Sometimes we use an abstraction to isolate a specific attribute from a more complex real-world item, such as the value of an amount of money, the age of an insurance policyholder or the circumference of a car wheel. Sometimes we use it as a shorthand for a real-world compound item, for example when we can deal with the notion of a customer, rather than the individual attributes of name, address, date of birth, list of insurance policies held, etc.

In a way, developing computer software involves starting with a very general abstraction (a requirements specification) and making it more and more specific as we progress through the development life-cycle (specification $\rightarrow$ designs $\rightarrow$ detailed designs $\rightarrow$ program code). In this sense, program code is less abstract than a specification, because it is more prescriptive. In specification, we reason with symbols that refer to complex aggregate entities (the *whats* of the system). In programming, we work with specific attributes of the specified system and perform concrete operations on them (the *hows*).

Abstraction and objects

In object oriented programming (OOP), we choose to devise abstractions by modelling the things we want to represent as objects. Part of the reason for this is that OOP allows the programmer to preserve an abstraction through most of the development life-cycle. By defining objects as compound constructions that protect their own internal data and provide a set of services to the outside world, it is possible to design an object to operate exactly as it is specified. All of the details of algorithms are implemented inside an object and hidden from users.

The advantages of this are enormous. For a start, a software developer can design objects to behave like idealized models of the real world they represent. Once the design is completed, the way that the object appears to the outside world need never change, even if the internal workings need to be radically altered. Figure 3.1 showed how we could think of an object as being composed of two structures – its internal

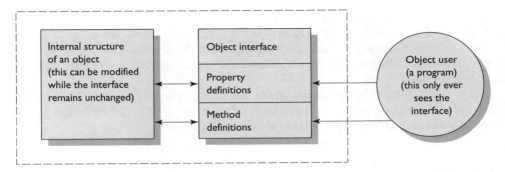

Figure 3.5 *The object interface allows the internal structure to change.*

structure and its interface. The interface part acted as a mechanism that protected the internals of the object from its users: see Figure 3.5.

Objects have many features that make them work well when we are developing abstractions of real-world systems in computer programs. However, the most important of these is the way that we can realize our abstractions in the object interface, and keep this separate from the internal structure of the object.

3.3   Data and process

Objects are a combination of data and process. The distinctive feature of object oriented programming is the way that data and process are combined into single entities. Data that distinguishes an object is referred to as its *attributes* or *properties*, and the procedures that manipulate it are its *methods* or *operations*. All of programming involves designing the interactions between data and process (see Figure 3.6).

In an object, the current *state* is given by the set of values held in all of its internal variables or data items. In Figure 3.6, this is the single member variable that stores the Balance of the bank account. Its behaviour is defined by the instructions (methods)

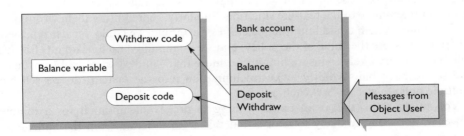

Figure 3.6 *Data and processes in a **BankAccount** object.*

that manipulate and access these variables. However, at a point in a program where none of the methods of a particular object are being executed, the entire object is represented purely by the state of its internal data. This is most of the time, since a computer can do only one thing at a time and there can be many objects within a single program.

It is essential that the design we create for an object represents it correctly all of the time a program is running. That means that the *data abstraction* embodied by the object's internal data must represent the object accurately.

Data abstractions

Since the data we hold in a computer is itself an abstraction, it is essential that it is an *adequate* abstraction. An abstraction is adequate if it incorporates all of the information necessary to allow it to do the job intended for it. We must therefore ensure that the variables we use capture every feature of the information we need.

For example, assume we wanted to write computer software to work with records of insurance policies. We need to ensure that we store enough information about each policy to enable us to perform all of the operations we would need to do.

Say, for example, we were required to be able to retrieve policy information that told us all of a customer's information. This might include:

- the customer's name,

- the address and contact details of the customer,

- the value of the policy,

- the liability (what the policy covers the customer for),

- any limitations on the policy (e.g. the customer might smoke cigarettes and this might imply that certain health considerations were not covered),

- the premiums and payment details,

- information on underwriters, etc.

Missing out any of these data items could make the system unusable, or worse, usable but unrepresentative of the real-life situation. Similarly, representing them wrongly on the computer system could limit the system. For example, we could decide to provide a variable to store the value of the policy, and we might allow up to six digits for this. Bill Gates is very likely to insure himself for more than can be expressed by six digits, and so we have built a fairly awkward limitation into the system (do we sell him multiple policies at £999,999 each?).

You might think this is an unlikely thing to do. Think about it for a minute, however, and you are likely to realize that this is no different from the millennium bug. Many programmers in the 1960s, 1970s and 1980s decided that dates beyond 1999 were so far off as to be not worth providing for, and so did not allocate enough digits to house dates further into the future. Assumptions that we make about data requirements can often come back and bite us.

Numeric precision

Besides simple specification errors like the millennium bug, there is also a fundamental limitation to computer representations of certain values. In software, numbers, text, true/false values (Booleans), times, dates, pictures and anything else we wish to represent is stored as a sequence of binary digits (ones and zeros). The trouble with this is that there are certain exact values that need to be stored as approximations.

For example, the number π (pronounced pi), which is the ratio of the circumference of any circle to its diameter, has an infinite number of digits after the decimal point (this has been proven). No matter how many digits we use, we cannot represent this number exactly in a computer program. That does not mean we do not get to do any computations involving circles. Just like any human doing that type of arithmetic, we work with approximations (children learning about the geometry of circles often use the value 3.14 for π; engineers might have to go to a precision of eight decimal places, giving 3.141 592 68 – both are approximations).

In fact, a computer will work with a much better approximation than most humans would, and π is normally represented to 15 decimal places. However, we would not want to represent every number to 15 decimal places (this would be a bit wasteful when storing, for example, the number of goals scored at a football match). There is usually a trade-off between numerical accuracy and storage and processing requirements. The higher the numeric precision used, the more space it takes to store a number and the longer it takes to do arithmetic on it.

When we wish to represent information of any type on a computer, we need to consider how to represent it carefully. Fortunately, most modern programming languages provide a range of data types to suit most purposes. Object oriented programming also helps, since when using this we are allowed to define new types of data and specify how they work. It is the job of the detailed designer of software either to select appropriate representations of information for a given task from the data types available, or to specify new classes of object that can do the job.

3.4 Expressions, declarations and statements

The fundamental building block of any computer program is a *statement*. This is a line of text that the computer (with the help of the programming language) will accept as an operation it can perform. This might be:

1. Assigning a value to a variable (e.g. X = 2)

2. Performing a calculation (and assigning its value to a variable) (e.g. x = 2 * y)

3. Calling on an existing code routine (e.g. Print X)

4. Calling an existing code function and assigning the result to a variable (e.g. x = Sqr(y), where Sqr( ) is a *function* that calculates the square root of a number)

5. Declaring a variable (setting aside storage space for it) (e.g. Dim X As Integer)

6. Defining structure within the program (by indicating that range of statements that a loop or selection statement will influence) (e.g. If x > 5 Then).

There are three different types of thing happening here. Statements can execute (1, 2, 3 and 4), make a declaration (5) or control other executable statements (6). Executable statements are the parts of a program that actually do something. Declarative statements are required to set up the program items needed to get the job done (variables, objects and code routines). Structure statements are there to prevent programs from just being a sequence of statements that execute one after the other blindly. If it were not for the first type, nothing would get done. If it were not for the second type, there would be nothing to do it to or with. If it were not for the third type, it would not be possible to make what has been done influence what else will be done.

Most programming languages allow these types of statement to intermix to a certain degree. For example, in Visual Basic, you can create a conditional block of statements using an `If..Then..End If` construct. For example, to verify the date and time of an appointment (Appt), we could use:

```
If (ApptDate < Date) Or _
  ((ApptDate = Date) And (ApptTime < Time)) Then
  MsgBox "Appointments must be in the future"
End If
```

The first line of this is both structural and executable. The `If..Then` part forms a conditional program structure that will execute the enclosed statement(s) only if the result of the condition is True. The sequence `(ApptDate<Date) Or ((ApptDate=Date) And (ApptTime<Time))` defines the actual condition. This is a fairly complex calculation comparing a date and time with the system date and time (accessed by calling the functions `Date` and `Time`). In the conditional group, it has the overall effect of checking whether a pair of variables storing a time and date refer to a point in time before the present time, and providing a message if they do. Note the use of brackets to ensure that the logical combinations (And and Or) group the individual conditions together in the right way.

Expressions

Assignment statements, where a value is assigned to a variable, often involve *expressions* – parts of statements that have a result. The simplest form of expression is a constant (e.g. **6**) or a simple variable (e.g. **x**). We can then have assignments such as:

```
Y = 6
Z = X
```

Most expressions in assignments are a bit more complex than this, involving arithmetic:

```
Z = 2 * Y + 6
```

(the actual expression is `2 * Y + 6`), or a call to a code routine that gives a result (i.e. a *function*):

```
Z = Sqr(y*y + x*x)
```

(in the above case, the function `Sqr()` returns the square root of the expression in the brackets). Note also that functions and arithmetic expressions can be combined.

It is important to distinguish between expressions and *statements*. In computer terms, a statement is something that will have an effect, such as performing a calculation and storing its result in some variable, displaying some information or causing an operation to be executed. However, an expression is simply some way of describing how we can calculate a value. An expression never states what is to be done with the value it equates to, and so can only ever be *part* of a statement. In Visual Basic in particular, you are allowed in some circumstances to enter an expression *as a statement*. However, this is always useless, since unless you state what is to be done with the result of the expression, the overall effect will be zero.

For example, in Visual Basic, it is legal to write the expression:

```
Sqr(100)
```

on its own as a line in a program. This will have the effect of calculating the square root of 100, *but will not do anything with it* – a thoroughly pointless exercise. However, the statement:

```
X = Sqr(100)
```

will have the overall effect of assigning the result of the expression to the variable X. The first does nothing, the second changes the value of a variable, even though both consume some of the computer's processor time.

QUESTION 3.4

(a) Write an expression that describes how the circumference of a circle is calculated, given its radius. (We can calculate the circumference by multiplying the radius by 2 times 3.14.)

(b) Write an expression that shows how to calculate the radius of a circle, given its circumference. (We can calculate the radius by dividing the circumference by 2 times 3.14.)

Declarations

Declarative statements are there to introduce new variables and code routines to the language you are working with. Some programming languages make only scant or optional use of declarations, but it is always considered good programming practice to use them and Visual Basic can be set up so that they are required. In Visual Basic, if we wished to set up three variables to store a whole number, someone's name and a date, we could do so as:

```
Dim aNumber As Integer
Dim aName As String
Dim aDate As Date
```

The keyword `Dim` is short for `Dim`ension, and directs the programming language to set aside enough storage space to accommodate a variable of the specified type. The three statements could also be combined as:

```
Dim aNumber As Integer, aName As String, aDate As Date
```

In either case, we have told Visual Basic that we want space allocated to store an integer (a whole-number variable that can store values in the range −32768 to +32767), a string (that can store sequences of text characters) and a date (that can store date and time values). Visual Basic also provides data types for storing floating point numbers (Single and Double), true/false values (Boolean) and many other varieties of data.

Packages of executable statements can also be declared, so that Visual Basic is made aware of them:

```
Sub SomeSubroutine()
  ' Executable statements go in here.
End Sub
```

In this case, we can write code for a **procedure** (a sequence of statements) that we might use repeatedly in a program and call on by name (**SomeSubroutine**). In a similar way, we can declare a **function** (a subroutine that returns a result):

```
Function SomeFunction() As String
  ' Executable statements go in here, including
  ' at least one statement that assigns a value
  ' to the Function as a result.
End Function
```

In OOP, the collective name we use for subroutines (subs) and functions is **methods**.

3.5   Inter-object communication

The declarations described above allow us to create simple variables based on simple data types provided by Visual Basic. These are the building blocks we use to create classes of object.

We can also create variables for working with objects. Having gone to the trouble of designing and developing a new class (e.g. **BankAccount**), it should be obvious that we will want to work with the class's objects in programs. Visual Basic allows us to create *reference variables* for this. A reference variable is a variable that allows us to refer to some object so that we can send it messages.

The statement:

```
Dim Account As BankAccount
```

creates a reference variable that *is able to act as a link* to a **BankAccount** object. Note that we do not say that **Account** is an object of the **BankAccount** class – that would be wrong. Instead, given that an object of the **BankAccount** class existed in a computer's memory, we could use the variable **Account** to access it. Figure 3.7 shows how an object reference variable operates.

Given the connection between a **BankAccount** object and an object reference variable as shown in Figure 3.7, we could access the account's properties and execute any of its methods by using the reference variable, for example:

```
Account.Deposit 100.00
Print Account.Balance
```

The **Account** reference variable could be defined as part of another class of objects, in which case we would be creating a message-link between objects of the two classes. We can interpret the statement:

```
Account.Deposit 100.00
```

as the Deposit message being sent to an **Account** object, with the value 100.00 representing the amount of the deposit. It would not be possible to send a message to an object without a reference variable.

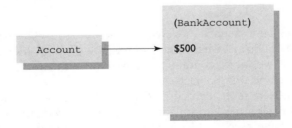

Figure 3.7   *A* **BankAccount** *object and an object reference variable (***Account***).*

3.6   Review questions

1. Why is some form of specialist notation often used when writing a detailed algorithm description?

2. Distinguish between a value and a variable.

3. Write the value of the following expressions:
   (a) $x * y/z$, where $x = 2$, $y = 12$ and $z = 4$
   (b) $x = y/z$, where $x = 2$, $y = 6$ and $z = 3$
   (c) $x > y * z$, where $x = 5$, $y = 4$ and $z = 11$
   (d) x Mod $y + 4$, where $x = 11$ and $y = 3$

4. Write a statement to assign the sum of y and z, all divided by 3, to the variable x.

5. Write a series of statements that will assign the larger of the values of y and z to x.

3.7   Practical exercises

In these practical exercises, you will learn how to:

- design a form to act as a user-interface for the **BankAccount** class developed in the previous chapter,

- create *event-handlers* to associate the behaviour of the form with interactions from the user,

- collect information from a program user using an **InputBox()** statement,

- manage a **BankAccount** object by making it respond to messages from a reference variable in the form.

> **Exercise 1:**   Setting up a form to use with a **BankAccount** object

In the previous chapter's exercises, we created a new class, **BankAccount**, and tested it by executing its methods in Visual Basic's Immediate window. Ideally we should use this class in a full working program to gain some idea of the overall dynamics involved in creating and using objects.

In the practical exercise at the end of Chapter 1, you were introduced to *forms*. These are Visual Basic's mechanism for defining user interfaces. We added simple controls to a form, and executed the resulting program. In this exercise, we will add controls to the form supplied by Visual Basic when we created the new project in the previous exercise. It is worth knowing that this form is in fact an object, and that we

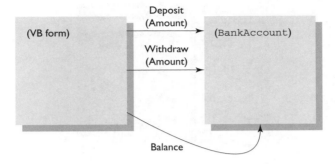

Figure 3.8   *Using a Visual Basic form to operate a* **BankAccount** *object.*

will be defining the way that the form object communicates with an object of our new **BankAccount** class (Figure 3.8).

Change the form's **Name** property.

A form, like every other user-interface object, has a **Name** property. We can change this in the Properties window by selecting the form in the Project Explorer, and then overtyping the current value of the **Name** property (Figure 3.9).

We now need to place some additional controls on the form to allow a user to interact with it. Since there are effectively two commands that can be sent to the **BankAccount** object, we will require a pair of command button controls, one to

Figure 3.9   *The form's properties, with the* **Name** *property changed.*

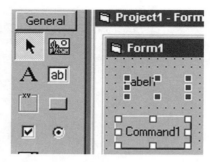

Figure 3.10   *The Label control and the* **Command** *button control on the tool box.*

initiate each command. The **Balance** message that the form will pass to the **BankAccount** will retrieve a value (the account balance) to be displayed, and so some form of display control will be required. We can use a standard **Label** control for this.

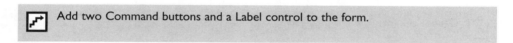

Add two Command buttons and a Label control to the form.

Figure 3.10 shows how the **Label** control and the **Command** button control appear on the tool box. Add two **Command** buttons and one **Label** to the form, and arrange them as shown in Figure 3.11.

To give the form an appearance that indicates the purpose of all of the elements on it, we will need to change some properties. Proceed as follows.

Set up the Command buttons.

We will make the top **Command** button operate as a **Deposit** button. To indicate this, we will change its **Name** property (so that any program code that refers to it will be more obvious in its function) and its **Caption** property (so that the user of the program will be aware of the button's purpose).

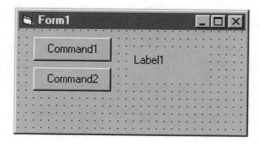

Figure 3.11   *Two Command button controls and a* **Label** *control arranged on the form.*

Figure 3.12   *Changing the* **Name** *and* **Caption** *properties for the Deposit Command button.*

Select the top Command button by clicking on it in the form. Grab handles will appear around its edges, as shown in Figure 3.12. Now move to the Properties window and change the **Name** property to **cmdDeposit**, and the **Caption** property to **Deposit**.

Repeat this procedure for the second **Command** button, naming it **cmdWithdraw** and changing its **Caption** property to **Withdraw**.

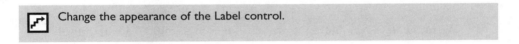

Change the appearance of the Label control.

To make the **Label** control stand out more from the surface of the form, we can change its background colour and apply a border to it. We should also change its **Name** property. Make the following changes:

- Change the **Name** to **lblBalance**

- Change the **BorderStyle** to **1 – Fixed Single**

- Change the **BackColor** to white

- Change the **Caption** to **0.0** (to signify that the account balance is initially zero)

- Change the **Alignment** property to **1 – Right Justify**

The form and controls should now appear as shown in Figure 3.13.

Figure 3.13   *The final appearance of the form and controls.*

Exercise 2:	Adding code to link the form to a **BankAccount**

> Add a reference variable to the form.

A single statement added to the top of the form code window will provide this:

```
Private Account As BankAccount
```

This statement declares an identifier '**Account**', associating it with the class **BankAccount**. When we later create the **BankAccount** object, we will use this identifier as a name by which we can access the object's properties and methods.

Overall, there are five interactions that need to be considered between the form and a **BankAccount** object. These are:

1.   When the form starts up, we need to create a **BankAccount** object.

2.   When the **Deposit** button is pressed, we need to initiate a deposit to the account.

3.   When the **Withdraw** button is pressed, we need to initiate a withdrawal.

4.   When either a deposit or a withdrawal is made, we need to update the balance label control with the current account balance.

5.   When the form shuts down, we should destroy the account object.

Each of these interactions is initiated by an *event*, that is, an external stimulus that the program is expected to react to. Each is an interaction between the form and a **BankAccount** object. Our first requirement will be to provide a variable that will allow us to refer to a **BankAccount** object.

Visual Basic is often referred to as an *event-driven* language, because of the way it allows programs to be controlled by such external influences. Operations can be triggered by events such as a form opening or closing, the user clicking the mouse cursor on a control, a key being pressed or some other stimulus.

The interactions that can occur between our form and a **BankAccount** object can be associated with:

1.   The **Form_Load** event, which fires when a form is first loaded into memory

2.   The **_Click** event associated with the **cmdDeposit** button

3.   The **_Click** event associated with the **cmdWithdraw** button

4.   The **Form_Unload** event, which occurs when the form is unloaded from memory.

Associating operations with an event is a simple matter because the design of Visual Basic is optimized for this type of association. We can create an *event-handler*,

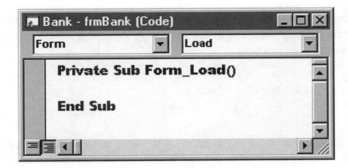

Figure 3.14   *The* **Form_Load** *event-handler outline.*

which is a subroutine that is automatically associated with an event, and enter calls to
the appropriate methods as statements in these.

 Add a Form_Load event-handler.

Double-click on the background of the form in its designer window. Visual Basic will
automatically bring up a code window (Figure 3.14), in which the outline of the
Form_Load event-handler is already in place.

The cursor should be flashing at the start of the blank line between the start and the
end of the event-handler. We wish to use this event to create a new **BankAccount**
object, and can do so by entering the following statement (exactly as we did in the
Immediate window):

```
Private Sub Form_Load()
   Set Account = New BankAccount
End Sub
```

 **Add event-handlers to deal with Deposit and Withdraw interactions.**

These event-handlers are necessarily more complex. As well as initiating the
appropriate methods of the **BankAccount** object, they must also get information from
the user regarding the amount of cash to be deposited or withdrawn, and then report
on the result of the deposit or withdrawal by updating the label control **lblBalance**.
In each case, we can make use of a Visual Basic facility called an *InputBox*.
InputBox() is a *function* that VB provides to allow us to enter some information into
a program. Since it is a function, it will return a value, which can then be used in a
program.

To create an event-handler for when the user clicks on a Command button, double-click on the button on the design window, and enter the statements necessary to perform the required operations:

```
Private Sub cmdDeposit_Click()
   Account.Deposit InputBox("How much to deposit")
   lblBalance.Caption = Account.Balance
End Sub
```

Note that two operations are associated with the `cmdDeposit_Click` event. The first calls on the `Deposit` method of the `Account` object, passing into it the value that the user enters into the `InputBox()`. The second calls on the `Balance` method of the `Account` object, passing its result to the `Caption` property of the label control.

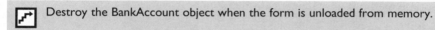 Destroy the BankAccount object when the form is unloaded from memory.

When the user clicks on the close button of a form (the small '×' in its top-right corner), it is reasonable to expect that the program is done. We can affirm this by deliberately destroying the `BankAccount` object. Again we can use an event-handler for this. It will be slightly more awkward to create this event-handler because it is not signalled by the *default* event as the others were (Load is the default event for a form, Click for a Command button).

To create the Unload event-handler, move the cursor into the Load handler, and then select the Unload event from the top-right combo-box (Figure 3.15).

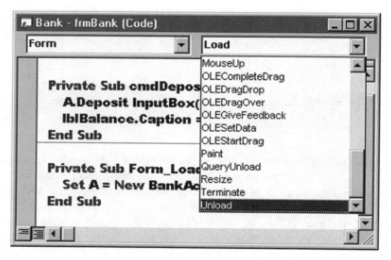

Figure 3.15 *Selecting an alternative event-handler.*

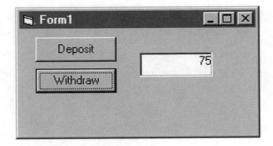

Figure 3.16   *The **BankAccount** program in operation.*

Visual Basic will create a second event-handler to cope with the Unload event:

```
Private Sub Form_Unload(Cancel As Integer)
   Set Account = Nothing
End Sub
```

Exercise 3:   Create an event-handler to handle a user's click on the Withdraw button

This exercise is left to the reader.

Exercise 4:   Test the program

Our Visual Basic program is now in a fit state to test. We simply need to run it and then make a few deposits and withdrawals to and from the account (Figure 3.16).

The full form code for the **BankAccount** program

```
Private Account As BankAccount

Private Sub cmdDeposit_Click()
   Account.Deposit InputBox("How much to deposit")
   lblBalance.Caption = Account.Balance
End Sub

Private Sub cmdWithdraw_Click()
   Account.Withdraw InputBox("How much to withdraw")
   lblBalance.Caption = Account.Balance
End Sub
```

```
Private Sub Form_Load()
  Set Account = New BankAccount
End Sub

Private Sub Form_Unload(Cancel As Integer)
  Set Account = Nothing
End Sub
```

3.8   Answers to questions

QUESTION 3.1

Expressions to represent a deposit to and a withdrawal from a BankAccount:

Deposit: `newBalance = curBalance + Amount`
Withdrawal: `newBalance = curBalance - Amount`

QUESTION 3.2

Eliminating the extra variable in the previous answers:

Deposit: `Balance = Balance + Amount`
Withdrawal: `Balance = Balance - Amount`

QUESTION 3.3

(a) A condition that could be used to determine if a withdrawal could be allowed:

```
Balance >= Amount
```

where Balance is the current balance in the account, and Amount the intended amount of the withdrawal. If this condition was true, a withdrawal could be allowed; if not, it should be forbidden.

(b) Use this condition:

```
If Balance >= Amount Then
  Balance = Balance - Amount
End If
```

If the condition is True, the withdrawal is made. Otherwise, nothing is done.

QUESTION 3.4

(a) If we call the circumference C and the radius R, and use Pi to refer to the circle constant 3.14 (approx.), the expression can be written as:

```
C = 2 * Pi * R
```

(b) Using the same definitions as in part (a), the expression would be written as:

```
R = C / (2 * Pi)
```

Note that the brackets are necessary to ensure that we divide C by the product of 2 and Pi, rather than dividing C by 2 and then multiplying the result by Pi.

3.9   Answers to review questions

1. *Why is some form of specialist notation often used when writing a detailed algorithm description?*   English text can be wordy, will take longer to write and read, and can contain ambiguities when used to describe subtle or complex scenarios. Using a specialized notation based on the rules of logic, it is possible to remove the redundancy inherent in English text, and produce a shorthand notation that is clear, simple and unambiguous.

2. *Distinguish between a value and a variable.*   A value is specific and cannot change (e.g. the number 3 will never represent any other number but 3). A variable is a holder for a value, and can hold different values at different times (e.g. the variable MyAge might currently hold the value 44, but at other times it might have held the value 38, and may at some other time hold the value 47). Variables are used in computer programs to store values that may change over time due to the action of the program statements.

3. *Write the value of the following expressions:*
    (a) $x*y/z$, *where* $x = 2$, $y = 12$ *and* $z = 4$ 6 (2*12/4)
    (b) $x = y/z$, *where* $x = 2$, $y = 6$ *and* $z = 3$ True (2 = 6/3)
    (c) $x > y * z$, *where* $x = 5$, $y = 4$ *and* $z = 11$ False (5 > 4*11, not true)
    (d) x *Mod* $y + 4$, *where* $x = 11$ *and* $y = 3$ 6 (11 mod 3 = 2, + 4 = 6)

4. *Write a statement to assign the sum of y and z, all divided by 3, to the variable x.*

```
x = (y + z)/3
```

5. *Write a series of statements that will assign the larger of the values of y and z to x.*

```
If y > z Then
   x = y
```

```
Else
   x = z
End If
```

Note that if both *y* and *z* had the same value, the condition `y > z` would be false and so the `Else` clause would win. However, since we can consider either value to be the larger since they are both the same, that would not be wrong.

CHAPTER 4

Simple programming in Visual Basic

Simple program statements on their own perform simple operations. They are the nuts and bolts of a programming language – the parts that are combined to form the inner workings of objects. We define an object's operations by packaging groups of statements so that together they perform significant actions. Objects individually and collectively are responsible for performing operations in object oriented programs.

By the end of this chapter, you should be able to:

- describe the standard objects instantiated in every Visual Basic program,

- write Visual Basic subs and functions,

- create modules of Basic code for use in any program,

- choose variables of the most appropriate type for use in programs,

- declare variables with appropriate scope in programs.

4.1 Introducing the Visual Basic programming environment

This chapter will formally introduce the programming language that is part of the Visual Basic development system. Visual Basic is not just an object oriented programming language. It also provides facilities for developing forms (windows) and user-interfaces, for implementing databases and for building new control objects for use within Visual Basic itself. You can also, if you wish, use it to program in a non-object oriented style. It is therefore wrong to think of Visual Basic as *just* the programming language. For the rest of this book, references to the Visual Basic programming language will simply use the term Visual Basic.

Getting started in programming

Good programming practice suggests that you should never approach the software development stage before you have a very clear idea of what you are going to do. That is, you should *design* a program before you write the program code. The previous chapters describe how you could go about designing a simple class of object, by specifying the properties each object should have and the methods all objects should have access to. In a real programming job, you are likely to have to develop a large number of classes to describe each type of object that will be used in the program. However, while you are learning to program, this is a difficult goal, since you are probably not aware of what is expected of you. You must learn to walk before you can try to run.

Before you go on to develop real programs, you should practise on simple exercises. Eventually, you will have gained enough confidence to undertake a real programming task, and then you should always follow the rule about clarifying your objectives. One worthwhile strategy is to practise by developing a simple class. You can try out most of the possible programming techniques by designing one class and working with one object, much as we did in the exercises at the end of Chapters 2 and 3. Such class designs may not do much, but they will make learning how to program much easier.

Start with the structure

The early stages of developing a piece of software involve figuring out what the program is required to do, then devising a structure or framework that will support these requirements. Following this, you would describe the structure or format of the information the program is to use in performing its tasks. You would then go on to devise an *algorithm* or process description that would describe the steps involved in performing each of the tasks specified in the requirements. Each of these should be a method of one or other object in the system.

Once you have devised an algorithm for a task, you then need to translate this to a working software routine. This stage represents a significant move from the design of a system to its implementation. It involves starting with a general description of how to do a job and then trying to translate this into a specific computer language. Assuming we already know the algorithm, and that it has been expressed in enough detail, the translation should be a straightforward process. As you gain experience, you should find that you are able express algorithms in less detail and add the detail as you implement the algorithm. For now, we will consider working with very detailed algorithms.

In the remainder of this chapter, we will examine the Basic language in which all Visual Basic code is written. Because we will be looking at a variety of features of the language, there will be no specific project on which to work. Instead, throughout the chapter, you will find a number of short samples of program code, each of which will illustrate a particular language feature, and, at the end of the chapter, a number of simple exercises.

4.2   Visual Basic program objects

Every Visual Basic program involves several objects, whether the programmer is aware of this or not. The `Global` object is the root of the whole application, and as such does not need to be referenced explicitly. In fact, since every Visual Basic program has a `Global` object, there is never any need to reference it explicitly. Instead, all of its methods and properties are continuously available throughout any program, and provide a wide range of facilities.

With no need to explicitly reference the `Global` object, there is no need to use the dot (.) operator we need to use when accessing the methods and properties of other

Table 4.1   *Objects that operate in any Visual Basic program.*

Name	Description	Typical use
App	The Application object – provides information about the application such as its name, the folder it is running from, etc.	FilePath = App.Path Sets the FilePath variable to the folder the program is running from
ClipBoard	This object provides for the transfer of information between Windows programs	ClipText = Clipboard.GetText Picks up text from the Windows clipboard
Forms	This is a collection of forms that are active in the current program	N = Forms.Count How many active forms?
Printer	This provides access to the current system printer	Printer.Print "Hello World" Printer.EndDoc Print the message, then eject the page
Screen	This object provides information about the screen format the program is running under	H = Screen.Height W = Screen.Width Measures the screen height and width

objects. Instead of:

```
X = Global.InputBox("Enter a number")
```

we simply use:

```
X = InputBox("Enter a number")
```

We can think of the **Global** object as providing all of the run-time services that are not provided for by other objects in a program. The **InputBox()** method referred to in the previous exercises and above, standard arithmetic functions, functions for manipulating dates, times and strings of characters, and a host of other features appear as if they are the methods and properties of **Global**.

In addition, Visual Basic provides us with a number of objects that appear as properties of the **Global** object. These are the objects listed in Table 4.1.

Using these objects, we can interrogate and control the environment that our Visual Basic programs are running under and so get the most from it. They are automatically instantiated when a Visual Basic program is run, and so are available for use at any point in a program.

4.3   Subs and functions

All Visual Basic program code is placed within **Sub** or **Function** declarations. If these are part of a class module or a form, we refer to them as the class *methods*. In some cases, the methods are *event-handlers* that are created automatically by the IDE (although you still have to define how they work by entering lines of Basic code). However, you can create a new user-defined sub or function in any form or class module by moving the cursor outside any existing subs or functions and typing the first line of the sub or function definition. If the contents of an existing VB form module were as shown in Figure 4.1, a new sub or function could be created by typing its first

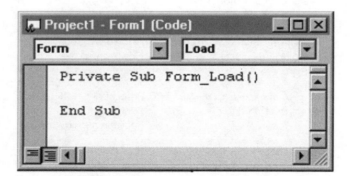

Figure 4.1   *An event-handler in a code window.*

'Objects'
combo-box

'Procedures'
combo-box

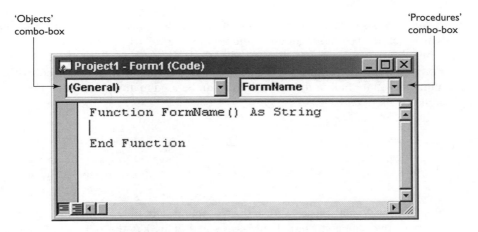

Figure 4.2   *A new function added to the code window.*

line *after* the `End Sub` of the existing sub. If, for example, you were to enter the line

```
Function FormName() As String
```

at the cursor position, and then press the Enter key, the result would be like that shown in Figure 4.2.

Note that the IDE has automatically inserted the `End Function` keywords. You would then normally continue by adding the lines of code that made up the body of the function.

There are two ***combo-boxes*** at the top of the code window. The left-hand one gives quick access to specific ***objects*** – controls on the form or specific parts of a class module. In this case, where we are adding a new function, it will be added to the '(General)' section of the form. This section contains variable declarations and subs/ functions that do not apply to any specific controls or parts of a class module. The right-hand combo-box gives quick access to ***procedures*** – the subs and/or functions in the General section, or the event-handlers attached to specific controls. Use these combo-boxes to navigate through a whole module of code quickly.

Since subs, functions and event-handlers contain every piece of code in a Visual Basic program, these combo-boxes can provide quick access to any routine in the current module. Subs, functions and event-handlers differ in the following ways:

- A *Sub* is a named part of a module with its own beginning and end. Optionally, it can have a set of *parameters* that specify data inputs to and outputs from the sub. Subs, or subroutines to give them their full name, are generally defined to do part of the work of a class or program and so break it up into smaller and more manageable pieces. Subs can also be defined for performing processing that is useful to a number of different parts of a class or program. For example, you could define a sub to make changes to a text string, such as correcting its case or hyphenating it. By defining it as a general sub in a form, it could be used to work on *any* text in the form or even throughout the program.

- A *function* is similar to a sub in that it is a named set of program statements with a defined beginning and end and an optional set of parameters. However, a function has the specific purpose of returning a *value* in place of a call to it. For example, if a function is defined to take a string of digits and return the numerical sum of all of them, a call to it can be used in any place that a number could be used, e.g.

```
X = SumDigits("12345")                ' Results in x=15
Print SumDigits("223")                ' Prints "7"
Y = Sqr(SumDigits("112"))             ' Sets Y to square root of 4
ListBox1.ListIndex = SumDigits("135")  ' Selects the 10th item
                                      ' in a listbox
```

Note that in Visual Basic, we use the '=' operator both for assignment and to compare two values to test if they are equal. This has the potential to cause confusion, but since Visual Basic can work out what is required from the context of the operator, it does not cause a problem in practice. Functions can be used to encode common calculations or operations for use throughout a program, or simply to make a program more readable. Some programmers use functions extensively rather than subs, since a function can always return a value that indicates whether it was successful at its task. For example, a function that reads information from a file can return a value that indicates how many values were read, or zero if the operation failed. Because a function is expected to return a value, its first (definition) line usually ends in **As SomeType**, where SomeType specifies one of the possible built-in Visual Basic data types (see later), or the name of a class.

- *Event-handlers* are special forms of sub, and therefore follow all the rules for subs. As their name suggests, they differ from normal subs because they are designed to respond to *events* from within and outside the program. A programmer never has to create an event-handler from scratch, since the Visual Basic IDE can create outlines for them automatically. VB will automatically assign a name and optionally a list of parameters to match the type of event it will be a response to. An event-handler is generally invoked automatically whenever the specified event occurs, e.g. a mouse click, a key press, or a form being opened on the screen. For example, to create the **KeyPress** event-handler

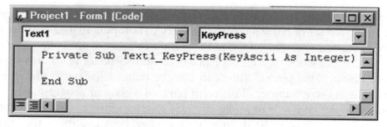

Figure 4.3 *An event-handler with a parameter.*

for a text box control, you would select the text box's name from the Objects combo-box, and then select the **KeyPress** event from the Procedures combo-box. Figure 4.3 shows what the IDE generates.

Note that a *parameter* has also been defined. This will be passed *into* the event-handler automatically when a **KeyPress** event occurs, and acts as a variable. It takes the form of an integer variable (whole number) which contains the ASCII code of the key that has been pressed. An ASCII code is a standard code used to represent letters, punctuation, digits and other characters in computers. The **KeyPress** event uses this code rather than the face value of a key to specify the key pressed, since the key pressed need not have a recognizable face value. For example, it could have been the *Esc* key or the *Enter* key on the keyboard, neither of which has a printable value.

Because of the way Visual Basic works, all the program statements you write will have to be placed in subs, functions or event-handlers. This is not a problem or limitation, since it has long been recognized that programs can be easier to write and maintain if they are structured in this way.

QUESTION 4.1

Subs and functions are used to break up the overall task of writing software. Instead of writing a single sequence of statements that will do the job, small chunks of code are developed that are made to work together to accomplish the overall task. Can you list a number of reasons why this is a good way of developing software?

QUESTION 4.2

Simple statements in a sub or function execute sequentially in the order that they appear. Consider the simple sequence of statements:

```
Print "Hello"
Print "Goodbye"
```

Where the keyword Print causes the message following it in quotes to be displayed on a form (window). Is the order in which these statements appear significant to the resulting output from the program?

Sample sub and function

```
Sub Greeting(someone As String)
  MsgBox "Hello " & someone
End Sub
```

The routine shown above is a sub (short for subroutine) with the name **Greeting**. It takes a piece of textual information (a **String**, referred to as **someone** from within the sub) and places it in a message box, preceded by the word 'Hello'. If this sub was *called* by the following statement:

```
Greeting "Fred"
```

it would have the effect of displaying a Windows message box containing the overall message 'Hello Fred'.

```
Function Product(n1 As Integer, n2 As Integer) As Integer
   Product = n1 * n2
End Function
```

The definition shown above is of a function called **Product**. It takes two pieces of information, referred to as **n1** and **n2** within the function, and produces a result that is the product of these two numbers (both of type **Integer**, a form of number with no fractional component). Because this routine is a function, a call to it can be used wherever a number or numeric variable could be used in a program. For example:

```
Print Product(3, 4)                   ' would print 12
Print 7 + Product(2, 5)               ' would print 17
MsgBox Product(4, 19) & " trombones"  ' would display 76 trombones
```

4.4 Modules and classes

When you create a Visual Basic program, you will often need to make choices regarding how to organize your program code. Visual Basic recognizes three different types of module, or file, of program code:

- Form modules

- Class modules

- Modules, or code modules

Each type can contain variable declarations, subs and functions. Both form modules and class modules contain the code required to describe the contents and behaviour of a particular class of object. A form module also contains a physical description of a form or screen window, indicating what controls appear on it, what they look like, and some aspects of how the form and controls will behave at run time.

Code modules, or simply modules, are rather different, in that the statements that go into one of these do not describe anything about a class of objects, but instead define an individual set of subs, functions and data descriptions. These can be thought of as the methods and properties of individual objects in the program – each code module defines *one* object instead of a class of objects. Objects defined as classes or forms have to be created or loaded when a program runs before you can access their methods or properties, but the code in a code module is available immediately.

Any number of code modules can be added to a Visual Basic program. Each code module that you add to a project will define another set of program-wide data items, subs and functions. Each module must have a unique name. To summarize:

- Form modules contain the data items, methods and event-handlers for each instance of a type of form. Every form of a particular class that is created and used in a program will have its own set of data items, called *instance variables*, which will describe the state of that form. Every form will also have the use of all of the subs, functions and event-handlers (or methods) defined for the class.

- Class modules contain the data items, methods and event-handlers for each instance of a type of object. Every object of a particular class that is created and used in a program will have its own set of data items, called *instance variables*, which will describe the state of that object. Every object will also have the use of all the subs, functions and event-handlers (or methods) defined for the class.

- Code modules contain the data items, subs and functions for use in a program. Only a single instance of each data item will exist throughout the program, but these may be made accessible to every object in the program.

As object oriented programmers, you should quickly get used to the idea of *instances* (Figure 4.4) of a class or form, each of which maintains its own state in instance variables. However, the purpose of the code placed in a code module may need to be clarified.

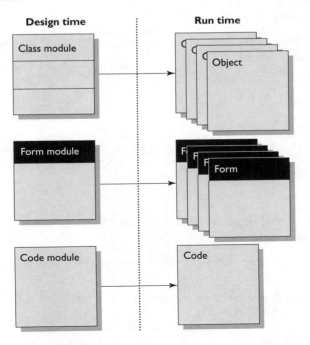

Figure 4.4   *Instances at run time.*

As an example, it may be necessary to keep track of the position and state of the mouse pointer in a graphics program. At first, it may seem that the best way to do this would be to create a **MouseState** class, so that we could use a **MouseState** object in the program. However, by creating a class, we will have to assume responsibility for creating a **MouseState** object the first time we need to use it, and for destroying it when we no longer need it. We will need to locate the **MouseState** variable in a convenient place in our program – one from which it will be available to all of the program code that needs to refer to it. Most importantly, we should make sure that only a single **MouseState** object is used, since there is only a single system mouse.

Now, if we were to define all of the required variables and routines in a code module, we would gain several advantages. Firstly, there is no need to create a **MouseState** object when the program starts, or destroy it when the program is done with it. Instead, all of the code in the module becomes available immediately when the program is run, and persists throughout the time the program stays running. Secondly, we can make the necessary routines and variables available to the whole program by defining them in the right way. The Public keyword can be used to define module variables and code routines that are to be available throughout the program. Finally, there will only ever be one instance of the code module available to the program, and so a single module of code representing our **MouseState** object is guaranteed.

```
' Three variables to store the mouse information...
Public MouseX As Integer
Public MouseY As Integer
Public ButtonState As Integer

' Subs and functions to control the mouse and retrieve
' information on it...
Public Sub MoveMouse(newX As Integer, newY As integer)
   ' ' '
End Sub

' ' ' '
' Remainder of Mouse module...
' ' ' '
```

Module structure

Every module in Visual Basic, whether it is a class, form or code module, has the code in it organized in a particular way.

Option Explicit

' ← *anything that follows one of these is a comment.*
' *Variable declarations go here.*

' *Sub and function declarations (including event-handlers) go here.*

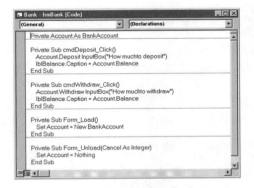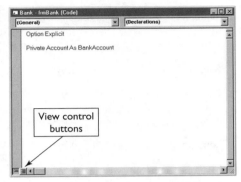

Figure 4.5   *Code view options in a code window.*

The keywords `Option Explicit` indicate that Visual Basic will refuse to recognize variables that have not been explicitly declared before they are used. They can be entered at the top of a module, or may be automatically inserted at the top of a module that has been created while the ***Tools/Options/Environment/Require Variable Declaration*** setting is in force. Option Explicit is a directive to Visual Basic that enforces a good programming habit – that of declaring all variables.

Between this and the first sub or function in the module, variables can be declared for use within the module (`Private`) or throughout the program (`Public`). Following these come the sub and function definitions. You can arrange the IDE so that it is possible to see only individual subs or functions or the declarations section above them, or to allow everything in the module to be viewed, either with or without a separating line.

Both pictures shown in Figure 4.5 are of the code window of the same form module, one in full-module-view mode and the other showing each sub and function in a separate pane. The environment setting that allows this tailoring is ***Tools/Options/ Editor/Default to Full Module View***, but a quick change between formats can be made by pressing one of the view control buttons at the bottom of the window.

4.5   Variables and data types

Visual Basic has a rich set of predefined data types that can be used in programs. Generally, these can be classed as *numeric* variables, *character* variables and *compound* variable structures. Table 4.2 lists the available types.

As you can see, the range of data types available will serve most of the programming purposes you have for them. Two types that are particularly interesting are ***Object*** and ***User-defined***. These types allow a programmer to extend the range of data types available. In particular, the use and definition of Object types will be a main feature of this book.

Table 4.2 *Data types in Visual Basic.*

Data type	Storage size	Range
Byte	1 byte	0 to 255
Boolean	2 bytes	True or False (the only two values allowed)
Integer	2 bytes	−32,768 to 32,767
Long (long integer)	4 bytes	−2,147,483,648 to 2,147,483,647
Single (single-precision floating-point)	4 bytes	−3.402823E38 to −1.401298E−45 for negative values; 1.401298E−45 to 3.402823E38 for positive values
Double (double-precision floating-point)	8 bytes	−1.79769313486232E308 to −4.94065645841247E−324 for negative values; 4.94065645841247E−324 to 1.79769313486232E308 for positive values
Currency (scaled integer)	8 bytes	−922,337,203,685,477.5808 to 922,337,203,685,477.5807
Decimal	14 bytes	±79,228,162,514,264,337,593,543,950,335 with no decimal point; ±7.9228162514264337593543950335 with 28 places to the right of the decimal; smallest non-zero number is ±0.0000000000000000000000000001
Date	8 bytes	January 1, 100 to December 31, 9999; also stores time, as a fraction of a day
Object	4 bytes	Any object reference (including forms and controls)
String (variable-length)	10 bytes + string length	0 to approximately 2 billion
String (fixed-length)	Length of string	1 to approximately 65,400
Variant (with numbers)	16 bytes	Any numeric value up to the range of a Double
Variant (with characters)	22 bytes + string length	Same range as for variable-length String
User-defined (using Type)	Number required by elements	The range of each element is the same as the range of its data type

For the rest, the following rules of thumb can suggest suitable usage:

- **Integer** variables are used for counting things, or for numeric values that will only ever be whole numbers. **Long** variables (long integers) may be needed where a lot of things are to be counted (more than ~32,000).

- Floating-point variables (**Single**, **Double**) are used for storing the values of physical things – sizes, weights, etc. Where the required precision is not crucial, a Single will do (up to 7 decimal places). Doubles are often used in scientific and engineering applications, and should be used when any of the transcendental functions (sin, cos, log, etc.) are required.

- **Date** variables can be used to record dates and times, and intervals between these.

- **Currency** variables are used for monetary values – the precision is always 15 digits, with 4 decimal places. This type maintains the necessary accuracy for financial calculations.

- **String** variables are used for text storage and manipulation. A Visual Basic string can be set to a fixed number of characters, or, more usually, can change its size to suit the data assigned to it. This can be up to 2 billion characters (computer memory permitting), which is enough for most uses.

- **Boolean** variables are used to record *binary* states. Any physical quantity that can be recorded as one of two possible states – Yes or No, True or False, Open or Closed, On or Off, etc. – can be stored in a Boolean variable. Visual Basic Boolean variables can take on the explicit values True or False; you can interpret these in any way you wish in a program.

- **Variant** variables are Visual Basic's default type – if you do not specify a type, VB will provide a variant. They are useful in a number of situations, such as where a subroutine is required to be able to accommodate a number of different types of information passed into its parameters.

Creating variables

Although it is not necessary to pre-declare variables before you use them, failure to do so is now commonly accepted as being a dangerous programming practice. Visual Basic can be set up to create a variable automatically the first time you refer to it. For example, if the statement:

```
X = 4
```

was used in a program at a point where there had been no prior reference to a variable **x**, this would result in the automatic creation of a new variable **x**, of a type that could be used to store a general number.

However, you should always declare a variable before you use it, in the same way that you should always fasten your seat belt before driving off in a car. You hope that it is not necessary but recognize that the safety inherent in the practice is worth the small effort required.

This leaves us with the questions of where and how to define a variable. Variables can be declared using one of three types of statement:

1. A `Dim` statement (short for Dimension) can be used within a sub or function or in the *general declarations* section of a module, form or class file. Good practice dictates that the `Dim` keyword is used within a sub or function only to declare variables that will be used only within that sub or function (commonly known as *local* variables).

2. A `Private` statement can be used in the general declarations section of a module, form or class module to create a variable that can be accessed within that module. Private variables in objects (defined in form or class modules) are the *instance variables* that store the state of an object – part of the internal workings of the object.

3. A `Public` statement can be used in the general declarations section of a module, form or class module to create a variable that can be accessed both within and from outside the module. Public variables in objects become part of the object interface to the object, as well as storing part of the state of the object. The principle of encapsulation suggests that while it is possible to declare a public variable within a class, it is not good practice. In the `BankAccount` class defined in the exercises at the end of Chapter 2, we found that declaring the `Balance` property as a public member variable made it possible to misuse the class. Variables that store the state of an object should be accessible only through a controlling subroutine as a property.

In any of these cases, the appropriate keyword is followed by one or more variable names and type declarations, using the `As` keyword. For example:

```
' A single variable..
Dim Counter As Integer

' Two private variables of different types..
Private UserName As String, UserBirthday As Date

' Two public variables of the same type..
Public AccountBal As Currency, TransAmount As Currency
```

These three statements would create variables of the specified types. The first declaration could be used anywhere in a program while it would be necessary to place the others in the `General Declarations` section of a class, form or module. The differences between these types of declaration are described next.

QUESTION 4.3

Select appropriate variable types for storing the information described below:

(a)   The number of goals scored at a football match
(b)   The length of a piece of string
(c)   The name of a customer
(d)   The price of a daily newspaper
(e)   Your birth date
(f)   The time of the next train
(g)   Whether a light is on or off
(h)   The diameter of the galaxy.

4.6   Variable scope in Visual Basic

All of the *executable* statements in a Visual Basic program are placed inside sub or function blocks. In this respect, Visual Basic is similar to the C language – all statements must be placed inside a structure that can contain one or more lines of code.

The end result is that Visual Basic programs are written in a modular manner that encourages good program structure. A strong feature of this structure is that it allows control over the placement of variables. By placing restrictions on where you can access specific variables in a Visual Basic program (or controlling a variable's *scope*), it becomes more difficult to create the circumstances where side effects can bring about errors in your code. In most cases, it is up to you, the programmer, to create variables that have the correct *scope* for the use you intend to make of them. *Scope* is a term that describes the range of places from where a variable can be accessed. There are three simple scope variations and one modified type of scope allowed in a Visual Basic program. These are local, module (or instance), global and static variables.

Local variables

This type of variable is created within a sub or function. As the name suggests, they are for local use (within the sub or function in which they are created) and cannot be accessed from outside. Because of this restriction, this type of variable declaration is only ever used for short-term data storage. Local variables are created at the point where a sub or function starts to execute, and are destroyed at the exit point of the sub or function.

Local variables can be considered safe to use, since their influence can never extend beyond the sub or function in which they were declared. This reduces the possibilities of side effects due to variable name conflicts (where two on more variables have been given the same name). On the other hand, they cannot be used for long-term data storage since their values do not persist beyond one call to the sub or function in which they are declared. A modified local variable declaration – a `Static` variable – does have this ability (see below). Finally, they cannot be used to communicate information between subs or functions, because they can be declared only within a single sub or function. An example follows.

```
Sub MySub()
' Typical Local variable declaration..
Dim Result As Integer    ' This variable exists only
                         ' within this sub.

  ' ' ' '

  Result = 10            ' This is legal, since Result
                         ' is in scope.
End Sub

Sub SomeOtherSub()
' No variables declared here.
  MsgBox Result          ' This statement can not access the
                         ' Result variable declared in MySub.
                         ' However, it may have access to
                         ' another variable called Result with a
                         ' Module or Global scope, if one exists.
End Sub
```

Module (or instance) variables

A *module* variable is declared in the declarations section (i.e. at the top) of a class, form or basic module. From this position, they can be accessed by every routine (sub or function) in that module. Module variables that are declared within a class type (i.e. a form or class) are *instance variables* or *member variables*, copies of which are created in every object of that type to become part of the object's state. That they can be accessed throughout a module makes them ideal for storing data that must be accessed by code in more than one sub or function.

For example, in a Visual Basic form it may be necessary to store the name of a file used to hold the contents of a **TextBox** or a **PictureBox** control. This type of variable may need to be accessed from more than a single sub or function – for example, event-handlers for Save and Load buttons on the form. In this case, we would create a **Private** module variable. This would allow us to access the filename when either saving or loading data.

Since this type of variable has module or private scope, it cannot be accessed by any code outside the module or form in which it was declared.

```
' Typical Module Variable Declaration
Private FileName As String
  ' ' ' ' The rest of the module..
```

Global variables

A *global* variable is one that can be accessed by any line of code in the entire program. Typical uses for this type of variable are to hold information that may be needed by any module or to store instance data that must be generally available to any users of an object. For example, the name of the directory (or folder) in which an application's data is stored is a useful piece of information that should be accessible from any part of a program. We might declare this type of variable in a code module.

Similarly, it might be necessary for users of an object of a given class to access a public instance variable that indicates something about the current state of the object. In this case, the instance variable would be a property of the class, since it was publicly accessible.

One major use of global variables defined inside a code module is to make some information that needs to be available throughout the entire program accessible. This could be, for example, the name of the folder that data files are be stored in.

```
' Typical Global Variable declaration, made in a code
' module..
Public DataPath As String
   ' ' ' '
```

The general recommendation is that you declare variables with the smallest possible scope that will allow them to do their job. The decisions to be made are simple:

- If a variable will be used only within a single sub or function, and is not required to keep its value between calls to the sub/function, declare it locally in that sub or function using the `Dim` keyword.

- If a variable is required to store a value that can be used throughout the class, form or module in which it is declared, declare it as `Private` at the top of the class, form or module.

- If a variable is to be used to communicate its value from one object to another, declare it as `Public`. If it is to contain information to be used throughout the entire program, but not part of a specific object, declare it as `Public` in a code module.

Static variables

Static variables are a variation of local variables. They are accessible only within the sub or function in which they are declared (they can be declared only in a sub or function), but retain their value between calls to it. The first time the sub or function is called, a static variable will be set to `0`, or an empty string `""` if it is a string variable. On subsequent calls to the sub or function, the variable will retain the value it had when the previous call was completed. Declare a static variable like this:

```
Private Sub MySub()
Static PreservedValue As Integer
  ' ' '
End Sub
```

In this case, the integer **PreservedValue** will initially contain a value of 0.

The sub shown below contains a static variable that keeps a count of the number of times it has been called:

```
Private Sub SomeSub()
Static CallCount As Integer
  CallCount = CallCount + 1
  ' '               ' Other statements that make use of the
                    ' CallCount variable.
End Sub
```

QUESTION 4.4

(a) Recall the idea of encapsulation described in the previous chapter. Given that some parts of a class need to be hidden from users of the class, and that some other parts need to be made accessible to the users, how will the idea of scope help with this?

(b) Given that a certain class defines four member variables, and that during a program run, 20 objects of that class are created and used, how many instance variables have there been in total?

4.7   Variants: all-purpose variables

Visual Basic provides a catch-all type of variable, called a *variant* type. A variant can take on whatever single value is assigned to it, regardless of what data type this value has. This can be very useful at times, when, for example, you wish to make use of a variable in a number of different contexts:

```
Private Sub cmdSquareRoot_Click()
Dim V As Variant            ' same as 'Dim V'
  V = txtInput.Text         ' Pick up a numeric string
                            ' from a text box
  V = Sqr(V)                ' Calculate its square root
  lblOutput.Caption = V     ' Display it (it will be
                            ' converted to a string)
End Sub
```

In the example event-handler shown above, a value is retrieved from a text box. Therefore, it must be a string. It is then replaced by its own square root, so it must be a number. Finally, the resultant value is passed to the Caption property of a label, so it must be a string again. In each case, Visual Basic has been able to figure out what type of variable was required, and convert the specified value to that type. It can do this because the variant variable V contains extra information about the current type of the variable, and code to perform conversions as required.

Note that programming in this way can be fraught with hidden dangers. For example, if the user had typed "abc" into the text box `txtInput`, Visual Basic would have tried to calculate the square root of "abc". Obviously this is not possible, and it would lead to an error that would cause the program to fail and end prematurely. To overcome this possibility, it would have been necessary to check whether the value entered had been numeric.

Variants have strengths and weaknesses when it comes to using them in programs. Many of the built-in functions in Visual Basic deal with variants since the language has to be as general-purpose as possible. However, a programmer developing an application is likely to be using variables for a specific purpose. Because of this, variables of specific types should be used whenever possible. They take up less memory, are faster to perform operations on, and require that the programmer be aware of the type of data that is stored in them. The last of these is a very important feature from a design point of view.

4.8   UDTs: do-it-yourself variables

No matter how many types of variable were already defined in Visual Basic, there would never be enough. The developers of Visual Basic could not possibly anticipate every type of data you would want to store and manipulate in a program. The reason object oriented programming is so powerful is that it gives a programmer the ability to create new data types as necessary. However, sometimes there is a need to create simple variable types that do not have any behaviour (methods) defined for them. For example, you might wish to pack a set of related information into a single variable for convenience, such as a person's name, date of birth and postcode, but use existing subs and functions to work with the information. In cases like this, object orientation is a bit like using a sledgehammer to crack a nut.

Visual Basic allows you to create *user-defined data types*, also known as *user-defined types* or *UDTs*. These are types of simple variables, defined as aggregates of existing types.

The idea is easier to demonstrate than to describe. Let's assume that I wish to write a program that allows me to store the names of my colleagues along with their telephone numbers. The program could be used as an on-line telephone directory.

In a Visual Basic program, I might think of storing these two pieces of information as pairs of variables. The first variable would hold the person's name, the second their phone number. However, as a human, I like to think of each of these phone-book entries as a single entity with two parts. Visual Basic allows me to do this by providing the user-defined type (UDT) structure:

```
Type PhoneEntry
  Name As String
  Telephone As String
End Type
```

It is possible to define this user-defined type only in a code module. Visual Basic does not allow their definition in class or form modules. However, I can *use* the new variable type anywhere in a project – as a local variable in an event-handler in a form, or as a private or public variable in a class, form or module. To declare a variable of the new type, I simply proceed as I would with any of the existing types, and use a dot '.' to access the internal member variables:

```
Dim PE As PhoneEntry
  PE.Name = "Fred Bloggs"
  PE.Telephone = "2468"
```

Note that, unlike an object defined in a class module, there is no need to use the keyword **New** to create the UDT before using it. In that respect, it is like one of the simple variable types; integer, string, etc. Once you have declared a UDT, you can use it in any situation where you would use an existing variable type, although Visual Basic Version 5 has one limitation in this respect. In VB5, it is not possible to make a function return a UDT variable, although VB6 does support this feature.

QUESTION 4.5

Describe the differences between an object and a variable of a user-defined type. Why would you use a user-defined type instead of a class in a program?

4.9 Objects and object references

Variables and UDTs are simple storage elements. Numeric variables store a number, string variables store a string and UDT variables store some combination of values. All of the operations performed on a variable are programmed as statements in which the variable is subjected to operators or sub or function calls. A distinct feature of variables is that they exist as soon as they are declared. Although no specific value has been put into a variable, it still contains a value – the *null* value.

A string that has had no value stored in it contains the empty string (""). A numeric variable that has had no number assigned contains zero (0 for integer types, or 0.0 for floating-point types). An unassigned date variable contains the zero date, defined in Visual Basic as 30 December 1899 (well, it had to be some date!).

In contrast, an object is not a simple storage element, but an assembly of data values (variables) and operations (functions/subs). An object occupies memory only when it has been explicitly created within a program using the keyword **New**. An *object variable* is a simple variable that stores a *reference* to an object in the computer's memory. Since it is a simple variable, an unassigned object variable does contain a *null* value. Visual Basic uses the name **Nothing** for this, so an object variable contains either a reference to an object or **Nothing**.

For example, assume we had defined (or added to our project) an object class called **MyClass**. This class would contain code to define one or more *member variables* or instance variables, a copy of which would be contained within each object of the class. It may also contain definitions of subs and/or functions (collectively referred to as *methods* when they are defined as part of a class). With the class defined, we could go on to declare reference variables for objects belonging to it:

```
Dim MyObject As MyClass
```

The **MyObject** variable contains a null value immediately after this form of declaration, i.e. the value **Nothing**, meaning no object. We can assign an object to the object variable using a **Set** statement. To create and assign a brand new object:

```
Set MyObject = New MyClass
```

The use of the **New** keyword creates an object of the specified class, and the use of the **Set** keyword *binds* it to the object variable **MyObject**. *It would be wrong to think of the object variable, **MyObject**, as the object – it simply refers to it.*

Another use of the **Set** keyword is to bind a reference variable to an existing object. This type of operation highlights the difference between objects and simple variables, since it allows us to create multiple references *to the same object*. For example, assume another object variable, **MyReference**, has been declared. Then we can connect this to our existing object:

```
Set MyReference = MyObject
```

We did not use the **New** keyword, so no new object has been created. Instead, we now have two variables that reference the same object: the one that was created in the first use of **Set** with the **New** keyword. We could depict this as in Figure 4.6.

Now, any operation we perform using the **MyReference** object variable will affect the same object that can be accessed using the **MyReference** variable, and vice versa. This is an important feature, since in some situations it is essential that we have more

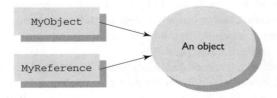

Figure 4.6   *Multiple references to a single object.*

than one variable referencing an object and we need to be aware of the ramifications of making changes to an object in these circumstances.

Destroying an object

Visual Basic allows you create as many references as you wish to an object. These can be made on the creation of an object by the **New** keyword, through simple assignments using the **Set** keyword, or by some other method, such as adding an object to a **Collection**.

As a program runs, objects are created and destroyed. The destruction of objects that are no longer needed is an important housekeeping task that Visual Basic performs for us. To do this, Visual Basic must recognize when an object is no longer needed. The method it uses is automatically to destroy objects that are not referred to by any reference variables or collections.

A reference to an object is removed if the reference variable goes out of scope, or if the reference is deliberately broken by setting the reference variable to **Nothing**, a Visual Basic keyword that means 'no object'.

```
Private Object1 As MyClass
Private List As New Collection

Public Sub SomeObjects()
Dim Object2 As MyClass
   Set Object1 = New MyClass    ' Creates an object
   Set Object2 = New MyClass    ' Creates a second object
   List.Add New MyClass         ' Creates a third object
   ' Can now go on to use these objects..
   ' ' ' '
End Sub                         ' Object2 is destroyed here

Public Sub NewList()
   Set List = New Collection    ' Destroys the existing
                                ' objects in the
                                ' collection as the New
                                ' one is created.
End Sub
```

In the example shown above, three objects are created. The variable **Object1**, which is defined as a **Private** variable in the module, refers to the first object. Its reference variable is defined at **Module** level. This will therefore remain in scope until the module (form, code or class module) is unloaded from memory or it is explicitly destroyed. For a code module, this will be when the program exits, or when the reference variable is **Set** to **Nothing**.

The second object is referenced by the **Object2** variable. Since this is local to the **Sub**, the object will be destroyed when the **End Sub** statement is met because the only variable that references it is going out of scope. The third object is never given a reference variable of its own, but is instead added to a collection as soon as it is created. When the collection goes out of scope, or when it is explicitly cleared out by assigning a new collection to the reference variable, the object will be destroyed along with it. This last point is important. If a new object is assigned to an object variable that already refers to another object, the other object will be replaced by the new one.

Of course, we could create other references to extend the life of an object. If we were to **Add** the second object to the collection (therefore creating a second reference to it), it would not be destroyed until it was removed from the collection or the collection itself was destroyed.

In a later chapter, we will write code to work with objects and go on to define new types of objects.

QUESTION 4.6

Is it right or wrong to say that an object variable *contains* an object?
Consider the following sub:

```
Sub MakeAnObject()
Dim NewObject As New MyObject
   Set TheObject = NewObject
End Sub
```

Given that the object variable **TheObject** is defined in the declarations section of a form module, will the object created in the sub still exist after the subroutine has completed?

4.10   Review questions

1. State whether the following would be more suitably implemented as subs or functions:
    (a) A routine that gets several pieces of information from the user, and passes these into a database
    (b) A routine that gets a single piece of data from the user
    (c) A routine to determine whether the floppy disk drive currently has a disk in it
    (d) A routine to write an item of data to a floppy disk file
    (e) A routine to find out whether the user wishes to save data to a file before the program exits.

2. A program to manage appointments bookings for a small dental practice has been through the first stages of design. The designers have decided that the following modules are necessary, but have forgotten to indicate whether they are to be code modules, class modules or form modules. Indicate the most suitable type of each module:
    (a) A module to define the structure and behaviour of a booking

  (b) A module to allow the user to view and enter the details of a session of
      treatment
  (c) A module to manage the operation of the system printer
  (d) A module to display and control the output of printed reports
  (e) A module to allow the system administrator to make data backups to a tape
      drive
  (f) A module to allow the system administrator to review the details of a booking
  (g) A module to manage all the bookings of any dentist in the practice.

3. Select appropriate variable types for storing and manipulating the following
   items of information for the dental practice described in Question 2 (see Table 4.2
   for possible types):
   (a) The time of a booking
   (b) A patient's name
   (c) A patient's address
   (d) Whether a patient belongs to the practice's standard health insurance scheme
   (e) A count of the bookings a dentist has for a specific date
   (f) The details of a patient's treatment, specifying duration, date, time of day,
       dental nurse present and a list of materials used
   (g) The cost of a treatment session.

4.11   Practical exercises: Basic programming

In this short collection of exercises, you will have a chance to put some of the concepts
described previously into practice. So that you do not spend most of the exercise
creating user-interfaces, we will set up a simple user-interface that will be used for all
the exercises. All the exercises will make use of only local variables, declared inside
event-handlers with the **Dim** keyword.

A simple user-interface

Rather than spend most of your time developing user-interfaces for these exercises, we
will set up a single form-based user interface that will allow us to try out various
aspects of the Basic language quickly and easily. We can use the form surface as a
space to send output to (using the **Print** statement). We can also use buttons placed on
the form to initiate actions in Basic code, and make use of the **InputBox** function to
allow the user to input data, and the **MsgBox** to display the results of calculations.

 Start a new project.

As in the previous exercises, start up Visual Basic or, if it is running already, select
File/New Project from the menus. When the form appears, name it **frmBasic**, name
the project **BasicProg**, and then save the project as usual, in a folder of its own.

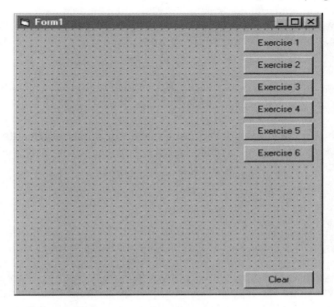

Figure 4.7   *The program's main form.*

Configure the form.

Resize the form to make it larger. Then add several buttons down its right-hand side, and change their Caption properties so that they appear as shown in Figure 4.7. In these exercises, we will be writing Visual Basic statements. We will make use of use each button's click event-handler to contain these statements. Note that the bottom button is captioned **Clear**. Since we will be printing directly on to the form surface, this button will allow us to clear the form surface.

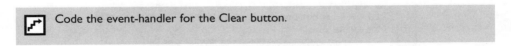

Code the event-handler for the Clear button.

Each Visual Basic form has a **Cls** method. Cls stands for 'CLear Screen', and acts as a command to clear away any printing from the form background. It does not affect any controls on the form. First, change the **Name** property of the Clear button to **cmdCls** in the Properties window, and then code the click event-handler as shown below:

```
Private Sub cmdCls_Click()
  Cls
End Sub
```

Now that we have put together a simple form to allow us to try out some Basic program code, we can proceed with the exercises.

Exercise 1:   Variables and statements: input and print a string

---

In Exercises 1–4, we will declare and use variables in simple statements.

Double-click on the button labelled Exercise 1. Add the following code to its click event-handler:

```
Private Sub Command1_Click()
Dim S As String
  S = InputBox("What is your name?")
  Print S
End Sub
```

Note that as you type certain of the keywords, Visual Basic tries to assist you by anticipating what you are typing. For example, by the time you type the **Str** of the word String on the first line, the **Auto List** shown in Figure 4.8 appears.

VB has guessed that the word you are going to type is **String**. If it is wrong, nothing is lost since you can continue to type the word you intended. However, if it is correct in its guess, you can simply press Enter to complete the word. Apart from a reduction in the amount of typing you need to do, this facility also serves to remind you of the available keywords.

If you run the project now, and then press the Exercise 1 button, the **InputBox** shown in Figure 4.9 will appear.

Note that it has a number of built-in facilities. The OK and Cancel buttons serve to close the box. Pressing OK will cause whatever you have typed to be returned to the

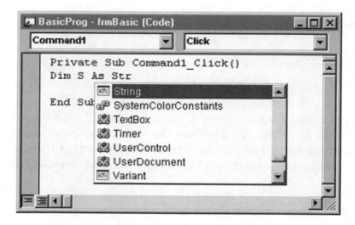

Figure 4.8   *A Visual Basic Auto List offering to complete a keyword.*

Figure 4.9   *An InputBox in operation.*

calling statement, while pressing Cancel will cause an empty string (i.e. one which contains no characters, often represented by an empty pair of double-quotes – "") to be returned. The box also has a default caption, given by the name of the project in which it appears.

If you type something in the InputBox and press OK, it will be printed at the top-left corner of the form. If you press the Exercise 1 button again and repeat the exercise, the text you enter will be printed below the output from the first time.

The three lines of program code in the event-handler did three things:

1. A String variable, **S**, is declared. Note that this is a local variable, which exists only while the event-handler is running, and is accessible only from within this event-handler.

2. An assignment is made to S, using the result from a call to **InputBox**, a standard Visual Basic function which prompts the user to enter some data.

3. The newly assigned value of S is printed on the form.

We could have used the input box to collect numbers or dates or any other type of data.

Suggested exercises

1. Change the type of the variable S to **Date**, and alter the prompt string passed to the InputBox function so that the user is asked to enter their birth date.

2. Change the variable declaration statement so that *two* variables are declared: one String type and one Date type (the two variables will need distinct names). Now change the body of the sub so that both variables are assigned from InputBox statements – one statement to collect the user's name, and the second to collect the user's birth date. Finally, amend the print statement so that both variables are printed out – place a comma between the variable names.

3. Re-code the sub so that an Integer variable is declared, and the user is asked to enter a number. Print out 10 times this number (the expression **N * 10** evaluates as the product of the variable N and the number 10).

Input numbers for calculation

Double-click on the Exercise 2 command button, and add code as shown below:

```
Private Sub Command2_Click()
Dim x As Integer, y As Integer
  x = InputBox("In what year were you born?")
  y = InputBox("What year is it now?")
  Print "You are "; y - x; " years old."
End Sub
```

Run the program and press the Exercise 2 button. This time, you will be asked to enter the year in which you were born, then the current year. By entering this information, the result printed on the form will be an estimate of your age, obtained by subtracting your birth year from the current year.

Suggested exercises

1. Add an extra print statement to the end of the sub that will print out an approximation of the number of **days** old the user is (the expression **(y-x)*365** can be used to calculate this). The additional statement should come before the **End Sub** line.

2. Change the form of the calculations so that the user is asked their **age** and the current year. The sub should then print out an estimate of the user's birth year. This exercise will require you to subtract age from current year.

Perform operations on strings

Although it is obvious that you can use Visual Basic statements to operate on numbers as we did in Exercise 2, it may be less apparent that it is also possible to operate on strings of characters. Visual Basic includes a number of standard functions for string manipulation. **UCase()** and **LCase()** are used to convert strings of characters to upper or lower case respectively, while **Left()**, **Right()** and **Mid()** are used to extract characters from the left, right and middle of a character string. There is a range of other string functions to find one string within another **(InStr())**, replace one sub-string within another **(Replace())**, create a string by repeating another string a number of times **(String())**, and a variety of other text-related tasks. Add the following statements (shown in bold) to the event-handler for the Exercise 3 command button:

```
Private Sub Command3_Click()
  S = InputBox("What is your name?")
  Print S, LCase(S), UCase(S)
  Print Left(S, 3), Right(S, 3), Mid(S, 2, 3)
End Sub
```

Run the program again and press the Exercise 3 button. Note the results of the LCase(), UCase(), Left(), Right() and Mid() functions as printed.

Suggested exercises

1. The Len() function operates on a string variable, returning the number of characters in it. Add an extra statement to print out the number of characters in the user's name.

2. Look up the UCase, LCase, Left, Right, Mid and Len functions in Visual Basic's on-line help. The easiest way to do this is to place the cursor on the required keyword in a code window and press the F1 key.

Exercise 4:   Perform date arithmetic

Visual Basic also allows you to work with dates and times. Add the following statements to the event-handler for the Exercise 4 command button:

```
Private Sub Command4_Click()
Dim today As Date
  today = InputBox("Enter today's date")
  Print "Next Week ";today+7; " Last week ";today-7
End Sub
```

Again, run the program and this time press the Exercise 4 button.

Suggested exercises

1. From the print statement in this exercise, you can see that the result of adding or subtracting a number to or from a date will be to calculate the date that number of days before or after it. Try amending the print statement to calculate the dates for tomorrow and yesterday.

2. A Visual Basic Date variable can store a time value as well as a date. We can use this feature to advance a given date by a fraction of a day. For example, adding 0.5 to a date will result in the same date, but at a time of 12:00 (since 12 hours is half a day). Try adding and subtracting various fractional values in the print statement.

Exercise 5:	Subs and functions: showing a message in all capitals

In Exercises 5–7, we create some useful subs and functions.

Double-click on the button labelled Exercise 5, and add the following code to the event-handler:

```
Private Sub Command5_Click()
    ShowCapitals "Here is a message. "
End Sub
```

Now move the cursor to the point just after the End Sub of the event-handler, and type the following sub definition (note the new code is shown in **bold**):

```
Private Sub Command5_Click()
    ShowCapitals "Here is a message. "
End Sub

Sub ShowCapitals(Msg As String)
    MsgBox UCase(Msg)
End Sub
```

Run the program and click on the button labelled Exercise 5. The message should be shown in all capitals. You can replace the function name **UCase()** with a similar one **LCase()** which converts text to lower case.

Note the way that the new subroutine outline is completed (adding End Sub automatically) as soon as you have entered the first line. Note also the way that a *parameter* has been specified in brackets. The code **Msg As String** means that this sub will now expect a string variable to be passed to it, and will refer to it as **Msg** locally. Note that this will be true whether the string passed is actually named **Msg** or not. In the test call to the sub within the event-handler, a string *value* is passed, and yet this is referred to as **Msg** within the sub.

Suggested exercises

1. Try calling the **ShowCapitals** sub *without a parameter*. Visual Basic will see this as an error. You should note the error message that VB throws up, so that you can recognize the same error when you make it in your own program code.

2. Replace the **MsgBox** call with a **Print** statement – it is possible to use either to display a single message or result.

Exercise 6:	Mixing upper and lower case

The sub in the previous exercise displayed an upper case version of a string. A much more useful sub would be one that capitalized proper names correctly. For example, the name 'fred' is more correctly displayed as 'Fred'. We can write a sub to convert any text into this mixture of cases by using both the **UCase()** and **LCase()** functions along with functions which extract *parts of a string:*

```
Private Sub Command6_Click()
   ShowNameCase("alistair")
End Sub

Sub ShowNameCase(N As String)
Dim First As String, Rest As String
   First = UCase(Left(N, 1))      ' 1st character from the left of N
   Rest = LCase(Mid(N, 2))        ' Everything from 2nd character on
   MsgBox First & Rest
End Sub
```

In this sub, two variables are used. The first, **First**, is assigned an upper case version of the first character in the string passed in **N**. The second, **Rest**, is assigned a lower case version of everything else in **N** (using the **Mid()** function to return everything from the second character on). These are then added together (using '**&**') and displayed in a **MsgBox** call.

Exercise 7:	Mixed case as a function

The **ShowNameCase** sub is of limited use – it can be used to *display words* in name case but nothing else. It would be far more useful if we could turn a string into name case and then do something else with it, such as add it to a database. We can do this by creating a **Function** that takes a string in any case and returns one in name case. We will need to amend much of the code from the previous exercise:

```
Private Sub Command6_Click()
Dim Name As String              ' Storage for a name
   Name = NameCase("alistair")  ' convert "alistair"
   MsgBox Name                  ' display the result
End Sub

Function NameCase(N As String) As String
Dim First As String, Rest As String
   First = UCase(Left(N, 1))      ' 1st character from the left of N
   Rest = LCase(Mid(N, 2))        ' Everything from 2nd character on
   NameCase = First & Rest
End Function
```

The **ShowNameCase** sub has been replaced with the **NameCase** function. Note that the first line now must indicate what type of data the function will return (**..As String**), and that the last line before the **End Function** has the task of returning the function result to the calling statement. The processing to convert to name case is the same.

Instead of a routine that simply takes a string and displays it in name case as previously, the **NameCase()** function will convert a string to name case and then return it to be dealt with in any way necessary. The result is a more general and therefore more useful routine.

Suggested exercises

1. Amend the above exercise so that the user can enter their name (use a call to **InputBox**) and have it converted to name case.

2. Add additional statements so that the user can enter their first and last names into separate variables (using two **InputBox** statements), and have both of them printed out in name case.

4.12 Answers to questions

QUESTION 4.1

In the early days of programming, a program was a single sequence of statements that did all of the required work. It was found that programs developed in this way quickly became complex and confusing for a number of reasons. In the same way that a book that was not divided up into chapters, paragraphs and sentences would be very difficult to read (and to write), so programs developed in this way had no discernible structure. It was difficult to follow the logic of the coding or to find errors in it if any existed. Subroutines were a way of breaking off a logical chunk of program code (logical, in that you would create a subroutine that performed a recognizable task, such as performing a calculation, collecting input from the user or sending a set of data to a file). One significant benefit of this soon became apparent. A subroutine that did a single, simple task well might be used several times in different parts of a program, thereby reducing the need to repeat passages of program code in different parts of the program. This led to efficient coding, and to a reduction in the number of errors, since if a subroutine was written only once and was known to be correct, it would be correct every time it was used. The list of good reasons for writing software in this way therefore includes:

- Makes program code easier to follow

- Makes program code easier to write

- Allows parts of a program to be reused

- Reduces the overall amount of coding necessary

- Reduces error incidences

- Reduces the amount of testing necessary.

QUESTION 4.2

The order in which statements appear in a program does have a significant effect on the resulting output. In the example given, the statements executed in order would display the messages in the sequence:

```
Hello
Goodbye
```

Obviously, the sequence is important since otherwise we would be saying there was no difference between that and 'Goodbye Hello'.

QUESTION 4.3

Appropriate variable types are as follows:

(a) The number of goals scored at a football match. **Byte** (or **Integer** for a match with very high scoring)

(b) The length of a piece of string. **Single** (since the length is likely to have a fractional part, such as 3.27 inches)

(c) The name of a customer. **String**

(d) The price of a daily newspaper. **Currency**

(e) Your birth date. **Date**

(f) The time of the next train. **Date** (this type also accommodates time values)

(g) Whether a light is on or off. **Boolean**

(h) The diameter of the galaxy. **Decimal**

QUESTION 4.4

(a) Scope control is essential for creating encapsulation. A **Private** member variable will be accessible only within the class module in which it is defined. It will be possible to access it to read or change its value from code that is in another module only via a call to a public **Sub** or **Function** – a method. This is exactly what is required in encapsulation: total control is exerted over the internal state of an object by ensuring that changes to it can be made to this state only by calling on methods.

(b) There will be a total of 80 instance variables, four for each object.

QUESTION 4.5

There are several differences between an object and a variable of a user-defined type. A UDT can contain only variable definitions, not methods. Also, all of the component variables in a UDT are automatically given `Public` scope. This makes a class definition better where is it necessary to control the range of values that can be applied to member variables, since the member variables can be made `Private` and access provided via methods.

A UDT is an aggregation of simple variables, so it is not necessary to use the `New` keyword to create one – once it has been declared, it exists. It is essential to use the `New` keyword to create an object of a class.

A UDT definition must be placed in a code module, and can be placed in the same code module as other UDT definitions. A class is always defined in a module of its own.

Since a UDT does not have to be created at run time as an object of a class does, it has less of an impact on machine resources than an object does. A UDT defined to have the same member variables as a class will take up less memory and be less work for the program to create and use.

QUESTION 4.6

(a)   It is wrong to say that an object variable contains an object. An object variable contains only a reference to an object in memory. It can therefore be used to manipulate the object by accessing its properties and methods.

(b)   The object created in the sub will still exist after the subroutine has completed. It will remain in memory until the form that the object variable `TheObject` is declared in has been unloaded from memory.

4.13   Answers to review questions

1.   *State whether the following would be more suitably implemented as subs or functions:*

(a)   *A routine that gets several pieces of information from the user, and passes these into a database.* A sub, since the routine performs an operation but has no need to return a result

(b)   *A routine that gets a single piece of data from the user.* A function (consider the `InputBox()` function)

(c)   *A routine to determine whether the floppy disk drive currently has a disk in it.* A function (the result would be Boolean)

(d)   *A routine to write an item of data to a floppy disk file.* A sub

(e)   *A routine to find out whether the user wishes to save data to a file before the program exits.* A function with a Boolean result.

2. *A program to manage appointments bookings for a small dental practice has been through the first stages of design. The designers have decided that the following modules are necessary, but have forgotten to indicate whether they are to be code modules, class modules or form modules. Indicate the most suitable type of each module:*

    (a) *A module to define the structure and behaviour of a booking.* A class module, since it will define the structure and behaviour of every booking

    (b) *A module to allow the user to view and enter the details of a session of treatment.* A form module, since it will need to be able to display information and provide controls to allow the user to manipulate it

    (c) *A module to manage the operation of the system printer.* A code module, since there is normally only a single system printer in use at one time

    (d) *A module to display and control the output of printed reports.* A form module, since it will need to provide facilities for viewing information and handling the user's control interactions

    (e) *A module to allow the system administrator to make data backups to a tape drive.* A code module

    (f) *A module to allow the system administrator to review the details of a booking.* A form module

    (g) *A module to manage all the bookings of any dentist in the practice.* A class module, since there are likely to be a number of dentists in a practice.

3. *Select appropriate variable types for storing and manipulating the following items of information for the dental practice described in Question 2 (see Table 4.2 for possible types):*

    (a) *The time of a booking.* **Date** (since a date variable also stores time of day information)

    (b) *A patient's name.* **String**

    (c) *A patient's address.* **String**

    (d) *Whether a patient belongs to the practice's standard health insurance scheme.* **Boolean**

    (e) *A count of the bookings a dentist has for a specific date.* **Byte** or **Integer** (**Byte** would suffice since 255 is probably more bookings than the world's fastest dentist could ever cope with in a day)

    (f) *The details of a patient's treatment, specifying duration, date, time of day, dental nurse present and a list of materials used.* A **user-defined type** with specific fields for a description of treatment (**String**), duration (Integer for minutes or a Date variable for a time period – hours:minutes:seconds), date and time (a **Date** variable for both combined), dental nurse (**String** for the nurse's name), list of materials (a **String** array)

    (g) *The cost of a treatment session.* **Currency**.

CHAPTER 5

Structured programming

Program statements in a group will normally execute in strict sequential order. All programming languages include constructs that let the programmer alter the sequence of operation, selecting alternative groups of statements to execute in different conditions, or to repeat certain groups of statements as necessary. Special-purpose statements are used to control the flow of others and add a level of structure to the internal operations of subs and functions. Visual Basic is rich in these structural forms.

By the end of this chapter, you should be able to:

- use selection and iteration constructs in Visual Basic programs,

- use arrays and collections in programs,

- use predefined objects in programs,

- handle errors in programming and by the user.

5.1 Program control constructs in Visual Basic

The methods you create for classes of objects need to contain more than just sequences of statements to be followed blindly. One of the most important features provided by programming languages is a facility to adapt the sequence in which statements are executed to fit in with the current state of objects in the program.

The natural structure of a group of Basic statements is a *sequence*. Statements in a sequence will be executed in the order in which they appear in the sub or function.

However, we often wish to make statements execute in some other order, either choosing which statements to execute or executing certain statements or groups of statements a number of times. Visual Basic, in common with all other programming languages, provides a number of options:

- One or more statements can be executed **If** a given condition evaluates to **True**.

- One or more statements can be executed **If** a given condition evaluates to **True**, or **Else** a different group of statements can be executed.

- A group of statements can be **Select**ed depending on which of a number of possible **Case**s a variable evaluates to.

- A group of statements can be executed once **For** each value in a given range.

- A group of statements can be repeatedly executed **While** a given condition evaluates to **True**.

- A group of statements can be executed in a **Loop**, **While** a condition remains **True** or **Until** a given condition becomes **True**.

All of these programming structures modify the execution of normal sequences of statements in some way. They are used in subs and functions to deal with varying conditions in the program or to repeat the same block of statements to process lists of information.

Conditions

All programming languages make use of the idea of a condition to guide the flow of the program. In Visual Basic, a condition is any type of statement that can evaluate to **True** or **False**. This can include:

- **True** or **False** keywords (which obviously evaluate to one or the other) or any other **Boolean** expression,

- the value of a **Boolean** variable or property (e.g. **Text1.Visible**),

- comparisons, such as equality (=) or inequality (<>) between two variables or values,

- comparisons, such as less than (<) or greater than (>) between two variables or values.

Conditions are used in **If..Then** statements, **While** statements, to control **Do..Loop** structures and in **Select Case** structures.

Selection structures

The standard selection structure, available in most programming languages, is **If..Then**. This structure evaluates a condition to determine whether it is **True** or

False, and then executes a controlled block of statements if the result was **True**. In Visual Basic, this takes the form:

```
If <condition> Then
  <controlled statements>
End If
```

For example:

```
If value = 0 Then
  MsgBox "The value entered was zero."
End If
```

A simple variation of this is a single line **If..Then** statement (in which no **End If** statement is required):

```
If <condition> Then <controlled statement>
```

The statement being controlled must appear in the same line as the **If** statement. For example:

```
If value = 0 Then MsgBox "The value entered was zero."
```

There is also a variant that allows an alternative set of statements to execute if the condition does not evaluate to **True**:

```
If <condition> Then
  <controlled statements>
Else
  <controlled statements>
End If
```

For example:

```
If value = 0 Then
  MsgBox "The value entered was zero."
Else
  MsgBox "The value entered was non-zero."
End If
```

The condition part of an **If..Then** statement can be derived in a number of ways. Any expression with a Boolean result is a suitable condition.

Examples of **If..Then** structures

```
' Conditions can come from Visual Basic controls..
If List1.ListIndex >= 0 Then
  ' There is a selected item in the list box named List1
  Text1.Text = List1.Text
End If
```

```
If txtUserName.Text = "John Smith" Then
  ' We can nest another If..Then structure inside this one..
  If txtPassword.Text = "abc123" Then
    LogInToNetwork
  Else
    MsgBox "Password Wrong"
  End If
Else
  MsgBox "Not a valid system user."
End If

' A Function can return a Boolean result to be used as a condition..
If ValidFileName(FName) Then LoadFile FName

' We can combine conditions using the keywords And and Or..
If examMark < 0 Or examMark > 100 Then
  MsgBox "Please enter the exam mark as a percentage."
End If
```

Using **If..Then** structures in a class

We can use an **If..Then..Else** structure in the **BankAccount** class developed in the exercise at the end of Chapter 2 to good effect. An obvious condition that would affect a **BankAccount** is whether there is any cash currently on deposit. In normal banking, an ATM (Automatic Teller Machine) would refuse to allow a user to withdraw cash if the withdrawal would result in the account balance going below zero. We can amend the **Withdraw** method to accommodate this rule:

```
Public Sub Withdraw(amount As Currency)
  If amount <= mvarBalance Then
    mvarBalance = mvarBalance - amount
  End If
End Sub
```

However, the way we have implemented this rule is not entirely satisfactory. If the account owner tries to withdraw more than they have in the account, the **BankAccount** object refuses to make the withdrawal, but there is no way to find out that this has happened without examining the Balance property. The problem is that the **Withdraw** method is implemented as a **Sub**, which does not return any result. If we were to implement it as a **Function** instead, it could be made to return a **Boolean** result to indicate the success or failure of the operation.

```
Public Function Withdraw(amount As Currency) As Boolean
  If amount <= mvarBalance Then
    mvarBalance = mvarBalance - amount
    Withdraw = True
```

```
    Else
       Withdraw = False
    End If
End Function
```

With this change, the account class can be used more securely. For example, in the form developed in the exercise at the end of Chapter 3:

```
Private Sub cmdWithdraw_Click()
   If Account.Withdraw(InputBox("Amount to withdraw")) Then
      lblBalance.Caption = Account.Balance
   Else
      MsgBox "There is not enough in the account."
   End If
End Sub
```

Note the change in the call to the **Withdraw** method. In the original exercise, it was called as a sub. In this case, it is called as a function, and this requires that the parameter (the return from the **InputBox** function) needs to be placed in parentheses. Since the result of the **Withdraw** method is a **Boolean**, it can be used directly as a condition in the **If..Then** statement that calls it.

If..Then structures are the classic way of adding conditional execution to a program. However, if there are a number of options, an **If..Then** structure can become quite difficult to follow. Take the example of working out how many days there are in a given month:

```
If MonthName = "Jan" Then
   Days = 31
Else If MonthName = "Feb" Then
   If (Year / 4) * 4 = Year Then
      Days = 29
   Else
      Days = 28
   End If
Else If MonthName = "Mar" Then
   ' ' ' '
   ' ' ' '         ' another 9 to go...
```

As you can see, the **If..Then..Else** form of the structure is adequate for the job, but it does not lead to elegant program code. Visual Basic has a useful alternative that is ideal for this type of job:

```
Select Case MonthName
   Case "Sep", "Apr", "Jun", "Nov"
      Days = 30
```

```
Case "Feb"
  If (Year / 4) * 4 = Year Then
    Days = 29
  Else
    Days = 28
  End If
Case Else
  Days = 31
End Select
```

The **Select Case** structure is ideal for this type of multi-way selection, and can do the work of many nested **If..Then..Else** structures if the problem circumstances are right. A structure is controlled by a single variable instead of a conditional expression. Which optional block of statements is executed depends on the value currently in the variable named after the keywords **Select Case**. Each alternative block is headed by a **Case** value or range of values. An **Else** case can be used to head the default action (the block of statements to be executed if the control variable does not match any of the specified cases).

QUESTION 5.1

A Boolean variable is one that can only store a True or False value. Given the following sub:

```
Sub Greetings()
Dim IsMorning As Boolean
  IsMorning = (Time < "12:00:00")
  If IsMorning Then
    Print "Good Morning"
  Else
    Print "Good Afternoon"
  End If
End Sub
```

and also given that the Visual Basic function **Time** returns a string of the appropriate format, what will be printed at exactly noon?

Can you extend the sub so that it will print 'Good Morning' before midday, 'Good Afternoon' before 5 o'clock in the evening and 'Good Evening' after this time?

If..Then, **If..Then..Else** and **Select Case** structures allow us to control which statements will be executed in a program, and therefore to direct how the program will react to prevailing conditions. These forms of statement can largely dictate the *structure* that the other statements in a program follow. Without them, all programs would blindly follow the sequence of statements in the order they were written, regardless of what was happening in the program.

Repetition structures

Repetition of a group of statements is known as *iteration*. When structured programming was first proposed in the late 1960s, it was suggested that the `While..Wend` (or `While..Do`, in the languages of the time) structure would cater for every situation in which iteration was necessary in programs. While this is certainly true, most programmers prefer the flexibility that a range of repetition structures can offer. Visual Basic has three, although of these, the `While..Wend` structure is the least powerful and can easily be dispensed with.

The `While..Wend` structure works like this:

```
While <condition>
   ' Statements to be executed repeatedly
Wend
```

The keywords `While` and `Wend` act as brackets around the group of statements we wish to execute a number of times. Before each execution of these statements, the condition after the `While` keyword is examined and, if it is `True`, the statements are executed. If the condition is ever `False`, control passes to the statement in the program that follows the `Wend` (meaning End While) keyword. For example:

```
While userName = ""
   userName = InputBox("Enter your name")
Wend
```

In the above example, the `InputBox` statement will be executed until the user types something into it and presses its OK button. We can therefore use this structure to make sure that the program's execution will not continue until some requirement is met (in this case, the user entering something as their name). Note, however, that if the `userName` variable already had a value in it, the logic of the `While` loop would have prevented the `InputBox` statement from ever being executed. Note also that it is essential that a statement or statements inside the loop can change the `While` condition (in this case, the user is given the chance to re-enter `userName` on each iteration). Otherwise, the `While` loop would continue iterating forever.

We will largely ignore the `While` loop because another, more flexible structure is available in Visual Basic. This is the `Do..Loop`, and we will examine it later.

The classic Basic repetition structure is the `For` loop. This requires an extra variable which is used as a counter by the `For..Next` structure. In its simplest form, the `For` loop takes the format:

```
For <loop_variable> = <initial-value> to <final-value>
   <Statements to be repeated>
Next
```

The loop variable used can be referred to inside the loop, giving access to a range of values counted out. For example, we can use a `For` loop to count through a range of values:

```
For value = 1 To 100
  Print value
Next
```

In the above example, each value in the range is simply printed out. However, we can make use of the loop variable in statements inside the loop, provided we do not attempt to change its value (since this would upset the flow of the **For** loop):

```
Table = InputBox("Which times-table do you wish")
For index = 1 To 12
  Print index, "X", Table, "=", index * Table
Next
```

This would result in a standard 'times-table' being printed out for the number entered at the **InputBox** statement. Assuming 5 was entered:

1 × *5* = *5*
2 × *5* = *10*
3 × *5* = *15*
4 × *5* = *20*
5 × *5* = *25*
etc.

It is possible to use **For..Next** loops to count up in increments other than 1. To do this, the **step** keyword is used:

```
For Size = 0 To 5 Step 0.2
  ' ' '
Next
```

Similarly, it is possible to use a negative increment to count down:

```
For Neg_Step = 10 To 1 Step -1
  ' ' '
Next
```

One very important feature of the **For** statement at the start of a **For** loop is that you can use variables or expressions instead of values to control the number of iterations. For example, a **For** loop can be used to calculate compound interest on an investment account:

```
Amount = InputBox("How much do you intend to invest?")
Period = InputBox("How many years of investment?")
InterestRate = InputBox("What is the interest rate (%)?")
For Interval = 1 To Period
  Amount = Amount + Amount * InterestRate / 100
Next
MsgBox "Return after investment will be " & Amount
```

In the above example, the number of iterations is the number of years the user enters in the **Period** variable. It is also possible to use variables or expressions to specify the initial value in the **For** loop (instead of 1) or to provide a **Step** increment that is different from the default 1.

The final repetition structure in Visual Basic is by far the most flexible (although **For..Next** is normally the most widely used). A **Do..Loop** structure can repeat **While** or **Until** a condition is **True**, and the terminating condition can be placed at the start of the structure (repeat zero or more times), or at the end (repeat one or more times). It is also possible to cause an exit from any point within the structure. The most common use of this is in implementing the classic **Repeat..Until** structure of the Pascal programming language:

```
Do
   ' Do Something
Loop Until <some condition is met>
```

For example, we could use this form of loop to force the user to enter a valid number:

```
Dim N As Variant, ValidN As Single
Do
   N = InputBox("Enter a number")
Loop Until IsNumeric(N)
ValidN = N
```

This example makes use of Visual Basic's **IsNumeric** function, that will test a string or variant variable and return a value of **True** if the content is a valid number. The **Do..Loop** will continue to iterate until the user enters a number, after which the number entered will be applied to the **Single** (floating-point variable) **ValidN**.

We can also negate the test for an exit condition by replacing the **Until** keyword with **While**:

```
Do
   userName = InputBox("Enter your name")
Loop While userName = ""
```

which would iterate until some text was entered into the **userName** variable. This is functionally similar to the example used to demonstrate a **While** loop, but will always ask the user to enter text *before* testing the variable for the first time. If instead we wanted to recreate the **While** loop exactly, we could use the alternative form:

```
Do While userName = ""
   userName = InputBox("Enter your name")
Loop
```

which makes the test at the entry point of the loop.

Using repetition structures in a class

In the simple **BankAccount** class we have been using as an example, there is little use for iteration, although a more realistic **BankAccount** class in which every single transaction was recorded would make good use of it. We will illustrate this in a future exercise. However, the **Form** class that we developed to work with the **BankAccount** class can make good use of iteration as a way of validating the user's input. For example, in the method to process a click on the **Deposit** button:

```
Private Sub cmdDeposit_Click()
Dim amount As String
  Do
    amount = InputBox("How much to deposit?")
  Loop Until IsNumeric(amount)
  Account.Deposit CCur(amount)
    lblBalance.Caption = Account.Balance
End Sub
```

Note that we have defined the **amount** variable as a **String** type, which we then validate using the **IsNumeric** function. This returns **True** if its String parameter can be converted to a number. The **Do..Loop** will continue to iterate until the user enters a valid numeric value. When iteration does finish, the standard **CCur()** function converts the numeric string to a valid currency value.

The repetition structures provided with Visual Basic allow us to create loops that work best in three types of circumstances. These are:

■ to execute one or more statements zero or more times, depending on a condition – use a **While** loop or a **Do While** loop or a **Do Until** loop, since the test is performed at the start and so the loop need never be entered,

■ to execute one or more statements one or more times, depending on a condition – use a **Do..Loop While** or a **Do..Loop Until**, where the test is done at the end of the loop, after at least one pass through it,

■ to execute one or more statements a number of times that is known or can be worked out before the loop commences – use a **For..Next** loop.

QUESTION 5.2

Select appropriate loop structures for the following tasks:

(a) to keep getting numeric values from the user, processing them in some way until a 0 is entered,
(b) to keep asking a user to enter a date until a valid one has been entered,
(c) to calculate and print out all of the odd numbers in the range up to 1000,
(d) to repeatedly halve the value of a variable until it becomes less than 100.

The '**With**' structure

Since Visual Basic supports the use of objects (forms, controls, etc.) in projects, it provides a **With..End With** structure to simplify coding that involves these. For example, consider the situation where you wish to assert a number of settings for a specific object on a specific form. From within the form (**frmNames**), we could manipulate a **ListBox** control, **lstUserNames**, this way:

```
Sub ManipulateListBox()
  lstUserNames.Clear
  lstUsernames.AddItem "John Smith"
  lstUsernames.AddItem "Mary Brown"
  lstUserNames.AddItem "Linda McGrath"
  lstuserNames.AddItem "Gordon Kennedy"
  lstUserNames.ListIndex = -1        ' No item selected
End Sub
```

A Visual Basic **ListBox** control stores and displays a list of values. In the example shown, four separate statements are used to add items to the list box. Performing the same operation from a different module (e.g. another form, or a procedure in a code module) is even more repetitive:

```
Sub ManipulateListBox()
  frmNames.lstUserNames.Clear
  frmNames.lstUsernames.AddItem "John Smith"
  frmNames.lstUsernames.AddItem "Mary Brown"
  frmNames.lstUserNames.AddItem "Linda McGrath"
  frmNames.lstuserNames.AddItem "Gordon Kennedy"
  frmNames.lstUserNames.ListIndex = -1
End Sub
```

Using a **With** structure, we can reduce the amount of typing (and, as a bonus, speed up the execution of the Visual Basic program):

```
Sub ManipulateListBox()
  With frmNames.lstUserNames
    .Clear
    .AddItem "John Smith"
    .AddItem "Mary Brown"
    .AddItem "Linda McGrath"
    .AddItem "Gordon Kennedy"
    .ListIndex = -1
  End With
End Sub
```

Inside a **With** structure, Visual Basic takes every line that begins with a dot ('.') as an extension of the object indicated after the **With** keyword. The result is much less typing, a clearer syntax and faster execution.

5.2   Arrays and collections

If you want to process a lot of data, you are likely to need to use a lot of separate variables to store the data you are processing. While this is self evident, what is less immediately apparent is that if you do this with normal variables, you would need to declare each separately. For example, to store the names of 1000 customers in variables, you would have **Dim** statements such as:

```
Dim Cust1 As String
Dim Cust2 As String
  ' ' '
Dim Cust1000 As String
```

Having laboriously set up all of these variables, you would then need to access each in separate statements:

```
' Get customers names from a file (Line Input# does this)...
Line Input #F, Cust1
Line Input #F, Cust2
  ' ' '
Line Input #F, Cust1000        ' Whew!
```

Obviously, large amounts of data are not handled this way in programs. Instead, a system of storing multiple variables under a single name with a subscript, known as an *array* is the standard way of dealing with a lot of individual variables that are being used to store similar data. For the above example, the Visual Basic statement to declare the data would become:

```
Dim Customers(1 To 1000) As String
```

This makes an array of 1000 string variables, all accessible using the name 'Customers'. To access an individual element, we simply use the array name followed by the number of the element in brackets:

```
Customers(100) = "Wendy Black"   ' to assign an element
Print Customers(550)             ' to access an element
```

Instead of using a literal number as the array *index*, we can make use of a variable. For example, to prompt the user to enter a name for each array element:

```
For Index = 1 To 1000
  Customers(index) = InputBox("Enter curtomer name")
Next
```

This will have the effect of assigning the first user-entry to **Customers(1)**, the second to **Customer(2)** and so on. Instead of the 1000 individual statements required to access 1000 individual variables, these three statements access all 1000 of the array elements. A **For..Next** loop is an ideal mechanism for dealing with the elements of an array, since it is easy to make it step through each element in turn. Of course, we could use an expression instead of the index variable to indicate a specific element of the array. If the variable **index** contained the value 3, then:

```
Customers(2 * index + 5)
```

would access the eleventh element of the array (since $2 \times 3 + 5 = 11$).

Arrays of simple variables are perfect for storing multiples of the same type of data. Normally, these would be members of a group of similar simple items. To create more complex data structures, we can work with arrays of user-defined types. For example, the UDT defined in Section 4.8 to store a person's name and telephone number becomes a much more useful data type, since we can now define enough of them to form a whole telephone book:

```
Private PhoneBook(1 To 100) As PhoneEntry     ' 100 entries
```

We can access each of the individual phone book entries using the array name and an index as previously. The dot notation can then be used to access individual component elements:

```
PhoneBook(10).Name = "Martin Green"
PhoneBook(10).Telephone = "4556"
```

It is also possible to define any of the component elements in a UDT as an array. We could, for example, provide each person's entry in our **PhoneBook()** array with several phone numbers by declaring the telephone component as an array, and so the statement:

```
Print PhoneBook(5).Telephone(2)
```

would have the result of printing out the second telephone number of the fifth entry in the phone book.

Declaring arrays

Visual Basic provides a number of ways to set up an array, allowing the number of elements and the range of indices to be declared quite flexibly. If I wished to set up a 10-element array of strings, I could use any of the following syntax variants:

```
Dim StrArr(10) As String
Dim StrArr2(1 To 10) As String
Dim StrArr3(0 To 9) As String
Dim StrArr4(-4 To 5) As String     ' counts element 0
```

Note that the first of these actually sets up an 11-element array using Visual Basic's default configuration, since element 0 is automatically included. In fact, **StrArr(9)** would be a 10-element array. If you are happier working with arrays whose first element is normally element number 1, then you can enter a directive to Visual Basic to make this the default at the top of a module:

```
Option Base 1
Public MyArray(10)     ' Elements 1 to 10
```

Arrays in objects and arrays of objects

We can use an array in a class definition to store multiple pieces of simple data. For example, in our **BankAccount** class, we could store details about the account owner (name, PIN number, etc.), including several lines of the customer's address:

```
Private mvarBalance As Currency
Public Name As String
Private mvarPIN As String      ' Private for obvious reasons.
Public Address(1 To 4) As String
```

Now, each instance we create of the **BankAccount** class will contain storage for up to four lines of address information that could be set up as follows:

```
Set Account = New BankAccount      ' Create the instance
Account.Name = InputBox("Enter customer's name")
' Now populate the address variables..
For index = 1 To 4
  Account.Address(index) = InputBox("Enter address line")
Next
```

We can also create arrays *of* objects. In this case, each array element would be an object reference variable that *could* refer to an existing object in memory. We might declare a suitable array for referencing 100 **BankAccount** objects as:

```
Private Accounts(1 To 100) As BankAccount
```

Since the array contains object *references*, we do not immediately get 100 bank account objects. Instead, each has to be instantiated in the usual way:

```
Set Accounts(index) = New BankAccount
```

This line of code could be placed in a sub. It would be necessary to keep track of the index variable so that we always assigned a new **BankAccount** to an object reference that currently had no object assigned to it. This requirement makes working with arrays of objects tricky and error prone, so most Visual Basic programmers use collections (described next) to group a number of objects together.

> **QUESTION 5.3**
>
> Since arrays are normally defined as having a particular number of elements, it is normal to use a **For..Next** loop with them. Can you think of situations where a **While** or a **Do..Loop Until** loop might be used to good effect?

Arrays are a very efficient way of storing large amounts of data. They occupy a minimum amount of storage space for the amount of information stored, and are very fast for Visual Basic to deal with – a seemingly ideal way to accommodate a lot of data. However, arrays have one major drawback. Normally, you need to know in advance how many items you wish to store in an array, so that you can dimension it to the correct size. Although there are ways around this (look up the **ReDim** keyword in Visual Basic's on-line help), arrays are still awkward to use in such circumstances. A **Collection** is like an array in many ways, but has the additional ability to accommodate a variable number of items without needing to be pre-dimensioned.

Collections

A collection is a 'smart array'. It dynamically resizes itself to accommodate the number of elements stored in it. Although Visual Basic collections can only accommodate lists of variants or objects, this is not a major restriction since we can store any simple value (from any of the existing Visual Basic variable types) as a variant. We can also use objects as more capable user-defined types, so it may be that collections are the better mechanism to use in object-oriented terms.

Here is a declaration of a simple collection we will use to store a list of numbers:

```
Private NumberList As New Collection
```

Note that **Public** or **Dim** could have been used instead of **Private**. We can see from this that a collection is a type of object. The **New** keyword is used to tell Visual Basic that it needs to set up a new collection object – without it, the **NumberList** variable could have been used to refer to an existing collection, but not to build a new one.

We can write a sub to add items to the collection as follows:

```
Public Sub InsertNumber(N As Variant)
   NumberList.Add N
End Sub
```

Note that it would have been possible simply to use the statement **NumberList.Add N** within the same module that the list was declared in, but by using a **Public** function, it can be used throughout the project. It is good practice to declare the data items as **Private**, and then use **Public** subs and functions to manipulate them. This prevents a programmer from dealing directly with the data and allows extra statements to be added to **InsertNumber** (in this case) to validate the data stored in the collection. For example, if we had wanted to restrict the collection to storing only positive numbers:

```
Public Sub InsertNumber(N As Variant)
   If N >= 0 Then NumberList.Add N
End Sub
```

A collection would be used for a similar purpose as an array; we are saved from needing to use a different identifier for each item of data.

The **Add** keyword is used to add data to a collection. To get at the data in the collection, we can use an index syntax similar to that we would use with an array:

```
For index = 1 To NumberList.Count
   Sum = Sum & NumberList(index)
Next
```

The first element in a collection is *always* element number 1. Note that a collection object has a **Count** property that indicates the current number of items in it, and an **Item()** property that appears like an array of the items in it. The syntax used above relies on the **Item()** property being the default property of the class, allowing us to dispense with the keyword. In fact,

```
NumberList(index)
```

is shorthand for, and exactly equivalent to,

```
NumberList.Item(index)
```

For..Each syntax

Visual Basic provides a slightly more elegant form of the **For..Next** structure for dealing with collections, as shown in this sub, which displays a whole list:

```
Sub DisplayList()
Dim S As String, N As Variant
  S = ""
  For Each N In NumberList
    S = S & N & vbCrLf
  Next
  MsgBox S
End Sub
```

The **For..Each** structure uses a reference variable (N) to access each element in the collection in turn. This variable has to be type-compatible with the members of the collection, i.e. a **Variant** or an **Object** type. Compare this with the index variable used in the standard **For** structure, which would normally be an integer type (**Byte**, **Integer** or **Long**).

To remove items from a collection, simply use the **Remove** keyword:

```
Sub ClearList()
  While NumberList.Count > 0
    NumberList.Remove 1          ' Keep removing first item
  Wend
End Sub
```

Note that in the above example, the **NumberList** is cleared by repeatedly removing the first item (specified by number). It is much easier to clear a collection by simply resetting it with the **New** keyword:

```
Set NumberList = New Collection
```

The best feature of collections is that they do not need to store items of the same type. The arrays we have seen store lists of strings, integers, etc., by virtue of the way they are declared (using the **As** keyword). However, collections are type-less, apart from the restriction on using only variants or objects. We can use them to store a list of all of the controls on a form, or, as we shall see later, a collection of user-defined objects of any type.

Collections of objects

If we have developed a class to represent a type of thing we need to deal with in a program, we can use a collection to accommodate as many objects of the class as we need in the program. For example, we could use a collection to deal with multiple instances of the **BankAccount** class developed in Chapter 2:

```
Private AccountList As New Collection

Public Sub NewAccount()
Dim Account As BankAccount
   Set Account = New BankAccount
   AccountList.Add Account
End Sub
```

Each call of the **NewAccount** sub will result in a new **BankAccount** object being created and added to the **AccountList** collection. The only limit to this is the amount of memory available on the computer on which the program is running. We could also use the **For..Each** syntax to access each **BankAccount** in turn:

```
Public Function TotalWorth() As Currency
Dim Account As BankAccount, total As Currency
   For Each Account In AccountList
      Total = total + Account.Balance
   Next
   TotalWorth = total
End Function
```

Using the **For..Each** syntax like this has a very specific meaning with a collection of objects. In effect, each iteration sets the Account reference variable to refer to each object in the collection in turn. Of course, once we have a reference variable to an object, we can access any of its properties or methods.

One perhaps obvious proviso regarding the use of collections of objects is that we can only add properly instantiated objects to a collection. Each object must have been created using the **New** keyword before it can be added to a collection. However, the collection does not check an object reference passed to it with the **Add** method to determine if it does refer to an actual object. Instead, it will blindly accept any reference passed to it. This will have the effect of causing a crash or at least an error condition when an attempt is made to access items later – for example, in a **For..Each** statement, the *run-time error* shown in Figure 5.1 would be displayed.

In this example, the sub shown adds a **BankAccount** reference to the **AccountList** collection. The **AccountList** correctly keeps a count of the items added to it. However, since no **New** keyword is used to create a **BankAccount** object, a null

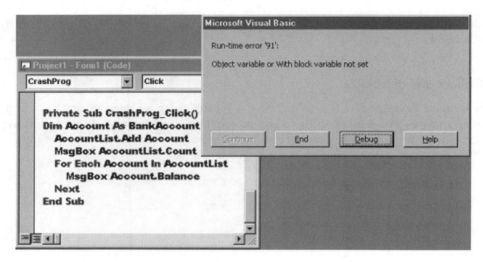

Figure 5.1   *Trying to access a non-instantiated object in a collection.*

reference is added. The result is that when an attempt is made to access the objects using a `For..Each` loop, Visual Basic throws up a run-time error.

QUESTION 5.4

It is also possible to create an array of objects, for example:

```
Private ObjList(1 To 10) Of SomeClass
```

Can you think of any advantages of this? When the array has just been declared, what will it contain?

5.3   Coping with errors

Various types of error can occur in a computer program. Some are mistakes in the use of the language rules or vocabulary. These are *syntax errors* and can be automatically identified by the Visual Basic IDE. You may already have noticed this type of error in a line in which you mistyped a keyword. Visual Basic responds by throwing up a message box identifying the error, and turning the offending line red in its code window. Because of this, these errors are generally easy to deal with.

Other errors can be due to flaws in the logic of the program you have written. Most of these can only be identified and removed by careful design and testing of your program. Errors such as attempting to access the eleventh element of a 10-element

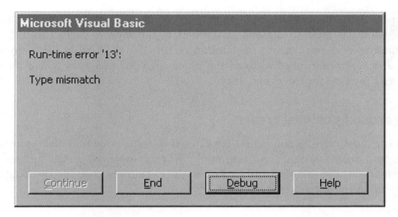

Figure 5.2   *The result of an invalid input in a Visual Basic program.*

array fall into this category. This is the most difficult type of error to eliminate, and is the reason why software development is more than simply programming. Using recognized design methods, ensuring that the code you write implements a valid design, and carrying out rigorous testing, are the main tools for the prevention and detection of this type of error.

However, an entire class of error can occur that is not attributable to the programmer or designer. These are errors that happen because the user has entered an invalid value (for example, entering alphabetic characters when a number is expected) or because some external entity such as a disk file or a printer is not present when it should be. These are generically called ***input/output errors***, and can only be handled automatically by the language in a very simplistic way. For example, the sub shown below will fail if the user enters a value that is not a date:

```
Sub Calculate_Age()
Dim DOB As Date
   DOB = InputBox("Enter your date of birth.")
   MsgBox "You are " & (Date - DOB)/365 & " years old."
End Sub
```

If the user enters a date, this sub will behave correctly by subtracting that date from the system date (given by the **Date** function), and then converting the resulting number of days to years by dividing by 365. However, if a character type of input is supplied, the date arithmetic embedded in the **MsgBox** statement will fail, causing the program to terminate abruptly with the error message shown in Figure 5.2.

This is not the most user-friendly response to a simple error, and most users would be (rightly) suspicious of a program that failed like this. The worst outcome of this type of error is that the program has now *terminated*. The user may have spent a long time entering data for processing and this error happens at the last stage, causing great frustration. As a programmer, you need to take control of the situation by making sure that errors of this type are handled in a way that will leave the user more aware of what has gone wrong and give the user an option to correct it.

There are several mechanisms for handling errors like this. All of them require that you, as a programmer, are aware of the places in your program where they could happen and provide for the eventuality.

Coding around potential errors

Perhaps the most obvious solution to an error is to write code that always anticipates an error and works around its eventuality. For example, to guard against a user entering text that did not equate to a date in the **Calculate_Age** sub, we could check the entry using the **IsDate()** function:

```
Sub Calculate_Age()
Dim DOB As String
  DOB = InputBox("Enter your date of birth.")
  If IsDate(DOB) Then
    MsgBox "You are " & (Date - Cdate(DOB))/365 & " years old."
  Else
    MsgBox "Invalid date."
  End If
End Sub
```

Note that the input variable is now a string type, useful since a string variable can accommodate any type of input. We then try to validate the string as a date using **IsDate()**.

We could go on to check all user input in programs in this way, but as this simple example shows, we could end up with the lines of error-handling code outnumbering the normal processing code. Visual Basic provides us with a couple of useful alternatives.

Ignoring errors

One alternative method is simply to turn off error handling altogether. Visual Basic traps any error condition and informs the user of it. By default, this also means that the program will end prematurely. We can suspend all automatic error handling in the current sub or function by inserting the statement **On Error Resume Next** at the start:

```
Sub Calculate_Age()
Dim DOB As Date
  On Error Resume Next
  DOB = InputBox("Enter your date of birth.")
  MsgBox "You are " & (Date - DOB) / 365 & " years old."
End Sub
```

In this case, the program will never exit prematurely because of invalid input. However, since errors are totally ignored, it will now be difficult to tell whether it is

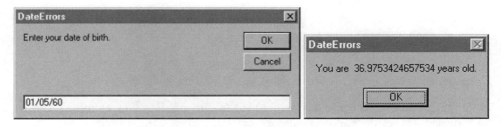

Figure 5.3   *The input and output from the* `Calculate_Age()` *routine.*

Figure 5.4   *Entering an invalid date with no error handling.*

providing the correct response, making it worse than useless in many situations. For example, in the program run shown in Figure 5.3, a correct date was entered. In Figure 5.4, however, the date entered is wrong because the first character is an 'l' (a lower case 'L') instead of a '1' (one). The resulting output is the same as if a date of 0/0/0 (one day before the first day in 1900) had been entered, because this is the base date the PC uses for calculations. By turning off error handling, our program has become simultaneously more robust and less reliable.

Handling errors

By far the best solution is to try to anticipate the types of error that can happen and provide an ***error handler*** for them. This is simply a section of code that will be run if any type of error occurs. For example:

```
Sub Calculate_Age()
Dim DOB As Date
  On Error GoTo err_Calculate_Age
  DOB = InputBox("Enter your date of birth.")
  MsgBox "You are " & (Date - DOB) / 365 & " years old."
err_Calculate_Age:
  If Err Then
    If Err = 13 Then    ' Type mismatch - we expected this.
      MsgBox "An invalid date has been entered."
      Resume
```

```
     Else
       MsgBox Error      ' Some errors can never be anticipated.
     End If
   End If
End Sub
```

Note that while a lot of code has been added to our sub, it is now as robust as if we had turned off error handling altogether, but copes with an error in a more informative and graceful way. If an error due to an invalid date occurs (Err=13, as shown in the error dialog in Figure 5.2), an appropriate message is displayed, leaving the user in no doubt of the cause. The **Resume** keyword causes control to return to the statement in which the error occurred, so the user can re-enter a date and continue. If any other error occurs (one that we have not anticipated, such as a processor fault), the user is given a message indicating the type of error (**Error** is a function that returns a description of an error).

The key points of this type of error handler are:

- An error handler is set up with the statement 'On Error Goto <Label>', where <Label> is a point in the code to which control should transfer when an error occurs.

- The start of the error handler is marked with a matching label (e.g. **err_Calculate_Age** in the example above).

- Expected errors can be dealt with specifically (e.g. the error **Err=13**, which is a type mismatch).

- Unexpected errors can be signalled to the user (using the **Error** function).

- The error handling code is guarded by an **If Err Then** condition, which is shorthand for **If Err<>0 Then**, i.e. if an error has happened. Without this, the error handling code would always be executed. As an alternative, you can insert an **Exit Sub** statement immediately before the error handler.

- The presence of the error handler means that *all code* after the **On Error** statement is protected, no matter how many lines of code the sub contains. Other, unanticipated errors will cause the default error response under the **Else** clause to be executed. At least the user will be aware that something has gone wrong.

In fact, **Err** is a globally declared Visual Basic object whose default property is the number that identifies the error. This object also has a **Description** property (**Err.Description**), which defines a string that is also returned by the **Error** function.

One of the biggest causes of frustration in software users is the occurrence of errors that cause hours of work to be lost. While no amount of error handling code can prevent errors from occurring, the use of error handling in critical routines can make these easier to tolerate. If the user of a program is warned that an error has happened, and the program does not just crash, it enables the user to recover gracefully from the error, saving data files and reporting its occurrence.

Why should using an error handler be preferable to simply writing extra code to ensure that error conditions are detected and corrected?

Types of error

Several types of error can occur when programming. The most prevalent groups that can occur at the programming stage are:

- syntax errors
- errors in logic
- run-time errors.

A syntax error is an error in the use of the language, for example:

```
For x = 1 Until 5...
```

Syntax errors are simple to deal with, since the programming language will refuse to accept them in code. Try to run a program with a syntax error in it and Visual Basic will either recognize the error immediately, or if it cannot do this, will find it when it comes into scope. In either case, the Visual Basic IDE will be able to highlight the exact cause of the error.

An error in logic is trickier, since the language cannot know your intention and is therefore most likely not to recognize this as an error. For example, you could misuse a loop structure in such a way that no exit condition is possible, resulting in an infinite loop. To the user, your program would simply 'hang', or stop responding to their input, even though nothing illegal has happened in the language. The only cure for this type of error is careful design.

Run-time errors are the group that we can deal with, since these often cause the language to try to do things it cannot and therefore cause a crash. As we have seen, run-time errors are mostly caused by unexpected user input or input from sources outside the program, or by unexpected results (such as a division by zero error). The best approach to dealing with this type of error is to become aware of the likely circumstances where they can occur, and use error handlers to deal with them. Every event-handler is a likely source of error, and should ideally be protected by an **On Error** definition.

In the end, the best approach to dealing with errors is to test program code. Become a naive user during testing, and enter obviously erroneous values to try to make errors happen. Better still, get someone to test your programs for you. They will not have your expectations of how the program should work, and so are more likely to enter invalid data that will cause trouble.

Error-free software is an almost impossible goal, but the best software is distinguished by the amount of effort that the developer has put into anticipating problems, and in testing for the program's response to them.

5.4 Review questions

1. Complete the following:
   (a) Extra program statements that control whether other statements will be executed or not are known as _____ structures.
   (b) Program statements that control the repeated execution of others are known as _____ structures.
   (c) A type of expression known as a _____ governs the **If..Then** structure.
   (d) A **Do..Loop** can be controlled by either a _____ condition or an _____ condition.
   (e) A _____ structure can be used to save having to type object references repeatedly over a number of statements.
   (f) The phrase _____ is used to introduce an error handler.

2. Multi-way selection structures can be made using either the **Select Case** structure, or an **If..Then..ElseIf..Else** group. Can you suggest situations in which either would be preferable?

3. It is possible to combine a number of conditions using the keywords **And** or **Or**. It is also possible to negate a condition using the keyword **Not**, e.g.

   ```
   If Not (x=2) Then...
   ```

   Write an **If..Then** structure that will set the **Boolean** variable **DataValid** to **True** if the variable **Age** is between 18 and 60 (inclusive), the variable **CanDrive** is **True**, **HasConvictions** has the value **False** and **FreeToTravel** contains either **"Monday"** or **"Thursday"**.

4. A programmer has written a sub in which a required date is to be entered, but has used an integer variable for it by mistake. Is this a syntax, logic or run-time error?

5. Write a series of statements that will assign the first five even values (starting from 2) to the variable X in turn.

6. Write a series of statements that will repeatedly halve the value of X until it becomes less than 10 in value.

7. An investment opportunity guarantees to provide 10% simple interest over the next 5 years (with simple interest, the capital does not grow from year to year). Write one or more statements that will calculate the final amount if you invest an amount A in this scheme.

8. An investment opportunity guarantees to provide 7% compound interest over the next 5 years (with compound interest, the previous year's interest is added to the capital for the calculation of the current year's interest). Write a sequence of statements that will work out the final amount if you invest an amount A in this scheme.

9. Incorporating the two previous algorithms, write statements that will determine which of the two investment schemes will provide the largest return.

10. Distinguish between an expression and a program statement.

5.5   Practical exercises: Using Basic's control structures

In this set of exercises, you will gain experience in using some of Visual Basic's control structures. As in the previous chapter's exercises, we will start this one by creating a simple form as a user-interface, with one command button per exercise.

Creating the user-interface for these exercises

As in the previous sets of practical exercises, start a new Visual Basic project and this time enlarge Form1 so that it can accommodate a number of command buttons. Placing these on the right of the form will prevent them from obscuring any text we print to the form in the following exercises. The form should have six command buttons and be configured as shown in Figure 5.5.

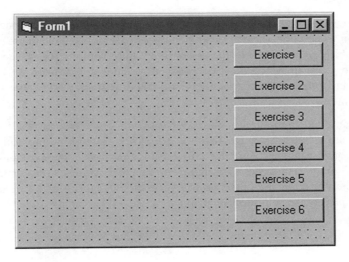

Figure 5.5   *The user-interface for these exercises.*

Exercise 1: Selection structures 1

Choosing whether to do something or not

We have already seen some uses of **If..Then** statements. In this exercise, we will decide whether or not to execute particular statements depending on a value entered to an **InputBox**.

Create a click event-handler for the button labelled Exercise 1, and enter the following code:

```
Private Sub Command1_Click()
Dim Inp As Integer
  Inp = InputBox("Enter a 1-digit number")
  If Inp Mod 2 = 0 Then
    MsgBox "You entered an even number"
  Else
    MsgBox "You entered an odd number"
  End If
End Sub
```

Note the **Mod** operator returns the *remainder* of a division. Therefore **Inp Mod 2** will return either **0** (if there is no remainder) or **1** – a suitable test for an even or odd number. We could have ignored the odd numbers in the above by simply missing out the alternative, **Else** clause (the **End If** is still required).

Suggested exercises

1. You can test the case of a character by comparing it with its upper case self. If they are the same, the character is in upper case; if not, lower case. A character variable can be passed to the **UCase** function to get an upper case version of it. Write a test in which the user is asked to enter a character, and this is then correctly identified as **Upper** case or **Lower** case by a message in a **MsgBox** statement.

2. Numeric and punctuation characters have no case. We can test for this, since for such a character **C**, **UCase(C) = LCase(C)**. Extend the previous exercise to categorize a single character entered as '**Caseless**', '**Upper Case**' or '**Lower Case**'. You will need to either nest one **If..Then..Else** structure inside another, or make use of the **ElseIf** syntax of Visual Basic's **If..Then** structure (see the on-line help files for this).

Exercise 2:   Selection structures 2

 Choosing from a number of possible options

`If..Then` and `If..Then..Else` are suitable structures for evaluating a single condition, which would turn out to be true or false. If, however, you had a condition that could have a number of outputs (such as an evaluation of the number of days in a month, given the month name), `If..Then..Else` is too limited.

```
Private Function DaysInMonth() As Integer
Dim NumDays As Integer
  Select Case Month(Date)
    Case 4, 6, 9, 11                ' i.e. Apr, Jun, Sep, Nov
      NumDays = 30
    Case 2                          ' i.e. Feb
      If Year(Date) Mod 4 = 0 Then
        NumDays = 29
      Else
        NumDays = 28
      End If
    Case Else
      NumDays = 31
  End Select
  DaysInMonth = NumDays
End Function
```

Enter this function into the form module of the project so far, and add the following statement to the click event for the Exercise 2 button as follows:

```
Private Sub Command2_Click()
  MsgBox DaysInMonth
End Sub
```

The **Select Case** construct has been used to choose from a number of possible options. Note that several options can be used as a single case (e.g. month number = 4, 6, 9 or 11). Also note the use of the **Month()** and **Year()** functions, and the **Date** function which returns the current date.

Suggested exercises

1. The control variable for the Select Case structure in the **DaysInMonth** function is **Month(Date)**, the result of passing the system date (from the **Date** function) as a parameter into the **Month** function. Change the code in the **DaysInMonth** function so that a month number can be passed to it, e.g. **DaysInMonth(3)**, to evaluate the number of days in March.

2. Make another change to the function so that the year number (currently calculated internally by the expression `Year(Date)`) is also passed as a parameter to `DaysInMonth`.

3. Regular geometric figures with different numbers of sides (up to 10) can be classified as shown in the following table:

Number of sides	Name
1, 2	Not a regular geometric figure
3	Triangle
4	Square
5	Pentagon
6	Hexagon
7 to 10	Polygon

Write a sub that uses a `Select Case` structure to identify a figure from the number of sides entered by the user. Once the user has entered a number of sides (into an `InputBox`), the figure should be identified by its name being displayed either by a `Print` statement or in a `MsgBox`.

Exercise 3: Repetition structures

 Doing something repeatedly.

In this exercise, we will try a number of the control structures that allow statements to be repeated in Visual Basic.

Add the following code to the Command3_Click event-handler:

```
Private Sub Command3_Click()
Dim Number As Integer, Name As String
  Number = InputBox("Enter an integer number")
  Name = InputBox("Enter Your Name")
  While Number > 0
    MsgBox Name & ":" & Str(Number)
    Number = Number - 1
  Wend
End Sub
```

Run the program and press the Exercise 3 button. After being asked for a number you will then be asked for your name. Whatever number you entered at the first **InputBox** will dictate how often your name will pop-up in a message box. A descending count will also be displayed. Note that the value you entered for **Number** will be wiped out by this process, since the loop iterations are counted by decrementing **Number** until it becomes 0.

It is possible to preserve the number in **Number** by using a second variable and a different type of loop. Edit the event-handler, adding a new variable declaration and replacing the loop code with that shown in **bold** in the following:

```
Private Sub Command3_Click()
Dim Number As Integer, Name As String, Count As Integer
  Number = InputBox("Enter a 1-digit number")
  Name = InputBox("Enter Your Name")
  For Count = 1 To Number
    MsgBox Name & ":" & Str(Count)
  Next
End Sub
```

Note that the number displayed along with your name increases in each message box. The **For..Next** loop automatically keeps track of how many times it has looped so far by incrementing the variable named immediately after **For**.

Suggested exercises

1. By placing an **InputBox** statement inside a loop, you can get input data repeatedly from the user. Write a sub that will ask the user to enter a number 10 times (use a **For..Next** loop). The number should be assigned to a variable **Number** of type **Single**.

2. Add a second numeric variable, **Total**, to the sub in the previous exercise. Add statements so that every number entered by the user is added to **Total**, and the final value of **Total** is displayed in a **MsgBox** after the loop has terminated.

3. Change the **For..Next** loop in the previous exercise to a **Do..Until** loop. Make the exit condition in the **Until** part stop the iteration when the user has entered 0.

We will see further uses for loop constructs in the next set of exercises.

Exercise 4:   Arrays of numbers

In these exercises, we will make use of Visual Basic arrays and collections to handle multiple items of data.

Create a simple numeric array.

Create an event-handler for the button labelled Exercise 4, and add the following code to it:

```
Private Sub Command4_Click()
Dim NumberArray(5) As Single, Index As Integer, Sum As Single
  ' Read in an array of numbers..
  For Index = 1 To 5
    NumberArray(Index) = InputBox("Enter a number")
  Next
  ' Calculate its average..
  For Index = 1 To 5
    Sum = Sum + NumberArray(Index)
  Next
  MsgBox "Average is : " & Sum/5
End Sub
```

In this example, a list of numbers is read from **InputBox()** function calls into an array. The contents of the array are then summed and divided by 5 (the number of numbers) to produce an average value. This is then displayed using a Message Box. Run the program and press the Exercise 4 button to try this.

Exercise 5: Arrays and collections

 Create a simple string array.

Visual Basic can work with arrays of any data type. Simply suffix the name of a variable with a number in brackets to create an array. If we wanted to work with an array of strings storing the words of a sentence, for example, we could use similar code to that in the previous exercise:

```
Private Sub Command5_Click()
Dim WordArray(5) As String, Index As Integer, Sentence As String
  ' Read in an array of words..
  For Index = 1 To 5
    WordArray(Index) = InputBox("Enter a word")
  Next
  ' String them together..
  For Index = 1 To 5
    Sentence = Sentence & " " & WordArray(Index)
```

```
   Next
   MsgBox "Sentence is : " & Sentence & "."
End Sub
```

(Note we have added an additional space character between each word.) The problem with arrays is that they are fixed in size. Visual Basic allows an array to be resized, but this is not automatic, and you need to keep track of the current size and increase it as required (look up **ReDim** in Visual Basic help for more information). With this limitation, the following code would cause problems because the **Do..Loop** leaves it up to the user how many words are to be entered:

```
Private Sub Command5_Click()
Dim WordArray(5) As String, Index As Integer, Sum As String
   ' Read in an array of strings..
   Index = 0
   Do
      Index = Index+1
      WordArray(Index) = InputBox("Enter a word")
   Loop Until WordArray(index)=""
   ' ' '
End Sub
```

Suggested exercise

1. It is possible to get around the problem of running out of array space in the above example by adding an extra exit condition to the **Loop Until** part of the loop definition. If the variable index has reached the value 5, we know we must stop the loop from iterating. Change the loop in the exercise to a **Do..Loop** as shown above, and alter the exit condition to limit the entries to no more than five.

 Create a collection.

Provided five or fewer words are entered, the previous program works perfectly well. If no word is entered at any iteration, the loop terminates. However, if the user goes on to add a sixth word, the program will crash, because the array has run out of capacity. A **Collection** can be used as an alternative to prevent this.

```
Private Sub Command5_Click()
Dim WordList As New Collection, S As Variant, Sentence As String
   ' Read in a collection of strings..
   Do
      WordList.Add InputBox("Enter a word")
   Loop Until WordList(WordList.Count) = ""
   ' String them together..
```

```
For Each S In WordList
  Sentence = Sentence & " " & S
Next
MsgBox "Sentence is : " & Sentence & "."
End Sub
```

In the above version of the event-handler, a `Collection` has been substituted for the array originally used. Now, we no longer need to keep track of the position that an entry will be placed in, because adding an item to a collection is performed with a simple `Add` method call. This places the new item into the next free position in the collection in the same way that we would add a number to a list – at the end. Because a collection is effectively open-ended, we do not need to worry about its capacity. There is an upper limit to the number of items a collection can accommodate, but this is set by the amount of memory the collection takes up and is usually very large.

Because we have used a collection, we can use the `For Each` structure to retrieve all of the items in it. Note that to start a collection, we need to use the `New` keyword, since a collection is an object.

Here, we have declared it with the syntax `..As New Collection`. We could instead have added a statement `Set WordList = New Collection` at any point before it was used in the sub. While an array is a simple container whose size is preset, a collection is a more intelligent container that provides certain methods – `Add` and `Remove` among them.

In this short sub, our collection is declared *locally*, within the sub itself. Since local variables are destroyed when they go out of scope, we can expect the collection object to be cleared at the end of the sub. Normally we would declare a collection at a higher level of scope: as a form- or module-level variable, for example. When using a collection, it is good practice to remove all of its elements and destroy it when it is no longer in use. If you fail to do this, the collection may simply stay in memory until the program ends, but it is always better to tidy up after performing a task. We can do this by adding the line:

```
   ' ' '
   Set NameList = Nothing
End Sub
```

By destroying the collection by setting its reference to `Nothing`, we also destroy each of the objects in it, provided there are no other references to them. Note that this will have no visible effect on the example program we are using, but may well have an effect in real software that must be used in a normal operational situation. Each collection item takes up memory, and this is a finite resource.

Suggested exercises

1. Move the declaration of the variable `WordList` in the previous exercise to the top of the form module (you can declare it as a `Private` variable in the **General Declarations** section). Now rerun the program and test what happens when you press the Exercise 5 command button several times.

2.   Add a new button to the form, name it `cmdClear` and give it the caption `Clear Collection`. Use this button to clear out the collection by adding the statement `Set WordList = New Collection` to its event-handler. Test that you can build up a collection using the Exercise 5 button, and purge it with the new button.

 Exercise 6:   Handling errors

Handling an error condition.

The following event-handler should be attached to the `Command6` button. The sub asks the user to enter two numbers and then tries to divide the first by the second. An error handler is used to trap a division-by-zero error condition.

```
Private Sub Command6_Click()
Dim n1 As Single, n2 As Single, n3 As Single
On Error GoTo err_Command6_Click
    n1 = InputBox("Enter a number")
    n2 = InputBox("Enter divisor")
    n3 = n1 / n2
    MsgBox n3
    Exit Sub
err_Command6_Click:
    If Err.Number = 11 Then
        MsgBox "Division by zero error - please re-enter divisor"
        n2 = InputBox("Enter divisor")
        Resume
    Else
        MsgBox "Error " & Err.Number & " : " & Err.Description
    End If
End Sub
```

The main point to note in this event-handler is the additional error handling, shown in **bold** text. Error handling is initiated by the insertion of an `On Error` statement at the start of the sub. Note that this comes before any executable statements, since we wish it to protect the whole sub. In this case, we use the `On Error GoTo` version, which says that in the event of any error, control should be transferred to the statements following the named *label*. Any unique identifier can be used as a label, but many programmers follow the practice of prefixing the name of the sub with the string `err_`.

Any run-time error in Visual Basic causes the creation of an error object. This is pre-declared with the name `Err` and is in scope throughout any Visual Basic program. `Err` provides us with information on the error that we can use to manage it.

We can do any processing we like in the error-handling section. To prevent the error-handling statements being executed every time, the sub executes the `Exit Sub` statement immediately before the label causes an immediate exit from the sub or function. Note that if no error occurs, this would be the last statement to execute within the sub.

In this case, a specific type of error is expected – a division by zero. You can look up the list of possible errors in the VB help system (search for ***Trappable Errors***). Division by zero results in an error number 11, and so we can test for this specific error and provide a workaround. In this example, the user is informed of the problem and asked to re-enter the divisor. A `Resume` statement then causes execution to continue with the statement that raised the error – the division.

It could well be that an error was due to a different, unexpected cause. In this case, we use the `Else` part of the error test to display Visual Basic's own error message and error number, using the `Description` and `Number` properties of the `Err` object.

Try running the code and pressing the Exercise 6 button. When asked for the two numbers, try entering 2 and 1. The answer of 2/1 should be displayed. Now try again with the values 2 and 0. In this case the error handler should come into play, allowing you to re-enter the divisor. Finally, try again, but this time enter an invalid value for either number (for example, a letter of the alphabet). This time, the error handler will display the details of the error, but will not provide any recovery option.

 Generating errors for test purposes.

One problem that you will find in error management in your programs is that you must test error-handling code by causing errors. Visual Basic allows error conditions to be simulated by providing a statement to *raise* an error on demand. This allows a programmer to create error conditions that would otherwise be unlikely to occur during the normal process of testing a program (but that would almost certainly happen in real life due to Murphy's law).

Since we need to be able to raise an error so we can test error handling, the following example event-handler contains an `On Error GoTo` statement, and a suitable label and `Exit Sub` statement as previously. We are doing nothing but demonstrating the facility to raise an error, so there is little extra code. Normally, an `Err.Raise` statement would be used at the start of a segment of code that *could* cause an error of the same type, but no such code has been added here.

The error raised in this example is error number 67, which indicates that there are too many files on a device. This would normally happen if you tried to add a new file to the root directory of a disk drive when it already contained the maximum number, and would cause a program to crash. This is not an error we would wish to cause for real on a system, since we would then have to tidy up the root directory afterwards. By raising the error in code, we can get the same effect on our program for testing purposes, but without the resultant mess in the computer's filing system.

In the error handler, we simply display Visual Basic's error description and then **Resume Next**, to go to the statement that follows the one where the error occurred. A simple **Resume** cannot be used here, since we would just keep raising the error. Try this out by adding an extra button to the form (**Command7**), and code its **_Click** event-handler as follows:

```
Private Sub Command7_Click()
On Error GoTo err_Command5_Click
  Err.Raise 67
  ' This is the "Too Many Files" error
  MsgBox "We got to this statement via Resume Next"
  Exit Sub
err_Command5_Click:
  If Err = 67 Then
    MsgBox Err.Description
    ' We could have code to delete some files here.
    Resume Next
  End If
End Sub
```

Using this technique, we will now know how our program will react when a 'Too Many Files' error occurs, and can try various strategies to recover from it.

Suggested exercises

1. Look back at some of the previous exercises and try to identify places where errors could occur. Rerun the exercises and attempt to cause the code to fail. One good strategy for this is to deliberately enter data that is of the wrong type – for example, enter a string when a number is expected, or enter an invalid date (31/22/2000). If you are successful, the error message generated by Visual Basic will give you the number of the error you caused. Add error handling code to prevent this from happening in future.

2. Look up 'Trappable Errors' in the on-line help to find out what types of errors could occur in your programs. Try to think how such errors could come about, and add error-handling statements to new programs to prevent them, where you think that specific types of error are likely. If in doubt, remember that user input is the most common source of run-time errors.

5.5   **Answers to questions**

Since, at noon, it is not before 12:00:00, `IsMorning` will be set to **False**, and the 'Good Afternoon' message will be displayed.

The sub can be extended to print 'Good Morning' before midday, 'Good Afternoon' before 5 o'clock in the evening and 'Good Evening' after this time as follows:

```
Sub Greetings()
Dim IsMorning As Boolean, IsEvening As Boolean
   IsMorning = (Time < "12:00:00")
   IsEvening = (Time > "17:00:00")
   If IsMorning Then
     Print "Good Morning"
   ElseIf IsEvening Then
     Print "Good Evening"
   Else
     Print "Good Afternoon"
   End If
End Sub
```

(a)   A `Do..Loop Until...` structure would be suitable, for example:

```
Do
   Number = InputBox("Enter a number")
   If Number <> 0 Then
     ' Process it
   End If
Loop Until Number = 0
```

(b)
```
Do
   DateEntry = InputBox("Enter a date")
Loop Until IsDate(DateEntry)
```

(c)
```
For number = 1 To 999 Step 2
   Print number
Next
```

(d)
```
While varValue >= 100
   varValue = varValue / 2
Wend
```

QUESTION 5.3

A `For..Next` loop is useful when a known number of items is to be processed, for example every item in an array. However, in many situations, an array may have empty elements. If the array elements are filled sequentially from the start, then a `Do..Loop` structure could be used to process only the elements that contain data, e.g. for an array of strings:

```
index = 1
Do While ArrayData(index) <> ""
  ' Process item ArrayData(index)
   index = index+1
Loop
```

QUESTION 5.4

Although a collection is the more usual structure to use with objects, if the number of objects required is known at the outset it can be more efficient to use an array. There will be no need to instantiate the data structure (as would be necessary with a collection, using the `New` keyword) and the simpler structure can simplify accessing and processing the elements in it.

Each element in the array will be a reference to `Nothing`, the null object. The declaration can be changed by adding the `New` keyword, which will ensure that an attempt to access an element of the array will be successful. However, with a declaration of this type (with the `New` keyword being used at the point of declaration), Visual Basic will defer the creation of the object until a reference is made to it, so the array elements will all still be `Nothing` until some attempt is made to access them.

QUESTION 5.5

An error handler can be used to catch unanticipated errors, but writing extra code to trap errors in input or calculation can only ever be used to save a program from crashing due to anticipated errors.

5.7 Answers to review questions

1.   (a) *Extra program statements that control whether other statements will be executed or not are known as* Selection *structures.*

     (b) *Program statements that control the repeated execution of others are known as* iteration *structures.*

     (c) *A type of expression known as a* Condition *governs the* `If..Then` *structure.*

(d) *A* `Do..Loop` *can be controlled by either a* While *condition or an* Until *condition.*

(e) *A* With *structure can be used to save having to type object references repeatedly over a number of statements.*

(f) *The phrase* On Error *is used to introduce an error handler.*

2. *Multi-way selection structures can be made using either the* `Select Case` *structure, or an* `If..Then..ElseIf..Else` *group. Can you suggest situations in which either would be preferable?* The `Select Case` structure is normally used where the different execution paths are to be selected by the value in a single variable – the month of the year example is a good example of this. Visual Basic's `Select Case` can be used more flexibly so that a different condition can be used for each case, though `If..Then..ElseIf` is a better structure for this. The major difference between them is that in `Select Case`, any number of cases can be simultaneously valid, and all the valid paths will be executed. In an `If..Then ElseIf` structure, all of the possible paths are mutually exclusive, so only one option will ever be chosen.

3. *It is possible to combine a number of conditions using the keywords* `And` *or* `Or`. *It is also possible to negate a condition using the keyword* `Not`, *e.g.*

```
If Not (x=2) Then...
```

Write an `If..Then` *structure that will set the* `Boolean` *variable* `DataValid` *to* `True` *if the variable* `Age` *is between 18 and 60 (inclusive), the variable* `CanDrive` *is* `True`, `HasConvictions` *has the value* `False`, *and* `FreeToTravel` *contains either* `"Monday"` *or* `"Thursday"`.

```
If (Age >= 18) And (Age <= 60) And CanDrive _
          And Not(HasConvictions) _
          And ((FreeToTravel = "Monday") _
          Or (FreeToTravel = "Thursday")) Then
   DataValid = True
End If
```

Note that the Boolean variable can be used without a comparison, since **`CanDrive`** is exactly equivalent to **`(CanDrive = True)`**. Note also the careful use of brackets to ensure that conditions are grouped in the right way.

4. *A programmer has written a sub in which a required date is to be entered, but has used an integer variable for it by mistake. Is this a syntax, logic or run-time error?* It is certainly a run-time error since it is caused by the wrong type of user input for the variable. However, since the correct user input will cause the failure, we might consider it to be a syntax error, since the correct input is being assigned to the wrong variable type, a fault in the programmer's interpretation of the language features. Alternatively, we could say it was a logic error since the programmer did not implement the logic of the program in the right way.

5. *Write a series of statements that will assign the first five even values (starting from 2) to the variable X in turn.* There are several possible solutions to this, but the most straightforward is to use a `For..Next` loop, specifying a step of 2:

```
For index = 2 To 10 Step 2
   X = index
Next
```

As an alternative, a simple `For` loop using the default step increment of 1 would save having to work out what the final value has to be. Multiplying by 2 makes sure the values are even. The first N even values can be coded as:

```
For index = 1 To N
   X = 2 * index
Next
```

6. *Write a series of statements that will repeatedly halve the value of X until it becomes less than 10 in value.* Obviously the solution to this will use a loop. Since the terminating point will come when a specific condition is met (X < 10), a `Do..Loop` is the most appropriate:

```
Do
   X = X / 2
Loop Until X < 10
```

7. *An investment opportunity guarantees to provide 10% simple interest over the next 5 years (with simple interest, the capital does not grow from year to year). Write one or more statements that will calculate the final amount if you invest an amount A in this scheme.* Since the interest formula used is simple, the first year's interest will be exactly the same as the last year's. Therefore, we can do this calculation by simply calculating a year's worth of interest and multiplying by 5:

```
YearInterest = A * 10 / 100      ' 10% = 10/100
FinalAmount = A + 5 * YearInterest ' Remember to add the principal
```

8. *An investment opportunity guarantees to provide 7% compound interest over the next 5 years (with compound interest, the previous year's interest is added to the capital for the calculation of the current year's interest). Write a sequence of statements that will work out the final amount if you invest an amount A in this scheme.* In this case, the compounded interest means that each year's interest will have to be calculated separately. We must therefore use a loop (there is an alternative method that uses logarithms, but ignoring that):

```
For Year = 1 To 5
   Interest = A * 7 / 100    ' Calculate 1 year's interest
   A = A + Interest          ' Compound it.
Next
```

9. *Incorporating the two previous algorithms, write statements that will determine which of the two investment schemes will provide the largest return.* In this case, we need to maintain a distinction between the result of the first algorithm and the result of the second, so that we have two results to compare. Since the first algorithm does not change the final value of A, this causes no problem, but this is something you need to be careful of:

```
YearInterest = A * 10 / 100
FinalAmount = A + 5 * YearInterest
For Year = 1 To 5
   Interest = A * 7 / 100      ' Calculate 1 years interest
   A = A + Interest            ' Compound it.
Next
If A > FinalAmount Then
   MsgBox "Compound interest at 7% is better"
Else
   MsgBox "Simple interest at 10% is better"
End If
```

10. *Distinguish between an expression and a program statement.* An expression is any combination of literal values, operators and function calls that results in a single value. Alone, an expression does nothing to alter the state of a program. A program statement is an assignment to a variable from an expression, or a sub call. In either case, a program statement can result in a change to the state of a program (i.e. one or more variables may take on new values).

CHAPTER 6

Object modelling the Visual Basic way

In previous chapters we have examined Visual Basic classes, the components that are used to provide objects with their capabilities, and ways that objects can be used to perform operations in programs. In this chapter, we will look at the practicalities of creating a realistic application using object oriented programming in Visual Basic.

By the end of this chapter, you should be able to:

- create classes that collaborate on a given task,

- devise *object models*, which are assemblies of objects that comprise a system or sub-system,

- build programs by assembling objects within simple code structures.

6.1 Object oriented programming in Visual Basic

Let's recap. The main design features of object oriented programming are:

- Classes, which are particular types of object with specific properties and behaviour

- Encapsulation, which is a principle used when defining a class of object to separate the internal representation of the object from the properties and methods that are used to operate it

- Properties, which are constructs that reflect the internal state of an object

- Methods, which are subs and functions defined for a particular class of object

- Messages, which are interactions between objects invoking methods or accessing properties.

So far, we have examined and written examples of Visual Basic code to demonstrate specific features of the language and object oriented programming. We have seen how the Visual Basic language provides us with the facilities to work with the predefined data types – integers, floating-point numbers, Boolean variables, strings, dates and currency values.

When it came to working with items of data that were more suited to real-world problems, we saw how objects, arrays, collections and user-defined types could all play a part in modelling some of the features of a real-world system. The time has come to examine how we can use object orientation (and, by extension, all of the features that make object orientation possible) to create coherent models of complex systems.

Modelling objects in Visual Basic

As object oriented programmers, we should try to avoid the use of highly abstract attributes (e.g. taste) since these would inevitably mean different things to different people. Visual Basic constrains us to creating properties that are either simple types that can be assigned to simple variables, or object types that can be assigned to existing classes.

Creating object-type properties is a way of hiding the complexity of using objects of a particular class by making an object of another class responsible for them. We could refer to this as an *object structure*. By defining object structures as components of programs, we are able to provide a complex assembly of components that can be treated as 'black boxes'; i.e. components that can be used without the user being aware how they work. If we strive to make assemblies of objects as logical and easy to work with as the individual objects that make them up, we can, in theory, build object models of arbitrary complexity.

Here's a simple example: suppose you wish to model a deck of cards for a game program you are writing. Using simple variables, you could keep an array of integers – 1 to 52 – and treat these as a pack of cards, dealing the cards by incrementing a counter variable to indicate the next card to be dealt. Users of this deck of cards will not appreciate having to remember that 1 is the ace of spades and 15 is the two of hearts. We therefore have the problem of associating a member of the array with a given card (ace of hearts, for example), and we will have to write routines to shuffle, deal and display cards (possibly even with pictures). Instead of trying to keep all of these balls in the air simultaneously, we could simply create two new types of object – one to represent an individual playing card and another to represent a whole deck of them.

Now, we could develop all of the features that we need to deal with single cards, decks of cards and hands of cards by defining a class structure. A card object can be

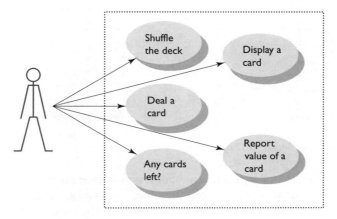

Figure 6.1 *The operations required in any card game.*

defined using a class, and other classes, deck and hand, can be used to manage multiple card objects as required by a card game, for example. Overall, we can consider this structure of object relationships to be our ***object model***.

Ignoring specific card games that we might wish to play with our object oriented, virtual deck of cards, we can depict the main operations needed to work with a deck of cards as in Figure 6.1.

The use-case diagram in Figure 6.1 shows us all of the operations that our virtual deck of cards will be required to provide. From this, we can determine the classes required by listing the objects that take part in it (**Card**, **Deck**) and enumerate some of the functionality required of each class: see Figure 6.2.

The **Card** class has a single **Property**, **Number**, and four **Methods**: **Suit** and **Rank** to determine what card is being represented (e.g. **Suit** = 'Spades' and **Rank** = 'Ace'), **Description** so that we can represent the card textually (e.g. 'Ace of Spades') and **Value** to determine the actual value of a card (e.g. Value = 11 for a Jack). The **Number** property will be an integer in the range 1 to 52, and we can use this to derive the other card information provided by the methods.

The **Deck** class has a property, **CardsLeft**, to indicate the number of cards not yet dealt, and its main property, **Cards**, which will represent all of the **Card** objects

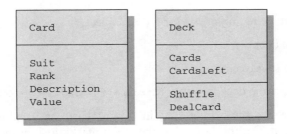

Figure 6.2 *Class diagrams for card games.*

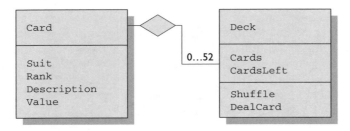

Figure 6.3 *The relationship between a card and a deck.*

remaining in the deck. It also has two methods, one to **Shuffle** the pack and another, **DealCard**, to deal a card. We can depict how these two classes relate to each other by illustrating how one class (the **Deck**) is an aggregate of the other, as in Figure 6.3.

These diagrams show us how a **Card** relates to a **Deck** of cards. Note that a deck of cards can contain anything between 0 and 52 cards, since dealt cards are removed from the deck (of course, when we are down to no cards, there is not really much of a deck left – a kind of object oriented Cheshire Cat). The diagrams also show us the interface methods required of each class. The next stage is to devise a method for representing each of the objects as pieces of data.

We could have represented a single playing card by providing it with two separate variables – one to indicate the suit it belongs to (a number in the range 1 to 4 would do), and a second to indicate which card in the suit (a number in the range 1 to 13 would do). Alternatively, the scheme chosen represents a card as a single integer in the range 1 to 52. While the first method has the advantage of being a simple and direct representation, the second, chosen method may have advantages when it comes to dealing with a whole deck of cards.

Here are the interface requirements for a single card object:

- Set the card by **Number** (1 to 52).

- Get the card's **Suit** (Clubs, Diamonds, Spades and Hearts) and **Rank** (Ace, 2 to 10, Jack, Queen and King).

- Get the card's **Description** based on number (1 to 52) (e.g. Ace of Hearts).

- Get the card's **Value** based on number (1 to 52) (e.g. 1 to 13 based on Ace = 1, King = 13).

Here are the interface requirements for a deck object:

- **Shuffle** the deck.

- Deal a card (**DealCard**).

- Indicate when the deck is empty (**CardsLeft** = 0).

At this stage, we are most interested in how a card or deck will appear to a programmer using it. Encapsulation has the job of masking all of the implementation detail, and allowing users to work with as natural an *interface* as possible. Once we have created the chosen implementation, we should be able to decide to reimplement it using the alternative suggested scheme, or indeed any other way we can imagine. It should make no difference to the interface.

To complete our choice of implementation, it would be best to add some more detail to the simple idea of representing a card by a single number. One important question we need to answer is 'what number will represent what card?'.

For example, we could use:

- 1 to 13: Ace to King of Clubs

- 14 to 26: Ace to King of Diamonds

- 27 to 39: Ace to King of Spades

- 40 to 52: Ace to King of Hearts

This gives us a way of converting a numeric representation of a card into a textual representation. We will control the internal representation (the single integer) from the user of the class by making it **Private** and making use of a **Let** property to allow program code to set it to a specific card.

Modelling a deck is actually easier, since our model can follow reality quite closely: a deck is a set of 52 cards, each different. We can use aggregation by providing a deck object with 52 references to card objects, either as a collection or as an array.

6.2   Creating a class

Recall that when we write the program code to represent a card, we are in fact writing the code to represent *any* member of the card class. Each object of a class has its own copy of all of the internal member variables, or instance variables. Each also can be manipulated by all of the class methods (subs and functions) and properties. We therefore start by adding a new class module to a Visual Basic project.

The first thing to do with any new class module is to set its **Name** property. Here, we shall start using a *convention* used by many Visual Basic programmers: a class name should be prefixed with a capital C, giving our card class a name **CCard**. This makes it easy to identify a variable declaration as being a class reference variable. We can now define the class fully in its code window:

```
' Class CCard - Description of a Playing Card

Private mvarNumber As Integer          ' Represented by an integer

Public Property Let Number(n As Integer)  ' Provides for giving the
                                          ' card an identity

  If n > 0 And n < 53 Then
    mvarNumber = n                        ' Set up the card.
  End If
End Property
```

```
Public Function Suit() As String
' Work out suit of card, based on 1..13 for Clubs,
' 14..26 for Diamonds etc...
  Select Case mvarNumber
    Case 1 To 13
      Suit = "Clubs"
    Case 14 To 26
      Suit = "Diamonds"
    Case 27 To 39
      Suit = "Spades"
    Case 40 To 52
      Suit = "Hearts"
  End Select
End Function

Public Function Rank() As String
' Work out rank (Ace to King) of card...
Dim r As Integer
' Convert card Number into a number in the range 1-13...
  r = (mvarNumber-1) Mod 13 + 1   ' Remainder after division by 13
                                  ' is a number 0..12.

  Select Case r
    Case 1
      Rank = "Ace"
    Case 2 To 10
      Rank = Str(r)                  ' Convert the ID number to a string
    Case 11
      Rank = "Jack"
    Case 12
      Rank = "Queen"
    Case 13
      Rank = "King"
  End Select
End Function

Public Function Description() As String
' Return the full description of the card..
  Description = Rank & " of " & Suit    'e.g. "King of Diamonds"
End Function

Public Function Value() As Integer
' Return its face value as a number..
  Value = (mvarNumber-1) Mod 13 + 1
  If Value > 10 Then
    Value = 10
  End If
End Function
```

The main points of note in this class definition are:

- The numeric variable that represents the card, **mvarNumber**, has been declared as **Private**. A user of the class cannot access this variable directly. Because of this, we can ensure that a **CCard** object is always a valid representation, since the **Property Let** definition of the **Number** property allows us to vet the value being assigned as being a number in the range 1 to 52.

- The function method **Suit** returns a string representation of the card's suit.

- The function method **Rank** also returns a string. The use of these two methods together will give us an easy way to represent a card descriptively. Note how the card **Rank** has been calculated:

    mvarNumber-1 $\rightarrow$ a number in the range 0 to 51

    (mvarNumber-1) mod 13 $\rightarrow$ a number in the range 0 to 12

    (mvarID) mod 13 + 1 $\rightarrow$ a number in the range 1 to 13

- The **Description** method simply joins up the **Suit** and **Rank** properties (with the word 'of') to form a card description.

- The function method **Value** returns a number that equates to one representation of the face value of a card. There could be alternative representations of this (for example, in a game where Ace was a high-value card). In this case, we have used the same calculation as for **Rank**, but then limited the value to no more than 10. The function returns a number.

At this stage, we would *save the class file* to make sure that when we test it, any error will not result in the loss of the work we have done.

Note that in the code we are able to call on a class method from the code of any other method of the class. For example, in the **Description** method, we make use of the **Rank** and **Suit** methods – these will automatically refer to the instance variables of the current object, and making use of them will save us from duplicating work within the class.

The *interface* of this class is the combination of property and methods – **Number**, **Rank**, **Suit**, **Description** and **Value**. These are the attributes and operations a user of the class will work with. With the class as defined above, we now have the ability to create a new card variable that has both an internal representation (a number from 1 to 52) and, more importantly, services or methods that allow us to find out more about it.

The decision to make **Number** a property while **Suit**, **Rank**, **Description** and **Value** have been made functions may appear arbitrary, especially since a function and a **Property Get** are treated equivalently by Visual Basic. Conventionally, a property is used to expose and provide access to a specific internal value in an object, while a function is used to derive a value from internal data. However, with the exception of **Number**, which has been implemented as a **Property Let**, all of the others could have been either **Property Get**s or functions.

The distinction made here has been that since **Number** represents an internal variable that we want to be able to change, a **Property Let** is necessary. However, the functions derive their results from the internal data but do not allow it to be changed. This is not written in stone, and it is preferable to consider how a class of object might be used when deciding whether a particular interface method should be a function, sub or property. Remember that we might decide to change how a card object is represented internally, and yet we would almost certainly want the interface to remain unchanged.

QUESTION 6.1

A **Property Get** is a method that returns a single value from inside an object. A **Property Let** is a method that takes a single parameter and assigns it to some internal data in an object. Assume we are designing a new class, **Rectangle**, which is to be given the following interface methods:

(a) Length, which indicates and allows us to set the length of the rectangle
(b) Width, which indicates and allows us to set the width
(c) Colour, which indicates and allows us to set the colour
(d) Size, which allows us to set the length and width in one step
(e) Area, which calculates for us the area of the rectangle
(f) Perimeter, which calculates the distance around the rectangle
(g) Display, which draws our rectangle object in the correct colour and size on a screen.

For each, state whether it should be a sub, function or pair of **Property Get** and **Let** routines.

Declaring objects

We can now declare variables that we can use to represent cards:

```
Dim C1 As New CCard, C2 As New CCard   ' Declare two card objects
C1.Number = 1                          ' This is the Ace of Clubs
C2.Number = Int(Rnd() * 52) + 1        ' This is a random card.
```

Both card objects declared above have been given **Number** values. The first has a **Number** of 1, which indicates that its **Suit** is Clubs and its **Rank** is an Ace (go back and examine the **Suit** and **Rank** methods to see why). Usually, if we were programming card games, we would probably want to assign random values to the cards. The Visual Basic **Rnd()** function lets us do this. The function returns a pseudo-random floating-point number in the range 0.0 to just less than 1.0. Since we need a random integer in the range 1 to 52 to select any card from a notional deck, we need to scale the value returned from **Rnd()**. By multiplying by 52, we can get a number in the range 0.0 to just less than 52.0 which, if we convert to an integer using the **Int()**

function, becomes an integer in the range 0 to 51. By adding 1, the possible range becomes 1 to 52, which is ideal for our purpose.

We can go on to use this randomly allocated card in a program, or create one to test in the *Immediate window*:

```
Set C = New CCard
C.Number = Int(Rnd() * 52) + 1
? C.Number
37
? C.Suit
Spades
? C.Rank
Jack
? C.Description
Jack of Spades
? C.Value
  11
```

Note the use of the **Set** keyword when we want to make a class variable refer to an object. Recall that a class variable, declared with a statement like

```
Dim C As CCard
```

acts as a *reference* to an object. However, we can only get an object by asking for one to be created. This is one of the main differences between simple variables and objects. A simple variable is just some storage space that we can put data in. If we do not put any specific data in it, it will take on the value 0, or the variable type's equivalent to zero ("" for a string, for example). An object *must be created explicitly*. The **New** keyword is used to create an object, as shown in the statement:

```
Set C As New CCard
```

This actually says: create a **New** object of the **CCard** class, and then **Set** the **C** variable to refer to it. If we were to enter this statement in the Immediate window, **C** will automatically become an object variable that we can assign a **CCard** to.

In a sub or function, we will normally assign a new object to an object variable of the correct type. We will therefore have to create variables of the correct type using **Dim**, **Public** or **Private** declaration statements. Inside a sub, function or property method, this would be:

```
Dim C As New CCard
```

while if we wanted to declare a suitable object variable for use in a form module, or a code module, or as an instance variable within a class, we would use either

```
Private C As New CCard
```

or

```
Public C As New CCard
```

6.3 References

The way that the *declaration* of an object variable is separated from the creation of an object allows us to be more flexible about how we use objects. For example, it is possible to refer to a single object with two or more object variables (Figure 6.4). Each indicates and deals with the same object, rather like a person with two phone lines – either number will put you in contact with them.

In Figure 6.4, if the object shown had a property called `Value`, the following sequence of statements would all affect the single object:

```
Reference1.Value = 4                      ' Object.Value = 4
Reference2.Value = Reference2.Value + 2   ' Object.Value = 6
Reference1.Value = 0                      ' Object.Value = 0
```

As it turns out, this can work to our advantage or our disadvantage, depending on how we use references, as you will see when we go on to create an object to represent a deck of cards. For example, examine the `Shuffle` routine of the `CDeck` class (later) with some care. In this, we reorganize an array of objects by switching the references around. Object references also allow us to create subs and functions that can manipulate an object, even though it was initially assigned to an object variable declared in a different routine or module.

Alternatives for creating a new object

To assign an object to a reference variable, we use the `Set` keyword. To create a new object, we can use either

```
Dim X As New SomeObjectClass
```

or

```
Dim X As SomeObjectClass
Set X = New SomeObjectClass
```

In the first of these, we are using a shorthand method of creating an object and a reference variable and making the assignment in a single, declarative statement.

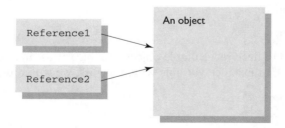

Figure 6.4 *An object with two reference variables.*

Visual Basic creates objects declared in this way on the first occasion when the object is accessed using a property or method call. In many situations, the programmer cannot predict when an object will be created for this reason. This mechanism is provided to make it easy to create and work with new objects in a program.

The second method uses a separate `Dim` statement to declare the reference variable, and a `Set` statement to perform the assignment. Doing it in this way, it is possible to decide exactly when the object instance is created. We may, for example, wish a new object to record the time at which it was first created, and we would have to use this method to make it possible to do this. This method is also used where we wish to create a number of new objects using the same reference variable, often to add them immediately to a collection. For example, the following sub will create a number of `CCard` objects as specified by its integer parameter, and add all of them to the collection `c`, declared as a module-level collection:

```
Public Sub CreateSomeObjects(n As Integer)
Dim O As CCard
Dim count As Integer
  For count = 1 To n
    Set O = New CCard
    C.Add O
  Next
End Sub
```

The sub `CreateSomeObjects` will create `n` objects, adding each to the collection `c`. No matter what value `n` has, we need only use a single object reference variable (`o`) to create the object.

QUESTION 6.2

Assume we have defined a class, `CHand`, with a method `Add` that accepts a `CCard` as a parameter (using the same syntax as a collection's `Add` method, as shown above). Write a subroutine, `DealTwoHands`, that takes two parameters, `Hand1` and `Hand2`, and adds five `CCards` to each of them.

Using `Property Set`

Since an object reference is a very specific type of variable assignment (i.e. it contains a reference to an object rather than a simple number or string), it cannot be applied using a simple assignment. Instead of the assignment:

```
X = SomeObject
```

when creating a reference to an existing object, it is necessary to use `Set`:

```
Set X = SomeObject
```

This is required because a simple assignment will actually copy a value from one variable to another. In a statement involving two simple variables:

```
A = B
```

we take the value stored in variable **B** and copy it into the storage space of variable **A**, resulting in two variables that hold the same value. We would not want object assignments to behave in this way, since logically that would also have the effect of *creating* a new object, for which we need to use the keyword **New**. The assignment syntax for an object reference reminds us that an object is not a simple variable.

This becomes a special case when we hold an object reference *inside* an object as a member variable. We may wish to assign a new object to it, but cannot use a simple **Property Let**, since this can deal only with simple data types. Visual Basic provides a **Property Set** type of property definition to deal with assigning references to internal object reference variables.

For example, if we had a new class of object, a **CHand**, that was to contain an array of cards, then we would need to have some way of passing a card into the **CHand** object. We could do this with a **Property Set**:

```
Public Property Set Card(C As CCard)
   Set mvarCard = C
End Property
```

The three types of **Property** methods (**Get**, **Let** and **Set**) allow for the three types of reference we might make to member variables inside an object:

- **Property Get**, e.g. **value = Object.Property**

- **Property Let**, e.g. **Object.Property = value**

- **Property Set**, e.g. **Set Object.Property = ExistingObject**

It is important to be aware of the distinction between these three types of object properties, and how they relate to the perceived attributes of an object.

QUESTION 6.3

A **CHand** class is to be given a property called **TopCard**, that can both **Get** and **Set** a single card reference variable **mvarTopCard**. Write both parts of this property.

6.4 The life of an object

Objects are created and destroyed as an application runs. For some objects, we would wish to create them and continue referring to them until the program run is finished. For others, we create them, make use of them to perform some service, and then

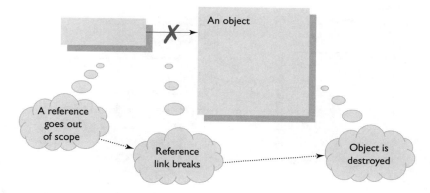

Figure 6.5 *Object references and lifetime.*

destroy them to save on machine resources. The factor that determines how long an object persists between its creation and its destruction is whether a reference to it exists. For example, we can create an object within a sub, attaching it to a local variable within the sub, as shown below:

```
Public Sub TransientObject()
Dim R As New SomeObject
    ' perform operations on the object referred to by R
    '
End Sub
```

Since the reference variable **R** will go out of scope when we exit this sub, there will be no reference to the object immediately after the **End Sub** statement. The object will be destroyed, and the next time this sub executes, a new object will be created. Figure 6.5 illustrates these ideas.

To keep an object alive, we need to create a more persistent reference variable. For example:

```
Private R As SomeObject          ' This is in the declarations
                                 ' section of this module

Public Sub LongerLivedObject()
  Set R = New SomeObject         ' Attach the object to the reference
  ' Use the object in some way
  '
End Sub
```

In the above example, the object assigned to the reference variable **R** will persist beyond the life of the sub that created it. This is because the reference variable has module-wide scope and so the object it refers to will persist while the module is in memory.

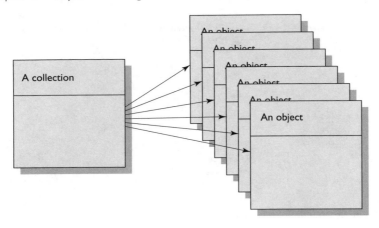

Figure 6.6 *Using a collection to maintain a list of objects.*

While small numbers of objects may be managed in this way, it is more usual to create objects and keep them alive by adding them to a collection (Figure 6.6). We can then reuse a single reference variable to create a large number of objects:

```
Private ObjectList As New Collection  ' Create a collection object.

Public Sub CreateObjects()
Dim R As SomeObject
  Do
    Set R = New SomeObject            ' Construct the object
    R.DoStuff                         ' May wish to do some operation
    ObjectList.Add R                  ' Now add it to the collection
  Loop Until MsgBox("Any more objects?", vbYesNo) = vbNo
End Sub
```

In the above example, the **CreateObjects** sub will continue to build new objects and add them to the collection until the user answers 'No' to the **MsgBox** statement.

Objects automatically expire when there are no longer any references to them. With local variables in subs, this is straightforward, since the end of the sub signals the end of the reference variable. With **Private** or **Public** reference variables within a module's declaration section, the objects persist until the module is unloaded (e.g. unloading a form from memory – see next chapter). Since a collection is simply another type of object, this would also be destroyed if no more reference variables referred to it (and so would any objects added to it).

However, sometimes we might wish to destroy an object explicitly; for example, we might have a type of object that gives us access to a file while it is alive. Creating the object could open the file, and then it would be natural to close the file by destroying the object. However, we might not want to wait until the object reference went out of scope.

In this case, we can kill off an object using the **Nothing** reference, as follows:

```
Public Sub ShortLife()
Dim R As SomeObject
  Set R = New SomeObject
  ' Now work with the object in some way
  '
  Set R = Nothing            ' Explicitly destroys the object.
  ' We can continue to do other operations
End Sub
```

In the above example, an object was created, assigned to a reference variable **R**, and operated on in some way. When we had finished with the object, setting its reference to **Nothing** simply destroys it – there is no longer an object attached to **R**. Note that this would have happened automatically at the end of the sub anyway, but sometimes it is better to maintain control over the persistence of an object. Note that the object will only be destroyed if the reference set to **Nothing** is the last reference to the object. If another variable or collection also refers to the object, setting one reference to **Nothing** will only have the effect of breaking the link between the object and that reference variable.

In the following example, we will see how a useful collection of our **CCard** objects can be managed. It is worth trying out this code to see how such a collection can be used.

6.5   Adding structure with a collection

A **CDeck** class

Of course, there is not a lot that can be done with individual playing cards. We could create an array of 52 of these to mimic a deck, but then we would have to worry about shuffling, dealing, etc. Far better would be to create a **CDeck** class:

```
Option Explicit

' Class CDeck
Private Cards(1 To 52) As New CCard    ' There are exactly 52 cards
                                       ' so an array is ok.
Private mvarNextCard As Integer        ' keep track for dealing

Private Sub Class_Initialize()
Dim index As Integer
  For index = 1 To 52
    Cards(index).Number = index
  Next
  mvarNextCard = 1
End Sub
```

```
Public Sub Shuffle()
Dim c As Integer, N As Integer, Crd As CCard
  Randomize                      ' Seed the random number generator.
  For c = 1 To 52
    N = Int(Rnd() * 52 + 1)      ' Get a random number, range 1..52
    Set Crd = Cards(c)
    Set Cards(c) = Cards(N)
    Set Cards(N) = Crd
  Next
  mvarNextCard = 1
End Sub

Public Function DealCard() As CCard   ' i.e. result is a CCard object
reference
Dim c As CCard
  If mvarNextCard <= 52 Then
    Set c = Cards(mvarNextCard)
    mvarNextCard = mvarNextCard + 1
    Set DealCard = c
  Else
    Set DealCard = Nothing             ' i.e. no object.
  End If
End Function

Public Function CardsLeft() As Integer
  CardsLeft = 53 - mvarNextCard
End Function
```

In the **CDeck** class, we use the principle of *aggregation* to store an array of **CCard** references within a deck. There are only two instance variables: the **Cards** array, and the **mvarNextCard** integer variable that indicates the next card to be dealt.

We have used the syntax:

```
Private Cards(1 To 52) As New CCard
```

to create an array of 52 instances of **CCard** objects. These objects will not be created at the point where the **CDeck** object is created but will be created on the first occasion where each of them is referenced.

We need to keep track of the cards in the deck – which have been dealt and which remain. Since a newly created deck will contain 52 cards, none of which have been dealt, we can make use of a single variable, **mvarNextCard**, to act as an indicator to the next card to be dealt, effectively indicating the top card in the deck. It is necessary to make sure that this is set to point to the first card whenever a new deck is created, otherwise it would have an invalid value (0). Visual Basic gives us a useful mechanism for making sure an object is made valid automatically when it is instantiated. It is based on the more general-purpose object oriented programming idea of the class *constructor*.

Constructors and destructors

The **CDeck** class has been given a new feature – a *constructor*. The **Class_Initialize()** method is a special-purpose sub that is run automatically whenever a new instance of the class is created. It is not called by another sub, but runs automatically in response to the object being created; the programmer therefore does not need to remember to use it. In this case **Class_Initialize()** can be used to make sure that the top card in the deck is indicated, by setting **mvarNextCard** to a value of 1. It is also used in this example to ensure that every card in the deck has a valid **Number** property before it is used. The simple form of the constructor here will assign each card consecutive numbers from 1 to 52, just like the neatly ordered cards in a deck that you have just unwrapped. You should think of a constructor as a set of instructions of how to build a new object of the class.

As well as a constructor, a class can also have a *destructor* method defined, that is invoked automatically whenever a member of a class falls out of scope or is explicitly destroyed by setting it to the special value of **Nothing**. In Visual Basic, a destructor has the name **Class_Terminate()**, and acts as an event-handler, being executed whenever an object is destroyed. Often it is not necessary to define a class destructor, since Visual Basic takes care of removing the object from memory. However, if an object makes use of any resources, such as disk files, screen area or a database, for example, then a destructor is useful for ensuring that all of the resources used by the object are released.

Dealing cards

The **DealCard** method returns a reference to one of the cards in the deck, and makes sure that that card will not be dealt again by incrementing the **mvarNextCard** counter that is used to keep track of what has been dealt. We would use this method to get cards from the deck to add to a hand of cards. Note that the **DealCard()** method returns **Nothing** when the entire pack has been dealt. The **CardsLeft()** function also exists to tell us explicitly when all cards have been dealt.

The **Shuffle** algorithm is worth closer examination. The sub works through the pack, swapping each card with a randomly selected one. Note the use of **Randomize** as the first statement. This makes sure that Visual Basic's random number generator produces a different pseudo-random sequence of numbers every time the deck is shuffled.

QUESTION 6.4

The **CDeck** class's **Shuffle** method goes through each object in the **Cards** array, swapping it with another, randomly selected card. An alternative algorithm would be to go through the pack assigning a random card to each position.

(a) What would be the drawback of the second method?

(b)   Why is the algorithm used much more likely to operate efficiently?

(c)   Which algorithm is closest to the way that a human dealer would shuffle a deck of cards?

Testing the CDeck class

Using the Immediate window, we can run a simple test to show that a **CDeck** object will do the required job:

```
Set D = New CDeck    ' This should execute Class_Initialize()
Print D.CardsLeft
52
For i = 1 To 52: Set C = D.DealCard: Print C.Description: Next
Ace of Clubs
  2 of Clubs
  3 of Clubs
  4 of Clubs
  ' ' '
Jack of Hearts
Queen of Hearts
King of Hearts
Ace of Hearts
Print D.CardsLeft
0
```

In the above Immediate window interaction, a **CDeck** object is created and then 52 cards are dealt in a loop. If we were to try to deal a 53rd card, the deck would return the reference **Nothing**, and any attempt to access any of the card's methods would result in the familiar *'Object variable or With block variable not set'* error message (Figure 6.7).

We can always check for this error condition by testing the type of the object returned from a call to **DealCard**:

```
Set C = D.DealCard
If C Is Nothing Then
  MsgBox "No card was dealt"
Else
  MsgBox "Card was " & C.Description
End If
```

Note that a new type of conditional test has been used here. The syntax

```
ObjectRef Is ObjectRef
```

is an expression that results in **True** if the object references on both sides of the **Is** keyword refer to the same object, and **False** otherwise. In this particular test, the object reference is being tested to see whether it refers to **Nothing**.

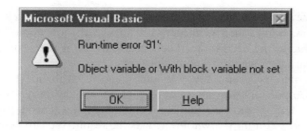

Figure 6.7   *Attempting to access the 53rd card.*

Once we know that the **CDeck** object can deal with 52 card references, we can try testing its other methods:

```
Set D = New CDeck
D.Shuffle
For i = 1 To 52: Set C = D.Deal: Print C.Description: Next
   Jack of Hearts     ' Now the cards appear in random order.
   6 of Spades
   ' ' '
   5 of Diamonds
   8 of Clubs
   King of Spades
```

By calling the **Shuffle** method of our newly created deck of cards, we get the cards dealt in the random order we would need if developing a computer-based card game. Armed with these two new classes, we can now go about programming card games without worrying about the trivia of representing cards or decks of cards.

QUESTION 6.5

A **CPokerHand** class has been defined with the following interface methods:

> **AddCard**, a sub that takes a **CCard** as a parameter
> **HandFull**, a function that returns a Boolean that indicates if all five cards have been added to the hand

Write a routine that creates an instance of a **CDeck**, shuffles it, and then deals cards to two **CPokerHand** objects, **Hand1** and **Hand2**, until both are full.

How does object orientation influence the way we write programs?

The example of the **CCard** and **CDeck** classes given above should be enough to suggest that object oriented programming can help to organize some of the more complex programming situations. The object model provides us with methods that we use to manipulate whole objects – cards and decks of cards. While it would be possible to do this using simple variables such as integers and strings, the job would have been much more complex due to the need to keep converting from the real-world objects to the numbers and characters we use to represent them.

In object oriented programming, we aim to solve problems by building up a solution from components, just as an auto-engineer would design a car as a lot of components (washers, gears, etc.) built into sub-assemblies (carburettor, suspension, electrical, etc.) and so on until a whole car was the result. We can keep on top of the complexity by making it unnecessary to know all of the details of a component in order to use it.

6.6   Review questions

1. In the `CDeck` card, an array of 52 `CCard` reference variables was used to house the deck. If instead a `Collection` had been used,
   (a) How would this have changed the coding of the `Shuffle` method?
   (b) How would it affect the `DealCard` method?
   (c) How would the `CardsLeft` method be best implemented?

2. We have two different ways of declaring and instantiating an object in a program. We can use `Dim Obj As New SomeClass`, to combine both operations, or we can use `Dim Obj As SomeClass` and then instantiate the object later with a `Set Obj = New SomeClass` statement. What would be the advantage of the second of these methods?

3. The three classes `CCard`, `CDeck` and `CHand` referred to in this chapter are interrelated in various ways. Recall that objects can have several forms of relationships – inheritance, composition, aggregation, message passing. For the relationships listed, suggest the most accurate form:
   (a) `CCard` and `CDeck`
   (b) `CCard` and `CHand`
   (c) `CHand` and `CDeck`

4. Complete the following:
   (a) The `Class_Initialize()` event-handler is a type of _____.
   (b) The `Class_Terminate()` event-handler is a type of _____.
   (c) Encapsulation control in classes is provided by the keywords _____ and
       _____.
   (d) In Visual Basic, the null object reference is given the keyword _____.

5. Explain the circumstances in which Visual Basic will automatically destroy an object.

6.7 Practical exercises: Working with an object model

In these exercises we will develop the `CCard` and `CDeck` classes described in the chapter.

Once you have completed these exercises, you should be able to:

- realize a simple object model in a Visual Basic project,

- implement a relationship between objects of different classes using aggregation and message passing,

- manage simple collections of objects.

| Exercise 1: | Creating the `CCard` class |

In this exercise, you will create the two classes that make up the card-playing object model.

Start a new VB project – select `Standard EXE` as the type. Rename the project from `Project1` to `Cards` by changing the Name property in the Properties window.

Right-click on the Project Explorer, and select `Add/Class Module` from the context menu. When the new class dialog box appears, select `Class Module`, and name the new class `CCard` in the Properties window.

Repeat this to add the `CDeck` class to the project.

Go to the `CCard` class's code window, and enter all of the code shown below.

```
Option Explicit

' Class CCard - Description of a Playing Card
Private cardNumber As Integer

Public Property Let Number(n As Integer)
  If n > 0 And n < 53 Then
    mvarNumber = n
  End If
End Property
```

```
Public Function Suit() As String
' Work out suit of card...
  Select Case cardNumber
    Case 1 To 13
      Suit = "Clubs"
    Case 14 To 26
      Suit = "Diamonds"
    Case 27 To 39
      Suit = "Spades"
    Case 40 To 52
      Suit = "Hearts"
  End Select
End Function


Public Function Rank() As String
' Work out rank (Ace to King) of card.
Dim r As Integer
  ' Convert card Number into a number in the range 1-13...
  r = (mvarNumber - 1) Mod 13 + 1
  Select Case r
    Case 1
      Rank = "Ace"
    Case 2 To 10
      Rank = Str(r)      ' Convert to a string
    Case 11
      Rank = "Jack"
    Case 12
      Rank = "Queen"
    Case 13
      Rank = "King"
  End Select
End Function


Public Function Description() As String
' Return the full description of the card..
  Description = Rank & " of " & Suit
End Function


Public Function Value() As Integer
' Return its value..
  Value = (mvarNumber - 1) Mod 13 + 1
  If Value > 10 Then
    Value = 10
  End If
End Function
```

Test the **CCard** class by instantiating an object in the Immediate window.

```
Set C = New CCard
C.Number = 1
Print C.Suit
```
VB responds with the appropriate suit..
```
Print C.Rank
```
VB responds with the card type (Ace, 2, 3 etc.)
```
Print C.Description
```
VB responds with a full text description of the card.

 Repeat the above test for other values of ID.

Exercise 2: Creating the **CDeck** class

 Add the following code to the **CDeck** class's code window.

```
Option Explicit

' Class CDeck
Private Cards(1 To 52) As New CCard  ' There are exactly 52 cards
                                     ' so an array is ok.
Private mvarNextCard As Integer      ' keep track for dealing

Private Sub Class_Initialize()
Dim index As Integer
  For index = 1 To 52
    Cards(index).Number = index
  Next
  mvarNextCard = 1
End Sub

Public Sub Shuffle()
Dim c As Integer, N As Integer, Crd As CCard
  Randomize                    ' Seed the random number generator.
  For c = 1 To 52
    N = Int(Rnd() * 52 + 1)    ' Get a random number, range 1..52
    Set Crd = Cards(c)
    Set Cards(c) = Cards(N)
    Set Cards(N) = Crd
```

```
    Next
    mvarNextCard = 1
End Sub

Public Function DealCard() As CCard  ' i.e. result is a CCard object
reference
Dim c As CCard
    If mvarNextCard <= 52 Then
      Set c = Cards(mvarNextCard)
      mvarNextCard = mvarNextCard + 1
      Set DealCard = c
    Else
      Set DealCard = Nothing          ' i.e. no object.
    End If
End Function

Public Function CardsLeft() As Integer
    CardsLeft = 53 - mvarNextCard
End Function
```

> Test the **CDeck** class by creating an instance of a deck in the Immediate window.

```
Set D = New CDeck
Print D.CardsLeft
52
Set C = D.DealCard
Print C.Description
Ace of Clubs
Print D.CardsLeft
51
```

Exercise 3:   Creating the **C21Hand** class

To test the card and deck classes properly, we will go on to develop a new class to represent a hand of cards in a simple game – 21 or Blackjack. We will continue to develop the full game in a later chapter.

The rules of 21 are simple:

■ There can be any number of players (within reason) plus a dealer, who also receives a hand.

■ Each player is initially dealt two cards, ending with the dealer, which in this case will be our Visual Basic program.

- Players play by asking the dealer for other cards (if necessary), the objective being to get as close as possible to a total value of 21. Settling on a score of less than 17 is not permitted. If a player's hand exceeds 21, that player has lost.

- The dealer is last to play, by adding cards to the hand until it has a score equal to or more than those of the other players, but not exceeding 21. If the dealer's hand has the same score as another player's, the dealer has the advantage.

For the game of 21, we will need to represent a hand of cards of any number from 2 up to some arbitrary (but quite small) limit. The **C21Hand** class should provide the following services:

- accept cards passed to its **Add** method,

- return the sum of the values of all cards added to it,

- return the number of cards currently in the hand.

We could impose additional requirements, such as a **Bust** function method that returns **True** if the hand value exceeds 21, and **False** otherwise, but the services listed above will suffice. Since a **CHand** object will accept a variable number of cards, it is sensible to accommodate these in a collection. The interface can be implemented by one sub (the **Add** method) and two functions (the **Value** method and the **Count** method). Additionally, we can use the **Class_Initialize** constructor to create an instance of the collection class when a **C21Hand** object is first created.

 Create the **C21Hand** class by adding a new class to the Project Explorer, and setting its Name property.

 Add the following code to the **C21Hand** class's code window.

```
Option Explicit

' Class C21Hand - represents a hand in the game of 21.

Private cards As Collection

Public Sub Add(C As CCard)
   cards.Add C
End Sub

Public Function Value() As Integer
Dim v As Integer, C As CCard
   For Each C In cards
     v = v + C.Value
   Next
   Value = v
End Function
```

```
Public Function Count() As Integer
  Count = cards.Count
End Function

Private Sub Class_Initialize()
  Set cards = New Collection
End Sub
```

 Test the new class in the Immediate window.

The following sequence of statements in the Immediate window should create an instance of the **C21Hand** class and add cards to it.

```
Set D = New CDeck
D.Shuffle
Set H = New C21Hand
H.Add D.DealCard
Print H.Value
  1
H.Add D.DealCard
Print H.Value
  11
```

Note that Visual Basic's responses (in italics) are unlikely to be the same when you try this, since the random number generator's purpose is to make the sequence of cards dealt unpredictable. You should be able to repeat this sequence of Immediate window commands and get a different result every time.

Suggested exercises

1. Create a new class, **CPokerHand**, which should accommodate five **CCards**. Add a method to it, **Flush**, that returns **True** if all of the cards have the same **Suit**. To check this, use a loop to compare the **Suit** of the first card with each successive one, set a flag (**Boolean** variable) to **True** before entering the loop, and then set it to **False** within the loop if any different suit is found. The final state of the flag will be the result of the method.

2. Test the **Flush** method of the **CPokerHand** class by assigning known cards to it and calling the method, either in an event-handler for a button on a form, or in code in the Immediate window.

6.8 **Answers to questions**

QUESTION 6.1

(a) Length: **Property** Get and **Let**

(b) Width: **Property** Get and **Let**

(c) Colour: **Property** Get and **Let**

(d) Size: sub

(e) Area: function

(f) Perimeter: function

(g) Display: sub

QUESTION 6.2

```
Public Sub DealTwoHands(Hand1 As CHand, Hand2 As CHand)
Dim count As Integer, C As CCard
  For count = 1 To 5
    Set C = New CCard
    Hand1.Add New C
    Set C = New CCard
    Hand2.Add New C
  Next
End Sub
```

Note that we could do this without having to declare and use C, the CCard reference variable:

```
Public Sub DealTwoHands(Hand1 As CHand, Hand2 As CHand)
Dim count As Integer
  For count = 1 To 5
    Hand1.Add New CCard
    Hand2.Add New CCard
  Next
End Sub
```

QUESTION 6.3

```
Public Property Get TopCard() As CCard
  Set TopCard = mvarTopCard
End Property

Public Property Set TopCard(card As CCard)
  Set mvarTopCard = card
End Property
```

QUESTION 6.4

(a) The second method, that of selecting cards randomly to add to the deck, would be inefficient because of the need to make all of the cards different. The first card dealt will always be unique, but from the second card on, there will be an increasingly likely chance that a random card added to the deck will already be in it. It would therefore be necessary to check each new card added to the deck to ensure that it was not already in it, and reject duplicates, selecting another random card. As the deck becomes full, it would get more and more likely that a card dealt was already in the deck, and by the last few cards it may take a large number of random cards before a unique one was found. Therefore, this shuffle algorithm would get slower and slower as the deck fills up.

(b) The algorithm used takes exactly 52 operations to shuffle a deck, one for each card. Swapping each card with a randomly selected card will thoroughly shuffle the deck with no need to check each stage for duplicates.

(c) The random-swap algorithm is a close analogue of a human shuffle. The alternative algorithm is closer to shuffling a deck of cards by pulling cards from a large box of randomly ordered cards, adding them to the deck if they were not already in it, and throwing away duplicates.

QUESTION 6.5

```
Public Sub TwoPokerHands()
Dim Deck As CDeck, Hand1 As CPokerHand, Hand2 As CPokerHand
  Set Deck = New CDeck
  Deck.Shuffle
  Do
    Hand1.AddCard Deck.DealCard
  Loop Until Hand1.HandFull
  Do
    Hand2.AddCard Deck.DealCard
  Loop Until Hand2.HandFull
End Sub
```

6.9   Answers to review questions

1. *In the* **CDeck** *card, an array of 52* **CCard** *reference variables was used to house the deck. If instead a* **Collection** *had been used,*

   (a) *How would this have changed the coding of the* **Shuffle** *method?* Only minor changes would be necessary – it would be safer to use the collection's **Count** property when determining the range of objects to exchange.

   (b) *How would it affect the* **DealCard** *method?* This would be the most significant change. Using the array form, a card that had been dealt never actually left the deck, but its reference was made unreachable because the **mvarNextCard** variable limited the range of card object that could be accessed. In a collection-based implemetation, it would be more appropriate to actually remove a card from the collection as it was dealt, using code such as:

   ```
   Public Function DealCard() As CCard
     If colCards.Count > 0 Then
       Set DealCard = colCards.Remove(1)
     Else
       Set DealCard = Nothing
     End If
   End Function
   ```

   We would no longer need the **mvarNextCard** variable, since the collection's **Count** property would take care of keeping track of cards for us.

   (c) *How would the* **CardsLeft** *method be best implemented?* **CardsLeft** could be directly implemented by returning the **Count** property of the collection.

2. *We have two different ways of declaring and instantiating an object in a program. We can use* **Dim Obj As New SomeClass**, *to combine both operations, or we can use* **Dim Obj As SomeClass** *and then instantiate the object later with a* **Set Obj = New SomeClass** *statement. What would be the advantage of the second of these methods?* With the first method, Visual Basic does not actually instantiate the object until it is referenced in a statement of executable code. While this is safe most of the time, it does have the effect of deferring the action of the **Class_Initialize()** event-handler until the object is actually created. The programmer effectively loses control over when the object is created and therefore when the **Class_Initialize()** method executes. The second method gives the programmer control, since the event-handler will fire when the **Set...** statement executes.

3. *The three classes* **CCard**, **CDeck** *and* **CHand** *referred to in this chapter are interrelated in various ways. Recall that objects can have several forms of relationships – inheritance, composition, aggregation, message passing. For the relationships listed, suggest the most accurate form:*

    (a) **CCard** *and* **CDeck** Aggregation

    (b) **CCard** *and* **CHand** Aggregation

    (c) **CHand** *and* **CDeck** Message passing

4. *Complete the following:*

    (a) *The* **Class_Initialize()** *event-handler is a type of* constructor.

    (b) *The* **Class_Terminate** *event-handler is a type of* destructor.

    (c) *Encapsulation control in classes is provided by the keywords* **Public** *and* **Private**.

    (d) *In Visual Basic, the null object reference is given the keyword* **Nothing**.

5. *Explain the circumstances in which Visual Basic will automatically destroy an object.* Visual Basic destroys an object when it can no longer be reached by any reference variables. This happens when the last variable referring to the object goes out of scope, either when the sub or function it is declared in as a local variable reaches its **End Sub/Function** statement, by the form it is declared in being unloaded, or by the object that its reference variable is declared in as part of a composition/aggregation relationship being destroyed.

CHAPTER 7

Graphical user-interfaces

Visual Basic gives the programmer two ways of creating new classes. The first is to use a class module and write code that describes the composition and behaviour of the new type of object. The second is by using the form designer. A Visual Basic form is a user-interface class, and the IDE provides design tools to allow the programmer to visually develop the appearance of a form and to programmatically define its methods and how it will react to events. The result is that Visual Basic makes the task of creating attractive and responsive Windows user-interfaces as easy as possible.

By the end of this chapter, you should be able to:

- create Visual Basic form classes that provide the user with a more intuitive way of controlling the actions of a program,

- construct simple programs that combine class modules and form modules,

- use event-handlers to make user interactions initiate object operations.

7.1 The user-interface

By concentrating on the structure and implementation of classes of objects to model system requirements, we have so far ignored a very important aspect of software development: the *user-interface*. This slightly de-humanizing term is commonly used to describe the set of mechanisms by which a human user of a computer system enters commands and accesses information to cause the system to do its job.

Visual Basic's immense popularity as a program development system owes more to its facilities for building user-interfaces than to any other single feature. Look at any Windows application program (including Visual Basic itself) and you will find that the most striking features are the ways that information is presented and the ways that you are able to interact with the application to make things happen. Visual Basic came to prominence due to its facilities for creating *graphical user-interfaces*, which rely on standard features such as on-screen buttons, edit boxes, list boxes, drop-down lists, scroll-bars, menus, etc. In this chapter, we will examine the principles of *event-driven programming*, the use of graphical user-interface elements and the construction of programs with user-interface modules.

Event-driven programming

With one exception, the type of programming we have examined in any depth in previous chapters can be described as the *imperative* model of programming. In this, the progression of the program is based on the sequence of executable statements that access object properties and *call* object methods to get jobs done. The exception has been the use of *constructors* and *destructors* in class design. These differ from the imperative model in one key respect: they are invoked automatically by the system.

The overriding principle of the imperative model of programming is that the entire operation of a program is dictated by the sequence set out by the programmer and the conditional logic directed by values input by the user. Any program developed to fit in with this model will progress according to the sequence shown in Figure 7.1.

The key feature of the *input–process–output* model is that the user is directed by the software to provide input data in some sequence dictated by the software. It may be that certain conditions cause the sequence to alter in some way. For example, an entry to an insurance database during which the user indicates that the record being entered is for a car insurance policy could trigger an extra sequence of interactions. The user may then be asked to enter details such as the make of car, length of time the insured has been driving, number of road accidents, etc. However, the information that the user provides to the program is always given in response to a sequence of operations dictated by the program.

This form of program control was popular for a long time because of the limited range of input and output devices available for early computers and their relative lack of processing power. A keyboard is quite a primitive form of input device and as such demands little in the way of processing power of the computer it is attached to. High-resolution graphics terminals and input devices based on a pointer controlled by a

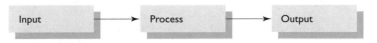

Figure 7.1 *Sequence model of an imperative program.*

mouse are now the norm, and operating systems such as Windows and programming languages like Visual Basic have evolved to take advantage of this form of user-interface and the necessary underlying processing power.

It should be apparent that most of the programs you use under Windows do not flow in the well-choreographed way that input–process–output style programs are supposed to. A user of a Windows program is likely to work in a less predictable way because of the number of potential input devices available.

As an example of the two different methods, consider the requirements of a program to calculate a person's wage, based on hours worked, rate of pay, overtime rate and bonus payments. We could write a Basic sub as a method of a **CEmployee** object, to perform the calculation as shown below:

```
' Member variables...
Private rate As Currency          ' Hourly pay rate
Private hours As Integer          ' Number of hours worked
Private overtimerate As Single    ' Multiplication factor for extra
                                  ' worked hours
Private bonuspayment As Currency  ' Cash bonus amount
Private pay As Currency

Public Sub CalculatePay()
   rate = InputBox("Enter hourly pay rate")
   hours = InputBox("Enter number of whole hours worked")
   overtimerate = InputBox("Enter the overtime pay multiply factor")
   bonuspayment = InputBox("Enter the amount of any cash bonuses")
   If hours > 40 Then
     pay = (40 * rate) + ((hours-40) * rate * overtimerate)
   Else
     pay = hours * rate
   End If
   pay = pay + bonuspayment
   MsgBox "Total pay for this period is : £" & pay
End Sub
```

In this sub, we have used input boxes to allow the user to enter values for pay rate, then number of hours, then overtime rate and then any additional bonus payments. If the user were to enter any of these values in the wrong order, the pay calculation would almost certainly be wrong.

Now consider how a normal Windows program might do the same job (from the user's point of view), as depicted in Figure 7.2.

In typical Windows fashion, the user is given a number of different controls in which to enter information. The **TextBox** control at the top will accept a line of text that can be treated as a number (or a currency value in this case). The **Spin** control for entry of hours worked allows the user to simply click on the up or down arrow to change the value selected. The **ComboBox** below this allows the user to pick from a drop down-list of available overtime rates. Another **TextBox** control is used to enter

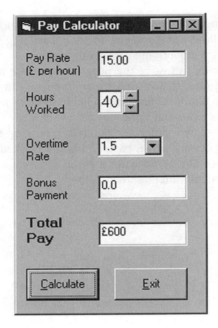

Figure 7.2 *A graphical user-interface.*

a bonus amount, and the overall result is displayed in the bottom text box. Two **CommandButtons** exist – the first (Calculate) is used to initiate a calculation sequence while the second (Exit) is used to quit the program.

This type of program must handle the user's interactions differently, since there is nothing to say that the user must enter Pay Rate, then Hours Worked, then Overtime Rate, etc. In fact the user could enter all of the required information in reverse order, or could enter a set of information, do a calculation and then change some figure to see what the effects of working a different number of overtime hours would be.

The key feature of this type of program is that the *user* dictates the sequence rather than the programmer. Since we cannot guarantee that immediately after the bonus payment entry we can go ahead and do the calculation, we must have some other way of controlling the program's operation.

The solution that Visual Basic takes is to attach *processes*, that is, sequences of operations, to *events*. In Visual Basic terms, an event is some occurrence that is initiated from outside the program. This is a flexible enough mechanism to allow us to initiate processes from any user-interaction, such as a key-press or a mouse click, or some system event such as a clock tick or a message from another program. In theory, controlling a program by reacting to events is as good a way as any of directing operations. However, practical considerations have to be taken into account: what if the user presses the calculate button without entering any information?

A programmer can take any of a number of strategies to ensure the user has entered all of the necessary information before performing a calculation. The options are:

- Do the processing only if all of the required information has been entered. This requires an additional bit of programming to test whether each of the possible entry fields has been filled, using an `If..Then` structure.

- Disable the `Calculate` button until all of the entry fields have been filled.

- Do the calculation using whatever information has been entered. In some cases this will result in a null answer. We would also have to be careful of any non-entries that were impossible to deal with – for example, if the content of a given field was to be used to divide into another (can you think of why this might cause problems?).

- Get rid of the `Calculate` button altogether, and simply react to every entry, producing a result or partial result at each stage.

It is likely that a programmer would use a combination of these techniques in a Visual Basic program to make the program responsive to the user and to prevent it from crashing due to lack of input data.

Event-handlers

The Visual Basic mechanism for attaching a particular process to a given event is to create an event-handler. As an example, here is the event-handler for a mouse click on the `Calculate` button in the Pay Calculator:

```
Private Sub cmdCalculate_Click()
Dim TotalPay As Currency
   If lblHours > 40 Then
     TotalPay = txtRate * 40 + txtRate * cboOtRate * _
                (lblHours - 40) + txtBonus
   Else
     TotalPay = txtRate * lblHours + txtBonus
   End If
   txtTotalPay = "£" & TotalPay
End Sub
```

This piece of code will execute automatically whenever its event occurs. There are a number of notable features, as explained below:

- All of the input *controls* on the form have been given names or identifiers. As in naming variables, care has been taken to make the name suggest the function of the control. By referring to the controls by name, we are referring to a ***default property*** of the control – usually the value contained in it. A Visual Basic text box control has the default property `Text`, which accesses the visible contents in the text box. We could also refer to specific properties, using a dot notation as we would for any object, e.g. `TextBox1.Font`.

- There are 13 controls on the form, seven of which are referred to in the event-handler. These are the three text boxes (`txtRate`, `txtBonus` and `txtTotalPay`), the two command buttons (`cmdCalculate` and `cmdExit`), a spin control (`spnHours`) to change the number of hours worked, and a combo-box control (`cboOtRate`) for allowing the selection of an overtime rate. There are also five label controls containing the text captions that indicate the purpose of each of the above controls (`Pay Rate (£ per hour)`, etc.), and another label control (`lblHours`) for displaying the `Value` property of the spin control. Only the last of these has been given a name since none of the others are referred to in program code.

- The event-handler itself is a sub, but has been given the name `cmdCalculate_ Click` *automatically* by Visual Basic. The combination of control name and event name separated by an underscore is Visual Basic's way of attaching events to controls. In most circumstances, this sub will not be called by another program statement but will execute automatically in response to the event.

- Although a single variable has been declared within the event-handler (`TotalPay`), we are making use of a number of different values from the various input controls, and are sending the result to another control. To all intents and purposes, these controls act as input variables to our sub. They are of course references to objects.

In the case of this program, we need to define only two event-handlers – one for each of the `CommandButton` controls. `CommandButtons` are probably the most simple control type to deal with, since most of the time we need only react to their `Click` event by executing a subroutine. However, most controls have a range of events they can react to. For example, a `TextBox` control can react to the list of events shown in Table 7.1.

In many cases, an event comes with additional information. For example, a `KeyPress` event is associated with a parameter (`KeyAscii`) that indicates which key was pressed. Therefore, a `KeyPress` event-handler for a `TextBox` control appears as follows:

```
Private Sub txtRate_KeyPress(KeyAscii As Integer)
   ' Code to handle the event..
End Sub
```

The `KeyPress` event's parameter – `KeyAscii` – indicates the ASCII code of the key being pressed. This code tells us which key – alphabetic, numeric, punctuation, or other – was pressed. By specifying a code instead of a string containing a single character, it makes it possible to deal with the special keyboard keys such as `Enter`, `Tab` and the cursor keys that do not have face values.

The list in Table 7.1 may initially seem to be a confusing array of events for a control to have to react to. However, as a programmer, you get to choose what events to support. You need only supply event-handling code for those events you want to react to. With some experience in event-driven programming, programmers quickly learn the most convenient combinations of events to deal with occurrences in a

Table 7.1 *Events that a* **TextBox** *control can respond to.*

Change	Executed when the text in the box changes
Click	Executed when the user clicks the mouse while the pointer is in the box
DblClick	Executed when the user double-clicks
DragDrop	Executes when an item is dropped on the control
DragOver	Executes when the mouse passes over the control while dragging
GotFocus	Executes when a cursor is activated in the text box
KeyDown	Executes when a key is pressed down while a cursor is active
KeyUp	Executes when a pressed key is released
KeyPress	Executes after a key is pressed then released
LinkClose	Executes when a control exchanging information with the text box terminates the link
LinkError	Executes whenever an error in link protocol happens
LinkNotify	Executes whenever an exchange event is sent out
LinkOpen	Executes when a link to another control is established
LostFocus	Executes when the active cursor is moved to another control
MouseDown	Executes when a mouse button is pressed down over the control
MouseUp	Executes when a depressed mouse button is released
MouseMove	Executes when the mouse pointer moves across the control
OLECompleteDrag OLEDragDrop OLEDragOver OLEGiveFeedback OLESetData OLEStartDrag	These events occur in response to various object linking and embedding operations – OLE is an inter-process communications protocol that allows two running programs to communicate information to each other

program. In the case of the Pay Calculator program shown, we could build a complete implementation of it by writing code for between two and four event-handlers. These would be:

- `cmdCalculate_Click`: This is the event-handler shown earlier, and we use it to perform the calculation assuming that the appropriate input information has been provided.

- `cmdExit_Click`: This is a very simple event-handler to react to the user clicking on the Exit button. As a minimum, it could contain the single command `Unload` to unload the form from memory.

- `txtRate_Change`: Optionally, we could use this event-handler to check the validity of any text entered into the text box. We could therefore screen for characters that did not make sense (in this case, any non-numeric characters).

- `txtBonus_Change`: Optionally, we could use this event-handler to check for a valid entry in the bonus text box.

QUESTION 7.1

An event-handler is a `Private` sub defined in a class – in most cases, form classes. Visual Basic automatically executes an event-handler if an appropriate event is passed to an object of an event-handling class. Do you think that this goes against the principle of encapsulation as defined for object oriented programming?

From what has been stated above, how do you think Visual Basic is able to differentiate between different events passed to an object or form?

7.2 Controls – properties, methods and events

To build up a user-interface, we place **controls** on a Visual Basic form at **design time**, i.e. when the program is being developed (rather than when it is being run). Every new Visual Basic project starts with a single form, initially referred to as `Form1`, on which we can place controls from the **tool box**. The controls are *drawn* on to the form in much the same way that items would be drawn in a graphics program (such as the **Paint** application supplied with Windows). A control that is newly added to a form is given **selection handles** so that it can be resized or moved to a new position on the form. For a newly added `CommandButton` control, this appears as shown in Figure 7.3.

Once a control is selected, it can be moved or resized or have any of its `Properties` altered. A control's properties are similar to the properties you might create for a new class of objects. These appear to the user of the control as simple data fields, but are in fact pairs of subroutines to assert a new value for a property and to retrieve its existing value, i.e. a `Let` or `Set` and a `Get` property.

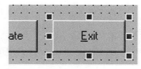

Figure 7.3   *A selected command button.*

For a control that will appear on a form at design time it is important that properties work in this way, since a programmer who changes a property during the design stages will generally want the new value to be applied immediately. Recall that a **Property Let** or **Set** routine contains executable statements that ensure that the new value of the property has an effect on the object immediately.

The most useful feature of Visual Basic controls is the way that they can be manipulated interactively while the program is in the design stages. Whenever a control is *selected* (i.e. displaying selection handles as shown in Figure 7.3), all of its *design-time* properties can be viewed and altered from the ***Properties window*** (see Figure 7.4). This feature of Visual Basic's development environment means that a programmer can set up all of the visible aspects of a program's user-interface (and many of its behavioural characteristics as well) without having to write any program code.

The properties shown are for a **CommandButton** named **cmdExit**. It is generally a good idea to use a name that describes both what type of control it is – **cmd** for **CommandButton** – and what its purpose is – **Exit**. Since there is such a wide range of

Figure 7.4   *Control properties in the Properties window.*

Table 7.2   *Standard Visual Basic controls and suitable name prefixes.*

Control type	Name prefix	Example
Form	frm	frmCustData, frmSearch
Command button	cmd	cmdOK, cmdExit
Text box	txt	txtName, txtDateOfBirth
List box	lst	lstCustomers, lstPurchases
Combo-box	cbo	cboPostCode, cboDeptHeads
Vertical scroll bar	vscr	vscrPage
Horizontal scroll bar	hscr	hscrColumn
Grid	grd	grdSalesData, grdTimetable
Label	lbl	lblTotalPrice, lblFieldHeading
Frame	fra	fraActionGroup, fraTools
Check box	chk	chkDiscount, chkMinor
Option button	opt	optUp, optDown
Timer	tim	timOverrun
Picture box	pic	picPhoto, picDiagram
Image	img	imgBackdrop
Data	dat	datCustDB, datSalesQuery
OLE control	ole	oleExcel, olePicture
Shape control	shp	shpArea, shpEccentricity
Line control	lin	linConector, linPointer

available Visual Basic controls and predefined objects, it makes good sense to stick with a predefined naming scheme when applying the **Name** property to a control. Table 7.2 is a list of control-name prefixes frequently used by Visual Basic programmers and recommended by Microsoft. By adopting this naming scheme you will be making sure that many other Visual Basic programmers will find your code easier to read.

When manipulating a selected control using the properties window at design time, we can set up its appearance (colour, text colour, border style, whether a control contains a picture or not, etc.) and some of its behavioural characteristics. For example, we can set the `Cancel` property to `True` to make the button react to a press of the `Esc` key on the computer's keyboard.

A Visual Basic control can react to events by executing an event-handler and can have its attributes manipulated by using its properties. Properties can be manipulated at design time using the Properties window and at run-time (while the program is executing) by lines of code. For example, to change the background colour of the command button while the program was running, we could place the statement:

```
cmdExit.BackColor = vbRed    ' Change background colour to red.
```

in an event-handler or some other sub or function. Controls can also be sent commands, which are the controls' `Methods`. For example, to move the button to a new location on the form, we could use the `Move` method, as follows:

```
cmdExit.Move 1000, 1000    ' Move top left corner to co-ordinates
                           ' 1000, 1000
```

Since controls can be used for widely different purposes, different types of control can have different combinations of properties and methods, and can react to a different range of events.

In general, all controls will have `Top`, `Left`, `Width` and `Height` properties, and the `Move` method. What other properties they have will depend on what they do. For example, a `TextBox` control has a `Text` property that reflects the text in the box, whether it was typed there by the user or set by program statements. `ListBox` and `ComboBox` controls have a `List` property, since both can maintain a list of strings of text. Similarly, a `TextBox` has a `SetFocus` method (to switch on a cursor in the box) while `ListBox` and `ComboBox` controls additionally have `AddItem` and `RemoveItem` methods (to allow text to be appended to and deleted from the list).

QUESTION 7.2

Suggest suitable names for the controls described below:
- (a) A text box to be used for entry of a customer's name
- (b) A list box containing a list of customer names
- (c) A picture box that displays a photo of a customer
- (d) Two list boxes, displaying a list of cities which are the potential starting place and destination of a journey
- (e) A form displaying a list of bank account transactions.

Making controls inter-operate

With very few exceptions, interactions between controls need to be effected by writing program code in event-handlers. For example, a typical interaction between a

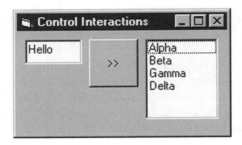

Figure 7.5 *A typical interaction between controls – how would we move the* **TextBox** *contents ("Hello") to the list?*

TextBox, a **ListBox** and a **CommandButton** might be to move the contents of the **TextBox** into the **ListBox** whenever the **CommandButton** is pressed (Figure 7.5). This is not difficult to do, but does require that you know how to address the required features of each control:

1. Which event-handler should house the program code? In this case the **Click** event-handler for the **CommandButton** control is probably the best for the job.

2. How do we access the contents of the **TextBox** control? In this case, its **Text** property.

3. How do we add an item to a **ListBox** control? By using its **AddItem** method.

Once we have answered these questions, the coding for the job is quite trivial:

```
Private Sub cmsAddText_Click()    ' This is the event-handler's name
   lstItems.AddItem txtItem.Text   ' Adds the text box contents to the
                                    ' list box
   txtItem.Text = ""               ' Clears the contents of txtItem
End Sub
```

Of course, for every interaction, there is likely to be a different combination of properties, methods and event-handlers to effect it. However, Visual Basic objects have been designed to be as easy to use as possible, and, using only a quite small bag of tricks, a Visual Basic programmer can perform quite a lot of different types of interaction.

QUESTION 7.3

In a **ListBox** control, an item that is selected (shown as a dark blue highlight across that item in the list) can be identified by number. This number is a property of the list box, **ListIndex** and is always counted from zero (i.e. the first item in the list is numbered 0). For example, the number of the selected item in a list box called **lstCustomers** is:

```
lstCustomers.ListIndex
```

An item can be removed from a **ListBox** by passing its number to the **RemoveItem** method. To remove the second item in **lstCustomers**, we could use the statement:

```
lstCustomers.RemoveItem 1
```

Note again that items are numbered from zero.

(a) Write a statement that will remove the selected item from the list box **lstCustomers**. (Hint – we need to replace the number '1' in the above sample.)

(b) If no item is currently selected in a **ListBox**, the **ListIndex** property returns the value −1. Write an **If..Then** conditional statement that could be used to control the removal of an item from the list box so that only a selected item would be removed.

7.3 Form classes

A Visual Basic form design is a class. This is a point that is easy to miss, since when you start up Visual Basic and start a new project, a new form is automatically added to the program whether or not you intend to develop a program along object oriented lines. However, it is a simple matter to demonstrate that a Visual Basic form is just another type of class, as the following short program demonstrates.

The form design shown in Figure 7.6 is simply the default form that is part of a new Visual Basic program with a single **CommandButton** control added. Adding the following code to the form's code window:

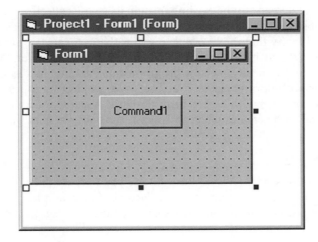

Figure 7.6 *Design window for a form class.*

```
Option Explicit

Private F As Form1

Private Sub Command1_Click()
  Set F = New Form1
  F.Show
End Sub
```

will have the result that each time the **CommandButton** is pressed, a new **Form1** object will be created and that form's **Show** method executed. This in turn causes a new version of the form to appear on the computer's display. We know that the **Set** and **New** keywords are used to manage objects in a program, and so the identifier **Form1** must be a class name. (Note that I have not renamed the form and controls according to the suggested naming scheme in this try-and-throw-away example – a case where even a good habit is more effort than it is worth.)

Are forms objects?

There is one logical problem about how this program works, since we can press the same copy of the command button over and over again and keep creating new form objects. In the previous chapter, we saw how creating an object and assigning it to an object variable would cause the destruction of an object already assigned to that variable – why is it that we can create as many forms as we like from this event-handler?

The answer to this is very straightforward: a Visual Basic application maintains a collection of all forms added in the global object. **Forms** is a collection accessible throughout any Visual Basic application and each element is a form. By pressing the command button repeatedly, we are deposing the existing form object from its reference by assigning a new form each time. Reference variable F will always refer to the most recently created form object. However, the Visual Basic application has already created a reference to the existing form in its **Forms** collection, and this ensures that the form object is not destroyed.

One other ambiguity that might occur to you is that a form class cannot be exactly the same as a class that is designed by a Visual Basic programmer. A Visual Basic form is created automatically when a program that contains its design is run. This does not happen with normal classes. A closer look makes this appear to be an even more weird feature, since although a form design is a class, not an object, the form object that Visual Basic creates when a program runs *has the same name as the class*.

Name overloading

An explanation of this is that Visual Basic allows you to reuse the name of a class as a reference variable – a feature known as *overloading*. For example, go back to any of the previous exercises in which a new class has been defined (e.g. the **CCard** class), and insert a statement:

```
Private CCard As New CCard
```

in the general declarations section of a form module. Visual Basic will allow you to use `CCard` as a reference variable to work with the object. Because both names will be used in different contexts, it has no problem in distinguishing the class name from the object reference variable.

In fact, a form design is always both a class and an object because Visual Basic's form designer always creates an appropriate reference variable for each form design, giving it the class name. The origins of this strange feature lie in the early versions of Visual Basic, before classes were introduced to the language. In those versions, Visual Basic could not be described as an object oriented programming language because there was no way to define objects. The GUI design features did exist, but were used to define form objects, not form classes. Since there was no `New` keyword, there was no way to create a form other than have Visual Basic do it for you when a program was run.

Later versions of Visual Basic introduced features that made it possible to create several copies of a form set up at design time. However, it was necessary to preserve the original behaviour of the earlier versions of the system by creating one form object of each type when a program was run. Otherwise, earlier programs written in Visual Basic would cease to work under the new versions. We simply have to accept that a form design is both a class and an object.

By recognizing that a form design is a class, we can make use of forms in programs in a more object oriented way:

- Forms can have `Private` member variables declared in their code. This allows us to use encapsulation, separating the inner workings of the form from its `Public` interface.

- We can define public methods and properties for a form, allowing us to deal with it in the same way as any other class of object.

- We can add forms to a collection, or make use of the collection of forms maintained by the Visual Basic application.

- Forms can be part of object interactions just as other objects can. We can aggregate forms within another object, or can aggregate other objects inside forms. We can also pass messages to form objects, or create other objects to do this.

- Most interestingly, a form design is a type of code inheritance, something that is not available to other Visual Basic classes. Every new form design is an extension of the existing form class that is used by Visual Basic to define a blank form. All of the properties and methods of a blank form automatically become properties and methods of a new form design.

In this and subsequent chapters, we will define and use forms in a way that capitalizes on their object oriented heritage.

QUESTION 7.4

By using form classes in Visual Basic, we can design programs in which user-interface objects can be used in a similar way as all of the other objects in a program. Why is this important from a design point of view? How do you think multiple copies of a form design might be used in a Visual Basic program? (Hint: look at the user-interface of the Visual Basic IDE, particularly the form design windows.)

7.4   Modular program structure

Visual Basic encourages *modular programming* as much as possible. You have met some of this already, since VB classes are separate modules (each residing in its own file). Each Visual Basic *form* class is also a module. By organizing things in this way, a programmer can build a program that contains form designs that were developed for another program, and only use a minimum of program code to make the forms in the new program inter-operate. Whenever you develop a form class, it is worth asking yourself whether the job it does might be required in other programs, and, if so, design it with reuse in mind. Ease of reuse depends on complexity, which in turn depends on the number of things you need to remember in order to reuse an item. It is therefore good practice to make reusable program components (such as forms and classes) simple to use by minimizing the number of operations built into them.

From a high-level point of view, we can consider an application program as a collaboration of a number of modules. Some will be form classes, providing the user with controls that allow the program to be operated. Others will be normal classes, providing the user with ways of creating and working with objects that are abstractions of the real-world objects being modelled. Finally, some will be code modules that simply contain subs and functions that do useful tasks in the program and that we may consider as being the properties and methods of the global object in the application program. Consider, for example, a simplified word-processing application. This might be structured as shown in Figure 7.7.

This program has a few component modules that interact to form the application. The main window (with the title bar 'My Word Processor') is the main module of the program, containing an area to type text into (probably a **TextBox** control) and a main menu. Menu commands cause interactions with other modules. For example, a command on the Edit menu would normally bring up the Search & Replace dialog box, while the management of files of text (to allow the program to load, save and edit files) could be consigned to a **CTextFile** class that contains the necessary methods.

By building the program in this modular way, we could reap the benefits of reuse. For example, we could reuse the **CTextFile** class in almost any program that dealt with files of text (programming editors, reporting systems, etc.), and we could reuse the Search & Replace form in, for example, a database system where we needed to be able to search for specific entries.

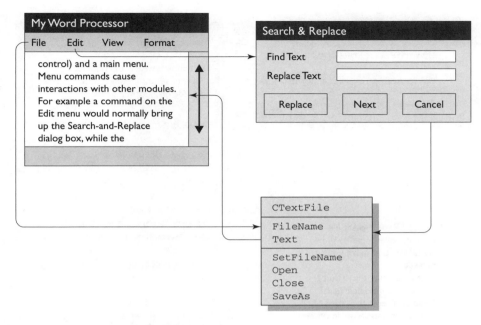

Figure 7.7   *A program composed of several component modules.*

Visual Basic deals with the modular structure of a project by constructing it as a set of files. Each form class in the program has its own file (where its design is stored so that it can be subsequently edited), each class occupies a file, and any additional code modules (containing variable declarations, subs and functions) occupy individual files. A project is, generally speaking, a collection of files, and so a VB program has a *project file* that indicates which component modules the project includes. For the above system, the Visual Basic project would be organized as shown in Figure 7.8.

Modules and scope

Recall the use of `Private` and `Public` keywords to allow certain member variables or methods in classes to be hidden from external code, or made available to external code. Until now, the concept of *external code* might have been vague or confusing. However, from the perspective of a specific module (class, form or code), external code is simply program statements in another module. Therefore, a `Public Sub` in this module can be accessed by a line of program code in any other module, while a `Private Sub` cannot be. The idea of *scope* is a bit like the concept of 'need-to-know' as applied by the security services. Information is made available on a need-to-know basis as a way of protecting the information itself and the users of the information. A spy will not be able to pass on information he or she has no knowledge of, but this may also lead to the spy not being put into a dangerous situation where he or she might be pressured to provide it. In software, you need to know enough about a

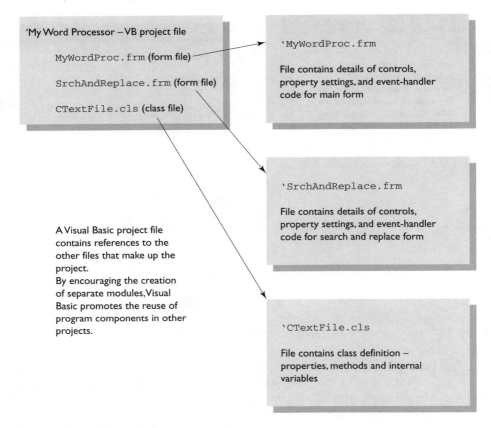

Figure 7.8 *The organization of a Visual Basic project.*

module to use it – any more information than that might encourage you to try to perform operations the module was not designed for, and that could cause errors.

7.5 An example user-interface

It is useful to look at a fuller example of a program with a graphical user-interface, so that we can appreciate how the component modules fit together and how operations are orchestrated. I will use the example of a program to mimic some of the operations of an ATM (Automatic Teller Machine or hole-in-the-wall bank).

In terms of requirements (which should always be clearly stated before any development work commences), we would expect this program to:

■ Allow a user to select a name from a list, and enter a four-digit PIN code (since we will have no facilities for reading a bank card in a Visual Basic simulation)

■ Provide the user with a range of banking options:
  – Deposit cash
  – Withdraw cash
  – Find out their account balance
  – Get a statement

■ Allow a list of accounts and balances to be set up in some way so that the remaining options will work.

The last requirement is not necessary for simulating the operations of an ATM, but is necessary so that we can ensure that there is data available referring to existing accounts.

To meet this specification, we could propose the design structure depicted in Figure 7.9.

Referring to the system diagram for the ATM simulation, we will need to create three separate modules. These are a `CAccount` class, the ATM entry screen form, and

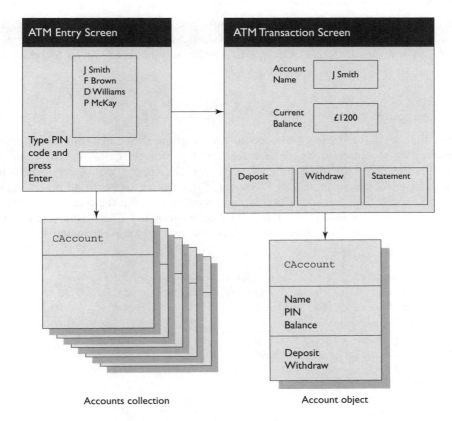

Figure 7.9 *Proposed structure for our ATM simulation program.*

the ATM transaction screen form. The fourth item shown, the Accounts collection, will be an instance of a collection object referenced from within the ATM entry screen. As you can see, some of the detailed design for the **CAccount** class has been done already. It will have three attributes to store and expose the **Name**, **PIN** number and **Balance** of the account, and two methods to initiate a **Deposit** and a **Withdrawal**. It may be that objects of this class will have other instance variables and/or methods, but this public interface is adequate for now.

QUESTION 7.5

Why is the model of a **BankAccount** depicted in Figure 7.9 not adequate? (Hint: consider how an account object might produce a statement of transactions.)

Developing the project to meet this design

The core item in the above design diagram is the **CAccount** class. Objects of this class are referred to in the Accounts collection, by the ATM entry screen and in the ATM transaction screen. Our starting point should therefore be to build this class.

The **CAccount** class

Given that we have defined the class in the diagram above in terms of its ***public interface***, we would need to make sure that it conforms to this specification. In line with the object oriented principle of *encapsulation*, we would define instance data (internal object variables) as *Private*, and only allow access to an object via its *Public* interface. The class definition is developed by entering the code shown below into a new ***class module***, created by selecting ***Project/Add Class Module*** from the Visual Basic menus. The class name would be set to **CAccount** in the Properties window.

```
Option Explicit      ' Visual Basic indicator that variables
                     ' are required to be declared before use.
' Private instance variables...
Private mvarName As String
Private mvarPIN As String
Private mvarBalance As Currency

' Public Interface...
Public Property Get Name() As String
  Name = mvarName
End Property
```

```
Public Property Let Name(newValue As String)
  mvarName = newValue
End Property

Public Property Get PIN() As String
  PIN = mvarPIN
End Property

Public Property Let PIN(newValue As String)
  mvarPIN = newValue
End Property

Public Property Get Balance() As Currency
  Balance = mvarBalance
End Property

Public Sub Deposit(amount As Currency)
  mvarBalance = mvarBalance + amount
End Sub

Public Sub Withdraw(amount As Currency)
  If amount < mvarBalance Then
    mvarBalance = mvarBalance - amount
  Else
    MsgBox "There is not enough in the account!"
  End If
End Sub
```

The code above defines the **CAccount** class. Access to the private instance variables is through the three *Properties* defined – **Name**, **PIN**, and **Balance**. We provide **Property Let** and **Property Get** methods for **Name** and **PIN**, but only a **Property Get** for **Balance**. This is because we will need to be able to read the balance of an account, but can only change the amount by making deposits and withdrawals, which we provide methods for (this is how any bank account works).

Note that while a deposit can always be made, any attempt to withdraw an amount more than is in the account will result in an error message being displayed (in the sub **Withdraw**). In effect this piece of code implements a *business rule* of the system. That is to say, the coding of the **Withdraw** method is a direct implementation of logic that is based on the workings of our notional bank, rather than on any specific programming requirements.

At this stage we can test (most of) the class in the Visual Basic Immediate window. This allows us to create object of the class, **Set/Get** property values and call on methods. The list of Immediate window commands and responses shown below shows a number of tests (the Visual Basic responses are shown in *italic* text). The response to an attempt to withdraw more than the account balance is shown in Figure 7.10.

Figure 7.10   *Bank account operations, showing the result of an attempt to withdraw more than there is in the account.*

```
Set A = New CAccount
? A.Balance
   0
A.Name = "J Smith"
A.PIN = "1234"
? A.Name
   J Smith
? A.PIN
   1234
A.Deposit 150.00
? A.Balance
   150
A.Withdraw 50.00
? A.Balance
   100
A.Withdraw 200
```

Now that we know that the **CAccount** class works, we can proceed with building the user-interface.

Developing the ATM entry screen

By starting a new Visual Basic project, we will automatically have been given a default main form. In normal circumstances, this will become the main form of the application. Therefore, we would change its name (e.g. to **frmATM**) and add controls as appropriate: a **TextBox** (for accepting the PIN number) a **ListBox** (to display the names of accounts) and a **Label** control (to display the entry prompt shown – 'Type PIN Code and Press Enter'). The result will be a Visual Basic form as shown in Figure 7.11.

By convention, the controls the user will interact with are given names that reflect their type and purpose (**lstAccounts** for the ListBox, and **txtPIN** for the TextBox). There is no need for such care with the label control, since this will not be referred to in program code.

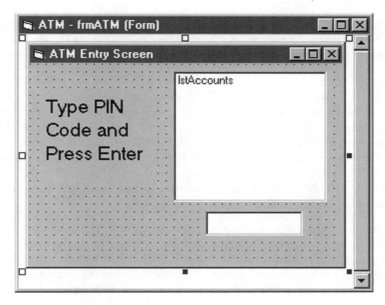

Figure 7.11 *The ATM entry form.*

Each control may also have some properties to set up. For the TextBox, the **PasswordChar** property allows us to indicate what character will be displayed for each password keystroke (an asterisk, *, is usual). For the ListBox, we can set the **Sorted** property to True so that the list of account names is displayed in alphabetically sorted order.

The ATM entry screen in operation

In operation, a user will select an account name from the list, and then enter a PIN number. Pressing the Enter key after this should cause the password to be checked against the name, and the appropriate account screen to be displayed if it checks out. In terms of events, the sequence should operate as follows:

1. When the application first executes, the collection of Account objects needs to be created. In a more realistic simulation, this information would be read from a file of account data, a facility that we will examine in a later chapter. For now, our simple simulation will construct a few account objects as it starts up. To do this, we will need to provide some *initialization code*. This is code that will be executed at the start of a run to put the application into a valid state. The most suitable event for initiating this is the **Form_Load** event for the ATM entry screen, since this will be the first event to 'fire' in the application.

2. The names of the accounts in the collection should be displayed in the list box. To do this, we can iterate through the collection, adding each account name found to the list box. We can also do this in **Form_Load** at start-up.

3. When an account is selected from the list box, the focus should move to the PIN TextBox. A cursor should then display in it allowing the user to type into the text box. We can use the Click event for the ListBox (`lstAccounts_Click`) for this.

4. Once the user has typed the PIN number, pressing Enter while in the PIN TextBox should cause the PIN to be checked against the Account name selected. If it fails to check out, an error message should be displayed; otherwise, the ATM transaction screen should be activated, with the details of the selected account in place. In this case we need to trap key-presses in the TextBox (using the `txtPIN_KeyPress` event) but only perform the PIN check when the Enter key has been pressed. We can place an `If..Then` structure in the event-handler to filter out other key-presses.

As shown in the design diagram, the Accounts collection will be available to the ATM entry screen, since this screen is responsible for checking PIN against Account name, for which access to all of the account objects is required. It will therefore be a simple matter to extract the appropriate account from the collection (we can use the Account name as the look-up key for the collection) to check the PIN entry.

Building and using the collection of account objects

This operation is crucial to the rest of the simulation – when the application starts up, we need to build a collection of account objects to work with. In a real application, we would have a disk file of objects (presumably created in some other application program) and would need to read the data from this file and create objects to encapsulate each record. In this simulation, we will simply create the objects within the `Form_Load` event-handler for the main form. We can create a `Private` sub in the form code to do this:

```
Private Sub BuildAccountList()
Dim A As CAccount
   ' Create the collection..
   Set Accounts = New Collection
   ' Now add some objects..
   Set A = New CAccount          ' Create an account
   A.Name = "J Smith"            ' Give it a name..
   A.PIN = "1234"                ' and a PIN..
   A.Deposit 100                 ' and a Balance..
   Accounts.Add A, A.Name        ' Then add it to the collection,
                                 ' using the Name property as a key.

   Set A = New CAccount
   A.Name = "M Brown"
   A.PIN = "4321"
   A.Deposit 150
   Accounts.Add A, A.Name
```

```
    Set A = New Caccount
    A.Name = "K Bright"
    A.PIN = "2468"
    A.Deposit 2500
    Accounts.Add A, A.Name
End Sub
```

Note that we can use a single **CAccount** reference variable to instantiate all of the objects. Since we are adding the objects immediately to the collection, we can reuse the **CAccount** reference variable to create the next object, knowing that the last one is still available from the collection.

By the end of the **BuildAccountList** process, we should have a valid collection of **CAccount** objects, each of which can be accessed individually by referring to it as part of the collection, or by assigning it to a reference variable while we work with it. For example, if we wanted to know the balance of an account in the collection that belonged to 'J Smith', we could use either of the following procedures:

```
MsgBox Accounts.Item("J Smith").Balance
```

or

```
Dim A As CAccount
   Set A = Accounts.Item("J Smith")
   MsgBox A.Balance
```

Note that although the second version is more long-winded, we might wish to perform a number of operations on this object, and so assigning it to a reference variable can make the sequence less tedious to type and faster in operation.

Building the list of accounts is a necessary starting point. However, the application requires that we make this list visible in a list box, so a procedure to fill up the list box from the collection will also be necessary:

```
Private Sub FillListBox()
Dim A As CAccount
   lstAccounts.Clear        ' Make sure the list is clear first.
   For Each A In Accounts
     lstAccounts.AddItem A.Name
   Next
End Sub
```

This short sub cycles through each **CAccount** object in the collection, extracting the **Name** property and placing it in the list box. Since it is possible that the contents of the collection may change (e.g. a customer joins the bank or leaves), this sub is also useful for updating the list box to be in step with the collection.

There is a strong advantage to exposing the collection's contents in this way. Recall that we can use a **Key** when adding an item to a collection, and that this key can then be used to retrieve the object (if, for example, we wished to perform some operation on an account). In our example, we will use the **Name** property of an account as the key value. However, you should be aware that this would not happen in real life, where two 'J Smith' entries would make it difficult to identify which account 'J Smith' identified. In a real situation, a bank would use an account number as a unique identifier for an account.

Since we fill up the **ListBox** with the **Name** property of each **CAccount**, we have a very easy way of referring to an object selected in the list box. This relies on a specific feature of a **ListBox** control: the selected item in the list (the one that is highlighted) is the **Text** property. Therefore, to retrieve the object referred to by the current selection in the **ListBox**:

```
Dim A As CAccount
   Set C = Accounts.Item(lstAccounts.Text)
   ' can go on to work with C...
```

The form code for the ATM entry screen

The entire code for this form is shown below:

```
Option Explicit

Private Accounts As New Collection    ' The accounts collection
Private thisAccount As CAccount       ' Reference to a selected account

Private Sub Form_Load()      ' Start-up code...
   BuildAccountList          ' Create the accounts collection
   FillListBox               ' Place account names in the list box
End Sub

Private Sub BuildAccountList()
Dim A As CAccount
   ' Create the collection..
   Set Accounts = New Collection
   ' Now add some objects..
   Set A = New CAccount       ' Create an account
   A.Name = "J Smith"         ' Give it a name..
   A.PIN = "1234"             ' and a PIN..
   A.Deposit 100              ' and a Balance..
   Accounts.Add A, A.Name     ' Then add it to the collection,
                              ' using the Name property as a key.

   Set A = New CAccount
   A.Name = "M Brown"
   A.PIN = "4321"
   A.Deposit 150
   Accounts.Add A, A.Name
   Set A = New Caccount
   A.Name = "K Bright"
   A.PIN = "2468"
```

```
    A.Deposit 2500
    Accounts.Add A, A.Name
End Sub

Private Sub FillListBox()
Dim A As CAccount
    lstAccounts.Clear                    ' Make sure the list is clear first.
    For Each A In Accounts
        lstAccounts.AddItem A.Name   ' Add name to list box.
    Next
End Sub

Private Sub lstAccounts_Click()
    txtPIN.SetFocus                      ' Place a cursor in the PIN box.
End Sub

Private Sub txtPIN_KeyPress(KeyAscii As Integer)
    If KeyAscii = 13 Then            ' Enter key pressed
        ' Dispose of the key code...
        KeyAscii = 0
        ' Get the account object indicated by the listbox..
        Set thisAccount = Accounts.Item(lstAccounts.Text)
        ' Check the PIN code entered..
        If thisAccount.PIN = txtPIN.Text Then
            AccessAccount thisAccount
        Else
            MsgBox "ERROR - Wrong PIN Code"
        End If
        txtPIN.Text = ""                 ' Clear out the last PIN entered.
    End If
End Sub

Private Sub AccessAccount(A As CAccount)
    ' Temporary code to test access...
    MsgBox A.Name & " " & A.Balance
End Sub
```

Note that for the moment we have provided a simple sub, **AccessAccount**, that demonstrates our access to the account object by displaying its details in a message box. Once the ATM transaction screen is designed, we will amend this code so that it passes the object to that form for further processing. *It is always a good idea to test a form in isolation before connecting it with other forms.*

We can now run the application and test our ability to access an account and the file handling within the **CAccount** class. When first run, the entry screen should appear with the account names that were set up in **BuildAccountList** in the list box. Selecting a name should highlight the name (automatic in Visual Basic) and place a text-entry cursor in the PIN box, as shown in Figure 7.12.

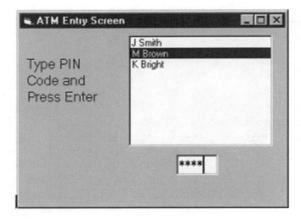

Figure 7.12 *The ATM entry form, with a name selected and a PIN number entered.*

Figure 7.13 *The result of the* **AccessAccount** *test method.*

When Enter is pressed, the system should respond with either an error message to indicate the PIN entered was wrongly entered, or a message box showing account details, as shown in Figure 7.13.

We can now go on to develop the ATM transaction form.

The ATM transaction form

Since we have done the bulk of the work of managing an account within the class module, developing this will be easy. The basic visual design of the form is as shown in Figure 7.14.

Note that **Label** controls have been used to display the name and balance; normally a **TextBox** would be used to display variable textual data, but in this case that would allow the user to edit the contents. We want to ensure that these controls display a true version of the account.

All of the controls whose name is shown above will be used in the correspondence between the ATM entry screen and the ATM transaction screen. It is therefore important to give these controls meaningful names, so that program code that refers to them is easier to follow.

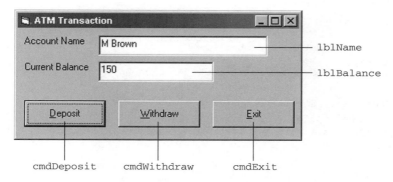

Figure 7.14   *The ATM transaction form.*

There is one further useful facility we can add to this form. The form will contain a reference variable to refer to the selected account object (**theAccount**). Following the principle of encapsulation, we should make this a **Private** member variable of the form. In order that this is made to refer to the account selected in the ATM entry form, we can add a **Property Set** method to the form that will pass the account object reference to the private member variable. The coding of this is simple:

```
Public Property Set Account(account As CAccount)
   Set theAccount = account
   lblName.Caption = account.Name
   lblBalance.Caption = account.Balance
   Me.Show vbModal
End Property
```

In fact, we have taken advantage of a side-effect of Visual Basic's object model for form objects. Whenever any property of a form is referred to in code, if the form is not already in memory, it is loaded into memory ready to use. By adding a new property to the form, we can arrange all of the necessary steps required for setting up and displaying the form in the coding of this property. As a result, a simple assignment in the ATM entry form code:

```
Set frmTransaction.Account = thisAccount
```

will also serve to load the form into memory, pass the account properties into the display labels (setting the two caption properties) and then display the form (**Me.Show vbModal** is the command to display the form that houses this code (**Me**) modally – modal simply means that the user will have to close the form to return to the ATM entry screen).

Most of the work of the ATM transaction screen is done in the event-handlers for the three buttons. In each case, the coding is simple. The full code for the form is shown below:

```
Option Explicit

Private theAccount As CAccount

Public Property Set Account(account As CAccount)
   Set theAccount = account
   lblName.Caption = theAccount.Name
   lblBalance.Caption = theAccount.Balance
   Me.Show vbModal
End Property

Private Sub cmdDeposit_Click()
Dim deposit As Currency
   deposit = InputBox("How much to deposit")
   theAccount.Deposit deposit
   lblBalance.Caption = theAccount.Balance
End Sub

Private Sub cmdWithdraw_Click()
Dim withdrawal As Currency
   withdrawal = InputBox("How much to withdraw")
   theAccount.Withdraw withdrawal
   lblBalance.Caption = theAccount.Balance
End Sub

Private Sub cmdExit_Click()
   Unload Me
End Sub
```

The deposit and withdraw buttons do the expected jobs, making use of **InputBox()** statements to get cash amounts from the user and then passing these to the account via the Deposit/Withdraw methods. For the Exit button, a simple **Unload Me** call will unload the specified form. The keyword **Me** is a simple reference to the current form in this case. In fact, this keyword works as a self-reference for any Visual Basic object. Note that there is no need to update the selected account object, since the reference **theAccount** is simply another reference to the account referred to in the ATM entry form as **thisAccount** and in the **Accounts** collection. As we update it in the **Transaction** screen, it is updated throughout the program.

Finishing touches

At this stage, our ATM simulation is almost complete. We could certainly improve on it by getting rid of the **InputBox** statements used in the ATM transaction screen (using other controls to collect user input). With a bit more work, we could get the program to fully simulate an ATM; this would involve more class design, since we would need to record each transaction as an individual object so that we could print or display a statement.

By far the most limiting feature of the current version is that every time the program is run, the account balances return to their initial values. To fix this, we will have to give the **CAccount** objects the ability to save the transient information stored in their member variables to a disk file and retrieve it again. This property of a class of objects, known as *persistence*, is a feature we will look at in a later chapter.

7.6   Review questions

1. Complete the following:
    (a) A Visual Basic _____ is a user-interface class definition.
    (b) Form designs can include descriptions of how the form should react to external stimuli, called _____-_____.
    (c) User-interface objects placed on a form are called _____.
    (d) An _____ is a signal from a control to a form that some external stimulus has occurred.
    (e) A Visual Basic form name is both an object identifier and a class name, a feature known as _____-_____.
    (f) Settings in forms and controls are known as _____.

2. Assuming we decided to progress with a fuller implementation of an ATM simulation, draw up an object model (specifying methods and properties for each class) that defines an account such that it contains a collection of transaction objects. Each transaction should have Amount, Type (Deposit/Withdraw) and Date properties.

3. A TextBox, **txtNewUserName**, and a ListBox, **lstUserNames**, are placed on a form along with a command button, **cmdAddUser**. Write an event-handler for the command button's **Click** event that will add the contents of the TextBox to the ListBox, and then clear the TextBox. Give the event-handler the name that the Visual Basic IDE would have automatically given it.

7.7   Practical exercises:
A class with an associated form

In this exercise, we will build a new class that can provide a useful facility to many programs. Objects of the **CScheduleItem** class will have Text, Date, Time, Alarm and Priority properties, making them suitable as entry objects in diary, agenda and personal information manager programs. A form to support the class will be designed, and will support creation and editing of **CScheduleItems**.

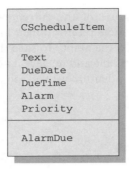

Figure 7.15   *Class diagram.*

Exercise 1:   Defining the `CScheduleItem` class

We can quickly define the required properties and methods of a `CScheduleItem`, making use of a simple class diagram (Figure 7.15).

The `Text` property will allow a message to be stored and retrieved, while `DueDate` and `DueTime` will do the same for the date and time setting. The `Alarm` property will indicate whether an alarm is set for this item, and the `Priority` property will allow one of three settings – `Low`, `Normal` and `High`. The `AlarmDue` method will return `True` if an alarm is set and it is time to sound it, `False` otherwise.

Internally, we will use a single variable of type `Date` to store both `DueDate` and `DueTime` properties, since the Visual Basic `Date` type allows this. `Text` will be stored as a string, `Alarm` as a Boolean and `Priority` as an `Enumeration`, a Visual Basic construct that allows us to store a simple numeric code with a meaningful name.

First, start a new Visual Basic project. Name the project 'Agenda' by selecting the project in the Project Explorer and entering this as the project's Name property in the Properties window.

Add a new class to the project, and give it the name `CScheduleItem` in the Properties window.

Start the class definition by creating an *enumeration* of priority values. A Visual Basic `Enum` is a definition of a type of variable that can take on one of a fixed set of possible values. Enter the following into the class's code window.

```
Option Explicit

Enum PrioritySetting
  psLow = 0
  psNormal = 1
  psHigh = 2
End Enum
```

Note that each priority setting has a prefix – `ps` – indicating that this is a PrioritySetting value. This is a Visual Basic programming convention used in all of the provided enumerations. We will now be able to create `PrioritySetting` variables that can take on one of the three defined values.

 Add the member variables to the class.

```
Private mvarText As String
Private mvarDateTime As Date
Private mvarAlarm As Boolean
Private mvarPriority As PrioritySetting
```

These four instance variables constitute the state of a `CScheduleItem` object. We should now provide property methods to allow the state variables to be accessed from external code.

 Add the `Property Get` and `Let` methods for the member variables.

```
Public Property Get Text() As String
  Text = mvarText
End Property

Public Property Let Text(ByVal NewValue As String)
  mvarText = NewValue
End Property

Public Property Get DueDate() As Date
  DueDate = Format(mvarDateTime, "Short Date")
End Property

Public Property Let DueDate(ByVal NewValue As Date)
  ' Ensure there is no time component in the new value..
  NewValue = Int(NewValue)
  ' Now add this date to the time part of the current
  ' DateTime setting..
  mvarDateTime = mvarDateTime - Int(mvarDateTime) + NewValue
End Property

Public Property Get DueTime() As Date
  DueTime = Format(mvarDateTime, "Short Time")
End Property
```

```
Public Property Let DueTime(ByVal NewValue As Date)
  ' Remove any date component of the new value..
  NewValue = NewValue - Int(NewValue)
  ' Add this to the date part of the current DateTime setting..
  mvarDateTime = Int(mvarDateTime) + NewValue
End Property

Public Property Get Alarm() As Boolean
  Alarm = mvarAlarm
End Property

Public Property Let Alarm(ByVal NewValue As Boolean)
  mvarAlarm = NewValue
End Property

Public Property Get Priority() As PrioritySetting
  Priority = mvarPriority
End Property

Public Property Let Priority(ByVal NewValue As PrioritySetting)
  mvarPriority = NewValue
End Property
```

Most of the above code is straightforward. However, the **Get** and **Let DueDate** and **DueTime** property methods require some further explanation.

Visual Basic date and time storage

Visual Basic uses a single data type to represent any instant in time within a wide range of dates and times. One **Date** variable can be used to store a date and a time simultaneously, using the simple method of storing whole days as the integer part of a floating-point decimal number, and the time as the fractional part. The integer part is the number of whole days since 30th December 1899, and the fractional part is the fraction of a 24-hour day. Therefore, 0.5 represents midday on 30/12/1899.

If we wish to separate the parts of a single **Date** variable into date and time components, it is a matter of extracting the integer part and the fractional part. Combining separate date and time parts requires us to reverse this. The Visual Basic **Format()** function can be used to return string components representing date and time (look up the help pages for the **Format** function and predefined date and time formats).

  Define the **AlarmDue** method.

```
Public Function AlarmDue() As Boolean
  If Alarm Then
```

```
      If (Now >= mvarDateTime) Then
         Alarm = False
         AlarmDue = True
      End If
   End If
End Function
```

This method simply checks whether an alarm is set, and if so, checks whether it has happened yet. If the alarm is due, the `Alarm` setting is cleared to prevent it continuing to be due for the rest of time. Note that we determine if the alarm is due by checking whether we are at or beyond the alarm time (>= operator). If we simply looked for the time being equal to the alarm time, there is a good chance that the alarm might be missed, since the check is only performed when the `AlarmDue` method is invoked.

 Save the project into a new folder.

This completes the `CScheduleItem` class definition. As usual, we should test the class fully before we try to use it in a project. Tests on this class can be made in Visual Basic's Immediate window. Before we commence testing, a useful tip is to declare an object variable of the appropriate type, since Visual Basic will then be able to provide help in the form of pop-up lists of methods and properties, as shown in Figure 7.16.

Visual Basic is only able to do this if it can determine the type of object it is dealing with. This in turn requires that the object must be assigned to a pre-declared variable, even if used in the Immediate window. We will start the tests by adding a code module to the project, and declaring a variable **As Public CScheduleItem** in it.

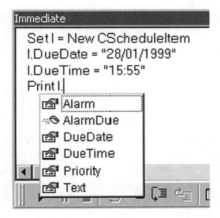

Figure 7.16   *Pop-up property and method lists.*

Add a code module to the project by right-clicking on the Project Explorer, and selecting **Add/Module**.

 Add a new object variable declaration to the top of the module.

```
Public I As CScheduleItem
```

Now when we assign an object to this variable and refer to the object, we will be offered a list of properties and methods.

 Enter the following sequence of statements into the Immediate window to test the various methods of the **CScheduleItem** object.

```
Set I = New CScheduleItem
I.DueDate = Date
I.DueTime = DateAdd("n", 2, Time)
I.Alarm = True
Print I.DueDate
  15/01/00
Print I.DueTime
  20:17:00
I.Priority = psNormal
Print I.Priority
  1
I.Text = "A Test Schedule Item"
Print I.Text
  A Test Schedule Item
Print I.AlarmDue
  False
Print I.AlarmDue ** NOTE At time of writing, It is
                15/01/2000 at 20:17:00
  True
Print I.Alarm
  False
```

Note that the date entered during this test was the current date (returned from the **Date** function). The time entered was two minutes ahead of the time when the test sequence was started. The **DateAdd** function adds the specified number (2) of time intervals ('n' = minutes) to the specified date or time (the return from the **Time** function). The statement marked ** was entered immediately after this time. When performing this test, you should adjust the date and time you set accordingly.

We can now go on to create a user interface that will work with objects of this class.

Exercise 2:   Creating the `frmScheduleItem` form class

The project that the new `CScheduleItem` class was added to will already have a form called `Form1`. We will start by renaming this form and adding the controls necessary for it to display a `CScheduleItem` object.

Rename `Form1` of the current project to `frmScheduleItem` by selecting the form's entry in the Project Explorer, and changing its `Name` property in the Properties window.

Add controls to the form so that it appears in the form design window as shown in Figure 7.17.

The *altered* properties of the controls on the form are listed in Table 7.3. All other properties have been left with their default values.

Note that in addition to these controls, labels have been added to indicate to the user what the various text boxes and other controls are for. Use the `Caption` property to change the text they display. There is no need to change the Name properties of these label controls, since they will not be referred to in program code. One useful tip is to set the `AutoSize` property of each of them to `True` so that they automatically grow or shrink to fit the text caption set for them.

Once you complete setting up the layout of the controls and changing their property values, save the project again.

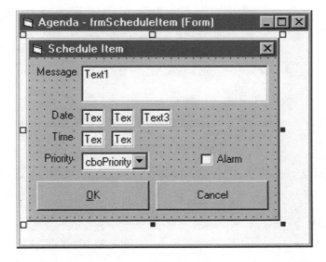

Figure 7.17   *A form design to act as a user-interface to a* `CScheduleItem`

Table 7.3 *Property settings for all of the user-interface controls on the form.*

Control type	Property name	Property setting	Description
Form	Caption	Schedule item	Gives the form a heading
	BorderStyle	3 – fixed dialog	Prevents the user resizing the form
TextBox	Name	`TxtText`	Displays the item's text message and allows it to be edited
	MultiLine	`True`	Allows a message of several lines to be added
TextBox	Name	`txtDay`	Display/edit the day part of a date
TextBox	Name	`txtMonth`	Display/edit the month part
TextBox	Name	`txtYear`	Display/edit the year part
TextBox	Name	`txtHour`	Display/edit the hour part of a time
TextBox	Name	`txtMinute`	Display/edit the minute part
ComboBox	Name	`cboPriority`	Display/edit the priority of a schedule item
	Style	2 – drop-down list	The user can only select from the drop-down list and is not able to type text into the box

	List	`Low`
		`Medium`
		`High`
			The list of possible priorities, displayed as text

CheckBox	Name	`chkAlarm`	Display/edit alarm status
	Caption	`Alarm`	
CommandButton	Name	`cmdOK`	The OK button of the dialog box
	Caption	`OK`	Note – defines an accelerator key
CommandButton	Name	`cmdCancel`	The Cancel button of the dialog box
	Caption	`Cancel`	
	Cancel	`True`	The cancel property makes the button respond to a press of the Escape key

Adding code to the `frmScheduleItem` form class

The form should now have an appearance that makes it suitable for using with an object from the `CScheduleItem` class. To complete it, we need to add code to associate the form with schedule item objects.

We can make this association in a number of ways. One method would be to give entire responsibility for displaying and managing the form to a `CScheduleItem` object. However, this would limit the types of interactions that the form could cope with, since all of the code controlling it would be in an object of a different class. Another method would be simply to place all of the code associating a schedule with a form in an application that used them both. However, this would go against the object oriented principle of encapsulation.

A preferable method of making form and schedule items work together is to pass a reference to a schedule item into the form. The form can then make use of the schedule item's properties to display the appropriate information, and could update the properties if the user of the form changed any of them. This is the method we will use, and so the starting point is to provide some way by which we can pass a `CScheduleItem` reference into the form.

 Open up the form's code window, and add a declaration for a **Private** object variable.

```
Option Explicit

Private mvarScheduleItem As CScheduleItem
```

An object of the form class can now store a reference to a schedule item. Using the reference variable, it can access the properties of a schedule item object and display them in its text boxes. To enable this to happen, we need a way of passing a reference to a `CScheduleItem` object into the form. We can use a **Property Set** for this.

 Create a **Property Set** method on the form.

```
Public Property Set ScheduleItem(SItem As CScheduleItem)
    Set mvarScheduleItem = SItem
    With mvarScheduleItem
      txtText =.Text
      txtDay = Format(.DueDate, "dd")
      txtMonth = Format(.DueDate, "mm")
      txtYear = Format(.DueDate, "yyyy")
      txtHour = Format(.DueTime, "hh")
      txtMinute = Format(.DueTime, "Nn")
      cboPriority.ListIndex =.Priority
```

```
    If.Alarm Then
      chkAlarm.Value = 1
    Else
      chkAlarm.Value = 0
    End If
  End With
End Property
```

The **Property Set** method shown will pass a reference to a **CScheduleItem** object to the form. Additionally, code has been added (inside the **With..End With** block) to cause the object's properties to be displayed on the controls on the form. Note that we do not need to spell out the **Text** property of each of the text boxes explicitly. **Text** is the *default property* of a **TextBox**, and is assumed if no other property is referred to.

The **ListIndex** property of the **ComboBox** control is set directly from the Priority property of the schedule item. This works because the actual values set in the **PrioritySetting** enumeration correspond well to the range of **ListIndex** values for the list box. The three items added to the List property of the list box have indices 0, 1 and 2, since all list box lists start at item number 0.

At this stage, we could test the form to see if it displayed a **CScheduleItem** object properly. This can be done from the Immediate window (Figure 7.18).

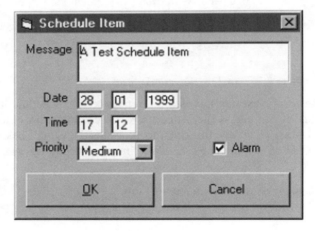

Figure 7.18   *A* **CScheduleItem** *being displayed by the* **frmScheduleItem** *form.*

Close down the form's designer window, and then enter the following sequence of commands into the Immediate window.

```
Set I = New CScheduleItem
I.DueDate = "28/01/1999"
I.DueTime = "17:52"
I.Priority = psNormal
```

```
I.Text = "A Test Schedule Item"
I.Alarm = True
Set frmScheduleItem.ScheduleItem=I
frmScheduleItem.Show vbModal
```

As a result, the form should display the details of the schedule item object. Neither of the buttons will work, and any changes made will not be reflected in the object after the form closes.

The final stages are to add code to make the form react to presses on either of the command buttons.

   Add event-handlers for the OK and Cancel buttons.

```
Private Sub cmdCancel_Click()
  Unload Me
End Sub

Private Sub cmdOK_Click()
  With mvarScheduleItem
    .Text = txtText
    If IsDate(txtDay & "/" & txtMonth & "/" & txtYear) Then
      .DueDate = txtDay & "/" & txtMonth & "/" & txtYear
    Else
      Exit Sub
    End If
    If IsDate(txtHour & ":" & txtMinute) Then
      .DueTime = txtHour & ":" & txtMinute
    Else
      Exit Sub
    End If
    .Priority = cboPriority.ListIndex
    .Alarm = (chkAlarm.Value = 1)
  End With
  Unload Me
End Sub
```

The code for the Cancel button is simple since it only has to close down the form. That for the OK button is more complex, since it must first update the schedule item object's properties. Note that the date and time strings are built up by adding together the day/month/year and hour/minute parts, incorporating '/' and ':' characters as appropriate. We also check the date and time entries using the **IsDate()** function, a useful function for determining that a string can be converted to the appropriate type. Visual Basic takes care of converting the resulting strings to date and time values as it applied them to the properties.

Save the project and test the classes.

At this stage, the important parts of the project are complete, and we should make sure it is all saved. One final test we can perform is that the class and form class work as expected in a program environment. One simple test we can make would be to create a sub in the code module added to the project earlier. This sub can be coded to create a **CScheduleItem** object, which we can then display, edit and interrogate.

Add the following sub to the code module in the project.

```
Public Sub TestClasses()
Dim SI As New CScheduleItem
Dim f As New frmScheduleItem
  Set f.ScheduleItem = SI
  f.Show vbModal
  MsgBox SI.Text
  MsgBox SI.DueDate
  MsgBox SI.DueTime
  MsgBox SI.Priority
  MsgBox SI.Alarm
  While Not SI.AlarmDue
     DoEvents                 ' Idle, but let other applications
                              ' use the processor
  Wend
  MsgBox "Alarm: " & SI.Text
End Sub
```

To run the test, simply enter **TestClasses** at the Immediate window. Note that when you fill in the time and date in the form, you should enter the current date, and a time that is only a few minutes from the current time at most, since Visual Basic will execute the **While** loop until that time arrives.

Suggested exercises

We will create a project that makes use of schedule items in a later chapter. As a guide to your own use of the classes, the following points will be useful:

- You can add schedule items to a collection, and therefore create a diary of entries. To test for alarms, a **Timer** control with an Interval property setting of around 10 seconds can be used. The **Timer** event-handler should then contain a **For..Each** loop, sending the **AlarmDue** method to each schedule item in the collection in turn, and react appropriately.

- The form is a separate class since a form always has a relatively large overhead of memory and processor demand. Forms should be created and destroyed as required rather than having one form object per schedule item.

- You may consider creating additional methods for the classes to make them more useful to your application. For example, you could add contact details or a duration setting for a scheduled item.

7.8 Answers to questions

QUESTION 7.1

Encapsulation is there to make sure that a casual user of a class is not allowed to access the internal mechanisms of a class programmatically. It works by making sure that the sensitive internal components are inaccessible by virtue of their `Private` declarations. Event-handlers are automatically given `Private` scope by Visual Basic, and so cannot be accessed programmatically. However, they do execute automatically in response to events. This, however, is more likely to strengthen encapsulation, since the class designer is given the ability effectively to define the circumstances under which an internal, `Private` method is called.

Visual Basic can differentiate between different events passed to an object or form in the following way. Every event-handler has a name that is automatically set by the IDE to indicate the object that sends the event and the specific event – e.g. `Command1_Click`. The Visual Basic event-handling system can work out where an event has come from and what caused it, and therefore which event-handler to execute.

QUESTION 7.2

Suitable names are as follows:

(a) `txtCustomerName`

(b) `lstCustomerNames`

(c) `picCustomerPhoto`

(d) `lstStart` and `lstDestination`

(e) `frmTransactions`

QUESTION 7.3

(a) A statement that will remove the selected item from the list box `lstCustomers` is
`lstCustomers.Remove lstCustomers.ListIndex`

(b) The following conditional statement could be used to control the removal of an item from the list box so that only a selected item would be removed:

```
If lstCustomers.ListIndex > -1 Then
   lstCustomers.Remove lstCustomers.ListIndex
End If
```

QUESTION 7.4

One reason is that we can think of a form as providing a service for an object – displaying it and allowing the program user to edit it. If the default form were used to provide this service, it would cause at best confusion and at worst program errors if more than one object were to access the form at a time. By using form classes in the same way as normal objects, i.e. using **New** to create an object of the class as and when it is required, each object working with a form will have its own instance of it. Multiple copies of a form design or form class would therefore exist in their own right to provide services to the object that instantiates them.

QUESTION 7.5

The picture of an account is not realistic, since in a real account, every transaction would have to be recorded for security, and to enable the production of statements. Each account would therefore have to incorporate not only just a record of the current balance, but also a history of how that balance was arrived at. The standard way of doing this is for an account to contain a collection of transaction records or transaction objects, and to recalculate the current balance by counting through each transaction in turn. A statement could then be generated by making each transaction generate a line of it.

7.9   Answers to review questions

1.   (a) *A Visual Basic* form *is a user-interface class definition.*

(b) *Form designs can include descriptions of how the form should react to external stimuli, called* event-handlers.

(c) *User-interface objects placed on a form are called* controls.

(d) *An* event *is a signal from a control to a form that some external stimulus has occurred.*

(e) *A Visual Basic form name is both an object identifier and a class name, a feature known as* name-overloading.

(f) *Settings in forms and controls are known as* properties.

2. *Assuming we decided to progress with a fuller implementation of an ATM simulation, draw up an object model (specifying methods and properties for each class) that defines an account such that it contains a collection of transaction objects. Each transaction should have Amount, Type (Deposit/Withdraw) and Date properties.*

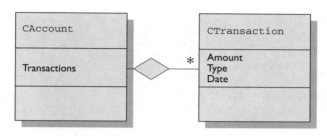

3. *A TextBox,* **txtNewUserName**, *and a ListBox,* **lstUserNames**, *are placed on a form along with a command button,* **cmdAddUser**. *Write an event-handler for the command button's* **Click** *event that will add the contents of the TextBox to the ListBox, and then clear the TextBox. Give the event-handler the name that the Visual Basic IDE would have automatically given it.*

```
Private Sub cmdAddUser_Click()
    lstUserNames.AddItem txtNewUserName.Text
    txtNewUsername.Text = ""
End Sub
```

CHAPTER 8

Objects as building blocks

One of the main points about object oriented programming is that applications are built by connecting objects together. Sharing the workload is a technique used in many forms of construction, and OOP makes it possible to think of programs as collaborations of actors doing a job. However, sharing the workload is only possible if some form of co-ordination is employed. In all large-scale endeavours, and even in organic systems, some form of executive structure is used to ensure that operations are properly directed. Object oriented programs too should be based on some form of structure.

By the end of this chapter, you should be able to:

- describe the importance of structure in an object oriented program,

- choose from a number of structural models when deciding on the organization of a piece of software,

- create associations and hierarchies of objects in an object model,

- model the structure of an application along the same lines as a real-world system.

8.1   Object oriented program structure

The emphasis of this book so far has been on the development of single classes and simple collaborations between objects of a small number of classes. However, it should be clear that object oriented programming is largely about creating structures, using objects as building blocks. Chapter 2 discussed the various ways that objects or classes could be associated with other objects or classes, and in this chapter we will go on to realize these associations in practice.

Several different forms of relationships between objects or classes were discussed:

- Inheritance, in which a class inherited either code (code inheritance) or interface definitions (interface inheritance) from an existing class to create a new class with additional or different capabilities

- Composition, in which an object that is a component of a new object performs some of the work of the new object's properties or methods

- Aggregation, in which members of one or more classes were incorporated into the definition of another class to create whole–part structures

- Message passing, in which a member of one class can elicit the services of one or more members of other classes by sending messages to it or them.

In Visual Basic, the central mechanism that allows us to implement these types of relationship is the use of object reference variables. We can extend an existing class by incorporating an object variable for that class into a new class definition and instantiating and using the object to perform some of the core services of the new class. We can create a composite or aggregate object by incorporating one or more object variables for existing classes into a new class and using these components as an assembly in the new class. Finally, we can create transient collaborations between objects by passing messages, or invoking the methods and accessing the properties of one object from another.

Why use structure, or 'avoiding the God object'

One question worth answering before we continue is 'why should we bother developing and working with complex structures of objects when we can simply create one object or class that contains properties and methods to do all that we need?'. The question is a good one, since it gets to the heart of object oriented programming. Before object oriented programming became popular, most software was written as a structured set of subroutines and functions that were not organized as methods of a range of classes. In object oriented terms, a program was a single object that contained declarations of every data member and definitions of every sub and function required. Structured programming, as this model of software development was called, relied on the ability of the programmer to organize the operations of a program to work on the appropriate data by creating the necessary associations between code and data in the program code itself.

The limitation of this form of programming was found to be the need to make these associations explicit. A programmer would organize the data within a program into some structure, for example a list, and would then create subs and functions to operate on this list. The programmer would need to remember what subs and functions worked with what bits of data, since there was no natural association between them.

Of course, since this was the normal way to create software, programmers did not see anything strange or inefficient with this way of working. In fact, the roots of object oriented programming as we have come to know it were formed in the imaginative way that programmers developed a form of object orientation within their structured program code.

Niklaus Wirth, one of the founding fathers of modern programming, presented a clear argument for the use of structure in software in a book entitled *Algorithms + Data Structures = Programs*. In this, he detailed how structured software could be developed by creating data structures, organizations of variables into logical structures such as lists, dictionaries, trees and graphs, and developing algorithms that would manage these structures in a consistent way.

This is an ideal that is still perfectly valid in object oriented programming, but as object oriented programmers we have the distinct advantage of not having to manage the associations between the algorithms and the data structures. Object structures contain their own algorithms, so we can concentrate on the conceptual requirements of the structure, trusting it to manage its components properly.

It is clear with the benefit of hindsight that the problem with structured programming was that programmers were putting all of the data and functionality into a single object – the program. A common error made by an experienced structured programmer when working with an object oriented language for the first time is to place the entire functionality of the program into a single, very complex object. The phrase 'the God object' has been coined to describe this flawed approach.

As object oriented programmers, we should aim to avoid creating the God object in our programs, and instead assign the various responsibilities of a program into a range of small and efficient classes, making the objects of these classes collaborate among themselves to achieve the overall aims of a system. By working in this way, we can reduce the complexity of complex operations by delegation, improve the maintainability of software by keeping classes and objects simple enough to be manageable, and reuse much of the work that we expend on a system in other systems.

QUESTION 8.1

From the previous paragraph: 'we can reduce the complexity of complex operations by delegation'. When a Visual Basic program starts to execute, either a form or a specially named subroutine in a code module, sub Main, has initial control:

(a) If a form is the program's entry point, what object delegates responsibility to others?

(b) If sub Main is the entry point, what object does the delegation?

(c) How is this delegation effected?

Structures in the real world

Look around and you will see that structures are an important feature of everything. In the natural world, we can see structure everywhere, from the organization of the known universe into galaxies, solar systems, planets and satellites, to the formation of proteins into DNA, single-cell creatures, plants, fish and animals. In all cases, complex things are made up of lots of small things, organized as assemblies in some way.

In the environments created by humans, we see the same types of organization. The construction of buildings is as assemblies of bricks, metals and aggregates into walls, floors, ceilings, these into rooms, corridors and floors, and these into blocks and terraces. Telecommunications networks are huge assemblies of simple components, interconnected by sub-assemblies of routers, switches and optical fibre cables. There seem to be few, if any, examples of complex systems that are not assemblies of assemblies of assemblies of simple components.

Most computer software is written to model real-world systems in some way. Banking, publishing, communications systems, and even humble word-processing and games playing are in some way models of the real systems of money, conversation, pen-and-paper and spacecraft strategy wars. It seems only sensible, therefore, to consider building software models to maintain models of the same organizational forms as those found in the real world.

Object structures

Considering the richness and complexity of systems that can be modelled in computer programs, there are surprisingly few fundamental structural forms commonly used in software. This is a good thing, since software development is a complex enough process without the programmer needing to consider which structure to use from a bank of several hundred or several thousand. Beyond the simple individual associations, such as the example of an object with a form that can display it, as demonstrated in the previous chapter, we can classify the structures that we would normally compose sets of objects into as follows:

- Lists, in which objects are organized into continuous sequences. These are most often realized in Visual Basic as arrays or collections.

- Trees, which are organized as having a *root* element, which is connected to two or more *branch* elements, which in turn may be connected to two or more branch elements and so on until each branch terminates in *leaf* elements. In particular, a *binary tree* is one in which each branch element has up to two branches or leaves attached to it. Examples of trees are family trees, hierarchical assemblies and organizational structures. These can be implemented as hierarchical object aggregations in Visual Basic.

- Graphs, which are interconnections of elements that do not follow the regular list or tree structures described. For example, road maps or electrical circuit diagrams are frequently modelled as graphs. These can be modelled by lists of object references in Visual Basic.

These types of structures are illustrated in Figure 8.1.

In practice, there are a large number of other possible structural forms, but all are refinements of the above fundamental forms. For example, queues and stacks are a form of list, binary-trees, B-trees and AVL trees are forms of tree structure, and graphs can be organized as unidirectional or bidirectional structures, and as partially or wholly connected structures.

The type of object structure we use in a program depends on several things:

- The type of organizational form of which we wish to create a model. For example, we would probably write an application for storing and analyzing family trees using a tree structure, and a program to maintain parts lists would use list structures.

- The level of storage efficiency we require. For example, a large road map would ideally be stored in a graph structure, but we might decide to implement it in arrays to make more efficient use of computer memory or processor power.

- The level of computational efficiency we require. For example, a tree structure is often used to enable very quick searching of a lot of information.

In fact, the choice of structure can be made more complex because how we model a structure in a design may not be how it is finally realized in program code. Binary trees are often realized in arrays for reasons of speed or memory efficiency, or because of programming language limitations. We can distinguish between a ***logical structure***,

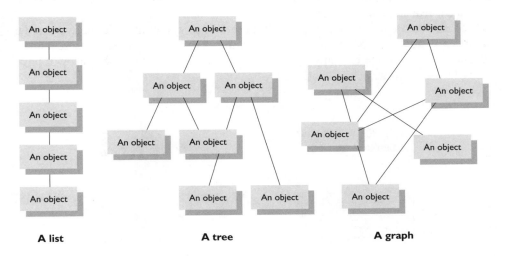

A list   **A tree**   **A graph**

Figure 8.1   *List, tree and graph structures.*

which is the idealized structure we would use to model a system and tends to be similar to the real-world structure, and a *physical structure*, that is the one we end up using in a program for reasons of efficiency, or reduced complexity, or some other expediency.

In the end, we tend to develop structural models that are right for the application we are developing, but that fit into the constraints of the programming language we use. In Visual Basic, arrays and collections are part of the language and so tend to be used for most of the structures we develop.

QUESTION 8.2

Most Microsoft applications have a structure based on the Collection class. Given that in real-world systems, there is a variety of structural forms (hierarchies, graphs, matrices, lists, etc.), how do you think this is possible? (For example, can you think of how a tree structure might be composed using only collections?)

8.2   An application example structure

In Chapter 7, we looked at the example of an Automatic Teller Machine, or AutoBank. The model we used of a bank account in this chapter was very simple, consisting of customer details and an account balance. It was pointed out in that chapter that this was not a very adequate model for several reasons, chiefly that unless we recorded the details of each individual transaction, we would not be able to produce a realistic bank statement.

We can use a class design diagram (Figure 8.2) to depict a more realistic model of a bank account. Note that the association between a **CBankAccount** and a **CTransaction** is a one-to-many aggregation. Generally one bank account will have many transactions associated with it.

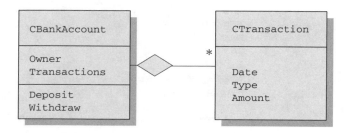

Figure 8.2   *A more realistic bank account model.*

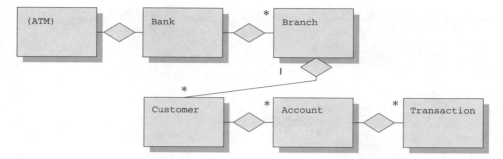

Figure 8.3   *A full ATM/bank model.*

QUESTION 8.3

When you first open a bank account, it will initially have no transactions associated with it.

(a)   How does this square with the one-to-many relationship described above?
(b)   What do you think is the logical (natural) structure of the one-to-many association between a bank account and its transactions?

In fact, although our model of a bank account is greatly improved by this structure, it still does not fully complete the picture, since an ATM allows access to many distinct bank accounts. In fact, the picture is even more complex, since the current generation of ATM machines allow customers from a wide range of different banks to access their accounts. A more realistic structure would be as shown in Figure 8.3.

Figure 8.3 shows something much closer to the real picture. An ATM allows a customer to access their account, which may be at a branch of any bank. The structural associations are that a bank may have many branches, each of which will have many customers. Each customer can have several accounts, which each have a number of transactions associated with them. The structure is almost a perfect hierarchy, apart from the connection between the ATM and all of the banks it can communicate with. The ATM passing a message to the bank that services a specific account makes this final association.

We can realize this structure in Visual Basic by using collections. A **CBank** object will have a **Branches** collection, and each **CBranch** will have a **Customers** collection. Each **CCustomer** object in this will have an **Accounts** collection, and so on.

8.3   Visual Basic collection classes

Visual Basic allows us to create collection classes, special-purpose classes that model the composition of an object by creating and maintaining a collection of other objects.

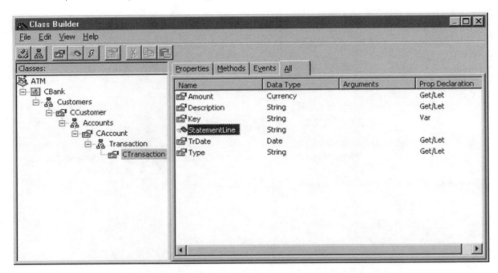

Figure 8.4 *Visual Basic's Class Builder add-in, showing an ATM class model.*

A collection class differs from the standard collection class provided with Visual Basic as it is designed to house a collection of a specific class of object, for example a banking transaction. Visual Basic's **Class Builder** add-in, a tool that is provided with the Professional and Enterprise versions of Visual Basic, can automatically generate collection classes based on a description of the component class defining the objects to be collected. Using this, it is an easy matter to set up a hierarchical structure of branches/customers/accounts, etc., or many other class models.

The class builder screen-shot shown in Figure 8.4 depicts the class structure of a somewhat simplified version of the full ATM model of Figure 8.3. It shows that an **ATM** object (at the top of the left-hand pane) contains a **CBank** object. Since this is an object reference, it can be used as a message-passing association, which is exactly what the model requires.

A **CBank** object contains a **Customers** collection. This is a customized collection class built by the class builder, and contains methods to add a new **CCustomer** object, remove a **CCustomer** object and provide a **Count** of **CCustomers** in the collection.

In addition, the **Customers** collection class provides a strange hidden method (that will be explained later) that goes by the name **NewEnum**. This method cannot be called on by a programmer using the collection class, but is used instead by Visual Basic to enable the **For..Each** syntax within the **CBank** class. This allows iteration through each object in the collection, making it possible to use code structures such as:

```
Dim C As CCustomer
  For Each C In Customers
    lstCustomers.AddItem C.Name
  Next
```

which would add each customer's name to a list box.

A similar collection class is defined as a component of the **CCustomer** class so that each **CAccount** owned by a customer can be iterated through. The **CAccount** class has a **Balance** method that returns the net account balance of the account by summing up all of the transactions. We could therefore use this collection to calculate the total worth of a **CCustomer** by iterating through each **CAccount** as follows:

```
' A Method of the CCustomer class...
Public Function TotalWorth() As Currency
Dim A As CAccount, TW As Currency
   For Each A In Accounts
     TW = TW + A.Balance
   Next
   TotalWorth = TW
End Function
```

At the lowest level of this object model, we have a **CTransaction** class, which models a single banking transaction. The right-hand pane of the Class Builder shown in Figure 8.4 shows all of the properties and methods defined for this class. A **CTransaction** has an **Amount** property, which is a currency value, and a **Description** property that stores a string description of the transaction (e.g. 'Cash Deposit'). A **StatementLine** method is a function that returns the **CTransaction** member data formatted as a single line string, as it would appear in a bank statement. It also has a **TrDate** that records the date of the transaction and a **TrType** property to indicate whether it was a deposit or a withdrawal.

A **CAccount** object can therefore use the **Transactions** collection generated by Visual Basic to retrieve aggregate account information, as the following method definitions for the **CAccount** class show:

```
Public Function Balance() As Currency
Dim T As CTransaction, B As Currency
   For Each T In Transactions
     If T.TrType = "Deposit" Then
       B = B + T.Amount
     Else
       B = B - T.Amount
     End If
   Next
   Balance = B
End Function

Public Function Statement() As String
Dim T As CTransaction, S As String
   For Each T In Transactions
     S = S & T.StatementLine & vbCrLf
   Next
   Statement = S
End Function
```

In the **Balance** method, we use **TrType** to determine whether a transaction's amount is to be added to or subtracted from the account balance. The **Statement** method adds together all of the **StatementLine** strings, placing a **vbCrLf** sequence between each to indicate the end of a line.

QUESTION 8.4

The **Balance** method in the **CAccount** class adds together all of the transactions in an account to calculate a final balance.

    (a) How could any initial account balance be taken into account in this?

    (b) What would be the major drawback of this method of storing all account transactions?

    (c) Can you think of a strategy that could be used to periodically clear the list of transactions in an account that is consistent with the model?

Collection class code

The interesting feature of the collection classes created in this way is the code that is automatically generated by the Class Builder to maintain the collection. The listing shown below is of the **Transactions** collection class, and was generated entirely (including the comments) by the Class Builder:

```
Option Explicit
' local variable to hold collection
Private mCol As Collection

Public Function Add(TrDate As Date, TrType As String, _
                Amount As Currency, Description As String, _
                Optional sKey As String) As CTransaction
  ' create a new object
  Dim objNewMember As CTransaction
  Set objNewMember = New CTransaction

  ' set the properties passed into the method
  objNewMember.TrDate = TrDate
  objNewMember.TrType = TrType
  objNewMember.Amount = Amount
  objNewMember.Description = Description

  If Len(sKey) = 0 Then
    mCol.Add objNewMember
  Else
    mCol.Add objNewMember, sKey
  End If
```

```vb
    ' return the object created
    Set Add = objNewMember
    Set objNewMember = Nothing
End Function


Public Property Get Item(vntIndexKey As Variant) As CTransaction
    ' used when referencing an element in the collection
    ' vntIndexKey contains either the Index or Key to the collection,
    ' this is why it is declared as a Variant
    ' Syntax: Set foo = x.Item(xyz) or Set foo = x.Item(5)
    Set Item = mCol(vntIndexKey)
End Property


Public Property Get Count() As Long
    ' used when retrieving the number of elements in the
    ' collection. Syntax: Debug.Print x.Count
    Count = mCol.Count
End Property


Public Sub Remove(vntIndexKey As Variant)
    ' used when removing an element from the collection
    ' vntIndexKey contains either the Index or Key, which is why
    ' it is declared as a Variant
    ' Syntax: x.Remove(xyz)
    mCol.Remove vntIndexKey
End Sub


Public Property Get NewEnum() As IUnknown
    ' this property allows you to enumerate
    ' this collection with the For..Each syntax
    Set NewEnum = mCol.[_NewEnum]
End Property


Private Sub Class_Initialize()
    ' creates the collection when this class is created
    Set mCol = New Collection
End Sub


Private Sub Class_Terminate()
    ' destroys collection when this class is terminated
    Set mCol = Nothing
End Sub
```

The collection class shown above is organized so that an application programmer who uses the class need never deal with an individual Transaction object. Can you think of reasons for and against this strategy?

When building a collection class like this, the Class Builder has to take a very simplistic view of the code that it generates, based on the small amount of information it has available. It knows nothing of the meaning of the structure we have laid out in it and so can only generate code to manipulate this structure as it would for any other collection class.

Components of a collection class

The collection class starts with a declaration, `mCol`, which is a normal collection object that will store all of the `CCustomer` objects added to the collection class object. Because this is an object variable, the collection object has to be instantiated in the `Class_Initialize()` and destroyed in the `Class_Terminate()`. (In fact, it does not have to be destroyed explicitly, since its object variable will be released when the collection class object goes out of scope, but the Class Builder takes a very belt-and-braces approach to much of the housekeeping code it generates.)

Other simple functions return the current `Count` of the internal collection object, `Remove` to remove an item, specified by key or number, from the internal collection object, and return an `Item`, using a `Property Get` to retrieve an object from the collection. Using the `Item` property, a user of an object of the `Transactions` collection class could access a specific transaction amount by using either of the syntax examples shown below:

```
SomeAccount.Transactions.Item(1).Amount   ' First CTransaction in
                                          ' the collection
SomeAccount.Transactions(1).Amount        ' Item is the default
                                          ' property of a
                                          ' collection class
```

Note that a collection class has a *default property* defined for it. This allows a programmer to omit the property name when accessing it. Recall that `Text` is the default property of a TextBox control, and so it is possible to nominate a default property in a user-defined class. The same mechanism can be used to define a default property in any user-defined class: simply place the cursor inside the property code, go to the **Tools** menu and select **Procedure Attributes**, press the **Advanced** button, and select **(Default)** from the **Procedure Id** combo-box.

The most useful method of the collection class is the `Add` method, since this is tailored to work with the specific type of collection. In this case, the `Add` method adds a new member to the Transactions collection by creating a new `CTransaction` object. The parameters passed to `Add` are all of the constituent components of a

CTransaction: TrDate, TrType, Amount and **Description**. In addition, you can supply an optional search key, **sKey**, so that a transaction can be retrieved by it. The **Add** method creates a new **CTransaction** object, applies these parameters to it as properties and then adds it to the internal collection, using a search key if one has been provided. Since it is defined as a function, it is also able to return a reference to the new **CTransaction** object. This allows us to work with that object as soon as it has been created:

```
Set objAccount = theBank.Customers("Joe Bloggs").Accounts("12345")
With objAccount.Transactions.Add "2/2/99", "Deposit", 150.00, _
                                 "Cash Deposit"
  MsgBox .StatementLine   ' .StatelemtLine is a method of the
                          ' newly added transaction.
End With
```

The above code fragment adds a new transaction of a cash deposit to account number '12345', belonging to customer 'Joe Bloggs'. The object reference returned by the **Add** method allows us to use object returned by the method call in a **With** statement. The **.Transactions** reference at the start of this **With** block is the **Transactions** property of the selected account object, and so we can use its **Add** method to create a new transaction for that account. Since a **CTransaction** object is returned from the **Add** method, we can immediately use it within the **With** block to refer to methods and properties of the transaction object – in this case to display its **StatementLine** method result in a **MsgBox**.

Creating a collection class in handcrafted code

We can define a Collection class without the aid of the Class Builder. It may be that you are using the standard version of Visual Basic, or one of the free versions (Control Creation Edition of Visual Basic 5 (VB5CCE) or the Visual Basic 6 Working Model). In either of these cases, you do not have the Class Builder. However, it is also good practice, since by writing the code you will gain a fuller understanding of how it works. We can build a collectable and collection class easily.

A collectable class

We could start by building a very simple class as an example of one that can be collected.

```
' CAnimal class - describes an animal and the noise it makes.
Option Explicit

Private mvarAnimal As String    ' e.g. "Pig"
Private mvarNoise As String     ' e.g. "Oink"

Public Property Get Animal() As String
  Animal = mvarAnimal
End Property
```

```
Public Property Let Animal(ByVal NewValue As String)
  mvarAnimal = NewValue
End Property

Public Property Get Noise() As String
  Noise = mvarNoise
End Property

Public Property Let Noise(ByVal NewValue As String)
  mvarNoise = NewValue
End Property

Public Property Get Key() As Variant    ' For general use.
  Key = mvarAnimal
End Property
```

This rather silly class simply defines objects to store the name of an animal and the sound it makes. Note that a **Key** method has been provided: we will make use of this method in this and later data structure examples. We can now use the **CAnimal** class in the definition of a new Collection class. Start by creating a new class module and defining its collection object:

```
' Animals collection class. This class maintains a collection of
' objects of class CAnimal.
Option Explicit

Private colAnimals As Collection
```

Before we can use this collection in an Animals collection, we need to ensure that it is available when we create an instance of the Animals class. For this, we use the **Class_Initialize()** method. At the same time, it is worthwhile to define the **Class_Terminate()** method so that we explicitly destroy the collection.

```
Private Sub Class_Initialize()
  Set colAnimals = New Collection
End Sub

Private Sub Class_Terminate()
  Set colAnimals = Nothing
End Sub
```

We now need to consider how to deal with the items we collect in this class. The standard methods we have to provide are **Add, Remove, Item** and **Count**. In addition, we will need to provide the hidden **NewEnum** method to enable the **For..Each** syntax. **Add** should provide parameters to allow us to set up the newly created **CAnimal** object:

```
Public Function Add(ByVal name As String, ByVal sound As String) _
                              As CAnimal
Dim objAnimal As CAnimal
  Set objAnimal = New CAnimal
```

```
With objAnimal
   .Animal = name
   .Noise = sound
End With
colAnimals.Add objAnimal, objAnimal.Key
Set Add = objAnimal
End Function
```

Note the use of the **Key** property of the **CAnimal** class when adding the animal object to the collection. We can retrieve the object from the collection by key or number. The **Count** and **Remove** methods are quite straightforward:

```
Public Property Get Count() As Long
   Count = colAnimals.Count
End Property

Public Sub Remove(ByVal theKey As Variant)
On Error Resume Next
   colAnimals.Remove theKey
End Sub
```

The error handler in the **Remove** method is important if you wish the collection to be robust. It allows the class to recover from an attempt to remove a non-existent item from the collection (as when, for example, you try to remove an item using a key that does not match that of any items in the collection). The default behaviour without this handler would be to terminate the execution of the program.

Now the **NewEnum** method:

```
Public Property Get NewEnum() As IUnknown
   Set NewEnum = colAnimals.[_NewEnum]
End Property
```

The coding of this property is so obscure as to seem like black magic. Visual Basic supports the definition of a hidden method, one that cannot be directly accessed by program code. In this case, a hidden **Property Get** is used as a method of enabling the **For..Each** syntax for a collection. The *enumerator* object returned by it is a component of every collection class, and is used automatically by Visual Basic. The type of this enumerator object, **IUnknown**, is defined so that *any* class of object can be returned by the property. In this case, we could change the **Property Get** method to return a **CAnimal**, since we know that this is what will be returned. However, the **IUnknown** (readable as 'unknown interface') is normal.

The enumerator object should be hidden to prevent a user from trying to work with it directly, since it is defined with public scope and would otherwise appear in the pop-up list of methods and properties provided when you type a '.' operator after an object reference. The underscore at the start of **_NewEnum** is not normally permissible Visual Basic syntax (but perfectly acceptable in C++, which Visual Basic is written in), and so the square bracket is a necessary trick that allows it to be used. You should hide the **NewEnum** property (Figure 8.5) as follows:

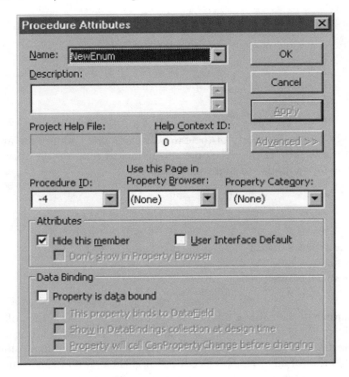

Figure 8.5   *Hiding the* **NewEnum** *method.*

1. On the **Tools** menu, click **Procedure Attributes** to open the **Procedure Attributes** dialog box. In the **Name** box, select the **NewEnum** method.

2. Click **Advanced** to show the advanced features. Check **Hide this member** to make **NewEnum** hidden in the type library.

3. In the **Procedure ID** box, type **−4** (yes, minus four, no point in asking why) to give **NewEnum** the procedure ID required by **For Each..Next**. Click **OK**.

Before we can use the **For..Each** syntax, it is necessary to create the **Item** property of the class, and to make it the *default* property:

```
Public Property Get Item(ByVal theKey As Variant) As CAnimal
On Error GoTo err_Item
  Set Item = colAnimals.Item(theKey)
  Exit Property
err_Item:
  Set Item = Nothing
End Property
```

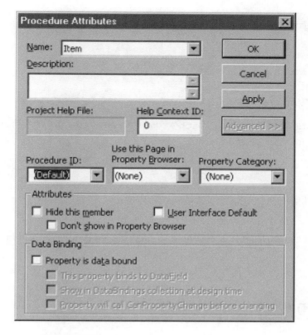

Figure 8.6 *Nominating a default property or method.*

Note that we have again set up an error handler to ensure an attempt to access a non-existent object has a sensible outcome. In this case, we return **Nothing**. To make this the default method (Figure 8.6):

1. On the **Tools** menu, click **Procedure Attributes** to open the **Procedure Attributes** dialog box. In **Name** box, select the **Item** property.

2. Click **Advanced** to show the advanced features.

3. In the **Procedure ID** box, select **(Default)** to make the **Item** property the default. Click **OK**.

The enumerator will now work properly to allow the use of **For..Each** with the **Animals** class. We can test out the new pair of classes in the Immediate window:

```
Set colAnimals = new Animals
Print colAnimals.Count
  0
colAnimals.Add "Pig", "Oink"
colAnimals.Add "Dog", "Bark"
colAnimals.Add "Cat", "Miaw"
colAnimals.Add "Cow", "Moo"
Print colAnimals.Count
  4
```

```
For Each A In colAnimals: Print "A " & A.Animal & " goes " & _
                                A.Noise: Next
A Pig goes Oink
A Dog goes Bark
A Cat goes Miaw
A Cow goes Moo
```

Note that the line beginning **For Each** *should be entered into the Immediate window without a break to work properly.*

QUESTION 8.6

Can you give a reason why it is desirable to hide the **NewEnum** method in a collection class?

8.4 Alternative object structures

Collection structures are certainly the Microsoft way of doing things. Use the object browser (press F2 in the Visual Basic IDE) to examine any of Microsoft's supplied classes in Visual Basic, or in the classes that are provided along with Microsoft Office applications, and you will find collections everywhere, in user-interface objects, database access objects and all of the other object models you can add references to. Microsoft Word and Excel ActiveX classes seem to contain little else.

This is certainly a good thing in many ways. With one predominant form of data structure, it does not take much effort to transfer the skills you have accumulated working with one object model to any other. Microsoft-style collections are also efficient and fast. However, a collection is no more than an assembly of code and object references written by Microsoft to provide a ubiquitous storage and retrieval mechanism for objects. Collections provide all of the benefits of a *hash-table*, a standard data list-type structure used by programmers to provide a time-efficient way of organizing information for quick retrieval.

There are a number of other standard structures that rarely get used in Visual Basic programs because collections are easy to work with. However, in some applications, it can be positively beneficial to use one or other of the more generally applicable structures. Let's look at some examples of these.

Alternative list structures

Arrays and collections are forms of list: a number of objects are placed into a structure that preserves their sequence in some way. In a collection, objects can be accessed via the **Item()** property. If we supply an integer number as a parameter, we can retrieve the items in the order in which they were **Add**ed to the collection. By adding items with the optional string **Key**, we can retrieve the objects by passing a copy of the **Key** to the **Item()** property. We can therefore access the collected items either in the order in which they were added (by number), or randomly (by key).

However, it is not too easy to add items to a collection so that they can be retrieved in some predefined order other than the insertion order. For example, if we wished to keep an alphabetically ordered list of items in a collection, we would have to do a fair amount of work when inserting items into the collection to make this possible. The following sub definition shows how this might be done with a standard collection of **CAnimal** objects (distinct from the specialist **Animals** collection we defined earlier), stored in order of the animal's name:

```
Public Sub AddAnimal(A As CAnimal)
Dim insertionPos As Long
   If colAnimals.Count = 0 Then
     ' This is the first item in the collection, so just add it..
     colAnimals.Add A, A.Animal
   Else
     ' There are already items in the collection, so
     ' we need to find the correct insertion position..
     insertionPos = 1
     ' Look for the first item whose key comes after the new
     ' item's..
     Do While insertionPos < colAnimals.Count
       If colAnimals(insertionPos).Animal > A.Animal Then
         ' Found it..
         Exit Do
       End If
       ' No, try the next..
       insertionPos = insertionPos + 1
     Loop
     ' It could be the new item should be the last, so check
     ' whether it should be before or after insertionPos..
     If colAnimals(insertionPos).Animal > A.Animal Then
       ' Insert before..
       colAnimals.Add A, A.Animal, insertionPos
     Else
       ' Insert after..
       colAnimals.Add A, A.Animal,, insertionPos
     End If
   End If
End Sub
```

The above sub works because it is possible to specify an insertion position when adding an item to a collection. The first requirement is to determine the correct position to insert the new item. This is done in the **Do..Loop**, iterating through each item in the collection until an item whose key should come after the new one's is found. Note that we use the **>** operator to compare two items. At the point where we find the item in the collection before which the new one should be inserted, the expression:

```
colAnimals(insertionPos).Animal > A.Animal
```

will evaluate to **True**. By using a comparison operator, we can create an ordered collection of numbers, currency values or, in this case, strings.

Once we have identified the correct insertion position, we can use one of two optional parameters at the end of the **Add** method to specify the insertion position. A collection object allows us to insert a new item either *before* or *after* an item already in the collection, specified by number or key. The statement

```
someCollection.Add obj, obj.key, 5
```

will insert the new item at position 5, immediately before the item currently at that position. Similarly, the statement

```
someCollection.Add obj, obj.key,, 5  ' Note the missing parameter.
```

will insert the new item *after* the item at position 5. The two last parameters are mutually exclusive. You cannot insert an item and specify a *before* and an *after* insertion position for obvious reasons. Using this **AddAnimal** sub, we can build a list in order, as shown in this sequence of Immediate window operations.

```
Set colAnimals = New Collection
Set A = New CAnimal
A.Animal = "Dog"
AddAnimal A
Set A = New CAnimal
A.Animal = "Pig"
AddAnimal A
Set A = New CAnimal
A.Animal = "Cat"
AddAnimal A
Set A = New CAnimal
A.Animal = "Horse"
AddAnimal A
Set A = New CAnimal
A.Animal = "Cow"
AddAnimal A
Set A = New CAnimal
A.Animal = "Elephant"
AddAnimal A
For Each A In colAnimals: Print A.Animal: Next
Cat
Cow
```

```
Dog
Elephant
Fish
Horse
Pig
```

Rather than repeating all of this code every time you needed to keep an ordered list of objects, it would make sense to create a new collection class, say `OrderedList`, for the purpose of keeping the ordered lists automatically. As the above code illustrates, the `Add` operation can be quite complex and is not optimally efficient, since the time it takes to add an item grows linearly with the size of the list. In our new class, we could simply amend the `Add` operation to make it insert items in our specified order.

Binary searching

One perhaps apparent feature of this type of list, whether based on a collection or an array, is that it is computationally expensive to insert an item into position. The longer the list, the more likely it will take a long time to insert an object, since it seems to be necessary to count through each item up to the correct insertion position. However, the benefits are that items can be retrieved in a specified order (encoded in the new `Add` method), and that an item can be retrieved very rapidly. This latter benefit comes from the ability to perform a *binary search* on the list to find an item.

A binary search is an algorithm for finding an item quickly in an ordered list. To understand how this algorithm works, think of how you look for some item in a long list if you know that the list is in some order – looking up a number in the phone book, for example.

Assume you have to look up someone's name in the phone book. The most likely method you would use is to open the book roughly half-way through, and check whether the names you find there are alphabetically before or after the one you are looking for. By dismissing half of the phone book in this stage, you have halved the amount of information you need to search. The same could be done with the remaining half of the phone book (open it at the middle and decide whether the name being sought is before or after this point), and so on until the correct page is found.

Let's assume a typical phone book has one million entries:

- Step 1 reduces the search to $\frac{1}{2}$ million entries

- Step 2 reduces it to $\frac{1}{4}$ million

- Step 3 to 125,000

- Step 4 to 62,500

- Step 5 to 31,250

- Step 6 to 15,625

- Step 7 to 7,813 (or less)

- Step 8 to 3,907 (or less)

- Step 9 to 1,954 (or less)

- Step 10 to 1000 (approx.)

- Step 11 to 500

- Step 12 to 250

- Step 13 to 125

- Step 14 to 64 (approx.)

- Step 15 to 32

- Step 16 to 16

- Step 17 to 8

- Step 18 to 4

- Step 19 to 2

- Step 20 ought to indicate the actual name.

Note that we have reduced a search through a million items to 20 steps, each of which involves a comparison to determine which half of the list to dismiss. That is the *worst case*, since it is possible we could have found the item during one of the comparisons. This is only possible if the phone-book entries appear as a sorted list.

The algorithm is known as a binary search because of the way we halve the scope of the search at each stage (binary means of order 2). We could write the algorithm more formally to work with an arbitrary set of data (*DataSet*):

```
StartPosition = 1
EndPosition = Number of items in the data set
Do
  MidPosition = (EndPosition + StartPosition) / 2   ' ½ way
  If DataSet(MidPosition) = ItemSought Then Exit Do ' Found it
  If SoughtItem > DataSet(MidPosition) Then
    StartPosition = MidPosition + 1       ' Look in 2nd half
  Else
    EndPosition = MidPosition - 1         ' Look in 1st half
  End If
Loop
```

Note that we need to be able to compare the item being sought with an item in the set (we have used the '=' and '>' comparison operators for this). Also, the above algorithm does not account for the possibility that the data sought may not be in the data set.

We can incorporate this algorithm into our **OrderedList** class by amending the **Item** method so that it retrieves an item using a binary search instead of by number or key. A good strategy to adopt is to make it a requirement of all objects added to an **OrderedList** to provide a **Key** property: some unique value that can be derived from the object data. Note that, since we can identify a suitable storage location using the same binary search algorithm, the **Add** method can be amended so it will benefit from it.

```
' COrdList class: a collection class for ordered lists.
Option Explicit

Private colData As Collection

Private Sub Class_Initialize()
  Set colData = New Collection
End Sub

Private Sub Class_Terminate()
  Set colData = Nothing
End Sub

' The binary search Function - note it is Private.
Private Function BinSearch(Key As Variant) As Long
Dim startPos As Long, endPos As Long
Dim midPos As Long
  startPos = 1
  endPos = colData.Count
  ' Use a binary search to locate position within list..
  Do While startPos <> midPos And endPos <> midPos
    ' Bisect the list..
    midPos = (endPos + startPos) \ 2
    If Key > colData(midPos).Key Then
      startPos = midPos + 1        ' Look in 2nd half
    ElseIf Key < colData(midPos).Key Then
      endPos = midPos - 1          ' Look in 1st half
    Else
      Exit Do
    End If
  Loop
  BinSearch = midPos
End Function

Public Sub Add(objItem As Object) ' objItem must have a Key property.
Dim insertPos As Long
On Error GoTo err_Add
  If colData.Count > 0 Then
    insertPos = BinSearch(objItem.Key)
    If objItem.Key > colData(insertPos).Key Then
      colData.Add objItem, objItem.Key,, insertPos
```

```
      Else
         colData.Add objItem, objItem.Key, insertPos
      End If
   Else
      colData.Add objItem, objItem.Key
   End If
   Exit Sub
err_Add:
   ' Re-raise the error..
   Err.Raise Err
End Sub

Public Property Get Item(ByVal Key As Variant) As Object
Dim atPos As Long
On Error GoTo err_Item
   ' Use binary search to locate item.
   atPos = BinSearch(Key)
   If colData(atPos).Key = Key Then      ' Did we find it?
      Set Item = colData(atPos)
   Else
      Set Item = Nothing
   End If
   Exit Property
err_Item:
   Set Item = Nothing
End Property

Public Property Get Count() As Long
   Count = colData.Count
End Property

Public Property Get NewEnum() As IUnknown
   Set NewEnum = colData.[_NewEnum]
End Property
```

Apart from the (radically) changed **Add** and **Item** methods, this collection class is exactly the same as the standard collection class developed earlier, including the requirement for hiding the **NewEnum** method and making the **Item** property the default. The **Add** method, besides having undergone a comprehensive rewrite, is now no longer a function. Since this one has not been written in such as way as to create the object before inserting it into the list, we do not need it to return an object. Instead, the **Add** method takes an **Object** parameter, which means that we can add any class of object provided it meets the other criterion – the object added must have a **Key** property. This requirement turns out to be a very telling one that will have to be addressed at some point. It will be dealt with further in Chapter 10 on Polymorphism.

The **Item** method takes a variant **Key** parameter and returns an object (of general type **Object**) with a matching key or **Nothing**. Note that error handling has become

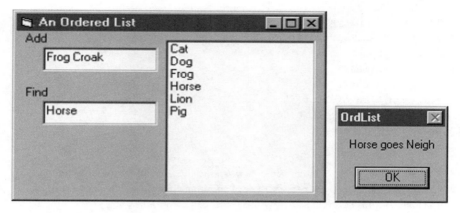

Figure 8.7 *Using an ordered list.*

important in this class because of the possibility of adding an object with a key that is already in the collection, and the possibility of searching for an item that does not exist in the collection. In the **Item** method, we can resolve the error by returning **Nothing**, thereby leaving it up to the user of the ordered collection to deal with the problem. However, in the **Add** method, the only possible resolution is to re-raise the error for the application programmer to catch.

The following is a simple test program (see also Figure 8.7) that demonstrates all of the features of the **COrdList** class.

```
Option Explicit

Private ordList As New COrdList

' This event-handler does its work when the Enter key is pressed.
' (i.e. KeyAscii = 13)
' It assumes a pair of words have been typed into txtAnimal, an
' animal's name and the noise it makes. A suitable object is
' created and added to the ordered list..
Private Sub txtAnimal_KeyPress(KeyAscii As Integer)
Dim A As CAnimal
   If KeyAscii = 13 Then
     KeyAscii = 0
     Set A = New CAnimal
     A.Animal = Left(txtAnimal, InStr(txtAnimal, " ") - 1)
     ' Text to the left of the space
     A.Noise = Mid(txtAnimal, InStr(txtAnimal, " ") + 1)
     ' Text to the right of the space
     ordList.Add A
     ShowList
   End If
End Sub
```

```
' This sub displays all of the items in the ordered collection
' in the lstAnimals list box..
Public Sub ShowList()
Dim A As CAnimal
  lstAnimals.Clear
  For Each A In ordList
    lstAnimals.AddItem A.Key
  Next
End Sub


' The event-handler does its work when the Enter key is pressed.
' It looks up the ordered collection based on the key entered in
' txtName, and reports on any object found..
Private Sub txtName_KeyPress(KeyAscii As Integer)
  If KeyAscii = 13 Then
    KeyAscii = 0
    If ordList.Item(txtName) Is Nothing Then
      MsgBox "Not in list"
    Else
      MsgBox ordList(txtName).Animal & " goes " & _
             ordList(txtName).Noise
    End If
  End If
End Sub
```

Note that the program makes use of the **Key** method of the **CAnimal** class, defined earlier.

> **QUESTION 8.7**
>
> List advantages and disadvantages in the use of ordered lists.

Queues and stacks

Beyond collections and ordered lists, in which easy access to individual items is an important feature, lies a category of list structures that deliberately limits access to the objects contained in it. A *queue* structure (Figure 8.8) is one in which objects are added to one end (the rear) and removed from the other (the front). The idea is familiar enough, since we are all used to queuing at the post office, at the ticket office and in shops. We join a queue at the back, shuffle up as the people at the front of the queue are served and new people join the end of the queue, and leave the queue when we reach the front and service becomes available.

Figure 8.8 *A queue structure.*

This structure is used in numerous situations in computer programming where the order of occurrences must be preserved. Windows and Visual Basic depend on the queue structure as the mechanism by which events are passed to applications. Events are added to the end of a queue, and removed from the front, so that the events are processed in the order they were generated. By this means, Microsoft Windows is able to service multiple programs, giving each access to the processor in an orderly and equitable way.

Queue structures are also useful in application programs such as transaction processing systems, multi-user databases or messaging systems, where the computer is able to keep up with the *average* load on the system but needs some help in dealing with occasional gluts.

A *stack* is a structure that in some ways is the opposite of a queue. Whereas in a queue, the first to join it will also be the first to leave, in a stack structure the first to join it will be the last to leave (and conversely, the last to join will be the first to leave). Stack structures are used in a number of ways in computer programs, but always as a mechanism to allow a process of some type to interrupt another temporarily.

A stack has a *top* and a *bottom*. Items at the top of a stack will be the next to be dealt with, but since another item can always be added to the top, items further down the stack will have to wait until the items above them have been dealt with. While a queue operates to allocate some resource (such as processor time or a shop assistant) on a fair basis, a stack operates to allocate the resource on a priority basis, with the assumption that the most recent addition is also the most important.

Almost all computer systems use stacks as a core element of their ability to work. Whenever a subroutine (sub or function) is executed, it is added to the top of a stack of items to be allocated the processor. When its execution has completed, it is removed from the stack. If another subroutine is called from within the current one, it is placed on top of the current one on the stack and so its execution must be completed before the current subroutine can complete its own execution. This system ensures that subroutine calls are executed in the required order.

There seem to be few real-world systems based on the stack principle. Due to its inherent unfairness, we would be unlikely to put up with a situation where anyone arriving after us in a shop, post office or bank would be dealt with before we were. This would be particularly annoying if the attendant were to break off from dealing with us to attend to the new arrival.

However, stacks are frequently used in systems where a number of optional strategies must be considered. Certain card games work on the stack principle: the last card added to a pile is the first to be removed. Computer chess games also work on the stack principle, where a move being considered is added to a stack before the subsequent moves that could follow this one are considered and so on. Effectively, a

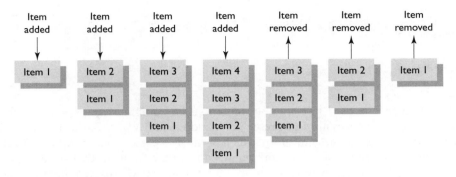

Figure 8.9   *A stack in operation.*

stack structure allows a system to proceed to a given stage and then unwind to a previous state (Figure 8.9).

Queues and stacks in Visual Basic

Since queues and stacks are other forms of list structure, we can use the ubiquitous collection class to implement them in a Visual Basic program. For example, to implement a queue structure in Visual Basic, we need only provide one sub and one function in addition to a collection object:

```
Private colQueue As New Collection

Public Sub JoinQueue(O As Object)
  colQueue.Add O
End Sub

Public Function LeaveQueue() As Object
  LeaveQueue = colQueue(1)
  colQueue.Remove 1
End Function
```

With a stack, we simply remove the last item (the item at position `Collection.Count`) from the collection instead. However, encapsulation should be used to hide the inner details and prevent the user from misusing the collection by accessing items that should not be accessible. For a *queue* class, we should provide the methods **Join**, a sub with an object parameter, and **Leave**, a function that returns an **Object** (which means we could use it to return any class of object).

```
' CQueue: A Simple Queue Class.

Option Explicit

Private colQueue As Collection
```

```
Private Sub Class_Initialize()
  Set colQueue = New Collection
End Sub

Private Sub Class_Terminate()
  Set colQueue = Nothing
End Sub

Public Sub Join(obj As Object)
  colQueue.Add obj
End Sub

Public Function Leave() As Object
  If colQueue.Count > 0 Then
    Set Leave = colQueue.item(1)
    colQueue.Remove 1
  Else
    Set Leave = Nothing
  End If
End Function
```

We have left it up to the user to deal with the situation of trying to remove an item from an empty queue: the queue will return **Nothing** in this case, and the application program can react accordingly as shown below:

```
Option Explicit

Private q As New CQueue

Private Sub cmdJoin_Click()      ' A Join button
Dim item As CItem
  Set item = New CItem
  item.Data = InputBox("Enter item to join queue")
  q.Join item
End Sub

Private Sub cmdLeave_Click()     ' A Leave button.
Dim item As CItem
  Set item = q.Leave
  If item Is Nothing Then
    MsgBox "Queue is empty"
  Else
    MsgBox item.Data
  End If
End Sub
```

With a stack structure, items are added with the **Push** method (you 'push' an item on to the top of the stack) and removed with the **Pop** method (the top item is 'popped' from the stack).

```
' CStack: a simple Stack class.

Option Explicit

Private colStack As Collection
Private Sub Class_Initialize()
  Set colStack = New Collection
End Sub

Private Sub Class_Terminate()
  Set colStack = Nothing
End Sub

Public Sub Push(obj As Object)
  colStack.Add obj
End Sub

Public Function Pop() As Object
  If colStack.Count > 0 Then
    Set Pop = colStack(colStack.Count)
    colStack.Remove (colStack.Count)
  Else
    Set Pop = Nothing
  End If
End Function
```

8.5   Tree structures

Selecting a structure to use in a program is largely a matter of design: where possible you use structures that are similar to the logical structure dictated by the application. As you have already seen, we can make use of the mainstay structure in Visual Basic, the collection, to create many forms of logical structure. However, in some cases, it is simply too difficult to create the underlying structure that is used in an application by implementing an existing physical structure.

One good example of a structure that would be difficult or inefficient to implement with collections is the *tree* structure. The classic example of this (Figure 8.10) is the tree structure that results when you trace back your ancestry, which is a *binary tree* (each branch having a maximum of two sub-branches).

We could use a similar structure to model the relationships between staff in a management hierarchy, or to describe assemblies of parts in a complex system. There is no need to restrict an element to having only two 'child' elements unless a tree is specifically a binary tree.

If we were to implement this structure with collections, either we would need to provide each member element of the tree with its own collection or we would have

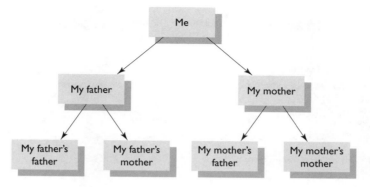

Figure 8.10   *An ancestry tree – a classic example of a tree structure.*

to encode the connections between elements as part of the objects themselves. The first method would be highly inefficient while the second would be computationally messy.

In fact, Visual Basic provides a much simpler solution to the problem. We can store references to other objects of the same class within each element object. This solves the structural problem of how to represent the connections between items. From this, it is a fairly simple matter to provide methods to add items, remove items and iterate through all of the items (or enumerate them).

First we should examine why it is desirable to use a tree structure. Recall the use of a binary search to speed up access to an ordered list structure. By halving the number of items examined at each stage, we could provide access to one of a very large number of items in a relatively few search operations.

A binary tree structure is the embodiment of a binary search algorithm. Each element in the tree treats all of its descendants as two halves. At the top of a well-structured binary tree (where each element has exactly two descendants), either direction leads to half of all the other elements. One level down, each element leads to one quarter of the items below that level, and so on.

A binary search of a tree is very simple: work down the tree deciding whether to go left or right at each junction. This property is usually exploited by ensuring that all items with a key value less than the current one are below it to the left, and all items with a key value above the current one are below it on the right. For example, the tree shown in Figure 8.11 is an ordered binary tree. Any item can be accessed with a minimum of two comparisons. Provided the tree remains in approximate balance (where all of the items above the lowest level have one or two descendants), even a very large tree can provide access to any item with only a few comparisons.

One realization that makes the implementation of tree structures very straight-forward is that every item in a tree is just a smaller tree. For example, in Figure 8.11 the item Foxtrot and the two items below it form a tree, that is a sub-tree of the entire structure. Therefore, operations on a tree structure tend to be the same at every level, allowing us to create very efficient code.

We can create a tree class in Visual Basic by providing all of the features necessary for management of a single item or *node*.

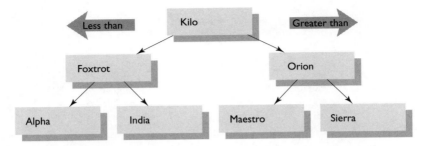

Figure 8.11 *An ordered binary tree.*

```
' CTree: An implentation of a Tree structure.
Option Explicit

Private nodLeft As Ctree      ' The sub-tree to the left of this one
Private nodRight As Ctree     ' The sub-tree to the right
Private nodData As Object     ' The data object at this node

' Properties to allow access to data object..
Public Property Get NodeObject() As Object
  Set NodeObject = nodData
End Property

Public Property Set NodeObject(objNode As Object)
  Set nodData = objNode
End Property

' A method to insert a new data object..
Public Sub Insert(objNode As Object)
  If nodData Is Nothing Then    ' We can insert at this node.
    Set nodData = objNode
  ElseIf objNode.key < nodData.key Then
    ' Insert on the left..
    If nodLeft Is Nothing Then
      ' We need to make a left sub-tree..
      Set nodLeft = New CTree
      Set nodLeft.NodeObject = objNode
    Else
      ' There already is a left subtree, so simply call Insert..
      nodLeft.Insert objNode
    End If
  Else
    ' Insert on right..
    If nodRight Is Nothing Then
      ' We need to make a right sub-tree..
      Set nodRight = New CTree
      Set nodRight.NodeObject = objNode
```

```
      Else
        ' There already is a right subtree, so simply call Insert..
        nodRight.Insert objNode
      End If
    End If
End Sub


Public Function Retrieve(vKey As Variant) As Object
    ' First check if this data node is a match..
    If nodData.key = vKey Then
      ' Yes, so return it..
      Set Retrieve = nodData
    ElseIf nodData.key > vKey Then
      ' No, so try smaller keys in the left sub-tree..
      If nodLeft Is Nothing Then
        ' No left sub-tree, so no match..
        Set Retrieve = Nothing
      Else
        ' Search the left sub-tree..
        Set Retrieve = nodLeft.Retrieve(vKey)
      End If
    Else
      ' Last option - try bigger keys on the right..
      If nodRight Is Nothing Then
        ' No right sub-tree so no match..
        Set Retrieve = Nothing
      Else
        ' Search the right sub-tree..
        Set Retrieve = nodRight.Retrieve(vKey)
      End If
    End If
End Function


Public Sub EnumerateOn(PC As Control)
    ' Enumerate on the left sub-tree..
    If Not nodLeft Is Nothing Then
      nodLeft.EnumerateOn PC
    End If
    ' Print the key value (could call a method here)..
    PC.Print nodData.Key
    ' Enumerate on the right sub-tree..
    If Not nodRight Is Nothing Then
      nodRight.EnumerateOn PC
    End If
End Sub
```

The **CTree** implementation shown has only one important property, **NodeObject**, having both **Get** and **Set** parts, and two important methods, **Insert** and **Retrieve**.

An extra method, **EnumerateOn**, is a simple example of the use of the tree structure to provide order to information. This method takes a control object, either a form or a PictureBox, as a parameter, and prints out the tree data on it. In a real application, this method would be replaced by one or more application-specific methods. The simple sequence

---

Sub Operate
  Operate on the left sub-tree **
  Operate on this node ***
  Operate on the right sub-tree ****
End Sub

---

is an example of the use of *recursion* in programming. Recursion occurs when a subroutine calls itself. In this case, it can be used to process an entire tree (by starting the call sequence from the root). The first statement (**) calls the sub **Operate** for the left sub-tree, which is all of the entries with a key value less than the root's. Within the root of the left sub-tree, this is repeated all the way down the tree until a leaf node is met. Since it has no left sub-tree to call the **Operate** sub for, it must continue with the next statement, which does the actual operation (e.g. printing the node data) for that node. As the call list unwinds, each node **Operate**s on itself, then its right sub-tree until we reach the root, at which the process continues in the same way with the left sub-tree under the root.

Because of the few methods defined for this tree class, it is a very easy class to use in a program, as shown next (Figure 8.12), but provides most of the advantages of a binary tree. The only important feature of a node object for insertion into a tree is that it provides a **Key** property, so we can reuse the **CAnimal** class defined for the **COrdList** example.

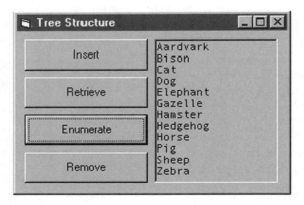

Figure 8.12   *Tree data enumerated on a PictureBox – note the alphabetical order, even though the items were entered randomly.*

```
' Test of CTree class. This code is in a form object, with three
' buttons, for Insert, Retrieve and Enumerate..
Option Explicit

Private Tree As New CTree

Private Sub cmdEnumerate_Click()
  picNodes.Cls                    ' picNodes is a picture box.
                                  ' Start by clearing it
    Tree.EnumerateOn picNodes
End Sub

Private Sub cmdInsert_Click()
Dim N As New CAnimal
  N.Animal = ("Enter an animal")
  Tree.Insert N
End Sub

Private Sub cmdRetrieve_Click()
Dim Key As String, N As CAnimal
  Key = InputBox("Key Value")
  Set N = Tree.Retrieve(Key)
  If N Is Nothing Then
    MsgBox "Not found"
  Else
    MsgBox N.Key
  End If
End Sub
```

Our **CTree** class has one apparent problem. There is no way to remove a node from the tree. Although it is possible to remove nodes from trees, it is a complex operation and less useful that you might imagine. The tendency is to create a tree structure to store data that changes infrequently or not at all – for example, a required look-up table in an application. The tree would be set up at the start of a run and used throughout the execution of the application, and so there would be no need to delete any nodes. It would provide the benefit of very fast look-up from a large collection of objects. However, some tree implementations would require a delete method, and possibly a method for re-balancing the tree to ensure that no branch could grow to be significantly longer than any other as items were added and removed.

QUESTION 8.8

Describe the main differences between the use of a tree structure and an ordered list.

A word about graph structures

A *graph* is a structure in which nodes are interconnected in any way other than as lists or trees. This description suggests that graph structures are more complex and more difficult to deal with than other types of structure: both true. However, a graph structure can address a range of problems that other structures are not adequate for. Typical examples of graph structures are network interconnection systems, map applications and circuit diagrams. In all of these cases, there is no simple algorithm to deal with the possible range of interconnections, since any node can connect arbitrarily with any other and can connect with any number of others.

A typical example of a graph structure is a system to model traffic flow in a town centre. Roads are the interconnections between junctions, which are the nodes in the graph. One junction will connect with several others, typically four in a grid system. Since it is possible for a junction to connect with more than four others (via an interchange roundabout, for example), it would not be adequate to model a node with only four connection points.

If all of the connections are one-way streets, we have a *directed graph*. The complexity increases if all or some of the roads are two-way, since then the node at either end must refer to its opposite. A picture of a very simple *undirected graph* (with all streets being two-way) for this type of application is shown in Figure 8.13.

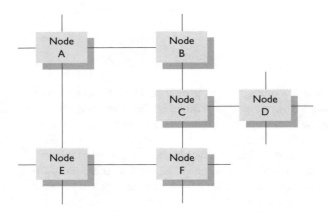

Figure 8.13   *An undirected graph structure depicting a fragment of a road system.*

Even in the small fragment of a road system shown in Figure 8.13, there is quite a high level of complexity. Table 8.1 shows the interconnection listing for this diagram.

In a computer graph structure, we would have to provide an arbitrary number of interconnection references within a node object. The best strategy for all but the simplest graph would be to provide each node with a collection of nodes. A typical implementation of a minimal node might be:

Table 8.1   *The interconnection matrix for the graph in Figure 8.13.*

From/to	Node A	Node B	Node C	Node D	Node E	Node F
Node A		X			X	
Node B	X		X			
Node C		X		X		X
Node D			X			
Node E	X					X
Node F			X		X	

```
' GraphNode class: models a node of an arbitrarily complex
' graph node.
Option Explicit

Private colConnectedNodes As Collection

Private Sub Class_Initialize()
  Set colConnectedNodes = New Collection
End Sub

Public Property Get Key() As Variant
  ' Generate some form of unique key.
End Sub

Public Sub ConnectTo(Node As CGraphNode)
If connectedNodes(Node.Key) Is Nothing Then
  colConnectedNodes.Add Node
  Node.ConnectTo Me
End If
End Sub

' Other stuff.
```

Using the scheme shown, it would be possible to set up a network of interconnected **CGraphNode** objects and provide mechanisms to manage the flow of vehicles, messages or other data through them. However, things become difficult when it is necessary to set up methods to traverse through all of the possible routes from any two arbitrary nodes, due to the computational complexity inherent in graphs in general.

The ***Travelling Salesman Problem*** (Figure 8.14) is a well-known problem of graph systems. It is based on the premise of calculating the most efficient route by which a travelling salesman might visit a number of towns interconnected by roads so that

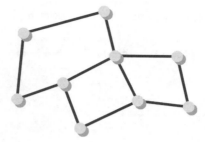

Figure 8.14 *The travelling salesman problem. What is the shortest route that will visit each town only once?*

each town is visited only once. For any more than a few towns, the calculation of the best (i.e. shortest) route becomes computationally difficult. For this reason, there are no common algorithms for analyzing graph structures that do not involve the brute-force approach of mapping out each possible route (possibly a huge number) and selecting the shortest one.

8.6 Review questions

1. Only a few fundamental physical data structures can be used to represent almost any logical structure required by an application. Why is this state of affairs preferable to programmers re-creating the exact structure necessary in an application?

2. Microsoft makes extensive use of collections in the class structures used in Visual Basic and their Office Applications. What advantages does this afford to an applications programmer working with Microsoft systems?

3. It is possible to step through each item in a collection using the syntax:

```
For index = 1 To coll.Count
  coll(index).DoSomething
Next
```

Why is the **For..Each** syntax preferable?

4. In the card game of Gin Rummy, discarded cards are placed on top of each other on the table between the players. A player can use his or her turn to pick up cards from the top of the discarded pile. In terms of the structures described in this chapter, how could the discarded pile be implemented?

5. How would you characterize the world's telephone network from among the structures discussed in this chapter?

8.7 Practical exercise: Using the COrdList structure

In this exercise, we will augment the **CScheduleItem** class and the **frmScheduleItem** form developed in the exercises at the end of Chapter 7. We will use a **COrdList** object to define a structure to house a number of schedule items, and a main schedule form to manage them.

 Re-open the Agenda project started in the previous exercise. Amend the existing **CScheduleItem** class, adding a **Key** property to it, as shown below.

```
Public Property Get Key() As String
   key = Format(mvarDateTime, "yyyy.mm.dd - hh:nn")
End Property
```

Note that a time format has been set up in the **Key** property as year, then month number, then day number, then hours, then minutes. In this format, a simple comparison using the '>' operator will allow us to compare items in date order. We can then use them in an ordered list to keep a list of schedule items.

 Add a new class module to the project, and give it the name **CAgenda**.

The **CAgenda** class will be a collection class that we can optimize for collecting schedule items. We can base this class on the **COrdList** class developed earlier in the chapter – this will allow us to maintain a list of **CScheduleItem** objects in key order (which is time and date order).

 If you have implemented the **COrdList** described earlier, add it to the current project by right-clicking on the Project Explorer, selecting Add/Class Module, choosing the Existing tab of the dialog box and browsing to find and select the **COrdList** file. If not you should add a new class module, and enter all of the **COrdList** class code (reproduced below) into it.

```
' COrdList class: a collection class for ordered lists.
Option Explicit

Private colData As Collection

Private Sub Class_Initialize()
   Set colData = New Collection
End Sub

Private Sub Class_Terminate()
   Set colData = Nothing
End Sub
```

```
' The binary search Function - note it is Private.
Private Function BinSearch(Key As Variant) As Long
Dim startPos As Long, endPos As Long
Dim midPos As Long
  startPos = 1
  endPos = colData.Count
  ' Use a binary search to locate position within list..
  Do While startPos <> midPos And endPos <> midPos
    ' Bisect the list..
    midPos = (endPos + startPos) \ 2
    If Key > colData(midPos).Key Then
      startPos = midPos + 1          ' Look in 2nd half
    ElseIf Key < colData(midPos).Key Then
      endPos = midPos - 1            ' Look in 1st half
    Else
      Exit Do
    End If
  Loop
  BinSearch = midPos
End Function

Public Sub Add(objItem As Object) ' objItem must have a Key property.
Dim insertPos As Long
On Error GoTo err_Add
  If colData.Count > 0 Then
    insertPos = BinSearch(objItem.Key)
    If objItem.Key > colData(insertPos).Key Then
      colData.Add objItem, objItem.Key,, insertPos
    Else
      colData.Add objItem, objItem.Key, insertPos
    End If
  Else
    colData.Add objItem, objItem.Key
  End If
  Exit Sub
err_Add:
  ' Re-raise the error..
  Err.Raise Err
End Sub

Public Sub Remove(ByVal key As Variant)
On Error GoTo err_Remove
  colData.Remove key
  Exit Sub
err_Remove:
  Err.Raise Err
End Sub
```

```vb
Public Property Get Item(ByVal Key As Variant) As Object
Dim atPos As Long
On Error GoTo err_Item
  ' Use binary search to locate item.
  atPos = BinSearch(Key)
  If colData(atPos).Key = Key Then    ' Did we find it?
    Set Item = colData(atPos)
  Else
    Set Item = Nothing
  End If
  Exit Property
err_Item:
  Set Item = Nothing
End Property

Public Property Get Count() As Long
  Count = colData.Count
End Property

Public Property Get NewEnum() As IUnknown
  Set NewEnum = colData.[_NewEnum]
End Property
```

> We now need to define the **CAgenda** class so that it acts as an optimized collection for **CScheduleItem** objects. This involves building a new collection class to wrap the **CordList** class in. Return to the **CAgenda** class's code window and add the following properties and methods.

```vb
' CAgenda class - a collection of schedule items..
Option Explicit
Private colAgenda As COrdList

Private Sub Class_Initialize()
  Set colAgenda = New COrdList
End Sub

Private Sub Class_Terminate()
  Set colAgenda = Nothing
End Sub

Public Sub Add(I As CScheduleItem)
  colAgenda.Add I
End Sub

Public Property Get Item(ByVal key As String) As CScheduleItem
  Set Item = colAgenda.Item(key)
End Property
```

```
Public Property Get Count() As Long
  Count = colAgenda.Count
End Property

Public Sub Remove(ByVal theKey As Variant)
On Error Resume Next
  colAgenda.Remove theKey
End Sub

Public Property Get NewEnum() As IUnknown
  Set NewEnum = colAgenda.NewEnum
End Property
```

Set the **Item** property as the default property of the **CAgenda** class (Tools/ Procedure Attributes, select the Item method, press the Advanced button and choose (Default) from the Procedure ID box).

Set the **NewEnum** property to be hidden, and give it a Procedure ID of −4, to enable the **For..Each** syntax.

We now have a collectable class (**CScheduleItem**), a custom collection class (**CAgenda**) and a custom form for schedule items (from Chapter 7). The last thing that we need for a complete Agenda application is a main form to provide access to all of the schedule item collection.

Add a new form to the project, and give it the name **frmAgenda**.

Add three button controls and a ListBox control as shown in Figure 8.15.

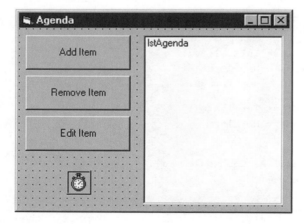

Figure 8.15 *A form for Agenda items.*

Table 8.2 *Properties of items and form for the Agenda application.*

Object	Property	Setting	Description
Form	Name	**frmAgenda**	Name of the form object
	Borderstyle	3 – fixed dialog	Makes the form a fixed size
	Caption	Agenda	
CommandButton	Name	**cmdAdd**	Button to add a schedule item
	Caption	Add	
CommandButton	Name	**cmdRemove**	Button to remove an item
	Caption	Remove	
CommandButton	Name	**cmdEdit**	Button to edit an item
	Caption	Edit	
ListBox	Name	**lstAgenda**	List of schedule items
Timer	Name	**timAlarms**	Periodic alarm checking
	Interval	10000	Every 10 seconds

Set the properties of the various items and the form as shown in Table 8.2.

You can of course set up the controls to have a more distinctive appearance than this, changing font, colours, etc.

Add a declaration for a **CAgenda** collection to the top of the form code.

```
Private Agenda As CAgenda
```

We need a sub to build a list of schedule items, so we can call on it each time the Agenda collection is changed. This will then be called whenever a schedule item is added or edited.

```
Private Sub RefreshList()
Dim SI As CScheduleItem
  lstAgenda.Clear
  For Each SI In Agenda
    lstAgenda.AddItem SI.key
  Next
End Sub
```

This simple sub makes use of the `For..Each` syntax defined for the `CAgenda` class to iterate through each schedule item, and places each item's `Key` into the list box.

 Add event-handler code to the form to make it behave as required by the application.

The Add button should create a new schedule item and add it to the collection:

```
Private Sub cmdAdd_Click()
Dim SI As CScheduleItem
Dim f As New frmScheduleItem
  Set SI = New CScheduleItem
  Set f.ScheduleItem = SI
  f.Show vbModal
  Agenda.Add SI
  RefreshList
End Sub
```

 The `Remove` event-handler should remove a selected event.

```
Private Sub cmdRemove_Click()
  If lstAgenda.ListIndex > -1 Then
    Agenda.Remove lstAgenda.Text
    RefreshList
  End If
End Sub
```

 The `Edit` event-handler should provide access to the selected schedule item.

```
Private Sub cmdEdit_Click()
Dim f As frmScheduleItem
  If lstAgenda.ListIndex > -1 Then
    Set f = New frmScheduleItem
```

```
    Set f.ScheduleItem = Agenda.Item(lstAgenda.Text)
    f.Show vbModal
    RefreshList
  End If
End Sub
```

 A **Timer** event-handler is required to periodically check for alarm conditions –
this will execute once every 10,000 ms or 10 s, as specified by the timer's Interval
property.

```
Private Sub timAlarms_Timer()
Dim SI As CScheduleItem
  For Each SI In Agenda
    If SI.AlarmDue Then
      MsgBox SI.Text, vbOKOnly, "Schedule Alarm"
    End If
  Next
End Sub
```

 Finally, we need to create the **CAgenda** collection when the form first loads, so
that it is ready to have **CScheduleItem** objects added to it.

```
Private Sub Form_Load()
  Set Agenda = New CAgenda
End Sub
```

Before we can run the application, we need to make sure that the agenda form is the
main application form.

 Go to Project/Properties, and from the General tab, set the start-up object to be
frmAgenda.

You should now be able to run the Agenda, add schedule items with or without
alarms, edit schedule items, remove items from the list and receive alarm notifications.
You can minimize the Agenda application's main form on your desktop, and it will
pop-up reminder messages for those **CScheduleItems** which have their **Alarm** property
set to True.

Persistence

Although the Agenda application works well enough, it still does not provide any way
to preserve its settings from run to run. We will look at various ways of doing this in
the next chapter.

8.8   Answers to questions

QUESTION 8.1

(a)   The form, being the entry point of the program, also assumes responsibility for delegating responsibilities to other objects. However, it could then instantiate a 'chief-executive object' responsible for the overall program, a bit like a minion introducing the chairman to the members of a board meeting.

(b)   The argument above applies, but in the case of sub Main, which is a method added to the global object, the global object has initial control.

(c)   Delegation comes from one object asking another to do a job by passing it a message. As a Visual Basic program starts, the entry point, either sub Main in the global object, or an event-handler on a form, can instantiate other objects. By passing messages to these other objects, task responsibility is delegated.

QUESTION 8.2

A collection object is a very versatile structure. It can, for example, be used as a component of a node on a tree or graph structure, so that other objects (which in turn may contain collections) can be attached to the node. We see later in this chapter how a collection can be used as the basis of other list-based structures – queues and stacks. Since a collection can store an arbitrary number of object references, it can be used as the basis for a range of alternative structures. A general principle that could be used is that if a node (or data-space) in a structure can access an arbitrary number of other nodes, a collection could be used. If it had to access only a small number of other nodes, a collection-based implementation might prove to be inefficient in memory and time.

QUESTION 8.3

(a)   In the one-to-many relationship shown, the 'many' side of the relationship can have zero or more items (the * asterisk shows this) – a `BankAccount` can have 0 or more transactions.

(b)   A list would be the logical structure of choice. In Visual Basic, we might implement this as a collection, since this imposes no limit to the number of transactions. An array would also be possible but less ideal, since its size would be an unnatural constraint.

QUESTION 8.4

(a) The obvious way to create an initial balance would be to create an initial Deposit transaction and add it to the account.

(b) Since the calculation of balance requires that the values of all transactions are added together, as the account matures the increasingly longer list of transactions will become a computational burden. The older the account, the longer it will take to calculate the balance.

(c) One way around the problem of increasingly longer transaction lists would be to periodically consolidate aged transactions by adding them together (up to some point several transactions before the most recent) and replacing all of the aged transactions with a single transaction of their total value.

QUESTION 8.5

For the strategy: the application programmer has a smaller class model to learn; since a Transaction is simply the result of a `BankAccount` method, the chance of a programmer introducing an error in handling transactions is removed. Against: the reduced public class model will be less versatile. For example, the strategy suggested in the answer to Question 8.4(c) could not be added by the applications programmer.

QUESTION 8.6

By hiding the `NewEnum` method in a collection class, there is no chance of an applications programmer misusing it.

QUESTION 8.7

Advantages of ordered lists: items can be found more quickly; the list contents can be enumerated easily; it is possible to determine if an item exists in a list without an exhaustive search. Disadvantages of ordered lists: it generally takes longer to insert an item; it is necessary to nominate some ordering key and provide access to it for items to be added to the list.

QUESTION 8.8

A tree structure allows items to be inserted and found quickly. In an ordered list structure, items can be located quickly using a binary search strategy, but inserting an item can be more time consuming, depending on the implementation, since it may be necessary to make a space in the list to accommodate the new item. It is possible to enumerate the items in a list quickly and efficiently, but only in one direction. Certain list implementations allow the items to be enumerated efficiently in either direction.

8.9   Answers to review questions

1. *Only a few fundamental physical data structures can be used to represent almost any logical structure required by an application. Why is this state of affairs preferable to programmers re-creating the exact structure necessary in an application?* Several reasons, but the most compelling of these are: any number of logical structures can be implemented using the small range of available physical structures; programming is difficult enough without having to learn the characteristics of a huge number of alternative structures; the main point about structure is that it forms a recognizable pattern in which items are put together – having access to a very large number of available structures defeats the advantages of this.

2. *Microsoft makes extensive use of collections in the class structures used in Visual Basic and their Office Applications. What advantages does this afford to an applications programmer working with Microsoft systems?* Since the collection is a ubiquitous structuring mechanism in Microsoft software, it is quick and easy to become familiar with any new Microsoft object model as it will always be similar in structure to others with which you are already familiar. Once you have learned to use the Word object model, it is very easy to learn to use the Excel object model.

3. *It is possible to step through each item in a collection using the syntax:*

```
For index = 1 To coll.Count
  coll(index).DoSomething
Next
```

Why is the **For..Each** *syntax preferable?* Using **For..Each**, a single object reference is attached in turn to every item in the collection, so the statement(s) that are then used to manipulate or query the item are simpler in form – **Obj.DoSomething**, *instead of* **coll(index).DoSomething**. A more important advantage to the use of **For..Each** is that **For..Each** will guarantee to enumerate all of the items in a collection, even if the collection changes during the enumeration. For example, we might decide to delete specific items in a collection using the code:

```
For index = 1 To col.Count
  If col(index).Type = expendable Then
    Col.Remove index
  End If
Next
```

Examine this code closely, and you might see that by deleting an item, you will also change the index of all of the successive items in the collection. Therefore, when an item is deleted, the next in the collection will escape the check for it being expendable. `For..Each` guarantees not to miss items out in this way.

4. *In the card game of Gin Rummy, discarded cards are placed on top of each other on the table between the players. A player can use his or her turn to pick up cards from the top of the discarded pile. In terms of the structures described in this chapter, how could the discarded pile be implemented?* A stack is the obvious structure.

5. *How would you characterize the world's telephone network from among the structures discussed in this chapter?* This is a graph – a number of arbitrarily interconnected nodes.

CHAPTER 9

Persistence

Software that could work only with information that was created since the computer system was switched on would be useless. All computer-based information, including programs, rely on a storage system that keeps data safe even when the system is switched off. Most computer systems operate a hierarchy of storage, at the top of which is the on-board working storage in the Central Processing Unit (the Pentium or other processor used by the system). Further down this hierarchy comes cache memory, then main memory, then off-line memory, which is normally disk storage. In terms of speed of access, the nearer the top of the hierarchy the faster the information can be accessed and manipulated. In terms of permanence, however, the lower down the hierarchy, the more permanent and more secure the data is. For users of computer systems, permanent storage is not an optional extra.

By the end of this chapter and after completing the practical exercise, you should be able to:

- discuss the various mechanisms by which the data in a system can be made persistent,

- implement simple stream-based persistence,

- use a relational database to create object-based persistence,

- compare the practical differences between stream-based and database-based persistence.

9.1   Persistence in software

Persistence is a term used to describe the way an application and its data can be made to have a life that extends beyond the exit point of the application. You will probably be painfully aware that the programs written as exercises up to this point have had the annoying habit of forgetting all of the information entered as soon as they were shut down. Obviously, real software does not do this. When you run Visual Basic, you are given the opportunity to load an existing project back into memory, so that you can continue from where you left off. In some systems, there is no need even to do this, since as soon as you run, say, a database application, it will return to the state that it was in the last time it was shut down.

Persistence is more than just a desirable property: it is essential for most types of computer work so that a job does not have to be completed in one session. This book has been written over a period of several months, and there were some brief periods of sleep during that time. Even had it been possible to write the whole text in one continuous session, it is very likely that the PC used would have crashed during such an extended period of use, and if no work had been saved in some way, it would have been lost. Without persistence, no one would write books, keep databases or even play games on a computer.

Files

The main way for computer programs to save information collected at run time is by using **Files**. Like a sheaf of paper-based information in a filing cabinet, computer files are mechanisms for storing information in an *ordered* way. The emphasis on the word 'ordered' is quite deliberate. Without some form of order, you would never be able to find any required piece of information in a filing cabinet. In computer terms, a *sequential file* is an ordered sequence of pieces of information.

Consider the term *rank and file*. This indicates a way of organizing lots of items (soldiers in this case) in rows (rank) and columns (file). File in this sense means *'an orderly line, as of soldiers one behind the other'* (Collins New English Dictionary). In a computer file, information is sent *in sequence* to some storage device (a disk, tape, network or whatever). When the information is retrieved, it will be returned in the same sequence it was originally sent out in.

Consider a program in which the user is asked to enter a sequence of names and exam marks. Instead of immediately processing these marks, they can instead be saved to a file for later retrieval:

```
open a file, F
get a Name from the user
While a Name has been entered
   get the Mark from the user
```

```
    write the Name and Mark to the file F
    get a Name from user
Wend
close file F
```

Note the need to ***open*** a file before saving information to it, and to ***close*** the file after its use. Also note the use of ***F***, a variable that identifies the file to our (pseudo-code) program. Finally, note the proper use of the ***while*** loop – first set up the exit condition to fail (get Name from user) and then, at the end of each iteration, set up the condition again.

Now we have a file of data, we can retrieve information from it for some form of processing. We have saved the items of data sequentially, and so the natural retrieval mechanism will be to read the items back in the same order:

```
open a file, F
While we are not at the end of file F
    read the Name and Mark
    print out the Name and Mark
    add the Mark to Total *
    add 1 to Count *
Wend
print out Total/Count (i.e. average mark) *
close file F
```

This example demonstrates the use of a ***sequential file***, which is the simplest form of file storage and retrieval. I have shown an additional bit of processing here (statements marked with an *) – the marks in the file have been averaged by the simple method of adding them all together and then dividing by the number of them. Note that the working of this pseudo-code *depends* on the file's contents being in the same order in which the file was written. It *expects* a sequence of names and marks in pairs.

File handling and file handles

Any programming language needs a mechanism for storing information in files and retrieving it again. In Visual Basic, a few keywords provide all of the necessary functionality: to open a file, to store information in it, to retrieve information from it and to close the file. Here is our pseudo-code example written in Visual Basic:

```
Sub CreateFile()
Dim F As Integer, Name As String
Dim Mark As Integer
    F = FreeFile
    Open "Marks.dat" For Output As #F
```

```
    Name = InputBox("Enter name")
    While Name <> ""
      Mark = InputBox("Enter mark")
      Write #F, Name, Mark
      Name = InputBox("Enter name")
    Wend
    Close #F
End Sub
```

As usual, the code has been topped and tailed as a Visual Basic sub (called **CreateFile**) so we will be able to call it when necessary. Apart from the statements required to package it as a sub and the variable declarations, one extra statement has crept in as part of the translation from pseudo-code to Visual Basic. The first executable statement, **F=FreeFile**, is necessary to ensure that the *file variable* used is a valid one. Visual Basic, in common with most other programming environments, uses an integer number as a file *handle*. This is simply a way of referring to the file (quite a complex construct) through a simple variable. Like anything that has a handle, the handle is simply a convenient mechanism for manipulating something that would not otherwise be easy to work with. We need to make sure that we are using a file handle that is not already in use in *any other program* running on the system. The best way to do this is to ask the operating system to supply us with one, hence the call to **FreeFile**.

Note we have used a **Write #** statement to send data to the file, and that our exit condition is that the user does not enter a name (so the **Name** variable contains an empty string).

```
Sub RetrieveFile()
Dim F As Integer, Name As String
Dim Mark As Integer
Dim Total As Integer, Count As Integer
  F = FreeFile
  Open "Marks.dat" For Input As #F
  While Not EOF(F)
    Input #F, Name, Mark
    Print Name, Mark
    Total = Total + Mark
    Count = Count + 1
  Wend
  Close #F
  Print "Average = ", Total / Count
End Sub
```

The **RetrieveFile** sub similarly needs to use a unique file handle, and so the call to **FreeFile** is repeated there. In this case, an **Input #** statement is used to read information back from the file. Note the use of the **EOF()** function (**End Of File**) to determine whether there is still information to be read.

The rules of sequential file handling are simple:

- You can only read back what you write and, with a sequential file, in the order in which it was written.

- The information returned must be assigned to variables of the correct type. Writing out a name followed by a mark, and then attempting to read back a mark followed by a name would cause an error. This is because we would be reading the mark into a string variable, which is OK, but would be reading the name into a numeric variable, causing a crash.

- You cannot read a file that has not been created. This most often happens when trying to read back a file but giving the wrong file name, or the wrong directory. If in doubt, be explicit with a file name (e.g. 'a:\Data\MyFile.dat'), and check whether it exists using the `Dir()` function in VB (see VB Help for more details).

- Always `Close` a file that has been opened once you have finished saving data into it or loading data back from it. The best normal solution is to Open, use and Close a file within a single subroutine. Visual Basic will close all files used by an application when the application exits, but leaving an open file just hanging around until this happens could cause it to be corrupted. House-keeping is best done as soon as it is needed.

- File handling requires external input, and so is error prone. Ideally, you should use Visual Basic's error handling mechanisms to prevent program crashes. As a minimum, you should check that a file has been opened as expected, which normally requires an error handler. If you are being diligent, check every file operation.

QUESTION 9.1

(a) Why should file access be any more error prone than other programming tasks?

(b) How could an error handler be used to allow the program to recover from a file-input error?

File types

As mentioned previously, a file is a sequence of similar items – student names and marks, bank account details, etc. The important feature is the type of item stored in the file, since without knowledge of this it would not be possible to read the information back in a way that made sense. For example, assume we had a data file containing a sequence of student names and marks, but had forgotten what was stored in the file. We could read the information back and interpret it in whatever way we liked. We might, for example, assume that we had a file of names where every second one was corrupted (and looked like a number), or we might assume that we had a file of pairs of names and passport numbers or whatever. Generally, a file has a specific *type* associated with it; the file type indicates the format of the information or how it is to be interpreted.

When we are dealing with files of similar items, this is simple to operate. For example, we can see that the following excerpt from a file contains three student names and their associated marks:

```
..."Joe Bloggs", 55, "Theresa Green", 72, "Wombat Snodgrass", 41,...
```

As far as a program is concerned, all that is necessary is to alternately read names and numbers. In fact, what the program is doing is to take a regular sequence of information and organize it as a table with two columns. Although the file itself is organized as a simple sequence of pieces of information, the program regards it as a name column and a mark column, as shown below:

```
...
"Joe Bloggs", 55
"Theresa Green", 72
"Wombat Snodgrass", 41
...
```

Sometimes we cannot interpret a file so easily. For example, it is common to store *text* in a file, as in Figure 9.1. In this case, we cannot assume that the file contents are divided up into logical units of information, but must find a more general way of interpreting it. A *text file* is a special type of file in which the significant type is a *character* of text. If we were to present the file excerpt in Figure 9.1 in tabular form, it would be:

```
F
i
l
e

T
y
...
```

```
File Types
As mentioned previously, a file is a sequence of similar items -
student names and marks, bank account details etc. The important
feature is the type of item stored in the file, since without knowledge
of this it would not be possible to read the information back in a way
that made sense. For example, assume we had a data file containing a
sequence of student names and marks, but had forgotten what was stored
in the file. We could read the information back and interpret it in...
```

Figure 9.1 *Part of a text file.*

Text files have another organizational form that can be applied – *lines* of text. In that case, the organization of the above file would simply appear as you would expect it to. From a program's point if view, a text file is a bit more complex, since in general the lines of text are not all exactly the same number of characters. Computer files resolve this difficulty by providing an ***end-of-line mark*** that acts as an indicator to a program that a new-line should start on the next character read. For example, the following code fragment would read an entire line-oriented text file and assign it to a single string variable. To preserve the line structure, `vbCrLf` is added to each line as it is read:

```
Line Input #n, L       ' Read a whole line from the file.
While Not EOF(n)       ' EOF() means End-Of-File
  S = S & L & vbCRLF   ' vbCRLF is the end-of-line mark.
  Line Input #n, L
Wend
...
```

The statement `Line Input...` reads in a line of text up to the next end-of-line mark (traditionally called a ***carriage-return line-feed*** sequence, referred to in Visual Basic as `vbCRLF`). What the code was doing was to read a file a line at a time and reassemble these lines so that the entire file, including its line format, was stored in the string variable `s`.

So far, the file formats we have looked at are based on sequences of characters, either as plain text, or grouped into some other format (such as names and marks). Visual Basic also supports ***binary files***. Where character-based files are constrained to containing only alphabetical, numeric and punctuation characters, a binary file can contain any value that can be expressed as a binary number. Binary files are often considered more awkward to work with than character-based ones. For one thing, it is not possible to load a binary file into a text editor (like Windows Notepad) and make sense of it – either such a file would not load, or it would appear to be total gobbledegook.

Binary files are used for efficiency. In terms of storage efficiency, more information can be stored in a given size of binary file because a character-based file contains a lot of redundant information. As for processing efficiency, reading an integer value from a character-based file requires that it be converted from characters (digits are just characters) to an integer number – storing 1 in a character file requires the reverse conversion.

Even better efficiency can be achieved by using a ***random-access*** file. This is a form of binary file that is optimally organized for speed of information storage and retrieval. The main requirement of a random-access file is that it must be possible to work out the exact size (in bytes – 8-bit binary numbers) of each item stored and retrieved. We will not deal with binary files or random-access files beyond this brief description in this book, but you should be aware that not all files contain just text characters. You can look up binary files in the Visual Basic help system for more information.

QUESTION 9.2

(a) The advantages of using a binary file are based on each record in the file being exactly the same length. Why should this make it possible to access certain data in a file much more quickly?

(b) Given a binary data file in which each record was 220 bytes long, what, in bytes, would be the position of the fifth record in the file?

9.2   Files of objects

Files can be used to store arbitrary data that has no apparent organization. However, it is usually much more useful to create files of specific *records* of data. In object oriented programming, a record will be all of the information contained in the member variables of a single object.

For example, if we had a collection of **CTransaction** items from the Bank Account example of the previous chapter, then we might decide to write the entire collection off to a file:

```
Dim T As CTransaction
Dim F As Integer
  ' Open a file to write to..
  F = FreeFile
  Open "Transactions.dat" For Output As #F
  For Each T In Transactions
     Write #F, T.TrDate, T.TrType, T.Amount, T.Description
  Next
  Close #F
  ...
```

The above listing assumes that we already have a collection of **CTransaction** items with the identifier **Transactions**. Reading this information back is a little more awkward, due to the need to *create* each transaction object before reading its information from the file, and then add it to the collection:

```
Dim T As CTransaction
Dim F As Integer
  ' Open the file for reading..
  F = FreeFile
  Open "Transactions.dat" For Input As #F
  While Not EOF(F)
     Set T = New CTransaction
     Input #F, T.TrDate, T.TrType, T.Amount, T.Description
     Transactions.Add T
  Wend
  Close #F
  ...
```

While this code will have the desired effect, there are several problems with it:

- The code needs to explicitly load each item of transaction data, and so depends on knowledge of what information a transaction object contains. This goes against encapsulation.

- The transactions are written out to and read from a whole file. There would be no opportunity to store more than one set of transactions in this file, because when reading the information back, there is nothing to differentiate one set from another. Effectively, we would need one file of transactions per account.

- The account information, presumably part of the object that the Transactions collection is a property of, would have to be stored in a different file, since we are constrained by the nature of files to have a regular structure where each item is a record of the same type.

All of these problems suggest that a simple file structure will not be sufficient to deal with anything but the most simply structured object oriented systems. For this reason, object oriented systems frequently rely on a storage structure built on top of a file-based system: a *stream*.

Files and streams

The name stream suggests a flow of information. Think about what can happen in a real stream or river. Whatever is dropped into the water will float downstream at the speed of the stream, and so maintain its relative position with respect to any other items dropped into it (provided they all float). However, unlike a file, where every item is expected to have the same structure, you can drop anything into a stream. Throw in a football, a stick and an old car tyre, and further down the stream, an onlooker will see a football, a stick and an old car tyre passing, in that order.

The problem with this scheme, if we are to use it to send objects to a storage medium, is that since we cannot expect every object to be of the same type, we need some way of identifying what type of object is next in the stream. We can see whether it is a football or old car tyre floating in a stream in the real world, but in a stream of data we need some other means of recognition.

If we send a **CAccount**, then each of its **CTransactions**, then another **CAccount** to a stream, we need to be able to identify this sequence of items as we read them back from the stream at a later date. The difficulty is due to the way that individual data members for one class of object look very much like individual data members from another. Based on the composition of the first item of member data, we could not tell whether an object being read was a **CAccount** or a **CTransaction**. There are two simple ways in which we can maintain the order of the original object sent to a stream when we retrieve them:

1. Store the objects in a hierarchy by storing the top-level object first, then a count of the number of second-level objects, and then each second-level object. The second-level objects in turn will store their own member data, followed by

a count of however many third-level objects there are, followed by each third-level object and so on.

2. Store an identification mark before each item to indicate what type of object it is. When reading the information back, read back an object type ID, then create the object and read its member data back, then the next object type ID, and so on.

Based on the first of these strategies, a sequence of accounts and transactions might appear as:

```
2
"Joe Bloggs", "1234"
2
#2/8/200#, "Deposit", 150.00, "Autobank Deposit"
#4/8/2000#, "Withdrawal", 25.00, "Cash Withdrawal"
"Mary Green", "1212"
3
#3/8/2000#, "Deposit", 150.00, "Autobank Deposit"
#4/8/2000#, "Withdrawal", 25.00, "Cheque Withdrawal"
#4/8/2000#, "Withdrawal", 25.00, "Autobank Withdrawal"
```

The first line is the number of **CAccount** objects (2). This is followed by the data from the first **CAccount** object (**Name** and **PINNumber**), followed by the number of transaction objects for that account (2), then one line per transaction object (**TrDate**, **TrType**, **Amount** and **Description**). Since we already know that there are two accounts in the stream, the next line must be account data for the second account, which is again followed by the number of transactions for that account. This structure could be used to cope with many more accounts and transactions.

Using the second strategy, the stream might appear as follows:

```
"CAccount"
"Joe Bloggs", "1234"
"CTransaction"
#2/2/99#, "Deposit", 150.00, "Autobank Deposit"
"CTransaction"
#4/2/99#, "Withdrawal", 25.00, "Cash Withdrawal"
"CAccount"
"Mary Green", "1212"
"CTransaction"
#3/8/2000#, "Deposit", 150.00, "Autobank Deposit"
"CTransaction"
#4/8/2000#, "Withdrawal", 25.00, "Cheque Withdrawal"
"CTransaction"
#4/8/2000#, "Withdrawal", 25.00, "Autobank Withdrawal"
```

In this case, we simply precede each object with an identifier (in this case a string, but an integer number is more common) that indicates its type. The program reading this data back would know to create and read a **CAccount**, then a sequence of **CTransactions** belonging to this account, then a second **CAccount** and its transactions.

Both of these strategies have some drawbacks. In the first case, the reading back of the entire hierarchy depends on the integrity of the code for writing and reading all of the objects in the hierarchy. If any of it has an error that makes the reading of the stream get out of synchronization, everything will be misread from that point on. The second method at least provides the possibility of getting back into synchronization since each object is delimited separately. However, the second method makes it the responsibility of one object in the system (the application itself, or its main form, or some delegated stream-handling object) to create each object and reassemble the hierarchy. This could get complex.

Worst of all, neither scheme provides for rapid access to any single object in the stream. If all objects took up exactly the same amount of storage space, we could always calculate the position in the file that, say, object number 27 was located at. We could then load up this object by quickly skipping past the first 26 and reading the next one. However, we cannot assume that all objects are the same size, and so could not use this scheme to provide immediate access to a single account. To read back any information, we always need to read back the entire stream.

These problems are inherent in the use of streams. Some commercial stream-based systems create a registration database so that reading an object identifier from a stream can automatically trigger the creation of that type of object.

As a rough guide, use a hierarchical stream if your application has a structure that uses a top-level object to manage a collection of objects, each of which might own a further collection and so on. Object identifiers are more useful with more ad-hoc structures, such as a top-level object that contains an aggregation of other objects of various classes.

QUESTION 9.3

To read back any information from a stream, we need to read back the entire stream. Why might this be a drawback in some applications?

Objects and streams

The principle of encapsulation was described as being the single most important feature of object oriented programming: never allow a user of a class of object (i.e. a programmer) to access the internal mechanisms or data. Instead, we provide services to allow objects to do everything for themselves: this saves us from breaking encapsulation and also makes it easier to work with objects.

When dealing with objects and streams, we need to uphold this principle. The most obvious thing to do is to provide all classes with a **LoadFromStream** and a **SaveToStream** method, so that all objects are able to store their data and recreate themselves from saved data on demand. The naive way of doing this would be to give every object the ability to open a file, store their data in it and close the file again. However, apart from the huge inefficiency that all of the file opening and closing would have, it would also require that each object had its own file, very inefficient in storage space, or was able to locate its own data within a file. This would be difficult when the object is newly created.

From an object's point of view, a stream should be an *open file* that data can simply be dropped into. We can then give any object access to the stream by simply passing it a *file handle*. For example, here are the **LoadFromStream** and **SaveToStream** methods for the **CTransaction** class:

```
Public Sub SaveToStream(ByVal Filehandle As Integer)
    Write #FileHandle, mvarTrDate, mvarTrType, mvarAmount, _
                    mvarDescription
End Sub

Public Sub LoadFromStream(ByVal Filehandle As Integer)
    Input #FileHandle, mvarTrDate, mvarTrType, mvarAmount, _
                    mvarDescription
End Sub
```

By making the assumption that the file is already open, a stream becomes a very simple mechanism to use. Our rules for handling streams become:

- Each item reads and writes its own data from and to a stream – the writer of the class can ensure that all member data is written and that the order for reading and writing is the same. Moreover, changes to an object's structure will be more easily accommodated, since the changes to the Load and Save methods will be local (within the class file for that object).

- A stream (file) is opened for writing before any write operations are executed. All data is written in a single session.

- A stream (file) is opened for reading before any read operations are executed. Systems are reconstructed from a stream by creating objects of the correct type immediately before a read operation. This requires that the system is able to construct objects of the correct class: a hierarchy of objects or an object identification mark can be used for this. For efficiency reasons, all of a stream should be read in a single operation, since it is difficult to find the position of a specific object in the stream without reading the stream up to that object.

- A stream should be closed immediately it has been written or read.

If we return to a simplified version of the ATM class model of Chapter 7, with classes **CAccount** and **CTransaction**, we can see how a stream would be managed for a hierarchical system. Recall that the structure of that example system was as shown in Figure 9.2. From this, we can see that the top-level object in the hierarchy is the ATM form, and so it should be this object that has the responsibility for opening and

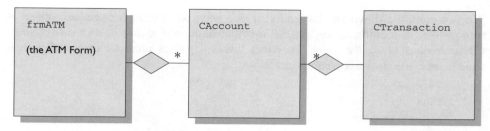

Figure 9.2   *A hierarchical class model.*

closing the stream. The form contains a collection of accounts (more precisely, it contains a reference to a collection of accounts), so we can consider it to be the top-level object in the application's hierarchy. This simplifies the required sequence of stream operations to

> *Open the stream*
> *Send the top-level object, and all of the objects that it owns to the stream*
> *Close the stream*

to send the application's data hierarchy to a stream, and

> *Open the stream*
> *Extract the top-level object, and all of the objects that it owns from the stream*
> *Close the stream*

to retrieve this data hierarchy.

The top-level object will need to deal with all of the objects it 'owns', or is directly responsible for in the hierarchy. To send these to the stream:

> *Write the number of CAccount objects in the collection to the stream*
> *For each CAccount in the collection*
>   *Ask it to write its data to the stream*
> *Next*

To retrieve them:

> *Read the number of CAccount objects from the stream*
> *For index = 1 To number of CAccount objects*
>   *Create a new CAccount object*
>   *Ask it to reads its data from the stream*
>   *Add it to the Accounts collection*
> *Next*

We can continue down the hierarchy in this way, so that each **CAccount** object is responsible for loading/saving its own member data, *and asking its own collection of CTransactions to do the same*. To effect this, each class must be provided with a **LoadFromStream** and **SaveToStream** method:

```
' ====================
' CTransaction class.
' ====================
' With this method, a single transaction saves itself to the stream..
Public Sub SaveToStream(ByVal Filehandle As Integer)
    Write #FileHandle, mvarTrDate, mvarTrType, mvarAmount, _
                    mvarDescription
End Sub

' With this method, a single transaction loads itself from the
' stream..
Public Sub LoadFromStream(ByVal Filehandle As Integer)
    Input #FileHandle, mvarTrDate, mvarTrType, mvarAmount, _
                    mvarDescription
End Sub

' ================
' CAccount class.
' ================
' With this method, a single account saves itself to the stream
' and asks each of its transactions to do the same..
Public Sub SaveToStream(ByVal FileHandle As Integer)
Dim T As CTransaction
    Write #Filehandle, mvarName, mvarPIN
    Write #FileHandle, Transactions.Count
    For Each T In Transactions
      T.SaveToStream FileHandle
    Next
End Sub

' With this method, a single account loads itself from the stream
' and asks each of its transactions to do the same..
Public Sub LoadFromStream(ByVal FileHandle As Integer)
Dim T As CTransaction
Dim count As Integer, index As integer
    Input #FileHandle, mvarName, mvarPIN
    Input #FileHandle, count
    For index = 1 To count
      Set T = New CTransaction
      T.LoadFromStream FileHandle
      Transactions.Add T
    Next
End Sub
```

At the top level of the hierarchy, the application's main form contains a collection of account objects. It should also have a **SaveToStream**/**LoadFromStream** pair of methods.

```
' =====================================
' frmATM class - the top level class.
' =====================================
' With this method, the main form of the application, which
' contains the collection of accounts, saves this collection
' to the stream..
Public Sub SaveToStream(ByVal FileHandle As Integer)
Dim A As CAccount
  Write #FHandle, Accounts.Count
  For Each A In Accounts
    A.SaveToStream FHandle
  Next
End Sub


' With this method, the main form of the application reconstructs
' the collection of accounts from the stream..
Public Sub LoadFromStream(ByVal FileHandle As Integer)
Dim A As Caccount, count As Integer, Index As Integer
  Input #FHandle, count
  For index = 1 To count
    Set A = New CAccount
    A.LoadFromStream FHandle
    Accounts.Add A, A.Name ' Use the Name property as a key.
  Next
End Sub
```

We could easily extend this to accommodate the full hierarchy of banks, branches, customers, accounts and transactions. At each level of object, **LoadFromStream** and **SaveToStream** code need only concern itself with the object data and the collection it houses.

At the top level (in this case the form), it is necessary to kick off the Load/Save processes at the appropriate times. A Load sequence should be activated when the top-level object is loaded into memory, a Save sequence when it is unloaded from memory. Since the top-level object is a form, we can use the **Form_Load** and **Form_Unload** events to initiate these procedures.

```
' frmATM class's event handlers..
' Form_Unload opens a file and sends the form's data to it..
Private Sub Form_Unload()
Dim fileHandle As Integer, fileName As String
  fileName = "ATMData.dat"
  fileHandle = FreeFile
```

```
   Open fileName For Output As #fileHandle
   Me.SaveToStream fileHandle        ' Me is this form.
   Close #fileHandle
End Sub

' Form_Load opens a file and extracts the form's data from it..
Private Sub Form_Load()
Dim fileHandle As Integer, fileName As String
   fileName = "ATMData.dat"
   ' We should check that this file exists (since it might be the
   ' first time the application has been run..
   If Dir(fileName) = "" Then Exit Sub
   fileHandle = FreeFile
   Open filename For Input As #fileHandle
   Me.LoadFromStream fileHandle
   Close #fileHandle
End Sub
```

A typical excerpt from a file created by this hierarchical stream operation is shown in Figure 9.3 (added comments are in *italics*).

Robust stream management

From the object point of view, streams provide an ideal mechanism for making objects and hierarchies of object persistent. However, an application programmer has to remember to do everything in the right order: assigning a file handle, opening the file, and asking objects to load or save themselves as required. Although there is nothing difficult about any of this, the fact that there are several operations makes it more likely that things can go wrong. An application will crash if you attempt to send an object to a stream that has not been opened, or use an invalid file handle, or make any of a number of other simple errors. The ideal situation would be to automate as much of the stream management as possible, and one way of accomplishing this is to

```
2       Number of accounts
"Joe Bloggs", "12345"
3       Number of transactions, acct #1
#12/1/99#, "Deposit", 150.0, "Cash Deposit"
#14/1/99#, "Withdrawal", 15.00, "Autobank London Golders Green"
#22/1/99#, "Withdrawal", 20.0, "Autobank Glasgow Buchannan Street"
"Mary Green", "15451"
2       Number of transactions, acct #2
#17/1/99#, "Deposit", 200.0, "Autobank Deposit Paisley Town Centre"
#24/1/99#, "Deposit", 100.0, "Autobank Deposit Paisley Town Centre"
```

Figure 9.3 *A file created by an example ATM stream (with additional comments).*

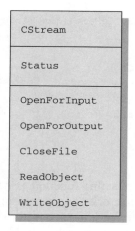

Figure 9.4   *A stream class.*

develop a **CStream** class. The class interface (all of the public methods and properties) is shown in the class diagram in Figure 9.4.

The **status** property can be used to determine the current state of a Stream object: whether file errors have occurred, whether it is currently working with an open file and what happened at the last operation. All of the other interface members are methods to cause the Stream object to do something.

OpenForInput and **OpenForOutput** have obvious purposes, but we can take the opportunity to make them more generally useful. Normally, we would open a file by providing a name and path, such as `"c:\My Documents\MyFile.str"`, to indicate the file name and the folder it was to be found or created in. We can deal with this situation easily by making the file name and path a parameter to the **OpenFor...** methods.

However, in some situations, it would be useful to simply ask for a file to be opened without having to worry about where or under what name. This might be useful where, for example, an application will have one file of object data that will always be associated with it. In this situation, we can ask the file object to derive a file name and path, based on the name of the application, the folder the application is running from, and a special file extension to indicate that this file is a stream. The application-specific information can be determined by accessing some properties of the **App** object that Visual Basic maintains for every project:

- **App.Path** is the name of the drive and folder the program is running from.

- **App.EXEName** is the name that has been given to the project, or the name of the executable program.

- We can use the custom file extension '**.str**' to indicate that this file is a stream.

Using this, we can create a function to generate a file name for a stream object:

```
Private Function GenerateFileName() As String
Dim FN As String
  FN = App.Path
  If Right(FN, 1) = "\" Then
    FN = FN & App.EXEName & ".str"
  Else
    FN = FN & "\" & App.EXEName & ".str"
  End If
  GenerateFileName = FN
End Function
```

The `If..Then..Else` construct in this function is necessary because of an inconsistency in the way that file directories are named in a Windows system. The root directory of a Windows file device is named with a drive letter followed by ':\'. Therefore the root directory of a floppy disk would be '`a:\`'. However, the directory path of any other folder under the root does not end with a '\' character. Therefore, depending on where an executable file is running from (the root or a folder), its name may or may not have a backslash appended to it.

If we assume that there is no backslash (the more general case), we need to insert one when naming a file path. However, if we do this, we will end up with a badly formed file name if a file is in the root directory, for example '`a:\\MyFile.str`'. The `GenerateFileName` function takes this into account by adding a backslash only if one is necessary to separate the name of the file from its path.

In `OpenForInput` and `OpenForOutput`, we can specify an `Optional` parameter so that the user of the stream class can choose to specify a file name and path or not. If the parameter is missing, we can simply call the `GenerateFileName` function.

`CloseFile` simply closes the stream's file and sets the status message appropriately. The `ReadObject` and `WriteObject` methods take an object reference as a parameter and then ask this object to read itself from or write itself to the stream. A requirement imposed by this method is that the class of the object passed to the stream must provide a `SaveToStream` and `LoadFromStream` pair of methods.

Here is the code for the `CStream` class:

```
Option Explicit

Private mvarFileName As String
Private mvarFileHandle As Integer
Private mvarStatus As String

' This method creates a filename to match the application's
' name and path. e.g. if the application is stored at location
' "c:\Data\" and has the name "Application.exe", the file name
' generated will be "c:\Data\Application.str".
Private Function GenerateFileName() As String
Dim FN As String
  FN = App.Path
```

```
   If Right(FN, 1) = "\" Then
     FN = FN & App.EXEName & ".str"
   Else
     FN = FN & "\" & App.EXEName & ".str"
   End If
   GenerateFileName = FN
End Function


' These methods open the file for output/input.
' The Optional parameter gives the programmer the opportunity
' to select a different file name.
Public Function OpenForOutput(Optional ByVal FName) As Boolean
On Error GoTo err_OpenFileForOutput
   If IsMissing(FName) Then
     FName = GenerateFileName
   End If
   mvarFileHandle = FreeFile
   mvarFileName = FName
   Open FName For Output As #mvarFileHandle
   mvarStatus = "File " & FName & " open for Output"
   OpenForOutput = True
   Exit Function
err_OpenFileForOutput:
   mvarStatus = Err.Description
   mvarFileHandle = 0
   OpenForOutput = False
End Function


Public Function OpenForInput(Optional ByVal FName) As Boolean
   If IsMissing(FName) Then
     FName = GenerateFileName
   End If
   If Dir(FName) <> "" Then
     mvarFileHandle = FreeFile
     mvarFileName = FName
     Open FName For Input As #mvarFileHandle
     mvarStatus = "File " & FName & " open for input"
     OpenForInput = True
   Else
     mvarStatus = "File " & FName & " does not exist"
     mvarFileHandle = 0
     OpenForInput = False
   End If
End Function
```

```
Public Sub CloseFile()
  Close #mvarFileHandle
  mvarFileHandle = 0
  mvarStatus = "File Closed"
End Sub

Public Function Status() As String
  Status = mvarFileStatus
End Function

' This method takes an object of any class as a parameter
' and asks it to save itself to the stream. Note that
' the object's class must have a SaveToStream method..
Public Sub WriteObject(O As Object)
On Error Goto err_WriteObject
  O.SaveToStream mvarFileHandle
  Exit Sub
Err_WriteObject:
  mvarStatus = "Error " & Err.Number & " on writing object. " _
                        & Err.Description
  Err.Raise Err.Number, "CStream::WriteObject", _
                        "Can not write object"
End Sub

' As for WriteObject, the object's class must have a
' LoadFromStream method..
Public Sub ReadObject(O As Object)
On Error Goto err_ReadObject
  O.LoadFromStream mvarFileHandle
  Exit Sub
err_ReadObject:
  mvarStatus = "Error " & Err.Number & " on reading object. " _
                        & Err.Description
  Err.Raise Err.Number, "CStream::ReadObject", _
                        "Can not read object"
End Sub

Private Sub Class_Initialize()
  mvarStatus = "Unassigned"
End Sub

Private Sub Class_Terminate()
  CloseFile
End Sub
```

Note that the `Class_Initialize()` event-handler sets the stream status to 'Unassigned' and `Class_Terminate()` closes any open file – both valid behaviour in the context of a stream object.

Now that we have a stream class, we can quickly add persistent behaviour to any of the applications developed previously. We must, however, remember to add the **LoadFromStream** and **SaveToStream** methods to every class involved. Returning to the bank account example, we can now use the stream class to simplify the persistence issue. The **SaveToStream** and **LoadFromStream** methods are largely the same, since the stream's **WriteObject** and **ReadObject** methods simply pass a file handle to the object to save or load itself as previously. However, at the top level, the code to open and close the stream (in **Form_Load** and **Form_Unload**) makes use of the **CStream** class:

```
' With this method, the main form of the application opens a file
' for use as a stream, then calls the stream's WriteObject method,
' passing itself as a parameter..
Private Sub Form_Unload()
Dim S As CStream
Dim A As CAccount
  Set S = New CStream
  If S.OpenForOutput() Then   ' No name - let the stream generate one.
    S.WriteObject Me
    S.Close
  End If
End Sub
' With this method, the main form of the application creates and
' opens a Stream object, then calls the stream's ReadObject
' method, passing itself as a parameter..
Private Sub Form_Load()
Dim S As Stream
  Set S = New CStream
  If S.OpenForInput() Then
    S.ReadObject Me
    S.Close
  End If
End Sub
```

By making use of the **CStream** class, the test for the existence of the file before a load is now simpler – check whether the stream's **OpenForInput()** method was successful.

QUESTION 9.4

Given what you know about streams, in which of the following applications would a stream-based filing system be suitable?

(a) A customer database with 10,000,000 customer records
(b) A text file editor
(c) A strategy game program in which the current state was required to be saved to disk before the program was terminated
(d) An airline booking system.

9.3   Objects and databases

While streams are a perfectly good persistence mechanism for saving and restoring the complete state of an object oriented system, this is often not required, and for some systems it may not be possible. Consider, for example, the database system for a large company. It is likely that there will be millions, or even billions, of records of data, each of which corresponds to the state of a single object. To load the state of the entire system into an object model would require a huge amount of computer memory, and would probably take a long while to do. Systems of this scale tend to work on the basis of single data records, small sets of data records or aggregate information about a lot of data records (for example, the total number of customer accounts, or the total customer credit amount).

We would neither be able nor wish to develop a system that would create an object model of the entire system in cases like these. Database systems work with large amounts of information, most of which is stored *off-line*, on a disk or some other form of permanent storage. Information is brought into main memory to be processed, and then sent back to off-line storage. New records are created in main memory and sent to disk when they have been fully entered.

In contrast, objects are kept in the computer's main memory, and so far we have only considered the use of permanent storage for keeping information when a program is not actually running. However, there is an entire class of object oriented program that is required to work with larger amounts of data than could be maintained as an on-line object model. These **object oriented databases** work on the principle that an object is reconstructed from a disk record if and when it is required. Matters get complicated when the objects in the object model in use are highly interconnected. In this case, reconstructing an object from a disk record may then have the knock-on effect of forcing the reconstruction of all of the objects that the first must refer to, and in turn all of the objects that they refer to, and so on. Various strategies are used to minimize the impact of these types of interconnections in object databases.

Fully functioning object oriented databases tend to be large and complex systems purpose-built for strategic purposes: large-scale Computer Aided Design and Manufacturing (CAD/CAM) systems, telecommunications data-management systems and similar applications with massive data requirements. We will not consider them further here.

Relational database systems

Visual Basic comes equipped with a full Relational Database Management System (or RDBMS), which is the same one as that used by Microsoft Access. It also provides a number of ways in which a programmer can connect a program to an Access database, from a very easy to use, form-based database model to a fully featured remote access database system.

A relational database is one in which all data is stored in *tables*, which are structures that can hold a number of records that all have the same composition. For

Name	Address1	Address2	PostCode	Telephone
Joe Bloggs	1 Acacia Ave.	Glasgow	G11 3XX	041 123 4567
Annette Curtin	2 High St	Stewarton	ST1 2EW	123 5678
Neil Doon	3 Low Rd	Kingussie	KG2 0QQ	234 4567
...	...	...	...	...

Figure 9.5 *A table, with rows and columns of data.*

example, a data table to hold customer information would be made up of a number of *rows*, each of which had the same number of *cells* of data in it. All of the cells from the same position in each row make up a *column* of data, as shown in Figure 9.5.

Organizationally, a row of a table constitutes a *record* of data, while a column contains a specific *field* of data. In the table in Figure 9.5, the first row (ignoring the title row) contains a record of data about a person (Joe Bloggs), while the first column contains the Name field of each record.

A relational database is composed of a number of tables (Figure 9.6), which are related to each other by the information in them. An example of a relationship would be where a customer record had one field that uniquely identified that record (usually a customer number), and this number also identifies all the records in a table of purchases that relate to this customer. The customer number in the customer table is known as that table's **primary key**, while the same number inserted into another table to relate it to this customer is then known as a **foreign key**.

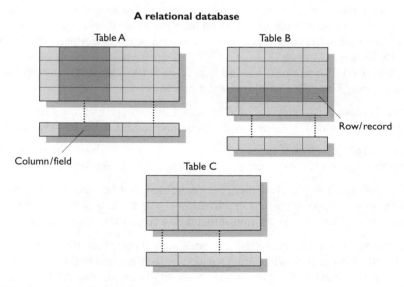

Figure 9.6 *A relational database.*

From our perspective as object oriented programmers, a relational database is made up of tables, each of which can contain the member data for all of the objects of a specific class. Compared to a true object oriented database, this is an inadequate system since each class's methods have been separated from the object data in a very non-object oriented way. However, we can make use of a relational database as a persistence mechanism. Provided we use the information in tables as simply the data from which objects can be reconstituted, the relational database model works well in supporting object oriented systems, particularly those in which objects are not required to be available on-line at all times.

Using ADO to manage a relational database

Microsoft currently provides in ActiveX Data Objects (ADO) a solid object hierarchy for the management of relational databases. ADO is part of their Universal Data Access (UDA) strategy, and replaces the more piecemeal approaches they have promoted over the years. Consequently, Visual Basic programmers no longer need to become familiar with the alphabet soup of database programming models that have confused their database connectivity choices since the early days of Visual Basic. ADO was introduced to Visual Basic in version 6.0, and it is this model we will use for examples here. Earlier versions of Visual Basic used a model known as Data Access Objects (or DAO), which is similar but not code compatible with the current model.

Two object libraries are provided to work with databases in VB6. The ADO object model and library provides user-level access to an existing relational database, allowing data records to be added, edited and removed and existing data sets to be retrieved. The ADOX object model and library provides facilities to create new database elements or alter the structure of a database. These two libraries separate the two complementary function groups of Data Manipulation and Data Definition. By making them distinct, Microsoft has simplified the process of deploying a database program, since users who only need to access a database will not need the facilities of the ADOX library.

ADOX and ADO are based around simple object models that can represent any database system. The ADOX object model provides:

- The *Catalog* class, which is used to access the *structure* of a database, allowing tables to be added, removed and restructured and indexes to be created

- The *Table* class, which is used to create new table structures, retrieve information on the structure of existing tables, and restructure tables

- The *Index* and *Key* class, which, between them, can be used to add indexes to a table to speed up data access and to allow the creation of *joins* between tables to form *virtual tables* that contain information from more than one actual table.

For our purposes, we can make use of the Visual Basic Data Environment, a tool included with VB6 (equivalents are provided with VB5 and VB4), to perform the work for which the ADOX classes would normally be used. The ADO object model provides a more user-oriented set of database access classes:

- The `Connection` class, which is used to form a connection to an existing database (analogous to the file handle you would use to open a stream file)

- The `Recordset` class, which is the main data retrieval class, used to return information from a relational database as a set of database records and to provide update access to sets of database records.

Both libraries contain other classes that can be used to define and manipulate information in relational databases, although we will make do with the classes mentioned.

In object oriented programming terms, these classes make up only the first layer of an adequate object oriented database solution. This layer is sometimes referred to as the *data access layer*. We can build application-specific and user-interface specific code on top of the standard database classes to make it easy to manage data in programs. The result is often referred to as a *three-tier* application, the tiers being:

- The data access layer, that deals with forming a connection with and getting information to and from the actual database

- The *business object* or *business logic* layer, that forms a set of business objects from the information in the database so that certain *business rules* can be imposed on the way the information is handled

- The *user-interface*, or *presentation* layer, that deals with presenting the business objects and allowing the user to interact with them.

This *three-tier* approach gives us a very flexible way of presenting a database to a user while imposing *business rules* on the way that the database is used. The benefits of this approach are the same benefits that object orientation can provide to any type of application, but have additional purchase in database-style applications:

- Objects can be used to manage all of the database-specific operations within the application, thereby making the application code itself easier to create and maintain. These are the *data access objects* that make up the *data access layer*.

- Changes to the underlying database need not affect the application code, since they can be made to the classes that provide database access.

- Changes to the business rules can be localized to the business object layer, so that it is often possible to avoid making changes to the database structure or access layer.

- The business logic layer can tightly control the way that the information in the database is used and updated. The *business objects* in this layer know how to interact with the data access layer but impose rules as to how this data can be used and changed, from the perspective of the environment they are used in. *Business rules*, such as a rule that makes it impossible for a customer to withdraw money from a bank account where the current balance would not cover the withdrawal, would be coded in this layer.

- We can make the information in a database appear as though it was a simple object model to the user-interface. Data access and business logic can be given an interface that provides apparently continuous access to every element in a large database even though only a few objects may be in memory at any one time, thereby simplifying the design of the *user-interface layer*. This layer simply handles events from the user and presents information from the lower layers.

- Once the two bottom layers are built, we can create a range of applications based on the same database and object model. This makes it possible to develop applications that are optimized for particular users within a larger organization. For example, applications for data entry and recall might be important in the front office of a company, while others might provide for the analysis of all of the information in the database to enable executives to make strategic decisions.

QUESTION 9.5

If we were to build the bottom two layers of a system to provide robust object access, what type of components would be required to form the top layer? How would it be possible to create a range of applications based on the pre-built bottom layers?

By developing an object model to act as an access layer between the application and the database, we will effectively be making on-the-fly translations from the relational data model to an object model and back again, as shown in Figure 9.7.

In many cases, the data access objects provided by Microsoft are sufficient to form the bottom tier. To make this scheme work, we need to create a robust and responsive interface between the business logic and data access layers.

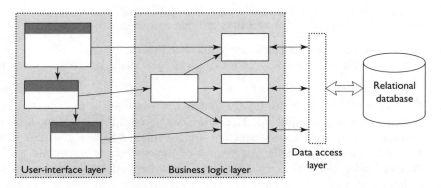

Figure 9.7 *Three-tiered application structure.*

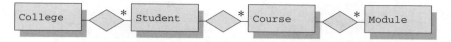

Figure 9.8 *An object model for managing student records.*

An example of data access in a three-tiered system

As an example, consider how a college or university might manage data on the modules taught to its students. There would be a need to keep records of the subjects each student has attended a course in, the results of any assessments they are subject to, and their progression and certification for each individual subject and their course as a whole. In terms of an object model, this might be composed as shown in Figure 9.8.

The object model in Figure 9.8 mirrors the way that information would be stored in database tables, apart from the top-level component, which would be an alias for the entire database. We would therefore require:

- A table of student records, containing Name, Address and Contact details

- A table of course records, containing data detailing the course of studies a student has registered for

- A table of module details, containing the subject name and performance data such as test and exam marks and marks for project work.

The structure of both the object model and the database tables is organized to be as unrestrictive as possible. Any individual who enrols at the college will have a single record in the database that stores their details. An individual can enrol for as many courses of study as the college will allow. Any specific course of study will comprise a number of modules to make up the qualification.

The three tiers of the system would be built as follows:

- The database and data access layer will provide access to the raw data in the tables, allowing new records to be created, existing ones modified and sets of records retrieved for analysis.

- The business logic layer will use the data access layer according to the rules of the college (allowing a student to enrol for only one course within an academic session, assuring a student has achieved the required marks in the components of a module before awarding a pass, etc.).

- The user-interface layer will provide methods and controls for creating new objects (aliases for data records), recalling existing objects, updating properties and analyzing the object model.

For example, the detailed object models for a course and a module might be as shown in Figure 9.9.

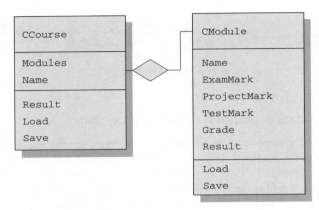

Figure 9.9 *The relationship between a course and its modules.*

While we could create the **CCourse** and **CModule** classes entirely in Visual Basic code, using a relational database would be much more efficient in this application. We would therefore devise two table structures, one to store course records and one to store module records. Using Access or Visual Basic's Visual Data Manager, we might create a database that contains the two table structures (among others) shown in Figure 9.10.

Note that the enrolment table contains relatively little information: simply a course name, an **CourseID** and a **StudentID**. The **Modules** property of the **CCourse** class is of course a collection, and in a relational database each module in this collection would become a record in the module table. The **CourseID** field is a necessity in a relational model, since this value will uniquely identify the enrolment record and every module record that relates to it (i.e. each module in its modules collection).

The **StudentID** field is used for the same purpose, but in the other direction. In this case, a student record will have a unique identification field (a matriculation number is normal in many colleges and universities), and we can identify each enrolment

Course table	
Field name	*Type*
StudentID	String
CourseID	Long integer
Name	String (30)

Module table	
Field name	*Type*
CourseID	Long integer
Name	String (30)
ExamMark	Byte
ProjectMark	Byte
TestMark	Byte

Figure 9.10 *Data tables for the object model in Figure 9.9.*

record as belonging to a particular student by repeating this number in each. In database terminology, **StudentID** is the *primary key* field of a **Student** record, and is a *foreign key* of a **Course** record. **StudentID** is used as a ***link field***.

Access to the database

Microsoft's ADO classes comprise the object model that provides the general access layer to any database. Creating a reference to the ADO library in the project enables use of the ADO classes. To do this, select **Project/References** from the IDE menus, and when the list appears, look for the **Microsoft ActiveX Data Objects 2.0 Library** entry, check it on, and press the **Apply** button. Of course, if you have a later version of this library, you should select that. (Earlier versions of the ADO libraries may not be completely compatible with the example code here.)

The listing below shows how the ADO objects could be used to connect an application to the **Module** table of our college database and return a set of **Module** records to match a particular **Course** record:

```
Public Property Get Modules(CourseID As Long) As Recordset
Dim C As ADODB.Connection, R As Recordset
Dim SQL As String
   ' Create and open a database Connection..
   Set C = New ADODB.Connection
   C.Open "Provider=Microsoft.Jet.OLEDB.3.51; " & _
          "Data Source=C:\ADOProject\College.mdb;"
   ' Build a SQL command as a string..
   SQL = "SELECT * FROM Module WHERE [Course ID] = " & CourseID
   ' Create a recordset based on this SQL command..
   Set R = New ADODB.Recordset
   With R
     .CursorType = adOpenDynamic        ' Style of connection
     .CursorLocation = adUseClient      ' Where record location
                                        ' is managed

     .LockType = adLockOptimistic
     .Open SQL, C
   End With
   ' Return the resulting recordset..
   Set Modules = R
End Function
```

Note that the above example uses a newly created connection object, with a string specifying what form of database is being used (**Provider=**) and where it is located. This string will be different for different versions of the ADO library in use. The easiest way to determine the correct connection string to use is to build a sample project with an ADODC data *control* on a form, right-click on the control, and select ADODC properties from the pop-up menu. You can then get the control's property page to build a connection string to your selected database that you can copy and paste.

The resulting recordset has been created by our specification set up in the SQL statement:

```
SELECT * FROM MODULE WHERE [Course ID] =
```

The final part of the **WHERE** condition, which is used to extract data records from a table which match a given criterion, is added within the **Property Get** routine by appending the numeric parameter – our course identifier. This **Property Get** will return a *dynaset*, or dynamic recordset, which is effectively a table in memory. The recordset contains the data from all matching records and exposes a single record at a time for reading or amending. For example, to determine the name of a module in the recordset, we could use

```
MsgBox R.Fields("Name")
```

and to update this same field, we could use

```
R.Fields("Name") = "Programming Principles"
R.Update
```

The ActiveX Data Object Library is a large and complex library, and the details of working with it are outside the scope of this book. However, Microsoft provides a great deal of on-line information regarding ADO programming, and there are many good books on the subject for those who wish to take database programming further.

We will look at the use of ADO as the data access layer for creating a useful business object layer for a small, sample object database application. (Note that this example can only be completed if you have an installation of Visual Basic 6.0 or later in either the Professional or Enterprise version, or a suitable installation of Microsoft Access 2000. If you do not have one of these, you will not have the ADO Library.)

9.4 A sample data-access application

In this example, we will develop a reduced model of the Student/Course/Module application partially described earlier. By making the simplistic rule that a student simply enrols for a number of modules, we can remove the Course section of the hierarchy, resulting in an object model that can be covered in a small example. The purpose of the example is to demonstrate the development of the middle, business object layer, although features and issues relating to the development of the other layers will be described and discussed as necessary.

Tables 9.1 and 9.2 can be created as an access database, using either Microsoft Access itself or Visual Basic's Visual Data Manager add-in. Field types and sizes are shown in the headings of the tables. The table design effectively provides for a one-to-many relationship between a student and that student's modules. For example, student 'Joe Bloggs' who has Matric (Matriculation Number) 'Jb1234' and lives at

Table 9.1 *Student table.*

Matric (Text – 8 character)	Name (Text – 50)	Address (Text – 50)
Jb1234	Joe Bloggs	1 High Street
Tg2468	Theresa Green	22 West Road
Pb3536	Peter Black	107 Long Road
...	...	...

Table 9.2 *Module table.*

Matric (Text – 8)	Name (Text – 30)	Exam (Byte)	Project (Byte)	Test (Byte)
Jb1234	Business IT	36	42	7
Jb1234	Database Sys.	28	33	6
Jb1234	Systems Analys.	32	38	8
Jb1234	Software Dev.			7
Tg2468	Database Sys.	29	35	8
Tg2468	Software Dev.	35	41	8
Pb3536	Systems Analys.	27	29	5
...	...	...	...	...

address '1 High Street' has completed three modules ('Business IT', 'Database Sys.' And 'Systems Analys.'). He also has one module to be completed ('Software Dev.') but has completed the Test part of the assessment of this module.

Now that the tables define the structure of the data in the application, we need to consider how the object model will work. This involves defining the business rules for the application and developing an object model that implements these as it provides access to the underlying data.

Note in Figure 9.11 that the `CStudent` class has a `Modules` property that will be implemented as a collection class. We will arrange the class so that this collection is automatically constructed once enough student information (a `Matric` code) has been provided.

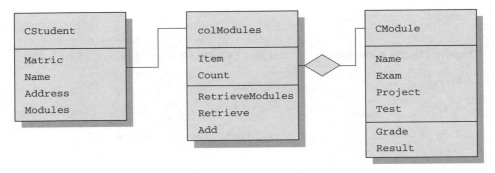

Figure 9.11 *Our simplified object model.*

The `CModule` class

We should start with the `CModule` class, since the other classes depend on this for operation. We can start by developing this class as we would any other class, by providing member variables and property methods to allow access to them:

```
Option Explicit

Private mvarName As String
Private mvarExam As Byte
Private mvarProject As Byte
Private mvarTest As Byte
Private mvarMatric As String

' Additional member variables for interacting with the database
' access layer..
Private mvarRS As Recordset
Private mvarBkMark As Variant
Private IsChanged As Boolean
```

In addition to the member variables required to support the class's properties, several other member variables are used for managing the database connection. **MvarMatric** keeps track of the Student class that owns this (and possibly other) module(s). **mvarRS** and **mvarBkMark** are used to maintain the connection to a recordset of modules (**mvarRS** is a set of records from the Module table while **mvarBkMark** is a *bookmark*, a Variant that is used by an Access database to record the location of a specific record in a recordset). Finally, **IsChanged** is a Boolean that we will set to **True** whenever one of an object's member variables is changed. It will then act as a flag to indicate when the underlying database record must be updated.

The standard property methods are used for accessing and changing property values. One small twist to these is the use of the **IsChanged** member variable, used in the **Property Let** methods.

```
Public Property Get Name() As String
   Name = mvarName
End Property

Public Property Let Name(ByVal NewValue As String)
   If mvarName <> NewValue Then
     mvarName = NewValue
     IsChanged = False
   End If
End Property

Public Property Get Exam() As Byte
   Exam = mvarExam
End Property

Public Property Let Exam(ByVal NewValue As Byte)
   If mvarExam <> NewValue Then
     mvarExam = NewValue
     IsChanged = True
   End If
End Property

Public Property Get Project() As Byte
   Project = mvarProject
End Property

Public Property Let Project(ByVal NewValue As Byte)
   If mvarProject <> NewValue Then
     mvarProject = NewValue
     IsChanged = True
   End If
End Property

Public Property Get Test() As Byte
   Test = mvarTest
End Property

Public Property Let Test(ByVal NewValue As Byte)
   If mvarTest <> NewValue Then
     mvarTest = NewValue
     IsChanged = True
   End If
End Property
```

Whenever a property changes, this change will have to be reflected in the database table that stores the module information. We could commit the change to the database immediately, but this could impact on the efficiency of the program, since we might make three changes one after the other, each triggering a database update.

Instead, we can use **IsChanged** to indicate that an update is necessary before the object is destroyed.

A method is required to retrieve a **CModule** object's data from the Modules table. This will take a recordset as a parameter, with the requirement that the required object's data is in the *current record* of the recordset:

```
Public Sub GetRecord(R As Recordset)
  If Not IsNull(R("Matric")) Then
    mvarMatric = R("Matric")
  End If
  If Not IsNull(R("Name")) Then
    mvarName = R("Name")
  End If
  If Not IsNull(R("Exam")) Then
    mvarExam = R("Exam")
  End If
  If Not IsNull(R("Project")) Then
    mvarProject = R("Project")
  End If
  If Not IsNull(R("Test")) Then
    mvarTest = R("Test")
  End If
  ' Keep a reference to this Recordset to allow easier updates..
  Set mvarRS = R
End Sub
```

The test **If Not IsNull(..)** is used to make sure that data has been added to a field before we try to read its value. Without this, the program would crash if we tried to read a **null** field (one which the user has not entered any value into). When we delete a module object, we must ensure that the underlying data record is also deleted:

```
Public Sub DeleteData()
  mvarRS.Delete
End Sub
```

If any of the properties in a **CModule** object have changed, we need to make sure it is possible to **Update** the underlying database:

```
Public Sub Update()
  If mvarBkMark <> "" And IsChanged Then
    mvarRS("Exam") = mvarExam
    mvarRS("Project") = mvarProject
    mvarRS("Test") = mvarTest
    mvarRS.Update
    IsChanged = False
  End If
End Sub
```

Note that if there have been no changes to the object data, no update operation will be executed. Note also that once we have updated the data, `IsChanged` should be reset to prevent unnecessary updates.

Two simple methods can provide business rules for a `CModule` by determining a `Grade` and `Result`, based on the sum of the assessment components. Assume that the Exam will be a mark out of 40, the Project a mark out of 50, and the Test a mark out of 10 – the sum of these is then a percentage. A Pass mark will be a mark of 40 or higher, while a re-sit is only allowed for a mark of between 30 and 39.

```
Public Property Get Grade() As String
Dim mark As Byte
  mark = mvarExam + mvarProject + mvarTest
  Select Case mark
    Case 70 To 100
      Grade = "A"
    Case 60 To 69
      Grade = "B"
    Case 50 To 59
      Grade = "C"
    Case 40 To 49
      Grade = "D"
    Case Is < 40
      Grade = "E"
  End Select
End Property


Public Property Get Result() As String
Dim mark As Byte
  mark = mvarExam + mvarProject + mvarTest
  Select Case mark
    Case Is > 39
      Result = "Pass"
    Case 30 To 39
      Result = "Resit"
    Case Is < 30
      Result = "Fail"
  End Select
End Property
```

Finally, we need to ensure that the Update method is called should this object be deleted:

```
Private Sub Class_Terminate()
  Update
End Sub
```

Now that we have a class for dealing with individual modules, we can build on this to create a collection of modules. Much of the database access code is placed here so that a single access session can be used for all of the modules in a collection.

A collection class for CModules

```
Option Explicit

' local variable to hold collection
Private mCol As Collection
Private RSModules As Recordset
```

The member variables for the collection are simple enough. One holds the standard collection object (mCol), while the other maintains a link with the underlying data table (RSModules).

Since the data for these comes from a table in the database, we need also to maintain a connection to this, using the RSModules recordset. A method, RetrieveModules, builds the collection, given a Matric string to match:

```
Public Sub RetrieveModules(Matric As String)
Dim SQL As String
Dim M As CModule
    ' Retrieve the module records from the database..
    SQL = "SELECT * FROM Module WHERE Matric = '" & Matric & "'"
    Set RSModules = New ADODB.Recordset
    With RSModules
      .CursorType = adOpenDynamic
      .CursorLocation = adUseClient
      .LockType = adLockOptimistic
      .Open SQL, gConn, adOpenDynamic
    End With
    ' Add an object to the Modules collection
    ' for each record..
    While Not RSModules.EOF
      Retrieve
      RSModules.MoveNext
    Wend
    RSModules.MoveFirst
End Sub
```

The RetrieveModules method shown above makes use of a Retrieve method to collect the data for each module. This method creates the CModule objects and appends them to the collection, sending the GetRecord message to each:

```
Private Function Retrieve() As CModule
Dim objNewMember As CModule
    ' create a new object
```

```
    Set objNewMember = New Cmodule
    ' Instruct it to get its data from the current record in
    ' the recordset..
    objNewMember.GetRecord RSModules
    mCol.Add objNewMember, objNewMember.Name
    ' return the object created
    Set Retrieve = objNewMember
    Set objNewMember = Nothing
End Function
```

Of particular interest is the line that calls the **GetRecord** member of the newly created **CModule** object. The **CModule** will extract its data from the current record in **RSModules**. We can then add the object to the collection as usual. In this example, we use the module name as a key, since we know a student will not be assessed twice for the same module, so the key will be unique within this collection.

When creating a brand new module, as opposed to one that is simply retrieved from a database image, we also need to ensure that the database is updated appropriately:

```
Public Function Add(ByVal pMatric As String, _
                    ByVal pName As String, _
                    ByVal pExam As Byte, _
                    ByVal pProject As Byte, _
                    ByVal pTest As Byte) As CModule
    ' Add a new database record..
    RSModules.AddNew
    RSModules("Matric") = pMatric
    RSModules("Name") = pName
    RSModules("Exam") = pExam
    RSModules("Project") = pProject
    RSModules("Test") = pTest
    RSModules.Update
    ' Now add a new object to the collection.
    Set Add = Retrieve
End Function
```

By calling the **Retrieve** method immediately after adding a new record to the underlying database, we immediately create a new **CModule** object that will read the data back from the database. The combination of the recordset object with the new record as the current one makes it possible for the new **CModule** to pick up the information and also to keep a reference to the correct position in the Modules table.

Since this is a collection class, we need also to provide the standard methods, **Item**, **Count** and **NewEnum**. The procedure attributes for the last two of these must be set up as shown in the previous chapter.

```
Public Property Get Item(vKey As Variant) As CModule
  ' The standard Item Property Get - must remember to set the
  ' Procedure ID to (Default).
  ' Can use module name or number as a Key..
  Set Item = mCol(vKey)
End Property

Public Property Get Count() As Long
  Count = mCol.Count
End Property

Public Property Get NewEnum() As IUnknown
  ' this property allows you to enumerate
  ' this collection with the For ... Each syntax
  ' Remember to set the Procedure ID of this
  ' member to -4, and Hide it.
  Set NewEnum = mCol.[_NewEnum]
End Property
```

We have a little more work to do than for a standard collection when we remove an item from the **Modules** collection, since we must also purge it from the database. The **DeleteData** method of the **CModule** class does this:

```
Public Sub Remove(vKey As Variant)
  mCol(vKey).DeleteData
  mCol.Remove vKey
End Sub
```

Finally, the two class event-handlers for **Initialize** and **Terminate** must deal with the collection object:

```
Private Sub Class_Initialize()
  ' creates the collection when this class is created
  Set mCol = New Collection
End Sub

Private Sub Class_Terminate()
  ' destroys collection when this class is terminated
  Set mCol = Nothing
End Sub
```

The student class

This class provides access to a student's name, address and collection of modules. The key field in the Student table is **Matric**, so we can arrange to build a student object once a **Matric** has been provided, since we can look up the rest of the information in the database. Again, we start by defining the member variables:

```
Option Explicit

Private mvarName As String
Private mvarAddress As String
Private mvarMatric As String
Private mvarModules As Modules
' These member variables are for database access..
Private mvarRS As Recordset
Private mvarBkMark As Variant
Private isChanged As Boolean
```

Beyond the normal set of member variables, one for each main property, we have added three extras. The first of these, **mvarRS**, is a **Recordset** reference variable, which we will use to maintain a connection with the Student table in the database while the object is in memory. The second is a Variant that we again use to store a bookmark for this particular record. The third, **isChanged**, is a Boolean variable we can use to indicate whenever a database update is required, as we did with the **CModule** class.

The simple property methods can be coded as usual, although again we need to ensure that the **isChanged** variable is set to true when an update is made:

```
Public Property Get Name() As String
  Name = mvarName
End Property

Public Property Let Name(ByVal NewValue As String)
  If mvarName <> NewValue Then
    mvarName = NewValue
    isChanged = True
  End If
End Property

Public Property Get Address() As String
  Address = mvarAddress
End Property

Public Property Let Address(ByVal NewValue As String)
  If mvarAddress <> NewValue Then
    mvarAddress = NewValue
    isChanged = True
  End If
End Property
```

The **Matric** property is a bit different. We will use the **Matric** property to retrieve a student record from the database. The **Property Get** will be as normal, but the **Property Let** can be given a more useful role. If, when the **Matric** property is updated, we can find a corresponding record in the Student table, we should retrieve that data. If not, we should create a new record with the given **Matric** setting. Note that when we retrieve a Student record, we are also in a position to build a collection of that student's **Modules**:

```
Public Property Get Matric() As String
   Matric = mvarMatric
End Property

Public Property Let Matric(ByVal NewValue As String)
Dim SQLGet As String, SQLNew As String, QUOTE As String * 1
' Matric is the primary key, so we can use a change in
' this to signal a change in Student and the Modules
' collection...
   QUOTE = "'"
   If mvarMatric <> NewValue Then
     ' Look up the matching student..
     mvarMatric = NewValue
     SQLGet = "SELECT * FROM Student WHERE Matric = " & QUOTE _
               & mvarMatric & QUOTE
     Set mvarRS = New ADODB.Recordset
     With mvarRS
        .CursorType = adOpenDynamic
        .CursorLocation = adUseClient
        .LockType = adLockOptimistic
        .Open SQLGet, gConn
     End With
     If mvarRS.RecordCount = 0 Then
       Set mvarRS = Nothing
       ' Need to create a new student.
       ' Start by creating a recordset of the Student table.
       SQLNew = "SELECT * FROM Student"
       Set mvarRS = New ADODB.Recordset
       With mvarRS
          .CursorType = adOpenDynamic
          .CursorLocation = adUseClient
          .LockType = adLockOptimistic
          .Open SQLNew, gConn
       End With
       ' Now add a new record..
       mvarRS.AddNew
       mvarRS("Matric") = NewValue
       mvarRS.Update
       ' Now we can retrieve this record (for consistency
       ' with the case where the student record already
       ' existed)..
       Set mvarRS = New ADODB.Recordset
```

```
        With mvarRS
            .CursorType = adOpenDynamic
            .CursorLocation = adUseClient
            .LockType = adLockOptimistic
            .Open SQLGet, gConn
        End With
    End If
    If Not IsNull(mvarRS("Name")) Then
        mvarName = mvarRS("Name")
    End If
    If Not IsNull(mvarRS("Address")) Then
        mvarAddress = mvarRS("Address")
    End If
    ' Make sure we have a bookmark..
    mvarBkMark = mvarRS.Bookmark
    ' Now need to build a Modules collection..
    mvarModules.RetrieveModules mvarMatric
    End If
End Property
```

The **Property Let Matric** method has the responsibility of keeping the entire Student/Modules object model in synchronization. It makes it a simple matter for a user of the class to access the details of a particular student or create a new one. Note that we use a one-character string variable, QUOTE, which has the value "'", to delineate the student's Matric in the SQL string. We can use this to add a single quote mark on either side of the **mvarMatric** variable to add it to a SQL string without the program code becoming difficult to read.

In order that we can access the details of individual modules, we must expose the modules collection as a **Property Get**. We must also provide an **Update** method, a **Class_Initialize()** and **Class_Terminate()** to manage the creation of the collection:

```
Public Property Get Modules() As Modules
    Set Modules = mvarModules
End Property

Public Sub Update()
    If isChanged Then
        mvarRS.Bookmark = mvarBkMark
        mvarRS("Name") = mvarName
        mvarRS("Address") = mvarAddress
        mvarRS.Update
    End If
End Sub

Private Sub Class_Initialize()
    Set mvarModules = New Modules
End Sub
```

```
Private Sub Class_Terminate()
  Update
  Set mvarModules = Nothing
End Sub
```

We now have a **CStudent** object that will manage its own collection of modules, including retrieval from the database and updates. Finally, we can test these classes in the Immediate window. A useful starting point would be a sub to create a connection object. This can be a global object, since we will wish to access it from various places. The sub can go in a code module, and be called in the on-load of the main form, or from the Immediate window.

```
Public gConn As ADODB.Connection

Public Sub CreateConnection()
  Set gConn = New ADODB.Connection
  gConn.Open "Provider=Microsoft.Jet.OLEDB.3.51; " & _
        "Data Source=C:\ADOProject\College.mdb;"
End Sub
```

At this point we have an object model that can be used as the bones of a number of different application programs, depending on the user's requirements. Before commencing the test, it is necessary to build the underlying database and populate it with a number of sample records, as shown in the tables earlier:

```
CreateConnection
Set S = New CStudent
S.Matric = "Jb1234"
? S.Modules.Count
   4
? S.Modules(1).Name
Business IT
S.Modules.Add "Jb1234", "Object Oriented Programming", 35, 41, 7
? S.Modules.Count
   5
? S.Modules("Object Oriented Programming").Grade
   A
? S.Modules("Object Oriented Programming").Result
Pass
```

From this stage, there is little or no difference between this and an object model with no persistence, so developing a user-interface will not be any different.

QUESTION 9.6

(a)   How does the three-tier structure help in the development of object oriented programs that use a database?

(b) List the advantages plus any disadvantages you can think of this structure.

(c) Can you think of an example of a situation where a single persistent object model might benefit from the ability to create a number of distinct user-interfaces?

9.5 Review questions

1. Complete the following:
   (a) A variable that maintains a link between a program and an open file is called a _____.
   (b) Files that contain raw numeric data that is not formed into readable characters are called _____ files.
   (c) Files that are organized into equal sized chunks of data for fast storage and retrieval are called _____-_____ files.
   (d) A stream is a file that contains the data from a sequence of _____.
   (e) A database that is composed of a number of logically interconnected tables is known as a _____ database.
   (f) A field in a database table that is used to relate records in it to records in other tables is a _____ field.
   (g) Data in the primary key field in a record in one table can be matched with data in the _____ key field in other tables to form a relationship.
   (h) The three object layers in a three-tier application structure are the _____ layer, the _____ _____ layer and the _____-_____ layer.

2. Why is the `FreeFile` function used when opening or closing a file in Visual Basic?

3. In Visual Basic, we can only send an object's data to a file, not its methods. Why do you think this is the case?

4. A file saved from a Visual Basic program contains a list of integer numbers. We do not know how many numbers are in the file. Write a program fragment that will read all of the numbers (assume the file is already open) and produce two resulting values – a count of the numbers and their total.

5. Describe the circumstances that could cause reading data from a file to generate a run-time error.

6. Explain why a stream-based filing system is inadequate for dealing with large numbers of objects.

9.6 Practical exercise:
Adding persistence to the Agenda project

The Agenda project that was started in Chapter 6 and continued in Chapter 7 is not, in its current state, persistent. In this short exercise, we will add the required methods and structures to make it so.

The first change to be made is that we must give the `CScheduleItem` class the facility to load and save its own instance data from/to a stream. The methods `Load` and `Save` will provide this.

```
Public Sub Load(ByVal stream As Integer)
   Input #stream, mvarText, mvarDateTime, mvarAlarm, mvarPriority
End Sub

Public Sub Save(ByVal stream As Integer)
   Write #stream, mvarText, mvarDateTime, mvarAlarm, mvarPriority
End Sub
```

The facility to load and save an entire collection of agenda items is built on this. We should not make any change to the `COrdList` class, since this is a general class that knows nothing about agenda items, and being a general class, we would not wish to amend it since this would restrict its usefulness to other applications. Fortunately, we have exposed all of the necessary information in the interface of the collection class to enable this.

 Add the `Save` and `Load` methods for the `CAgenda` class.

```
Public Sub Save(ByVal stream As Integer)
Dim I As CScheduleItem
   Write #stream, colAgenda.count
   For Each I In colAgenda
     I.Save stream
   Next
End Sub

Public Sub Load(ByVal stream As Integer)
Dim I As CScheduleItem
Dim count As Integer, index As Integer
   Input #stream, count
   For index = 1 To count
     Set I = New CScheduleItem
     I.Load stream
     colAgenda.Add I
   Next
End Sub
```

The `Load` and `Save` methods of the `CAgenda` class deal with the collection of `CScheduleItem` objects by saving/loading the number of items first. When saving, it is a simple matter of asking each schedule item to save itself to the stream. When loading, it is necessary to create a schedule item object for each entry in the stream before asking it to load its own data.

Finally, the top-level object in the program (the **frmAgenda** form) must open the file/stream before asking the agenda object to load itself or save itself. Since we wish the agenda to load up immediately on running the program, we should use the **Form_Load** event-handler to initiate the load sequence. The **Form_Unload** event can be used as a trigger to save the agenda. One useful tip is the use of **App.Path** to provide the name of the folder the application is running from. The agenda file will be saved to this folder, which will simplify matters if we ever decide to relocate the agenda executable – simply move its data file with it.

 Create the **FileName** variable in the **frmAgenda form**.

```
Private FileName As String
```

 Code the **Form_Load** and **Form_Unload** methods to kick off the stream operations.

```
Private Sub Form_Load()
Dim filehandle As Integer
  Set Agenda = New CAgenda
  If Right(App.Path, 1) = "\" Then
    FileName = App.Path & "Agenda.dat"
  Else
    FileName = App.Path & "\Agenda.dat"
  End If
  If Dir(FileName) <> "" Then
    ' The file exists, so..
    filehandle = FreeFile
    Open FileName For Input As #filehandle
    Agenda.Load filehandle
    Close #filehandle
    RefreshList
  End If
End Sub

Private Sub Form_Unload(Cancel As Integer)
Dim filehandle As Integer
  filehandle = FreeFile
  Open FileName For Output As #filehandle
  Agenda.Save filehandle
  Close #filehandle
End Sub
```

This completes the stream management for the Agenda application. It is possible to make the program a bit more user-friendly by making it easier to enter schedule item details. For example, we can arrange that a new schedule entry be set for the current date and time to simplify data entry.

 Add a `Class_Initialize` method to the `CScheduleItem` class to set the default entry to the current date and time.

```
Private Sub Class_Initialize()
   mvarDateTime = Now     ' This sets the date and time to the
                          ' current date and time.
End Sub
```

This will save the user some typing when adding a new item to the agenda. When the **frmScheduleItem** form loads, it should display the current date and time setting from the current item.

One final piece of polish we can add to the Agenda application is to save the user some typing when entering new details or editing existing details in a schedule item. We can use the **GotFocus** and **LostFocus** events of the various text boxes on the **frmScheduleItem** form to preselect the text in the box. By doing so, if the user chooses to type anything into the text box, it will immediately replace the existing text and save the user having to backspace over the existing contents. Two properties, **SelStart** and **SelLength**, control the amount of text selected in a text box. **SelStart** is effectively the cursor position in the text box, and **SelLength** the number of characters beyond this that are selected.

 Add code on the form to preselect text when the user places the cursor in any of the text boxes.

```
Private Sub txtDay_GotFocus()
   txtDay.SelStart = 0                      ' Puts cursor at the start
   txtDay.SelLength = Len(txtDay.Text)     ' Selects all of the text
End Sub

Private Sub txtHour_GetFocus()
   txtHour.SelStart = 0
   txtHour.SelLength = Len(txtHour.Text)
End Sub

Private Sub txtMinute_GetFocus()
   txtMinute.SelStart = 0
   txtMinute.SelLength = Len(txtMinute.Text)
End Sub
```

```
Private Sub txtMonth_GetFocus()
  txtMonth.SelStart = 0
  txtMonth.SelLength = Len(txtMonth.Text)
End Sub

Private Sub txtYear_GetFocus()
  txtYear.SelStart = 0
  txtYear.SelLength = Len(txtYear.Text)
End Sub
```

This completes the Agenda project. You can now use the ***File/Make Agenda.exe*** menu item in the Visual Basic IDE to compile this to a project that you can distribute to other computer users. Note that if you do distribute the program, you will have to ensure that the Visual Basic runtime support file, **MSVBVMXX.DLL** (where **XX** should be replaced by the version number of Visual Basic, 40 for version 4, 50 for version 5 or 60 for version 6), is on the target PC. This file is required for *any* Visual Basic project to run on a machine.

9.7 Answers to questions

QUESTION 9.1

(a) One reason why file access could be any more error prone than other programming tasks is that it is likely to be different parts of a program, or even different programs, that are responsible for writing and reading a file. However, the most compelling reason is that file access involves the use of systems outside the control of the program, and this leads to a higher probability of a run-time error. For example, an expected file might not exist, or may be on a removable disk that has been removed from the drive.

(b) The details of how an error handler could be used to allow the program to recover from a file-input error would depend on the nature of the error, but typically, an error handler would be put into force at the point immediately before a file was opened. Any error in opening the file, or in trying to read or write information from or to it, would cause the error handler to be invoked. This could minimally inform the user of the nature of the error and then abandon the file access, or more comprehensively, allow the user to make changes (e.g. the name of the file for a problem in opening a file) or perform some other recovery strategy. The key feature of the error handler is that it operates instead of the default action that is the program terminating with an error message.

QUESTION 9.2

(a) If every record in a file is the same length, then simple arithmetic can be used to determine the location of the start of a given record. Operating systems (and programming language file handling functions) provide the ability to go directly to a specified location in a file and start reading or writing information at that point, and so the ability to work out the location of a specific record of data enables this facility to be used to the full.

(b)   The first four records would take up $4 * 220 = 880$ bytes of storage, so the fifth record would start at the 881st byte in the file. In general, record N would start at byte number $(N - 1) * 220 + 1$.

QUESTION 9.3

In an application that stores a very large amount of information, e.g. a database system, it would be impractical to have to load all of the information to retrieve a part of it. Even if we choose to discard items as we read past them so that the entire stream does not have to be read into memory, if would be very inefficient to read an item that is near the end of the stream, since we would need to read past all of the preceding items to get to it. Most applications that use streams work by reading the entire stream into memory as they start up – streams are used as a way of restoring the previous state of an application. More complex data requirements almost always use some form of random file access.

QUESTION 9.4

A stream-based filing system would be suitable as follows:

(a)   A customer database with 10,000,000 customer records: not at all suitable

(b)   A text file editor: possible for small text files, but as file sizes increase, a stream-based application would become less viable

(c)   A strategy game program in which the current state was required to be saved to disk before the program was terminated: very suitable, unless the strategy game involved a very large number of complex objects

(d)   An airline booking system: not at all suitable.

QUESTION 9.5

Forms would be required to form the top layer.
The two bottom layers form an object model. We could build different forms to provide different levels of access to the business logic layer. For example, in the College project described, it would be possible to develop forms that simply allowed student information and module results to be accessed in a read-only mode by not providing any way to change information in the object model. This interface would be suitable for

providing students with on-line access to their data. A teacher could be given access via a different form that allowed marks to be altered. An administrator could use a form that allowed student information (name and address plus any other enrolment data) to be altered as necessary.

QUESTION 9.6

(a) The three-tier system makes it possible for the applications programmer to be unaware of the database system in use and how to work with it. By presenting the programmer with a more logical and consistent business model of the information, it is possible to make sure that inconsistent operations are not allowed.

(b) Advantages: database layer protects the underlying information from illegal operations; business logic layer provides programmer with a conceptually simple object model; business logic layer can be altered to change business rules without affecting either of the other layers; database layer can act as a consistent interface to changing data structure; database layer can provide access to legacy database information without the business logic or application programmer being aware of this. Disadvantages: initially more complex to set up; requires programmers to follow strict rules.

(c) The answer to Question 9.5 provides a good example of a situation where a single persistent object model might benefit from the ability to create a number of distinct user-interfaces.

9.8   Answers to review questions

1.
(a) *A variable that maintains a link between a program and an open file is called a* handle.

(b) *Files that contain raw numeric data that is not formed into readable characters are called* binary *files.*

(c) *Files that are organized into equal sized chunks of data for fast storage and retrieval are called* random-access *files.*

(d) *A stream is a file that contains the data from a sequence of* objects.

(e) *A database that is composed of a number of logically interconnected tables is known as a* relational *database.*

(f) *A field in a database table that is used to relate records in it to records in other tables is a* key *field.*

(g) *Data in the primary key field in a record in one table can be matched with data in the* foreign *key field in other tables to form a relationship.*

(h) *The three object layers in a three-tier application structure are the* data access *layer, the* business logic *layer and the* user-interface *layer.*

2. *Why is the* `FreeFile` *function used when opening or closing a file in Visual Basic?* It is used to get a file handle from the operating system that is guaranteed to be valid and not currently in use by another application.

3. *In Visual Basic, we can only send an object's data to a file, not its methods. Why do you think this is the case?* Visual Basic class methods are subs and functions. These are defined in the Visual Basic program for specific classes. It would be awkward and dangerous for Visual Basic to allow this information to be accessible to programmers at run time (when file accesses are made) since a bit of bad programming could totally destroy the capabilities of a class at a stroke. There would also be a potential paradox, since the program code to load and save objects would presumably be sent to a file, but could not be loaded back from a file since the necessary instructions would not be in memory until they had been read from the file. More fundamentally, methods belong to a class, not any specific object of the class.

4. *A file saved from a Visual Basic program contains a list of integer numbers. We do not know how many numbers are in the file. Write a program fragment that will read all of the numbers (assume the file is already open) and produce two resulting values – a count of the numbers and their total.*

```
Count = 0
Total = 0
While Not EOF(theFile)
   Input #theFile, aNumber
   Count = Count+1
   Total = Total + aNumber
Wend
```

5. *Describe the circumstances that could cause reading data from a file to generate a run-time error.* There are several possible causes. The file might not exist, or might be saved with a name different from that expected, or in a different location, or have been stored in a removable disk (i.e. a floppy). The program might be trying to read the data in the wrong format (e.g. an integer instead of a floating-point number); the program might be trying to read past the end of the file; the file could be corrupt; a user might remove a disk from the drive while it is being accessed; or the file being read might be unavailable because another program is writing to it.

6. *Explain why a stream-based filing system is inadequate for dealing with large numbers of objects.* One principle in a stream-based system is that it is an all-or-nothing system. Either the whole stream is read, on none at all. For a very large number of objects, a system would be unlikely to have enough main memory to accommodate them all.

CHAPTER 10

Polymorphism

Visual Basic provides the facility to define a class as an *interface*, or *abstract class*, which can then be inherited by other classes, *concrete classes*, to provide type-compatibility. In this chapter, we use this facility to create classes that are type-compatible as a means to simplify program structure and improve generality.

By the end of this chapter, you should be able to:

- create *interfaces* that define the range of properties and methods a class must provide,

- use interfaces in new class definitions to create *polymorphic* classes, i.e. classes that have compatible interfaces and can be used interchangeably,

- create programs that make use of polymorphs to simplify their control structure.

10.1   Interfaces

Imagine a world in which jargon in communication was taken to extremes. If you spoke to your doctor, you would have to speak in a language suitable for medical conversations, using the jargon that a doctor would. If you spoke to a lawyer, you would have to converse in purely legal terms (your brother might have to be referred to as 'the party of the first part'). In fact, everyone that you spoke to would only understand you if you spoke in their particular specialist jargon, and you in turn would insist on speaking to people using only the jargon of your own specialist subject.

In this world, there would be very few conversations. You would have to study law before having a night in the pub with your lawyer friend, and would live in fear of a doctor's appointment. No one but other nuclear physicists would speak to nuclear physicists. Now compare this to the real world. We all have specialist jargon we need to use sometimes to enable rapid and effective communication. However, we also speak an 'everyman' version of the language that serves us for all of the non-specialist communication we get involved in. Doctors speak doctor jargon with other doctors, and talk down to our level (mostly) when we consult them. Similarly, lawyers make a living out of having a specialist jargon that most of us cannot speak or understand, but translating it into common terms for us mere mortals.

Sometimes it needs to be the same with software objects. Most classes are developed to fulfil a specialist purpose, and because of this, their interfaces tend to be made up of keywords that fit that purpose. For example, we might develop a student marks system, in which each subject that a student studies has its information encapsulated in a `Subject` object. This might have properties called `Name`, `Exam`, `Project` and `Test`, and methods called `Grade` and `Result`. This class interface is quite specialized, since these names would not be appropriate to an arbitrary class (with the possible exception of the `Name` property).

However, consider the more general case of a class (any class) whose objects we wish to be able to send to and retrieve from a stream. In example classes in Chapter 9 on Persistence, we developed classes to which we gave two methods, `SaveToStream` and `LoadFromStream`. Provided these methods took an integer parameter that was the file handle, they would work with other code that sent objects to a stream and retrieved them from it. In fact, we relied on classes having these methods with the appropriate parameter, since without them, the objects could not have been sent to a stream using the code that we used. We made it a proviso that if a class was to be *streamable*, it had to provide a pair of methods called `SaveToStream` and `LoadFromStream` that took an integer file handle as a parameter.

We have met other examples like this. All of our collection classes had a default `Item` property, a `Count` property, `Add` and `Remove` methods and a hidden `NewEnum` method. Without these, they would not have worked as proper collections, since Visual Basic makes some assumptions about collection classes (in particular, it insists on using the `NewEnum` method to enable its `For..Each` syntax). In effect, Visual Basic will only be able to work with a collection class that provides these methods.

Interfaces

Ideally, we should be able to specify that a class supports a specific set of *interface methods*, instead of having to list all of the methods it must support separately. Visual Basic provides a way of doing this. We can say that a class ***implements*** a certain interface. We can also define an interface by creating a class that contains only the specified members *in outline*. Each property, sub or function in an interface has a first line defining the name, type of routine and parameters, and a last line, the **End Function**, **End Sub** or **End Property** statement, but no actual code.

For example, we can easily create an interface definition for a class that is able to save itself to a stream and load itself from a stream. We would start by creating a new class and complete the interface with the following code:

```
' IStreamable - an interface definition for objects that can be sent
' to and restored from a Stream.

Public Sub LoadFromStream(ByVal fileHandle As Integer)
  ' Method to load an object from a stream
End Sub

Public Sub SaveToStream(ByVal fileHandle As Integer)
  ' Method to save an object to a stream
End Sub
```

It is a convention to give an interface class a name beginning with a capital I, standing for 'Interface'. In the listing of the **IStreamable** interface, the most striking feature is the total lack of executable code. We have stated method names and parameters for any object that supports this interface, but have not said what these methods will do. Nor have we specified any member data for the class. In this respect, an interface is an *abstract class*. It specifies how methods are to be called, but not what they do, or what specific information they should work with.

Implementing an interface

When a class supports all of the methods specified in an interface class, we can say it *matches* the interface. However, this relationship is not a strong enough one to build a large and complex application in which many classes interact. If we wish to guarantee that one class provides all of the methods defined in a particular interface, Visual Basic allows us to specify that it **Implements** that interface. For example, we can create a new class that will be guaranteed to be able to work with a **CStream** object as defined in the previous chapter by including the **IStreamable** interface class in the Visual Basic project, and then making this statement at the top of the class file:

```
Implements IStreamable
```

Now, the Visual Basic IDE will provide outline methods for all of the interface functions on demand. To implement one of the stream methods, we can select it from the combo-boxes at the top of the class's code window. Visual Basic will provide a method outline in the same way it does when adding an event-handler.

As shown in Figure 10.1, **IStreamable**, the interface that the new class implements, is now available in the top-left combo-box of its code window. The top-right combo-box provides a list of the methods to be implemented. In this case, the two methods **LoadFromStream** and **SaveToStream**, will appear. Visual Basic will now refuse to run the program that this new class belongs to until at least empty versions of these two methods have been implemented.

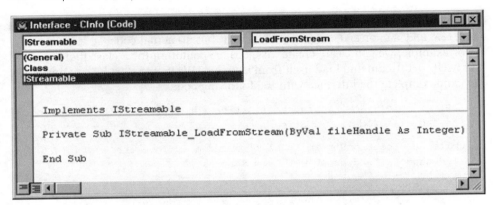

Figure 10.1   *Generating an outline for an interface method.*

Note that when an interface method is implemented, Visual Basic adds the interface name to the method name within the implementing class. Instead of

```
Private Sub LoadFromStream(ByVal fileHandle As Integer)
```

the implemented method is called

```
Private Sub IStreamable_LoadFromStream(ByVal fileHandle As Integer)
```

This allows Visual Basic to identify the implemented methods and which interface they belong to, since it is possible for a class to implement any number of interfaces.

Changes to the `CStream` class

We should remember that an interface defines how two sides of an interaction will operate. If we are to define an `IStreamable` interface class, we also need to ensure that the class that uses objects with this interface, `CStream`, is changed to match it.

Before we continue with the creation of a class to match the `IStreamable` interface, we need to make the `CStream` class enforce its compatibility with this interface. Previously, the `ReadObject` and `WriteObject` methods of that class took parameters of class `Object`, a generalization we made to ensure that *any* object could be sent to and retrieved from a stream. Now, we are deliberately restricting the range of classes that are stream-compatible by insisting that they implement the `IStreamable` interface, and we need to amend the `CStream` class to suit. The necessary changes are shown below:

```
Enum StreamErr
  errCanNotWriteObject = 0
  errCanNotReadObject = 1
End Enum
```

```
    Public Sub WriteObject(O As IStreamable)   ' Note can only write
                                               ' IStreamables
On Error GoTo Err_WriteObject
  O.SaveToStream mvarFileHandle
  Exit Sub
Err_WriteObject:
  mvarStatus = "Error " & Err.Number & " on writing object. " _
                    & Err.Description
  Err.Raise vbObjectError + errCanNotWriteObject, _
      "CStream::ReadObject", "Can not write object to stream."
End Sub

    Public Sub ReadObject(O As IStreamable)   ' Note can only Read
                                              ' IStreamables
On Error GoTo err_ReadObject
  O.LoadFromStream mvarFileHandle
  Exit Sub
err_ReadObject:
  mvarStatus = "Error " & Err.Number & " on reading object. " _
                    & Err.Description
  Err.Raise vbObjectError + errCanNotReadObject, _
      "CStream::ReadObject", "Can not read object from stream"
End Sub
```

Note that, as well as amending the **WriteObject** and **ReadObject** methods of the **CStream** class, an *enumeration* has been added (this must be placed before any methods in the class file) to provide symbolic names for some useful error numbers. This makes the error handling code in the classes easier to follow.

We can now go on to complete an **IStreamable** class. In this case, the class will be trivial, containing only a String and a Number, with associated properties. The important methods in this new **CInfo** class are the **IStreamable** interface methods.

```
' CInfo class - a demonstration of the IStreamable interface.

Option Explicit

Implements IStreamable

' Member variables for data storage..
Private mvarString As String
Private mvarNum As Single

' Property methods for data access..
Public Property Get StringData() As String
  StringData = mvarString
End Property

Public Property Let StringData(ByVal NewValue As String)
  mvarString = NewValue
End Property
```

```
Public Property Get NumData() As Single
  NumData = mvarNum
End Property

Public Property Let NumData(ByVal NewValue As Single)
  mvarNum = NewValue
End Property

' IStreamable interface methods..
Private Sub IStreamable_LoadFromStream(ByVal fileHandle As Integer)
  Input #fileHandle, mvarString, mvarNum
End Sub

Private Sub IStreamable_SaveToStream(ByVal fileHandle As Integer)
  Write #fileHandle, mvarString, mvarNum
End Sub
```

We now have a class that is *guaranteed* to support the proper interface methods for a
CStream object. Note that this does not mean that the methods will be coded
correctly, or even that the code in them will do anything at all related to streams,
simply that the class provides the expected method names and that these take the
appropriate parameters.

We can add these classes (**CStream**, **IStreamable** and **CInfo**) to a Visual Basic
project, and easily provide code to send any **CInfo** objects to a stream and get them
back again:

```
Public Sub WriteStream()
Dim S As CStream
Dim Info As CInfo
  ' Build a CInfo Object...
  Set Info = New Cinfo
  Info.StringData = "Hello Mum"
  Info.NumData = 3.1415926
  ' Now send it to the stream..
  Set S = New CStream
  If S.OpenForOutput Then
    S.WriteObject Info
    S.CloseFile
    Set S = Nothing
  Else
    MsgBox S.Status
  End If
End Sub

Public Sub ReadStream()
Dim S As CStream
```

```
Dim Info As CInfo
  ' Build a CInfo Object...
  Set Info = New Cinfo
  ' Get its data from the stream..
  Set S = New CStream
  If S.OpenForInput Then
    S.ReadObject Info
    S.CloseFile
    Set S = Nothing
  Else
    MsgBox S.Status
  End If
End Sub
```

Of course, since we are using a stream, we could send as many objects as we wish to it, and bring them back again. However, the most important point is that we can send *any* class of object that implements the **IStreamable** interface. If a collection class also implemented this interface, we could send it to the stream and bring it back again (as we did less rigorously in the previous chapter). More importantly, by making the requirement to provide methods to load from and save to a stream explicit, we could *guarantee* that the code would at least be compatible with the calls made by the stream class.

Polymorphism

By creating classes that conform to an interface, we can build whole ranges of classes that are compatible in some respect. For example, if we ensure that all of our classes implement the **IStreamable** interface, we know that we will be able to send all of our objects to a stream, regardless of what job they were developed to do. The term for this type-compatibility in object oriented programming is *polymorphism*. Literally translated from Greek, this word means *many forms*, and its use in object oriented programming refers to the *is-a* relationship used to describe how classes that are related by inheritance can be regarded.

In the case of classes that implement the **IStreamable** interface, we can say that there are many forms of streamable objects, or that these classes are polymorphs of the more general streamable class.

Polymorphism is used in object oriented programming to simplify the way we treat objects. Instead of having to interrogate an object in a collection to determine if it can be sent to a stream, we can make sure that all of the objects in the collection conform to the **IStreamable** interface. This may at first seem to be a dubious benefit, since we need to put in some effort when we first create the interface, and later when we build each class that conforms to it. However, all that we are really doing is putting a bit of rigorous practice on a more formal footing.

In some of the examples of alternative collection classes and other object structures that were used in Chapter 8, we had to make it a condition of an object that could be placed in a collection that it provided a **Key** property. This was so that the collection class could determine how to insert the object to keep the collection in order. We now have a stronger way of enforcing this type of rule, since we can write the **Add** method so that it takes an **ISortable** parameter. Of course, **ISortable** would be an interface class, and would specify a single property method, **Key**. Any class we wanted to add to an ordered collection would have to implement this interface, and Visual Basic would enforce the type-compatibility for us.

QUESTION 10.1

(a) How many methods will the **ISortable** interface class have to specify?

(b) Write the **ISortable** interface class as a short exercise, and indicate how the **COrdList** class would have to be changed to work with that type of object.

10.2   An example of polymorphism

Computer aided drawing

Computer Aided Drawing (CAD) programs allow a user to draw regular figures such as lines, circles and rectangles on a computer screen, and make it possible to edit the drawing by moving or resizing the figures. It is a relatively simple matter to draw figures on a screen, but a much more complex problem to make these editable. To understand why this is, consider the simple drawing shown in Figure 10.2.

Assume we wish to make the circle shown in the drawing larger. The circle could have been drawn in a Visual Basic program by using the Circle method of a form or PictureBox object. The actual expression to do the job would be something like:

```
PictureBox.Circle (XPosition, YPosition), Radius
```

where **PictureBox** is the **Name** property of a Visual Basic PictureBox control, **XPosition** and **YPosition** give the distance from the left and top of the picture box to the centre of the circle, and **Radius** gives the distance from the centre to any point on its circumference. We can redraw the circle larger by simply increasing the Radius value. However, doing this would not erase the existing circle (which is now simply a

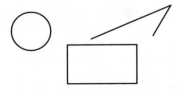

Figure 10.2   *A simple drawing made by computer.*

pattern of dots or *pixels* on a display), and having changed the value of Radius, we would still have to reissue the command to do the drawing again.

Because of this, a proper CAD program has the requirement to keep a record of the size and position of every figure drawn, so that these can be edited. Using current programming practice, every figure on a drawing is an object. If we were to resize a circle object that was being displayed on the screen, the proper sequence of commands would be:

- draw over the original circle in the background colour,

- change the Radius property of the circle object, and

- draw the circle object in the proper foreground colour.

Since the circle is an object, we can make it the circle's responsibility to do this, and provide lines, rectangles, and whatever other figures we support in our CAD package with the same set of capabilities.

Alternatively, we could:

- change the Radius property of the circle object,

- clear the display, and

- redraw the entire list of objects (including the resized circle).

This method also requires that each object is able to draw itself, and that the CAD program maintains a collection of every object that has been drawn. Each of these methods has its advantages and disadvantages, and several commercial CAD programs make use of both methods, using each in the circumstances it is most suited to.

Once we have defined a range of classes to represent various shaped figures in a CAD system, we will want to simplify the way that we work with these as much as possible. For example, to redraw all of the figures on a PictureBox control, we might use a sequence of statements such as:

```
For Each Figure in colDrawing
   Figure.Draw PictureBox
Next
```

We rely on each figure providing the **Draw** method and supporting a **PictureBox** parameter, and we might similarly rely on a range of other methods to provide the ability to select, move, resize and re-colour a figure. By far the best way we have of doing this in Visual Basic is to make sure that every figure class we build implements a common interface, **IShape** for example.

QUESTION 10.2

When we develop a class that implements an interface, we need to code all of the interface methods within the class. What advantage does this give us?

Table 10.1 *Members of the **IShape** interface.*

Name	Type	Purpose
Left	Property Get/Let	Horizontal position of a figure
Top	Property Get/Let	Vertical position of a figure
Width	Property Get/Let	Width of a rectangle enclosing the figure
Height	Property Get/Let	Height of a rectangle enclosing the figure
Draw	Sub Method	Draws the figure on a picture box (specified by a parameter)
MoveBy	Sub Method	Moves a figure by an amount along and down, specified in parameters
Visible	Property Get/Let	Specifies whether a figure will be drawn or not
Here	Function Method	Indicates whether a pair of co-ordinates passed as parameters is within the figure

The **IShape** interface should provide the properties and methods shown in Table 10.1.

We may well decide to add more methods to the interface at a later time, but these will be adequate for now for the purposes of creating figures in a drawing.

```
' IShape - an interface class for CAD drawing figures.
Option Explicit

Public Property Get Left() As Single
End Property

Public Property Let Left(ByVal NewValue As Single)
End Property

Public Property Get Top() As Single
End Property

Public Property Let Top(ByVal NewValue As Single)
End Property

Public Property Get Width() As Single
End Property

Public Property Let Width(ByVal NewValue As Single)
End Property
```

```
Public Property Get Height() As Single
End Property

Public Property Let Height(ByVal NewValue As Single)
End Property

Public Sub Draw(Pic As PictureBox)
End Sub

Public Sub MoveBy(Pic As PictureBox, DeltaX As Single, _
                  DeltaY As Single)
End Sub

Public Property Get Visible() As Boolean
End Property

Public Property Let Visible(ByVal NewValue As Boolean)
End Property

Public Function Here(ByVal X As Single, ByVal Y As Single) _
                  As Boolean
End Function
```

The crux of this interface definition is that we can create a shape by specifying a *bounding rectangle* that it will fit within. For rectangular shapes, this is obvious, but we can do the same for many shapes, as shown in Figure 10.3.

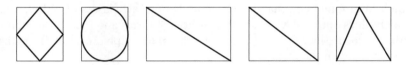

Figure 10.3 *Various shapes and how they can be defined by a bounding rectangle.*

Drawing on a screen

Drawing a shape object that belongs to a class that implements **IShape** is a simple matter. Simply set the **Top**, **Left**, **Width** and **Height** properties to the required values (similar to the same properties in a Visual Basic control object), set the **Visible** property to True, and call the **Draw** method passing a PictureBox control reference as a parameter. Making all of this work in the context of a drawing application is where the real work starts, and it is here that the definition of the Interface class and the principle of polymorphism work for us.

If you follow the example of Windows Paint or almost any other drawing package available, drawing a shape on a screen should proceed as follows:

1. The user selects the type of shape to draw by using a menu selection, pressing a button or some other user-interface control.

2.   The user moves the mouse cursor over the drawing area, and initiates drawing a figure by depressing the left mouse button and holding it down. The position where the button was pressed indicates one corner of the bounding rectangle.

3.   The user drags the mouse cursor to stretch out the bounding rectangle to the required shape and size.

4.   The user releases the mouse button to finish the drawing operation. The position where the mouse button was released indicates the opposite corner of the bounding rectangle.

5.   The selected shape and the opposing corners of the bounding rectangle define the shape to be drawn. The application creates a new object that meets this definition and adds it to a list of drawn shapes.

Some of these steps can become quite elaborate, depending on the amount of feedback you provide to the user. For example, in step 3, it is normal to show a 'rubber-band' bounding rectangle as the mouse moves over the display, letting the user see the area the drawn shape will cover. Before we see how we would create classes to implement the graphic shapes in a CAD application, an overview or reminder of Visual Basic graphics would be in order.

Graphics in Visual Basic

Because objects manage all of the user-interface tasks in a Visual Basic program, all of the built-in graphics commands are methods of a few classes of object. The most common graphics output devices are the surfaces of forms and PictureBox controls. A PictureBox is ideal since it can be used to separate graphic output from the user-interface elements on the form.

There are surprisingly few primitive graphics commands. Basically, the `Line`, `Circle` and `PSet` methods of output devices generate all graphics output. These methods generate lines, circles and individual points on a display device, but also variations on their basic shape. The `Line` method can also be used to draw rectangular shapes, filled or unfilled, while the `Circle` method can be used for ellipses, arcs and 'pie slices'.

Table 10.2 shows an example, applying commands to a PictureBox `Pic`.

You can read more detail on the graphics methods in the Visual Basic help files.

Drawing modes

All of the objects that have graphics methods support various *drawing modes*. These allow the individual picture elements (pixels) on the display to be drawn in a number of ways by combining them with the background colour they are being drawn on. The `DrawMode` property of forms and PictureBoxes can be set to a range of values, the most useful of which are `vbCopyPen` and `vbXORPen`. `vbCopyPen` provides normal drawing so that a black line drawn on a white background will appear black.

Table 10.2   *The effects of Visual Basic's drawing methods.*

```
Pic.Line (x1, y1) - (x2, y2)
```

x1, y1 is top-left
x2, y2 is bottom-right

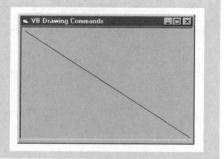

```
Pic.Line (x1, y1) - (x2, y2), _
         Colour, B
```

x1, y1 is top-left
x2, y2 is bottom-right
Colour is the drawn colour

```
Pic.Line (x1, y1) - (x2, y2), _
         Colour, BF
```

x1, y1 is top-left
x2, y2 is bottom-right
Colour is the fill colour

```
Pic.Circle (x1, y1), Radius
```

x1, y1 is centre
Radius is the circle's radius

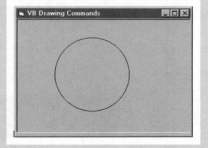

Table 10.2 (cont.)

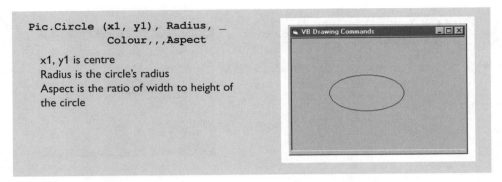

```
Pic.Circle (x1, y1), Radius, _
          Colour,,,Aspect
```

x1, y1 is centre
Radius is the circle's radius
Aspect is the ratio of width to height of
the circle

However, `vbXorPen` mode can be used to draw reversibly, by inverting the colour of the pixels being drawn. For example, a line drawn in white on a white background will appear black. However, if the same line is drawn again in the same place (over the black line), the pixels will revert to white. This mode turns out to be ideal for allowing drawn elements to be moved around a display, since by repeatedly drawing them and then drawing over the original, a shape can be made to erase itself. We can make use of this facility for allowing shapes to be 'dragged' around the display.

Building the application – a simple prototype

Before we can make use of any classes that implement the `IShape` interface, we need to code the core drawing behaviour into a form. This form will be told how to draw

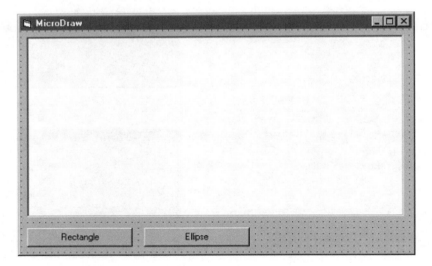

Figure 10.4 *A prototype CAD window.*

an arbitrary graphic shape (corresponding to the **IShape** interface), and poly-morphism can then be used to deal with concrete shapes by creating classes that **Implement** this interface. We can start with a minimal set of drawing code, based around a PictureBox control, on a form as shown in Figure 10.4.

The white area in the form design in Figure 10.4 is a PictureBox control that has been named **P**. The two buttons will allow us to select a shape to draw in the prototype, although a toolbar or menu would be used in a full application to provide a 'professional' look and feel to the program. For now, when the user clicks on either button, that will define the next shape to be drawn. We will need to provide various *status variables* in the form code to record what is happening.

```
Option Explicit

' Definitions of program states..
Enum CurrentOpType
   coNothing = 0
   coDrawing = 1
   coDragging = 2
End Enum

' The collection of shape items..
Private DrawList As Collection

' Storage for useful coordinate values..
Private StartX As Single, StartY As Single
Private LastX As Single, LastY As Single
Private DeltaX As Single, DeltaY As Single

' Used to indicate current shape being drawn..
Private DrawType As String
' and the current operation..
Private CurrentOp As CurrentOpType
```

'States' of the form

The enumeration at the top of the form code defines the various states the program can be in at any time. Depending on what the user is currently doing, the program is either in idle mode (**coNothing**), drawing (**coDrawing**) or dragging a shape (**coDragging**). Defining these as an enumeration and providing a variable to indicate the current state will simplify much of the logic of the program. The various events that the form receives from the PictureBox will cause the form to move from state to state, depending on the current state and the event that arrives. This is a complex set of interactions that we will need to manage very carefully.

DrawList is the collection of drawn items. As each item is drawn, it will be added to this collection. In order to draw on the screen and provide appropriate feedback to the user, we need to record the cursor location in certain states: when the mouse button is pressed at the start of a draw operation (**StartX**, **StartY**) and whenever the mouse cursor position changes (**LastX**, **LastY**). It is also useful to calculate the *delta* or change in the cursor position whenever it moves (**DeltaX**, **DeltaY**). Finally, **DrawType** will be set to the name of whatever shape is to be drawn next, and **CurrentOp** will record the current status of the program.

The first operation of the program should be to create the collection of drawing items. We can use the **Form_Load** event for this:

```
Private Sub Form_Load()
  ' Create the shapes collection..
  Set DrawList = New Collection
End Sub
```

All of the drawing operations will be coded in three event-handlers for the PictureBox, **MouseDown**, **MouseMove** and **MouseUp**, and these will be used to define how the form moves from state to state. All three of the event-handlers provide information on the position and status of the mouse in parameters: **Button** is an integer that indicates which button is currently pressed (Left = 1, Right = 2); **X** and **Y** indicate the current mouse position relative to the top-left corner of the PictureBox. Using these, we can draw a simple shape, specified by the **DrawType** string, as follows:

```
Private Sub P_MouseDown(Button As Integer, Shift As Integer, _
                        X As Single, Y As Single)
  StartX = X
  StartY = Y
  Select Case CurrentOp
    Case coNothing
      ' No code here yet.
    Case coDrawing
      ' If a draw command is active, start the draw..
      If Button = 1 Then      ' Left button pressed.
        P.DrawMode = vbXorPen
        P.DrawStyle = vbDot
        P.Line (StartX, StartY)-(X, Y), vbWhite, B
      End If

    Case coDragging
      ' No code here yet.
  End Select
  ' Record where the cursor was..
  LastX = X
  LastY = Y
End Sub
```

Note that this is an event-handler, and so is created in outline by the Visual Basic form designer. Place the picture box on the form, size it appropriately, change its name to **P**, and then double-click on it to generate an event-handler, and select

MouseDown from the events combo-box to get the outline event-handler. Then add the code listed above.

When the mouse button is pressed, the above event-handler fires, and we immediately record the mouse cursor location. What else is to be done depends on the current state (given by **CurrentOp**). In time, we will add code to allow drawn objects to be moved around the display, and so two of the operation states are yet to be coded. If, however, the current operation is a drawing one, and the left mouse button has been pressed, we can start the drawing operation off.

To draw a *rubber-banded* bounding box, we can make use of the **DrawMode** property of a PictureBox control. **vbXorPen** is a drawing mode that can be used to either draw or undraw a line on the control. The *exclusive-or* operation used to determine what colour to change the display pixels to works in such a way that, providing we are drawing in white on white, it reverses the last drawing operation. If we draw the same line twice over, the second time erases the first.

Using this, we start off the drawing operation by drawing a bounding box of zero size, at the current mouse location (at this point, **X = StartX**, and **Y = StartY**). We will draw the bounding box as a dotted rectangle. Finally, in this event-handler, we record the last mouse cursor location (currently the same as the starting location). More of the drawing work is done in the **MouseMove** event-handler:

```
Private Sub P_MouseMove(Button As Integer, Shift As Integer, _
                    X As Single, Y As Single)
' Start by recording how far the cursor has moved since the last
' operation..
  DeltaX = X - LastX
  DeltaY = Y - LastY
  Select Case CurrentOp
    Case coNothing
      ' No code here yet
    Case coDrawing
      ' Re-size the bounding box..
      If Button = 1 Then
        P.Line (StartX, StartY)-(LastX, LastY), vbWhite, B
        P.Line (StartX, StartY)-(X, Y), vbWhite, B
      End If

    Case coDragging
      ' No code here yet
  End Select
  ' Record the last cursor position..
  LastX = X
  LastY = Y
End Sub
```

In this handler, we erase the previous bounding box by drawing over it exactly, using XOR (exclusive-or) mode and drawing in white again. We are using a dotted line

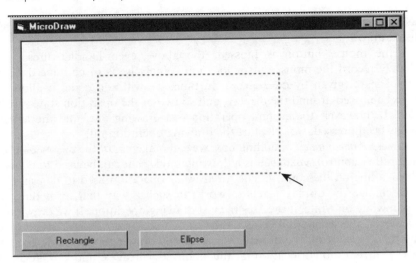

Figure 10.5 *Dragging out a bounding box.*

style, so this will appear as shown in Figure 10.5. We can then draw the new bounding box in exactly the same way, using the latest update of the mouse co-ordinates. Finally, we again record the last mouse co-ordinates, to enable us to undraw the bounding box.

The final drawing operation happens when the mouse button is released:

```
Private Sub P_MouseUp(Button As Integer, Shift As Integer, _
                      X As Single, Y As Single)
Dim S As IShape
  Select Case CurrentOp
    Case coNothing
      ' Nothing to do..
    Case coDrawing
      ' Get rid of the bounding box..
      P.Line (StartX, StartY)-(LastX, LastY), vbWhite, B
      ' Create the new shape object..
      Set S = GetNewDrawShape(DrawType)
      ' Set up position and size..
      S.Left = StartX
      S.Top = StartY
      S.Width = X - StartX
      S.Height = Y - StartY
      S.Visible = True
      ' Add it to the draw list..
      DrawList.Add S
      ' Set up for drawing the shapes..
      P.DrawMode = vbCopyPen
```

```
        P.DrawStyle = vbSolid
        P.ForeColor = vbBlack
     Case coDragging
        ' Nothing to do..
   End Select
   ' Draw everything..
   DrawShapes
   ' Tidy up..
   DrawType = ""
   CurrentOp = coNothing
   ' And record the current position..
   LastX = X
   LastY = Y
End Sub
```

In this method, we need to create an **IShape** object, so a suitable reference variable is declared. Since the current operation is a drawing one, all of the code for the **coDrawing** case is executed. This erases the final state of the bounding box, and then creates a new shape object. This is done using the **GetNewDrawShape** function (defined later), to which a string parameter is passed to state what *type* of shape it should be.

The function returns an object that implements the **IShape** interface. The parameter to the function, a string such as **"Rectangle"** or **"Ellipse"**, selects which class of shape the function returns. Its size and position are then set up and it is added to the draw list. Finally, every shape in the draw list is drawn in the call to the **DrawShapes** sub, status variables are cleared and the last mouse location is recorded again.

QUESTION 10.3

In this application so far, we have used the **IShape** interface when dealing with drawn objects. How will we need to change this code so that it can work with concrete classes of object such as rectangles and lines?

Drawing shape objects

To complete the rudimentary drawing code, we need to provide methods to select the type of item to be drawn, and we need to write the code for the **GetNewDrawShape** function, and the **DrawShapes** sub. First, selecting shapes to be drawn:

```
Private Sub cmdEllipse_Click()
  DrawType = "Ellipse"
  CurrentOp = coDrawing
End Sub
```

```
Private Sub cmdRectangle_Click()
  DrawType = "Rectangle"
  CurrentOp = coDrawing
End Sub
```

These two event-handlers are for mouse clicks on the buttons shown in Figures 10.4 and 10.5. Their action is simply to set the **DrawType** string that indicates the type of item to be drawn, and the current operation. The **DrawType** string is used in the **GetNewDrawShape** function:

```
Private Function GetNewDrawShape(desc As String) As IShape
Dim S As IShape
  Select Case desc
    Case "Rectangle"
      Set S = New CRectangle
    Case "Ellipse"
      Set S = New CEllipse
  End Select
  Set GetNewDrawShape = S
End Function
```

In its current state, this function will create a shape from one of two classes: a **CEllipse** or a **CRectangle**. We can extend this to make it able to create any of a large range of shapes. The most important feature of the function is that whatever type of shape it creates, it is returned as an **IShape** object. The mouse event-handlers neither know nor care what type of object is being created provided it meets the requirement of being an **IShape**. This is polymorphism (and the answer to Question 10.3).

The **DrawShapes** method is quite simple: clear the display, then go through each shape in the **DrawList** collection asking them to draw themselves.

```
Private Sub DrawShapes()
Dim I As IShape
  P.Cls
  For Each I In DrawList
    I.Draw P
  Next
End Sub
```

The most important feature of this sub is that it does not know or care what classes of shape it is drawing – each **IShape** object knows what it is and draws itself appropriately.

Building the shape classes

Before we can go on to test the form, we must first provide the two shape classes, **CEllipse** and **CRectangle**. Both must implement the **IShape** interface, which is largely a matter of adding code to all of the interface methods. The only (slightly) awkward method is the one that is different for each class – **Draw**. To create the **CEllipse** class, add a new class to the project and name it **CEllipse**, then add code to this as shown below:

```
' CEllipse class definition.
Option Explicit

Implements IShape

Private mvarLeft As Single
Private mvarHeight As Single
Private mvarTop As Single
Private mvarWidth As Single
Private mvarVisible As Boolean

Private Sub IShape_Draw(Pic As PictureBox)
Dim rad As Single
  If mvarVisible Then
    ' To draw an ellipse, work out its radius (rad),
    ' aspect ratio (mvarHeight / mvarWidth) and
    ' centre (mvarLeft + mvarWidth / 2), (mvarTop + mvarHeight / 2).
    ' The biggest axis is always taken as the radius..
    If mvarWidth > mvarHeight Then
      rad = mvarWidth / 2
    Else
      rad = mvarHeight / 2
    End If
    Pic.Circle ((mvarLeft + mvarWidth / 2), _
                (mvarTop + mvarHeight / 2)), _
                  rad,,,, (mvarHeight / mvarWidth)
  End If
End Sub

Private Property Let IShape_Height(ByVal RHS As Single)
  mvarHeight = RHS
End Property

Private Property Get IShape_Height() As Single
  IShape_Height = mvarHeight
End Property

Private Function IShape_Here(ByVal X As Single, ByVal Y As Single) _
                            As Boolean
Dim cx As Single, cy As Single, rad As Single
  ' We need to find out if the mouse cursor is within the shape's
  ' bounding rectangle. This is the case if X is between the
  ' left and right edges and Y is between the top and bottom..
```

```
    If X >= mvarLeft And X <= (mvarLeft + mvarWidth) And _
       Y >= mvarTop And Y <= (mvarTop + mvarHeight) Then
      IShape_Here = True
    Else
      IShape_Here = False
    End If
End Function


Private Property Let IShape_Left(ByVal RHS As Single)
  mvarLeft = RHS
End Property


Private Property Get IShape_Left() As Single
  IShape_Left = mvarLeft
End Property


Private Sub IShape_MoveBy(Pic As PictureBox, DeltaX As Single, _
                          DeltaY As Single)
  If mvarVisible Then
    ' If it is currently visible, we should erase it..
    Pic.DrawMode = vbXorPen
    IShape_Draw Pic
  End If
  ' To move a shape, update its Left and Top properties
  ' and then redraw it..
  mvarLeft = mvarLeft + DeltaX
  mvarTop = mvarTop + DeltaY
  If mvarVisible Then
    ' If it is currently visible, we should redraw it..
    Pic.DrawMode = vbXorPen
    IShape_Draw Pic
  End If
End Sub


Private Property Let IShape_Top(ByVal RHS As Single)
  mvarTop = RHS
End Property


Private Property Get IShape_Top() As Single
  IShape_Top = mvarTop
End Property


Private Property Let IShape_Visible(ByVal RHS As Boolean)
  mvarVisible = RHS
End Property
```

```
Private Property Get IShape_Visible() As Boolean
   IShape_Visible = mvarVisible
End Property

Private Property Let IShape_Width(ByVal RHS As Single)
   mvarWidth = RHS
End Property

Private Property Get IShape_Width() As Single
   IShape_Width = mvarWidth
End Property
```

The **CRectangle** class is coded in almost exactly the same way, with only the **Draw** method being in any way distinct. To create this class quickly, add a new class to the project, call it **CRectangle**, copy the **CEllipse** code, paste it into the **CRectangle** code window, and edit the **IShape_Draw** method as shown below:

```
Private Sub IShape_Draw(Pic As PictureBox)
   ' Drawing a rectangle is much easier..
   If mvarVisible Then
      Pic.Line (mvarLeft, mvarTop)-(mvarLeft + mvarWidth, _
                mvarTop + mvarHeight),, B
   End If
End Sub
```

At this stage, it is possible to test the program, and you should be able to draw either elliptical or rectangular shapes by selecting the appropriate type and dragging it out on the picture box. It should draw black single-width solid lines.

QUESTION 10.4

Using the **CRectangle** shape class as a template, create a new class, **CLine**, that can be used to draw lines in the CAD program. (Hint: the only required difference in the class will be in the **Draw** method – look up the **Line** method in Visual Basic help, or Table 10.2.) You will also need to provide a command button and its **_Click** event-handler for selecting a line to draw (similar to those for the ellipse and rectangle classes) and amend the **GetNewDrawShape** method to deal with a **"Line"**.

As it is, the CAD application adequately demonstrates the power of polymorphism. It would now be a simple matter to create a range of different shape classes, all of which would implement the **IShape** interface. Each would fit into the existing drawing framework with only minimal changes to the form code – additional user-interface controls to select the new types of shape, and a small modification to the **Select Case** structure in **GetNewDrawShape**.

10.3 Extending the CAD application – getting the most from polymorphism

Up to this point, the CAD project is fine for drawing simple shapes and not much more. Ideally, it should allow the drawn shapes to be moved and changed in size, colour or line settings. To permit this, we will need to make the PictureBox event-handlers react in different ways depending on the current form state.

We need to add several key features to the application and its classes to support this. A **CDrawSettings** class will be required to encapsulate the colour, line and style settings of drawn objects, along with a control on the form to display the current settings. We will also need to extend the various PictureBox event-handlers to cope with the richer range of possible program states. First the **CDrawSettings** class:

```
' CDrawSettigs - a class to encapsulate the various settings a drawn
' object may take on.
Option Explicit

Private mvarColour As Long                      ' Object's line colour
Private mvarLineStyle As DrawStyleConstants ' Line style
Private mvarLineWidth As Byte               ' Line width
Private mvarFillStyle As FillStyleConstants ' Fill style
Private mvarFillColour As Long              ' and Fill Colour


' The Clone method returns a new copy of this object with its
' current settings.
Public Function Clone() As CDrawSettings
Dim S As New CDrawSettings
  With S
    .Colour = mvarColour
    .FillStyle = mvarFillStyle
    .LineStyle = mvarLineStyle
    .LineWidth = mvarLineWidth
    .FillColour = mvarFillColour
  End With
  Set Clone = S
End Function

Public Property Let FillColour(ByVal vData As Long)
  mvarFillColour = vData
End Property

Public Property Get FillColour() As Long
  FillColour = mvarFillColour
End Property
```

```
Public Property Let FillStyle(ByVal vData As FillStyleConstants)
  mvarFillStyle = vData
End Property

Public Property Get FillStyle() As FillStyleConstants
  FillStyle = mvarFillStyle
End Property

Public Property Let LineWidth(ByVal vData As Byte)
  mvarLineWidth = vData
End Property

Public Property Get LineWidth() As Byte
  LineWidth = mvarLineWidth
End Property

Public Property Let LineStyle(ByVal vData As DrawStyleConstants)
  mvarLineStyle = vData
End Property

Public Property Get LineStyle() As DrawStyleConstants
  LineStyle = mvarLineStyle
End Property

Public Property Let Colour(ByVal vData As Long)
  mvarColour = vData
End Property

Public Property Get Colour() As Long
  Colour = mvarColour
End Property
```

The most unusual feature of this class is its **Clone** method. We need to give each shape object its own settings, which means we need to create a **CDrawSettings** object for each. This can be simplified by keeping a single **CDrawSettings** object within the program's form. This object can change in response to various user-interface events to change colour, line-style, etc. However, at the point where we create a new object, we can capture the *current* settings in a new **CDrawSettings** object and pass this to the shape object as its own copy. The **Clone** method simply creates a new object of the class from an existing object of the class, and passes a reference to it back to the caller.

The **IShape** interface and each of the implementing classes must be given a matching **Settings** property. First the **IShape** interface, to define the interface method:

```
Public Property Get Settings() As CDrawSettings
End Property

Public Property Set Settings(NewSettings As CDrawSettings)
End Property
```

Now add implementations to both the **CEllipse** and **CRectangle** classes (remembering to get the outline of each method by selecting **IShape** in the top-left combo-box and the property names in it in the top-right combo-box in the code window for the class). Both **IShape** property methods and a **CDrawSettings** member variable will be necessary.

```
Private mvarSettings As CDrawSettings

Private Property Set IShape_Settings(RHS As CDrawSettings)
    Set mvarSettings = RHS.Clone
End Property

Private Property Get IShape_Settings() As CDrawSettings
    Set IShape_Settings = mvarSettings
End Property
```

These will be the same for both **CRectangle** and **CEllipse** classes.

Selecting an object

If we are to provide the facility to move or otherwise edit an existing drawn shape, we will need to provide a way of selecting it from the drawn image on the PictureBox. We have already provided the interface class with a **Here** method that can be used to identify an object given a pair of co-ordinates within its bounding rectangle. First, we need some extra variables within the form object to refer to objects being selected:

```
' Useful shape object references..
Private mUnderMouse As IShape
Private mSelection As IShape
```

mUnderMouse is an object reference variable we can use to indicate an object that the mouse cursor is currently hovering over. **mSelection** will be used to refer to an object that is currently selected, i.e., the mouse is hovering over it and the left mouse button is depressed. We can now use the **Here** method to select from the **DrawList**, using the **MouseMove** event-handler. The **mUnderMouse** object reference is set in the **MouseMove** event-handler by a call to the **ItemUnderMouse** method described later:

```
' When a mouse button is pressed over the picture box..
Private Sub P_MouseDown(Button As Integer, Shift As Integer, _
                        X As Single, Y As Single)
    ' where is it?..
    StartX = X
    StartY = Y
    ' what is currently going on?..
    Select Case CurrentOp
      Case coNothing
        ' If there is a shape under the mouse, make it the selection..
```

```
        If Not mUnderMouse Is Nothing Then
          Set mSelection = mUnderMouse
          CurrentOp = coDragging
          P.ForeColor = P.BackColor
          P.DrawMode = vbXorPen
        End If
      Case coDrawing
        ' If a draw command is active, start the draw..
        If Button = 1 Then
          P.DrawMode = vbXorPen
          P.DrawStyle = vbDot
          P.Line (StartX, StartY)-(X, Y), vbWhite, B
        End If
      Case coDragging
        ' Nothing to do, since we can only START a drag here.
    End Select
    ' Record where the cursor was..
    LastX = X
    LastY = Y
End Sub
```

In the updated version of the **MouseDown** event-handler shown above, code has been added to set a reference to an object in the **DrawList** at the point where a mouse button is pressed and there is no current operation. For this to work, an object reference, **mUnderMouse**, must have been previously set. We can identify the object currently under the mouse cursor in the **MouseMove** event:

```
' When the mouse cursor moves over the picture box..
Private Sub P_MouseMove(Button As Integer, Shift As Integer, _
                        X As Single, Y As Single)
Dim thisItem As IShape
  ' Start by recording how far the cursor has moved since the
  ' last operation..
  DeltaX = X - LastX
  DeltaY = Y - LastY
  ' Now find if there is anything under the mouse cursor..
  Set thisItem = ItemUnderMouse(X, Y)
  ' What is currently going on?..
  Select Case CurrentOp
    Case coNothing
      ' Should we change the cursor shape?..
      If thisItem Is Nothing Then
        P.MousePointer = vbCrosshair
```

```
      Else
        If Not thisItem Is mUnderMouse Then
          P.MousePointer = vbSizeAll
        End If
      End If
      ' Record the ref. to the item under the mouse for
      ' the next time..
      Set mUnderMouse = thisItem
    Case coDrawing
      ' Should re-size the bounding box..
      If Button = 1 Then
        P.Line (StartX, StartY)-(LastX, LastY), vbWhite, B
        P.Line (StartX, StartY)-(X, Y), vbWhite, B
      End If
    Case coDragging
      ' Should drag the current item..
      mSelection.MoveBy P, DeltaX, DeltaY
  End Select
  ' Record the last cursor position..
  LastX = X
  LastY = Y
End Sub
```

The updated **MouseMove** event-handler does several things. Firstly, if the mouse cursor has moved to a position above one of the drawn objects, the cursor shape is changed to indicate this to the user. This feedback will help the user to determine whether it is possible to select an object or not, using a call to **ItemUnderMouse**. If the item reference returned by this function has changed since the last call to it, changing the **MouseCursor** property of the PictureBox changes the appearance of the mouse cursor. If an object reference is returned, the **mUnderMouse** member variable is set to this object reference. If the current state of the program is **coDragging**, then the **mSelection** object under the mouse cursor is dragged by sending it the **MoveBy** message, passing **DeltaX** and **DeltaY** variables to indicate how far to move.

The **MouseUp** event-handler also needs to be updated:

```
Private Sub P_MouseUp(Button As Integer, Shift As Integer, _
                    X As Single, Y As Single)
Dim S As IShape
  Select Case CurrentOp
    Case coNothing
      ' Nothing to do..
    Case coDrawing
      ' Get rid of the bounding box..
      P.Line (StartX, StartY)-(LastX, LastY), vbWhite, B
```

```
        ' Create the new shape object..
        Set S = GetNewDrawShape(DrawType)
        ' Set up position and size..
        S.Left = StartX
        S.Top = StartY
        S.Width = X - StartX
        S.Height = Y - StartY
        ' Make the shape's settings..
        Set S.Settings = mSettings.Clone
        S.Visible = True
        ' Add it to the draw list..
        DrawList.Add S
      Case coDragging
        ' Drop the current selection..
        Set mSelection = Nothing
    End Select
    ' Draw everything..
    DrawShapes
    ' Tidy up..
    DrawType = ""
    CurrentOp = coNothing
    ' And record the current position..
    LastX = X
    LastY = Y
End Sub
```

If currently drawing, the final stage of drawing the shape and adding it to the **DrawList** is the point where the draw settings should be applied. These settings are made within event-handlers attached to various additional controls on the form, as will be explained later. If currently dragging an object, releasing the mouse button should cause it to be dropped.

An extra function is required within the form code to set a reference to the item currently under the mouse cursor:

```
Private Function ItemUnderMouse(ByVal X As Single, _
                              ByVal Y As Single) As IShape
  Dim I As IShape, S As IShape
    Set I = Nothing
    For Each S In DrawList
      If S.Here(X, Y) Then
        Set I = S
        Exit For
      End If
    Next
    Set ItemUnderMouse = I
End Function
```

This function simply passes the **Here** message to each object in the collection until one of them returns **True**. If none do, the function returns **Nothing**, otherwise it returns a reference to the object under the mouse.

When shapes are drawn on to the PictureBox, their **Settings** property must now be taken into account:

```
Private Sub DrawShapes()
Dim I As IShape
  P.Cls
  For Each I In DrawList
    With I.Settings
      P.DrawMode = vbCopyPen
      P.ForeColor = .Colour
      P.FillColor = .FillColour
      P.FillStyle = .FillStyle
      P.DrawWidth = .LineWidth
      P.DrawStyle = .LineStyle
    End With
    I.Draw P
  Next
End Sub
```

All that happens here is that the draw settings for the PictureBox control are changed to suit the shape currently being drawn. To make it possible to change these settings, we add several controls to the form as shown in Figure 10.6.

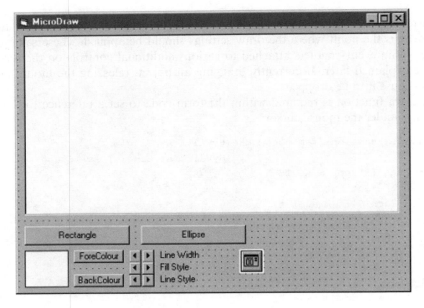

Figure 10.6 *Additional form controls for making shape settings.*

Table 10.3 *Additional form controls for asserting shape settings.*

Control type	Property	Value
Command button	Name	`cmdFore`
	Caption	`ForeColour`
Command button	Name	`cmdBack`
	Caption	`BackColour`
Horizontal scroll bar	Name	`scrWidth`
	Min	1
	Max	10
Horizontal scroll bar	Name	`scrFill`
	Min	0
	Max	7
Horizontal scroll bar	Name	`scrStyle`
	Min	0
	Max	6
Shape control	Name	`shpSettings`
Common dialog control (*need to add a control reference from the Project/ Components menu – Microsoft Common Dialog Control*)	Name	`dlgSettings`

The added controls are listed in Table 10.3.

The various event-handlers for these controls are shown below:

```
' A button to set the background colour..
Private Sub cmdBack_Click()
  dlgSettings.ShowColor
  shpSettings.FillColor = dlgSettings.Color
  mSettings.FillColour = dlgSettings.Color
End Sub
```

```
' A button to set the foreground colour..
Private Sub cmdFore_Click()
  dlgSettings.ShowColor
  shpSettings.BorderColor = dlgSettings.Color
  mSettings.Colour = dlgSettings.Color
End Sub

' Button to change the fill style..
Private Sub scrFill_Change()
  shpSettings.FillStyle = scrFill.Value
  mSettings.FillStyle = scrFill.Value
End Sub

' Button to change the line style..
Private Sub scrStyle_Change()
  shpSettings.BorderStyle = scrStyle.Value
  mSettings.LineStyle = scrStyle.Value - 1
End Sub

' Button to change the line width..
Private Sub scrWidth_Change()
  shpSettings.BorderWidth = scrWidth.Value
  mSettings.LineWidth = scrWidth.Value
End Sub
```

Finally, we need an extra member variable for the form. This will store the current settings to be made for any new drawn element:

```
Private mSettings As CDrawSettings
```

When the form is first loaded, we need to instantiate a **CDrawSettings** object and assert its initial values:

```
Private Sub Form_Load()
  ' Create the shapes collection..
  Set DrawList = New Collection
  ' Create a CDrawSettings instance..
  Set mSettings = New CDrawSettings
  With mSettings
    .Colour = vbBlack
    .FillColour = vbBlack
    .FillStyle = vbFSTransparent
    .LineStyle = vbSolid
    .LineWidth = 1
  End With
End Sub
```

We are now ready to test the CAD application. In the revised state, it should now indicate when the mouse cursor hovers over a drawn element, and should allow elements to be picked up with the mouse and dragged to a new position. By interacting with the various settings controls, you should also be able to change the colour, fill-colour, fill-style and line width of the shapes you draw.

Adding shape classes

To extend the range of shapes that can be drawn in this project, simply add new classes that implement the **IShape** interface. If you follow the example of the **CRectangle** class, it is a simple matter to copy an existing shape class and change the coding of the **Draw** method to draw the new shape. Suitable shape classes to add would be lines, triangles, diamond shapes, etc., since in all of these cases, a bounding rectangle can be used to define the final appearance of the shape. Note that a shape object drawn by drawing a succession of lines (such as a triangle or diamond shape) cannot be filled in the same way that the **CRectangle** or **CEllipse** objects were. Instead, you would need to make use of a call to the Windows flood-fill routines, which is inherently more awkward.

   Note that the extension of the range of shapes relies on the use of polymorphism in this application. Without the ability to create objects that match a common interface, it would have been a much more awkward task to add a shape to a drawing, and editing a shape would have been similarly awkward.

Possible refinements

As it stands, the CAD application allows shapes of various classes to be drawn and moved. It should be a simple matter to allow shapes to be removed from a drawing. It should also be possible to change the size of a shape by altering its bounding rectangle, although in this case it would be necessary to create *drawing handles*, similar to the ones used in Visual Basic for changing the size of a control. This is beyond the scope of this book. It is also possible to change the appearance of a shape by editing its colour, fill-colour, line style or line width. The best approach to this would be to create a form to go with the **CDrawSettings** class, allowing a set of draw settings to be edited by selecting a shape, possibly using a right mouse button click.

10.4   Polymorphism – the key to OOP

In an early book on object oriented programming by Greg Voss, object oriented programming was described as **'programming by sending messages to objects of unknown class'**. We should now have a clearer picture of what this means and why it is important. Effectively, the statement makes the point that the most important feature of object oriented programming is polymorphism: the ability to treat objects of different classes in the same way. Of course, polymorphism itself relies on the facilities of encapsulation and inheritance, and as such is only the most important feature provided the others already exist. However, we should consider it the *goal* of good object oriented programming to maximize the use of polymorphism so that we can simplify the broad structure of programs without compromising on their flexibility.

In the next chapter, we will go on to investigate software patterns, which are design templates that allow us to maximize the way that polymorphism is used in programs.

QUESTION 10.5

With reference to the quote above, how is it possible for a programmer to create program code in which the class of object being dealt with is unknown?

10.5   Review questions

1. Complete the following:
   (a) A class module that is used only to define the form of the Public methods and properties of a range of classes is known as an _____.
   (b) A class can be guaranteed to conform to an existing interface if it uses an _____ statement that names it.

2. A single class can implement many interfaces – true or false?

3. In early chapters of this book, a distinction was made between the methods that a class provided, and the messages that were sent to a class, even though they seemed to be the same thing. Distinguish between methods and messages in the light of what you have read about interfaces and polymorphism.

4. Suggest a way in which the Visual Basic IDE uses polymorphism. (Hint: consider the range of controls available for user-interface design.)

10.6   Practical exercise:
Extending the Agenda project

In this exercise we will add an additional facility to the Agenda project, that will allow us to keep a list of To-Do items in the agenda items list. To enable this, we will have to restructure the existing CScheduleItem class so that it implements an interface that the CToDo class will also implement. This will require us to factor out a common set of properties and methods for both classes.

A To-Do list item is an entry in the agenda that indicates a task that is to be completed. The task is kept in a prioritized list (a ToDo List) until it can be signed off as completed, at which point it is dropped from the list.

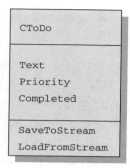

Figure 10.7 *A* **CToDo** *item class.*

A ToDo item is modelled in the class diagram shown in Figure 10.7.

If we compare this with a schedule item (Figure 10.8), we can identify the common features.

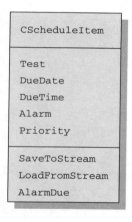

Figure 10.8 *A* **CScheduleItem** *class.*

From this we can see that the common properties between the two classes are the properties **Text** and **Priority** and the methods **SaveToStream** and **LoadFromStream**. The common interface class therefore becomes as shown in Figure 10.9.

Figure 10.9 *An interface class for agenda entries.*

We can build this **superclass** (a class definition from which other classes inherit) as a Visual Basic interface class as follows.

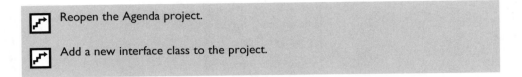

 Reopen the Agenda project.

Add a new interface class to the project.

Right-click on the project explorer, select **Add Class Module,** and choose to add a new class. In the Properties window, change the name of the new class to **IAgendaItem.**

Code the interface class as follows.

```
Option Explicit

Enum PrioritySetting
    psLow = 0
    psNormal = 1
    psHigh = 2
End Enum

Public Property Get Text() As String
End Property

Public Property Let Text(ByVal NewValue As String)
End Property

Public Property Get Priority() As PrioritySetting
End Property

Public Property Let Priority(ByVal NewValue As PrioritySetting)
End Property

Private Sub LoadFromStream(ByVal fileHandle As Integer)
End Sub

Private Sub SaveToStream(ByVal fileHandle As Integer)
End Sub
```

Note that we have moved the **PrioritySetting** enumeration into the interface class. Since both of the agenda item classes will have a priority setting, the interface is a good place to put this item. Note, however, that this is only possible because the enumeration is not a program feature that requires any storage space. We could not, for example, place a common *variable* in the interface class, since it would be ignored by Visual Basic.

Amend the `CScheduleItem` class so that it implements the common interface.

Make the following changes (shown in **bold**) to the `CScheduleItem` class:

```
Option Explicit

Implements IAgendaItem

Private mvarText As String
Private mvarDateTime As Date
Private mvarPriority As PrioritySetting
...

' These replace the Property Get and Let of the existing
' Priority methods...
Private Property Let IAgendaItem_Priority(ByVal RHS As _
                                          PrioritySetting)
  mvarPriority = RHS
End Property

Private Property Get IAgendaItem_Priority() As PrioritySetting
  IAgendaItem_Priority = mvarPriority
End Property

' These replace the property get and let of the existing
' Text methods...
Private Property Let IAgendaItem_Text(ByVal RHS As String)
  mvarText = RHS
End Property

Private Property Get IAgendaItem_Text() As String
  IAgendaItem_Text = mvarText
End Property

' The methods for handling stream operations need to be changed..
Private Sub IStreamable_LoadFromStream(ByVal fileHandle As Integer)
  Input #fileHandle, mvarText, mvarDateTime, mvarPriority
End Sub

Private Sub IStreamable_SaveToStream(ByVal fileHandle As Integer)
  Write #fileHandle, mvarText, mvarDateTime, mvarPriority
End Sub

' The remainder of the class stays the same.
```

At this stage, you can test the interface class and the alterations to the `CScheduleItem` class by first adding the following code to a code module in the project.

```
Enum AgendaItemType
  ScheduleItem = 1
  ToDoItem = 2
End Enum

Public Function CreateAgendaItem _
              (ItemType As AgendaItemType) As IAgendaItem
Dim AI As IAgendaItem
Dim f As Form
  If ItemType = ScheduleItem Then
    Set AI = New CScheduleItem
    Set f = New frmScheduleItem
    Set f.ScheduleItem = AI
  End If
  f.Show vbModal
  Unload f
  Set CreateAgendaItem = AI
End Function
```

Note that the statement **If itemType = ScheduleItem Then** is currently of little use, since the function will only create **CScheduleItem** instances. This will soon be amended.

 You then create a new **AgendaItem** using the Immediate window.

```
CreateAgendaItem ScheduleItem
```

This should cause the **frmScheduleItem** form to be displayed at the point of creating a new item. If this works as expected, you can now proceed to creating a second class that implements the **IAgendaItem** interface.

 Add the new **CToDo** class.

```
' CToDo class - models to-do list entries.

Option Explicit

Private mvarPriority As PrioritySetting
Private mvarText As String
Private mvarCompleted As Boolean
```

```
Public Property Let Completed(ByVal vData As Boolean)
   mvarCompleted = NewData
End Property


Public Property Get Completed() As Boolean
   Completed = mvarCompleted
End Property


Private Property Let IAgendaItem_Priority( _
                   ByVal RHS As PrioritySetting)
   mvarPriority = RHS
End Property


Private Property Get IAgendaItem_Priority() As PrioritySetting
   IAgendaItem_Priority = mvarPriority
End Property


Private Property Let IAgendaItem_Text(ByVal RHS As String)
   mvarText = RHS
End Property


Private Property Get IAgendaItem_Text() As String
   IAgendaItem_Text = mvarText
End Property


Private Sub IStreamable_LoadFromStream(ByVal fileHandle As Integer)
   Input #fileHandle, mvarText, mvarDateTime, mvarPriority
End Sub


Private Sub IStreamable_SaveToStream(ByVal fileHandle As Integer)
   Write #fileHandle, mvarText, mvarDateTime, mvarPriority
End Sub
```

Note that the property methods that are implemented solely by the CToDo
class are made public, while the ones that implement the interface methods are
private.

 This class will also require a special-purpose form so that the user can create
objects.

Create a new form, and organize components on it as shown in Figure 10.10.
Component properties should be set according to Table 10.4.

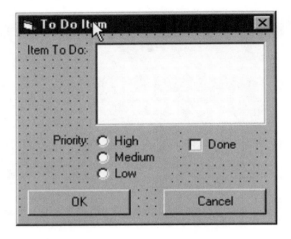

Figure 10.10 *A form class for agenda items.*

Table 10.4 *Setting of component properties.*

Control type	Property	Setting
Form	Name	`FrmToDo`
	Caption	To Do item
	BorderStyle	3 – fixed dialog
TextBox	Name	`txtText`
	MultiLine	`True`
	Text	
OptionButton	Name	`optHigh`
	Caption	`High`
OptionButton	Name	`optMedium`
	Caption	`Medium`
OptionButton	Name	`optLow`
	Caption	`Low`

Table 10.4 (cont.)

CheckBox	Name	chkDone
	Caption	Done
CommandButton	Name	cmdOK
	Caption	OK
Label	Caption	To Do item
Label	Caption	Priority

Add the following code to the form.

```
Option Explicit

' Note, a reference variable to both the class and its
' interface type..
Private mvarToDo As CToDo
Private mvarItem As IAgendaItem

' Set the form's reference to a ToDo Item..
Public Property Set Item(T As CToDo)
  ' Deal with the interface specific parts (Priority and Text)..
  Set mvarItem = T
  txtText.Text = mvarItem.Text
  Select Case mvarItem.Priority
    Case psHigh
      optHigh.Value = True
    Case psNormal
      optMedium.Value = True
    Case psLow
      optLow.Value = True
  End Select
  ' Now deal with the class specific part (Completed)..
  Set mvarToDo = T
  If T.Completed Then
    chkDone.Value = 1
  Else
    chkDone.Value = 0
  End If
End Property
```

```
' No changes to referred item..
Private Sub cmdCancel_Click()
  Unload Me
End Sub

' Change the referred item..
Private Sub cmdOK_Click()
  mvarItem.Text = txtText
  If optHigh.Value Then
    mvarItem.Priority = psHigh
  ElseIf optMedium.Value Then
    mvarItem.Priority = psNormal
  Else
    mvarItem.Priority = psLow
  End If
  If chkDone.Value = 0 Then
    mvarToDo.Completed = False
  Else
    mvarToDo.Completed = True
  End If
  Unload Me
End Sub
```

Amend the test routine to allow the creation of either type of agenda item.

```
Public Function CreateAgendaItem(ItemType As AgendaItemType) _
                             As IAgendaItem
Dim AI As IAgendaItem
Dim f As Form
  If ItemType = ScheduleItem Then
    Set AI = New CScheduleItem
    Set f = New frmScheduleItem
    Set f.ScheduleItem = AI
  ElseIf ItemType = ToDoItem Then
    Set AI = New CToDo
    Set f = New frmToDo
    Set f.Item = AI
  End If
  f.Show vbModal
  Unload f
  Set CreateAgendaItem = AI
End Function
```

Note that regardless of what type of agenda item we create, the agenda item and form variables are the same. Once we have created the item, we need not care what type of item it is unless we want to retrieve or set some class-specific property (e.g. the **Completed** property of a ToDo item).

 Test the new class and its form by creating a **ToDo** item in the Immediate window.

```
Set I = CreateAgendaItem (ToDoItem)
```

Conclusions

In this practical exercise we have created an interface class (`IAgendaItem`) that defines how objects of more than one class can be manipulated in a program. The benefit of the interface class is that Visual Basic will check the type-safety of any class we access through it, and prevent any program in which incompatible classes are used from being deployed. Interfaces are Visual Basic's way of providing polymorphism, a mechanism by which a range of objects of different classes can be used interchangeably.

Interestingly, polymorphism works in two ways in Visual Basic: one interface can take on many forms of object (the standard way that polymorphism is used in object oriented programming), but also one class can implement a number of interfaces, so an object can appear in many forms. We saw this in example programs where the way an object was accessed depended on what interface type it was attached to.

It is worth spending some time getting to grips with polymorphism. It is a part of object oriented technology that helps to manage complexity by masking the range of types it is often necessary to deal with in a program. As such, it should be strongly featured in the object oriented programmer's tool box.

10.7   Answers to questions

QUESTION 10.1

(a) The **ISortable** interface class will have to specify one method – Key.

(b)   ' ISortable Interface Class Code
          Public Function Key() As Variant

The **CordList** class would have to be altered to work with objects that implemented the **ISortable** interface, instead of the more general object type that was previously used to allow a range of classes to work with it. The two methods that this would affect are:

```
Public Property Get Item(ByVal Key As Variant) As ISortable
Public Sub Add(objItem As ISortable)
```

QUESTION 10.2

Since each class's interface methods are coded separately, we can ensure that the best possible implementation is used in each case. Programmers who use C++, Smalltalk and other object oriented languages will see this as a distinct disadvantage, since code inheritance allows them to automatically inherit much of the code in classes that inherit from others. However, in the Visual Basic form of OOP (and in Java in some circumstances), reimplementing an interface leads to more efficient code and less reliance on code that you may not be familiar with.

QUESTION 10.3

We will not need to change the application so that it can work with concrete classes of object such as rectangles and lines. The main point of polymorphism is that we can design and implement for the general case, and later concrete implementations will be guaranteed to conform.

QUESTION 10.4

```
Private Sub IShape_Draw(Pic As PictureBox)
   If mvarVisible Then
     Pic.Line (mvarLeft, mvarTop)-(mvarLeft + mvarWidth, _
               mvarTop + varHeight)
   End If
End Sub
```

QUESTION 10.5

It is possible to be unaware of the class of an object, and yet to be aware of its interface type. This is the basis of polymorphism. Look back at the implementation of the CAD program, and specifically at the implementations of the **MouseDown**, **MouseMove** and **MouseUp** event-handlers for the PictureBox. None of these subs are aware of the class of object they are dealing with. In fact, the only sub on the form that makes any reference to a specific class of drawn object is the **GetNewDrawShape** function – every other sub or function deals with an **IShape interface**.

10.8   Answers to review questions

1.   (a)   *A class module that is used only to define the form of the Public methods and properties of a range of classes is known as an* interface.

(b)   *A class can be guaranteed to conform to an existing interface if it uses an* `Implements` *statement that names it.*

2.   *A single class can implement many interfaces – true or false?* True

3.   *In early chapters of this book, a distinction was made between the methods that a class provided, and the messages that were sent to a class, even though they seemed to be the same thing. Distinguish between methods and messages in the light of what you have read about interfaces and polymorphism.* A message is a call to a class interface. An interface can be implemented by any number of classes, each of which has its own method for dealing with it.

4.   *Suggest a way in which the Visual Basic IDE uses polymorphism.* Every control that can be placed on a Visual Basic form has the common properties Name, Left, Top, Width, Height, Index, Enabled and Tag. These are most likely to be an interface definition shared by all VB controls. By defining this interface, the Visual Basic form designer greatly simplifies the work of placing, moving and resizing controls on a form.

CHAPTER 11

Patterns in object oriented programming

Object orientation is a means to an end. With it we hope to develop programs that are well organized and therefore robust and maintainable. However, for large or complex applications, it is merely a starting point. How we connect objects together is as important as how we design and develop the classes that define the objects in the first place. As the field of object oriented programming has matured, design techniques that address this question have come to the fore. Current practice is to take a leaf from the book of real life. In many disciplines, we connect components together to form well-defined and well-understood assemblies – *patterns*. By reusing a pattern that we have used many times before in similar circumstances, we can be secure in the knowledge that many of the problems we might encounter have been met and solved before.

By the end of this chapter, you should be able to:

- characterize certain programming structures as patterns of objects,

- identify a number of specific patterns and describe their use in applications,

- recognize the role that polymorphism can play in the development of reusable structures in applications,

- implement examples of certain software patterns.

11.1 Software patterns

Objects give us the ability to create new types of variable, and use them in a range of applications. Object structures add the facility to create collections of objects organized to optimize aspects of efficiency such as speed of access. We can deal with individual entities and collections of similar entities using the techniques described so far in this book.

However, applications programs are rarely composed entirely of homogeneous collections of objects that can be modelled in a single collection or hierarchy. When developing a collection, we are more likely to be confronted by the need to connect together a wide variety of objects in a less orderly way. This can lead to the belief that each application has a unique structure that must be crafted individually. In particular, we can be left with the impression that reuse of program code is an ideal that can only be realized for individual classes and very simple structures.

One aspect of why we still find it difficult to reuse elements of programs we created last week in new programs this week is that OOP can only partially address the problem of structure in programs. Structure is the framework of software, and, in most cases, goes beyond what can be accomplished by a single object or class, or by a specific form of collection. If we wish to build an application that models a complex view of reality in software, we will probably need to model the interconnections between all of the components of the real-world system (i.e. the objects) as much as the software components themselves.

OOP shows us how to create classes and collections of objects, but we are left to assume that these alone will form the basis of our software model of a real-world system. **Software design patterns**, or simply **patterns**, provide the next step. Once we have a methodology for constructing models of the components of the world we wish to model, we have need of a model for connecting them together in assemblies, and this is provided by patterns.

Christopher Alexander proposed the idea of design patterns in a book in 1977. To quote a passage of this, 'Each pattern describes a problem which occurs over and over again in our environment, and then describes the core of the solution to that problem, in such a way that you can use this solution a million times over, without ever doing it the same way twice'. In Alexander's discipline of architecture, the patterns were structures such as entrances, mezzanines and town squares. In software, we can use much the same approach to generalize the design of specific algorithms, ways of constructing objects and data structures. The core text in this area is *Software Patterns*, by Gamma, Helm, Johnson and Vlissides, and this has become a key text in computer science since its publication in 1994.

In this chapter, we will examine specific examples of software patterns and implementations of them in Visual Basic. Gamma *et al.* divide software patterns into three groups: **creational patterns**, **stuctural patterns** and **behavioural patterns**. These describe ways of creating objects in programs, ways of forming connections and collaborations between objects and organizations of objects that define operations or algorithms. We have already used some of these patterns in the example programs of earlier chapters, so the key point of this chapter is that we should be able to recognize a pattern and therefore apply it to a variety of situations. The important feature of using patterns is the philosophy, which takes us a step beyond objects and into the next phase of software development.

In a previous chapter we examined the idea of structure in object oriented software. How do you think the idea of software patterns differs from a structure?

11.2 Creational patterns

This type of pattern is used to generate objects conforming to a specific super-class or interface. It allows us to separate the mechanism used to create objects from the logic of the application in which they are created. A typical non-pattern method of doing this is to have a case structure in the module in which new objects are created, e.g. in an event-handler on a form. This is then used to create a specific class of object (the *product* class) given a specific cue (e.g. a menu or toolbar selection).

The Factory Method pattern

As an improvement on this way of doing things, our simple CAD program in the previous chapter used a function call within the event-handler where drawn objects were created, as shown below:

```
Private Sub P_MouseUp(Button As Integer, Shift As Integer, _
                      X As Single, Y As Single)
Dim S As IShape
  Select Case CurrentOp
  ...
    Case coDrawing
      ' Get rid of the bounding box..
      P.Line (StartX, StartY)-(LastX, LastY), vbWhite, B
      ' Create the new shape object..
      Set S = GetNewDrawShape(DrawType)
      ' Set up position and size..
      S.Left = StartX
      S.Top = StartY
      S.Width = X - StartX
      S.Height = Y - StartY
      S.Visible = True
```

```
      ' Add it to the draw list..
      DrawList.Add S
      ...
    End Select
  ...
End Sub
```

The statement in *italics* is a call to a function whose job is to create objects. We pass the function a value that indicates the type of object we want, and it returns an object of the required type. This function is known as a ***Factory Method*** and is one of the standard patterns described by Gamma *et al.*

DrawType was a variable set by a button click event-handler, although we could just as easily have used a selection from a menu or toolbar. The function that created instances of the shape objects was, in that example application, a method of the user-interface form. However, it would be better practice to place this code in a separate module, since it is normally a good idea to separate user-interface from program logic.

The Factory Method pattern has the following benefits:

■ Objects are created at a central location (the Factory Method) of the application, and so object creation and the user-interface operations that lead to object creation are kept distinct. This makes the user-interface and object creation features easier to test is isolation.

■ We can add new objects (e.g. new Shape classes) to the application more easily, since we simply need to amend the Factory Method function.

■ Use of the Factory Method enforces polymorphism, since the method has only a single return interface type, and so all classes of object that it can return must implement this interface.

■ We can use the Factory Method to perform some other useful tasks in setting up a new object once it has been created but before it is returned to the application.

The classic structure of a Factory Method function is shown below:

```
Public Function GenerateObject(objectType As objectTypeIdentifier) _
                        As InterfaceType
  Select Case objectType
    Case type1:
      Set GenerateObject = New CObjectType1
    Case type2:
      Set GenerateObject = New CObjectType2
    ...
  End Select
End Function
```

In this, **objectType** is some variable used to identify the type of object required. An integer or string can be used, but an enumeration, as used in the CAD program, is better. **InterfaceType**, the return type of the function, is a specification of the *super-class* that the generated object must belong to.

In Visual Basic, it is possible to lever some extra functionality from a Factory Method by giving it some of the responsibilities of a **constructor**, a sub or function that places an object into a desired state. For example, in our CAD example, we could have greatly simplified the **MouseUp** event-handler that the call to the Factory Method was placed in by passing additional parameters to it to describe the required position and size of the object:

```
Public Function GetNewDrawShape(desc As String, left As Single, _
        top As Single, width as Single, height As Single) As IShape
Dim Shape As IShape
  Select Case desc
    Case "Rectangle":
      Set Shape = New CRectangle
    Case "Ellipse":
      Set Shape = New CEllipse
    Case "Line"
      Set Shape = New CLine
      ...
  End Select
  ' Now set up shape object...
  Shape.Left = left
  Shape.Top = top
  Shape.Width = width
  Shape.Height = height
  GetNewDrawShape = Shape
End Function
```

The Factory Method is a useful pattern in programs where a variety of 'product' objects of compatible types are required. By centralizing the creation of the various product classes, we can simplify the development and maintenance effort required by the program and improve its logical structure.

The Prototype pattern

The Factory Method used in the CAD example still requires a certain amount of the main application logic to be altered. It is not possible to leave main application logic untouched entirely when adding new product classes, since we would need to amend the way that the type of new product objects are selected by a user. In the CAD application as it was, we would need to add a new CommandButton to the form for a new product class, for example **CTriangle**, and provide an event-handler so that the type identifier could be set to indicate that type (**DrawType = "Triangle"**). In this type of application, it would not be too onerous a task to provide this.

However, it should always be a design goal to minimize the number of changes required in an application when we augment its functionality. Typically, new product classes need to be linked into an application and routes to their constructors provided.

Using the Factory Method, it was necessary to update the `GenerateObject` function used whenever a new product class was introduced to the application. It was also necessary to add control methods to allow us to choose instances of the new classes to instantiate. Although not a particularly onerous set of requirements for the provision of an extensible range of products, it is always worth looking for ways to reduce the update burden.

The ***Prototype pattern*** has a similar objective to the Factory Method pattern, allowing us to delegate the creation of new objects to a structure that is well suited to the job. However, it is often the case that the best way of creating a new object is to copy an existing one. The Prototype pattern hinges on a requirement that all objects of product classes are able to *clone* themselves. Clones are autonomous copies of objects of their own class. The cloning process could create an *exact copy* of the prototype or, where the prototype is simply being used as an object generator, could simply create another instance of the prototype's class.

We also used an example of this pattern in the CAD application, when we provided a `CDrawSettings` class, which had a `Clone` method:

```
' The Clone method returns a new copy of this object with its
' current settings.
Public Function Clone() As CDrawSettings
Dim S As New CDrawSettings
  With S
    .Colour = mvarColour
    .FillStyle = mvarFillStyle
    .LineStyle = mvarLineStyle
    .LineWidth = mvarLineWidth
    .FillColour = mvarFillColour
  End With
  Set Clone = S
End Function
```

We used the `Clone` method to create a *brand new* set of settings, based on the current values in the prototype object. This allowed us to provide each shape object with its own settings rather than the copies of a single set that would have resulted by simply setting a reference variable.

We could also have used the Prototype pattern to create the shape objects in the first place, by using a collection of prototype shapes in conjunction with a Factory Method. A major advantage of this is that instead of a case statement that would need to be updated with the addition of each new type of shape object, we could leave it up to the prototype to identify itself:

```
Public Function GetNewDrawShape(desc As String, left As Single, _
        top As Single, width as Single, height As Single) As IShape
Dim Prototype As Ishape, Shape As IShape
   For Each Prototype In Prototypes
      If Prototype.Ident = desc Then
         Set Shape = Prototype.Clone
         Exit For
      End If
   Next
   ' Now set up shape object...
   Shape.Left = left
   Shape.Top = top
   Shape.Width = width
   Shape.Height = height
   Set GetNewDrawShape = Shape
End Function
```

Now the Factory Method does not need to be changed whenever we add new prototypes. Note, however, that as well as the **Clone** method, another new method would have to be added to the **IShape** interface. The **Ident** method would be required to return unique identifier, in this case a string that was different for each class that implements the interface.

The Prototype pattern can be extended to deal automatically with a number of the limitations of using the Factory Method alone. For example, we could provide the **IShape** interface with additional methods that allow them to interact more intelligently with the user-interface of a program. By giving the interface an **AddToList** method, or even a **ToolbarButton** property, we can make it the responsibility of each prototype either to add itself to the user-interface or to provide the user-interface with the information required to update itself. We could code three methods of the base (interface) class, **AddToList**, **Clone** and **IDString**, as shown below:

```
' IBase interface class..

   ...
Public Sub AddToList(C As ComboBox)
End Sub

Public Function Clone() As IBase
End Function

Public Property Get IDString() As String
End Property
   ...
```

A concrete class that implements this method could then use it to insert its own identification string into a combo-box, so that the class appeared on the user-interface:

```
' CSomeClass - a prototype class.

Implements IBase

   ...
Private Sub IBase_AddToList(C As ComboBox)
  C.AddItem IBase_IDString
End Sub

Private Property Get IBase_IDString() As String
  IBase_IDString = "CSomeClass"
End Property

Private Function IBase_Clone() As IBase
  Set IBase_Clone = New CSomeClass
End Function
   ...
```

It would now be a simple matter to create a collection of prototypes and register each of these with a combo-box on a form so that the user could create one of any of the listed types. We would do this in a public method that could be called by any form with a ComboBox (or ListBox, if we changed the parameter type) on it:

```
Private ProtoList As Collection

Public Sub RegisterPrototypes(C As ComboBox)
Dim I As IBase
  Set ProtoList = New Collection
  Set I = New CSomeClass
  ProtoList.Add I, I.IDString
  Set I = New CSomeOtherClass
  ProtoList.Add I, I.IDString
  Set I = New CSomeThirdClass
  ProtoList.Add I, I.IDString
  For Each I in ProtoList
    I.AddToList C
  Next
End Sub
```

Of course, the purpose of all this is to simplify creating objects from the application's point of view, so we will need a Factory Method function in the same module:

```
Public Function GenerateObject(ID As String) As IBase
Dim I As IBase
  For Each I In ProtoList
    If I.IDString = ID Then
      Set GenerateObject = I
      Exit For
    End If
  Next
End Function
```

Now to create a new object, the user simply selects a type from the combo-box and initiates some event that calls on the `GenerateObject` Factory Method. It is not at all necessary to amend the form code that the event-handlers reside on, so all maintenance required to extend the range of classes can now be done within the code module that contains the `RegisterPrototypes` and `GenerateObject` routines.

Other creational patterns

Gamma *et al.* specify five creational forms of pattern. In addition to those described here, there are:

- **Abstract Factory**, which provides an interface for creating *families* of related or dependent objects without specifying their concrete classes

- **Builder**, which separates the construction of a complex object from its representation so that the same construction process can generate different representations

- **Singleton**, which ensures that only a single instance of a class can be created and provides a global point of access to it.

In all but the last of these, the specific goal is to separate the creation of product objects from the application in which they are managed. This allows the use of polymorphism to be maximized. The *Singleton* pattern is used when only a single object of a class can be allowed. For example, Visual Basic provides a *Printer* class and a single *Printer* object of this class. There would be no point in creating another printer object, and so it is not allowed.

QUESTION 11.2

    (a)   Creational patterns are used in programs where objects are created interactively by the user. Explain the key feature that a creational pattern would bring to the design of this type of application.

    (b)   How does a Prototype pattern differ from a Factory Method?

11.3 Structural patterns

Structural patterns are concerned with the mechanics of building complex structures in software while maintaining the general goal of promoting reusability and abstraction. This can be used to allow incompatible classes to inter-operate, complex hierarchical structures of objects to be maintained uniformly within an application, or for a variety of other reasons where the clean structure of an application would be compromised by a proliferation of classes or objects.

A typical use of structural patterns would be to integrate a range of existing classes into an application where their interfaces were not compatible; for example, we might wish to add an existing class into the `IShape` hierarchy described previously. This could be for reasons of compatibility with another part of the application, or simply because we have a class that does most of what we want but that is currently incompatible with `IShape`. The **Adapter** pattern is suitable for this purpose.

The Adapter pattern

As its name suggests, this pattern has the job of making one class fit the interface of another, a bit like an electrical adapter that you might take abroad to allow the use of your electrical appliances. By using this pattern we can, for example, make a class conform to another pattern we are using, even though it was never intended for use in that specific way.

For an example of this pattern, we can again return to the graphics application. Imagine a class, `CCircle`, had already been developed, but followed the template shown below:

```
' CCircle class
Option Explicit

Private Const PI = 3.1415927
Private mvarX As Integer
Private mvarY As Integer
Private mvarRadius As Integer

Public Property Get X() As Integer
  X = mvarX
End Property

Public Property Let X(ByVal NewValue As Integer)
  mvarX = NewValue
End Property

Public Property Get Y() As Integer
  Y = mvarY
End Property

Public Property Let Y(ByVal NewValue As Integer)
  mvarY = NewValue
End Property

Public Property Get Radius() As Integer
  Radius = mvarRadius
End Property
```

```
Public Property Let Radius(ByVal NewValue As Integer)
   mvarRadius = NewValue
End Property

Public Function Circumference() As Single
   Circumference = 2 * PI * mvarRadius
End Function

Public Function Area() As Single
   Area = PI * mvarRadius * mvarRadius
End Function
```

The **CCircle** class shown is simple to implement. It does not, however, do what we require of an **IShape** implementor. We could of course amend the class by making it implement the **IShape** interface in addition to what it does, but this requires that we be allowed to modify its source code; in some development environments, that may not be the case for good project management reasons. In this case, an Adapter class could be used to create an interface between the **CCircle** class and the **IShape** interface. It would *contain* a **CCircle** object.

```
' CCircleAdapter class.
Option Explicit

Implements IShape

Private mvarCircle As CCircle
Private mvarSettings As CDrawSettings
Private mvarVisible As Boolean

Private Sub Class_Initialize()
' Create the circle object..
   Set mvarCircle = New CCircle
End Sub

Private Sub Class_Terminate()
' Destroy the circle object..
   Set mvarCircle = Nothing
End Sub

Private Sub IShape_Draw(Pic As PictureBox)
   If mvarVisible Then
     With mvarCircle
        Pic.Circle (.X,.Y),.Radius
     End With
   End If
End Sub

Private Property Let IShape_Height(ByVal RHS As Single)
   mvarCircle.Radius = RHS \ 2
End Property
```

```
Private Property Get IShape_Height() As Single
    IShape_Height = mvarCircle.Radius * 2
End Property

Private Property Let IShape_Left(ByVal RHS As Single)
    mvarCircle.X = RHS + mvarCircle.Radius
End Property

Private Property Get IShape_Left() As Single
    IShape_Left = mvarCircle.X - mvarCircle.Radius
End Property

Private Property Let IShape_Top(ByVal RHS As Single)
    mvarCircle.Y = RHS + mvarCircle.Radius
End Property

Private Property Get IShape_Top() As Single
    IShape_Top = mvarCircle.Y - mvarCircle.Radius
End Property

Private Property Let IShape_Width(ByVal RHS As Single)
    mvarCircle.Radius = RHS \ 2
End Property

Private Property Get IShape_Width() As Single
    IShape_Width = mvarCircle.Radius * 2
End Property

    ...
' Other properties and methods: Draw, MoveBy, MoveTo, Visible etc.
    ...
```

Although, in this case, it would have been easier to simply define a new **CCircle** class for the application, this is not the general case. Using the adapter pattern, we have a circle object that is able to communicate geometric information, and yet it behaves in the same way as a standard **IShape** class. Note that while the methods of the Adapter class interface need to be coded, we simply delegate calls to the native **CCircle** methods to the enclosed circle object.

In general, the Adapter pattern allows us to mix and match objects of classes from a wide range of applications and interfaces, without the need to make any alterations to any of the existing classes.

The Composite pattern

This pattern allows us to work with complex hierarchical structures of objects in the same way that we would work with single objects. It is based on a hierarchical tree structure.

Continuing the earlier example of a graphics application, we may decide to implement a Group command so that we can compose a number of graphics primitives into

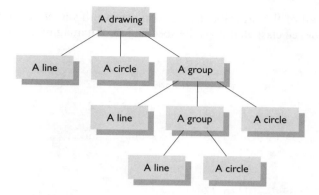

Figure 11.1   *A drawing made up of composite elements.*

a single object. The resulting complex object should be addressable as a single object for the purposes of editing, moving deletion, copying, etc. Figure 11.1 is an example of the sort of structure we require.

Items in this drawing structure are either *primitives* or *groups*. However, we will be making the drawing and editing code in the application unnecessarily complex if we make it necessary to distinguish between these two types of drawn item. The composite pattern allows us to avoid making the distinction by preserving the compatibility of both single items and groups. We can do this be amending the common interface so that every drawn item implements a composite interface:

```
' IShape - a shape class that allows for composite shapes...
Option Explicit

Public Property Get Left() As Single
End Property

Public Property Let Left(ByVal NewValue As Single)
End Property

    ...
' Other standard shape primitives...
    ...

' Now for the composite specific interface methods...
Public Sub Add(Shape As IShape)
End Sub

Public Function Remove(Shape As IShape) As Boolean
End Function

Public Function GetChild(n: integer) As Ishape
End Function
```

We will make all of the drawable classes conform to this interface, but we can now create a **CComposite** class that does the specific job of managing composite groups of objects:

```
' CComposite class - used to manage groups of shape objects.
Implements IShape


' We need a structure to hold other shapes in...
Private Shapes As Collection


Private Sub Class_Initialize()
  Set Shapes = New Collection
End Sub


Public Property Get IShape_Left() As Single
' The left extent of this composite shape will be defined by the
' left-most shape within it...
Dim minleft As Single, S As IShape
  minLeft = Shapes.Item(1).Left
  For Each S In Shapes
    If S.Left < minLeft Then
      minLeft = S.Left
    End If
  Next
  IShape_Left = minLeft
End Property


Public Property Let IShape_Left(ByVal NewValue As Single)
' We need to update the left property of every shape in this
' composite so that the whole composite moves left...
Dim delta As Single, S As IShape
  delta = NewValue - IShape_Left
  For Each S In Shapes
    S.Left = S.Left + delta
  Next
End Property


Public Sub IShape_Draw(Pic As PictureBox)
Dim S As IShape
  For Each S In Shapes
    S.Draw Pic
  Next
End Sub
```

```
...
' Other standard shape primitives...
...

' Now for the composite specific interface methods...
Public Sub IShape_Add(Shape As IShape)
  Shapes.Add Shape
End Sub

Public Function IShape_Remove(Shape As IShape) As Boolean
Dim index As Integer
  For index = 1 To Shapes.Count
    If Shape Is Shapes.Item(index) Then
      Shapes.Remove index
      IShape_Remove = True
      Exit Function
    End If
  Next
End Function

Public Function IShape_GetChild(n: integer) As IShape
  If n <= Shapes.Count Then
    IShape_GetChild = Shapes.Item(n)
  Else
    IShape_GetChild = Nothing
  End If
End Function
```

Of course, if the shape class is to be a primitive rather than a composite, the **Add**, **Remove** and **GetChild** methods are simply left empty. Using the new form of the shape class, we can quickly code new shapes by adding existing ones together to form a composite. Figure 11.2 illustrates the stages in this process.

Of course, the method shown above for creating a new triangle shape is not very useful, since it is not interactive. However, we could provide a way for user-defined composite shapes to be built at run time by allowing multiple items to be selected and the selected items to be grouped. Each item in the group could then be added to a **CComposite** instance.

The composite pattern is used extensively in computer aided drawing, but is also a feature of many types of interactive software. For example, multiple documents can be combined to form composite documents, and groups of database records can be formed so that a common operation can be performed on each member.

Other structural patterns

The set of structural patterns described by Gamma *et al.* covers the range of possibilities for building flexible software structures and maximizing the use of OOP principles. Among these are:

```
Public Function New Triangle ( ) As IShape
Dim C As CComposite
Dim L As CLine
   Set C = New CComposite
   Sel L = New CLine
   L.Left = 500
   L.Top = 0
   L.Width = 500
   L.Height = 1000
   C.AddL
   Set L = New CLine
   L.Left = 0
   L.Top = 1000
   L.Width = 1000
   L.Height = 0
   C.Add.L
   Set L = New CLine
   L.Left = 0
   L.Top = 0
   L.Width = 500
   L.Height = 1000
   C.Add L
   New Triangle = C
End Sub
```

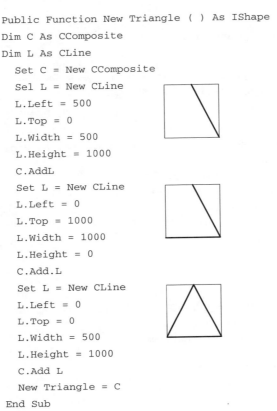

Figure 11.2   *Building up a triangle composite from line-segments.*

- **Bridge**, that allows us to use a range of abstractions (e.g. abstract base classes) with a range of implementations (concrete classes) in such a way that a given concrete class can be appointed a *different* abstract class. In effect, two separate class hierarchies are maintained: one for abstractions and another for concrete implementations. By enclosing a member of the base implementation in the base abstraction, it becomes possible to make generalized changes to the abstract classes that proliferate throughout the implementation classes.

- **Decorator**, that allows us to extend an object dynamically, by attaching a member of a helper class. The decorator pattern allows us to avoid sub-classing in the case where we wish to extend the functionality of specific objects. The example given in Gamma *et al.* is the addition of Border and Scrollbar objects to a plain TextViewer. By creating Border and Scrollbar as *Decorator* classes, we can avoid having to create a subclass of the TextViewer class, and also have the ability to apply Decorator objects to other viewer classes.

- **Façade**, which allows us to provide a single uniform interface to a complex set of interfaces. For example, we might consider a Visual Basic form with added properties to access the data in controls as a Façade pattern.

- **Flyweight**, which allows a large number of small items to share a single object. An example of this is the use of Flyweight objects to represent any of a large number of characters in a word processor. Each character has font, size, style, colour, etc., attributes, but instead of occupying an object each, a single flyweight object can act as the interface to a large number of characters.

- **Proxy**, which is a way of making one object act as a surrogate for another to provide control access. For example, we could use a proxy instead of dealing directly with a printer object. Since the printer object may have to access the network and verify the status (on-line, etc.) whenever it is accessed, the proxy could be used to maintain a copy of the printer status and allow us to control the printer. Meanwhile, the proxy would only contact the real printer object when it was necessary for printing.

QUESTION 11.3

(a) How does the Composite pattern differ from a simple collection of objects?

(b) What advantage does the Adapter pattern bring to existing classes in applications?

11.4   Behavioural patterns

So far, we have examined patterns that provide for the flexible creation of objects and optimization of software structures. Behavioural patterns are about the generalization of algorithms and the assignment of responsibilities among objects. The behavioural patterns codify how objects communicate with each other in a way that can assist our understanding of control flow in a program. Instead of managing control flow, you deal with object interconnections; this in turn manages control flow.

Behavioural patterns are the most diverse group. This is probably because the history of computing has concentrated more on algorithms rather than structures. Structure is a feature that supports good algorithms, but algorithms make the data work.

The Observer pattern

This is also known as *Subject–Observer*, since it allows us to define the interaction between an object (the subject) and another object that is interested in its state (the observer). The purpose is to set up an automatic interaction between subject and observer so that updates need not be performed by the application code. Visual Basic is particularly suited to the pattern because a number of the built-in user-interface controls are potential subjects or observers.

Assume, for example, that we wish to make sure that all of the controls that are currently displaying state information about a specific object are kept up to date. We might, for example, have displayed two or more forms, each of which displays specific properties of an object, and these forms might also allow us to edit the object.

The Observer pattern allows us to keep the two or more observer forms in synchronization with the current state of the object by providing a **Notify** method. The subject class keeps a list of all of its current observers, and dispatches the **Notify** message to each whenever its state changes. The end result is an automatic update of all observers, without any need to code the updates into the application program.

For example, a simple subject class is shown below:

```
Option Explicit

' Subject specific member variables...
Private mvarHeight As Single
Private mvarWidth As Single

' Observer pattern data...
Private mvarObservers As Collection

' Use this method to add to the list of observers...
Public Sub AddObserver(NewObs As Form)
  mvarObservers.Add NewObs
End Sub

' Call whenever the state of an object changes in a way that is
' significant to the observers...
Public Sub Update()
Dim O As Form
  For Each O In mvarObservers
    O.Notify Me
  Next
End Sub

' Normal object state stuff...
Public Property Let Width(ByVal vData As Single)
  mvarWidth = vData
  Update            ' Note - updates observers.
End Property

Public Property Get Width() As Single
  Width = mvarWidth
End Property
```

```
Public Property Let Height(ByVal vData As Single)
  mvarHeight = vData
  Update               'Note - updates observers.
End Property

Public Property Get Height() As Single
  Height = mvarHeight
End Property

Private Sub Class_Initialize()
  Set mvarObservers = New Collection
End Sub
```

With the subject class able to maintain a list of observers (in this case forms, but an observer object does not need to be visible), we can now turn to the creation of observer objects. The only pattern requirement for these is that they must implement a **Notify** method and have some way of accessing the subject's state:

```
Option Explicit

Public Sub Notify(S As CSubject)
  With S
    S_Pic.Width = .Width
    S_Pic.Height = .Height
  End With
End Sub
```

Note that in this case, we have simply passed a reference to the subject directly to the observer. However, this may require us to break encapsulation in some cases, and then more specific parameters would need to be defined for the **Notify** method. The above code changes the **Width** and **Height** properties of a **Shape** control named **S_Pic**. The form therefore provides a graphical representation of the changes in the subject's state (Figure 11.3). A second form can provide a textual representation of the same state variables:

```
Option Explicit

Private Subj As CSubject
Private Pic As frmPicObserver

Private Sub Form_Load()
  Set Subj = New CSubject
  Subj.AddObserver Me
  Set Pic = New frmPicObserver
  Pic.Show
  Subj.AddObserver Pic
End Sub
```

```
Public Sub Notify(S As CSubject)
  txtWidth.Text = S.Width
  txtHeight.Text = S.Height
End Sub

Private Sub txtHeight_KeyPress(KeyAscii As Integer)
  If KeyAscii = 13 Then
    KeyAscii = 0
    If IsNumeric(txtHeight.Text) Then
      Subj.Height = CSng(txtHeight.Text)
    End If
  End If
End Sub

Private Sub txtWidth_KeyPress(KeyAscii As Integer)
  If KeyAscii = 13 Then
    KeyAscii = 0
    If IsNumeric(txtWidth.Text) Then
      Subj.Width = CSng(txtWidth.Text)
    End If
  End If
End Sub
```

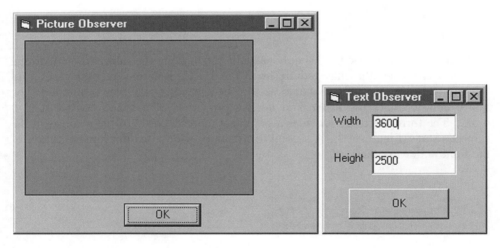

Figure 11.3 *Two observer forms in operation.*

Subject–Observer is a very simple method for keeping a number of objects in synchronization. In Visual Basic, it is ideal for providing a number of alternative views of a single object or structure, but it can also be used as a method for keeping objects in touch with each other.

The Iterator pattern

This pattern exists to allow us to work our way through the items in a collection without knowing or caring what form the collection takes. For example, we could store our **IShape** objects from earlier examples in a standard Collection, an array or even a tree structure. By using an iterator we can dispense with the need to change the application code if we decide to change the data structure.

The iterator pattern also allows us to be flexible in the way we define a *traversal* (i.e. iteration across the members) of the aggregation. We could define a number of iterators that allowed us to traverse a set first-to-last, last-to-first or even filtering out members that did not match a specific criterion.

So that an appropriate type of iterator is always used, we make it the responsibility of a collection class to create its own iterator. For example, if we were to provide an iterator for an ordered list class (**COrdList**, described in Chapter 7), we would amend the **COrdList** class to enable it to create an iterator object:

```
' COrdList class: a collection class for ordered lists.
Option Explicit

Private colData As Collection
Private mvarIterator As IIterator

Private Sub Class_Initialize()
  Set colData = New Collection
  Set mvarIterator = Nothing
End Sub

Public Sub CreateIterator(type As String)
  If type="Backwards" Then
    Set mvarIterator = New CBackwardIterator
  Else
    Set mvarIterator = New CForwardIterator
  End If
  Set mvarIterator.Collection = colData
End Function
```

Note that the **CreateIterator** function sets the **mvarIterator** member to be an interface object, **IIterator**. This allows us to create several iterator classes that implement the interface. The iterator interface defines four standard methods:

```
' IIterator interface definition

Public Function First() As Object
End Function

Public Function Next() As Object
End Function
```

```
Public Function Current() As Object
End Function

Public Function IsDone() As Boolean
End Function
```

The **IIterator** interface defines the core behaviour required of all iterators. In the example above, the **First, Next** and **Current** methods return objects of class **Object**; this is any class of object. In most concrete examples, an iterator class would be defined to work with a specific class or interface. From here, we can go on to define concrete list and iterator classes. For example, with our **COrdList** class, we might amend it as follows:

```
' COrdList class with Iterator.

...
' Class definition as before.
...
Public Property Get Iterator() As IIterator
  Set Iterator = mvarIterator
End Property
```

We can now provide the required iterator class:

```
' Class CForwardIterator

Private mvarCurrent As Integer
Private mvarCollection As Object
Private mvarDone As Boolean

Private Function IIterator_First() As Object
  If mvarCollection.Count > 0 Then
    mvarCurrent = 1
    mvarDone = False
    Set IIterator_First = mvarCollection.Item(1)
  Else
    mvarDone = True
    Set IIterator_First = Nothing
  End If
End Function

Private Function IIterator_Next() As Object
  If mvarCurrent < mvarCollection.Count Then
    mvarCurrent = mvarCurrent+1
    Set IIterator_Next = mvarCollection.Item(mvarCurrent)
  Else
    mvarDone = True
    Set IIterator_Next = Nothing
  End If
End Function
```

```
   Private Function IIterator_Current() As Object
     If mvarCurrent > 0 And mvarCurrent <= mvarCollection.Count Then
        Set IIterator_Current = mvarCollection.Item(mvarCurrent)
     Else
        Set IIterator_Current = Nothing
     End If
   End Function


   Private Function IIterator_IsDone() As Boolean
     IIterator_Done = mvarDone
   End Function
```

It is a simple matter to provide an alternative iterator – in this case one that traverses a collection backwards rather than forwards. All that is necessary is to provide alternative versions of the **IIterator_First** and **IIterator_Next** methods:

```
   ' Class cBackwardIterator.
   ...
   ' Code as per the cForwardIterator class, with the exception of...
   Private Function IIterator_First() As Object
     If mvarCollection.Count > 0 Then
        mvarCurrent = mvarCollection.Count
        mvarDone = False
        Set IIterator_First = mvarCollection.Item(mvarCurrent)
     Else
        mvarDone = True
        Set IIterator_First = Nothing
     End If
   End Function


   Private Function IIterator_Next() As Object
     If mvarCurrent > 1 Then
        mvarCurrent = mvarCurrent-1
        Set IIterator_Next = mvarCollection.Item(mvarCurrent)
     Else
        mvarDone = True
        Set IIterator_Next = Nothing
     End If
   End Function
```

Now that we have defined the iterator classes and amended the collection class to select an appropriate iterator object, we can easily deal with all of the objects in a collection in an order defined by the iterator. For example, if we have a collection, **c**, of **CInfo** objects, each of which has a **Text** property, we can search for a specific phrase, forwards or backwards, using code as follows:

```
Public Function SearchCollection(searchFor As String, _
                                 direction As String) As CInfo
Dim I As CInfo
  C.CreateIterator direction
  Set I = C.Iterator.First
  While Not C.Iterator.IsDone
    If InStr(I.Text, searchFor) >0 Then
      Set SearchCollection = I
      Exit Function
    End If
    Set I = C.Iterator.Next
  Wend
  Set SearchCollection = Nothing
End Function
```

Although the iterator-based search requires more code than a **For..Each** traversal, it gives us the advantage of allowing us to search in a given direction, or using a given algorithm, or even applying a particular filter on the items returned by the iterator. For example, we could have coded the **First** and **Next** methods to skip past items that did not contain a certain property value, or even created a specialized searching iterator class. Most importantly, we would use the same code to traverse a structure whether it was a tree, graph or collection or had some other form.

Other behavioural patterns

The behavioural patterns section of the book by Gamma *et al.* is the richest collection. These patterns are there to simplify and generalize algorithms in some way, and are all recognizable as ways of keeping to the abstract solutions devised for a system design during the implementation stages. The remaining ones are:

- **Chain of Responsibility**, which separates an operation from the request for it, thereby providing for a range of possible operations in response. The example given by Gamma *et al.* is of a context-sensitive help system, in which a request for help starts at the specific context of the request and works up a hierarchy until the most specific available level of help is found.

- **Command**, which encapsulates a request for an operation as an object, thereby allowing the request to be parameterized with respect to client, stored or logged.

- **Interpreter**, which allows the grammar of a language to be represented so that syntax can be easily maintained.

- **Mediator**, which is a pattern for defining the interactions between different objects, thereby removing the need for the interacting objects to refer explicitly to each other. This preserves the independence of either end of the interaction.

- **Memento**, which is a way of keeping a snapshot of an object's internal state without violating its encapsulation.

- **State**, which is a pattern for allowing an object to vary its behaviour when its internal state changes. The object appears to change class depending on its state.

- **Strategy**, which allows a range of algorithms to be used interchangeably, allowing different algorithms to be used in different situations.

- **Template Method**, which defines skeletal algorithms, steps of which are delegated to subclasses to enable an algorithm to be used in a wider range of situations without change.

- **Visitor**, which represents a generalized operation to be performed on the elements of an object structure. The operation can be changed without changing the class of the elements operated on.

QUESTION 11.4

Behavioural patterns allow us to encapsulate algorithms within reusable classes. How do such patterns differ from subroutines and functions that allow us to implement an algorithm in code?

11.5   Review questions

1. Complete the following:
    (a) Software patterns that are used to assist in the generation of new objects in an application are called _____ _____.
    (b) Software patterns that are used to assist in interconnecting objects in an application are called _____ _____.
    (c) Software patterns that are used to assist in the design of algorithms in an application are called _____ _____.

2. Name the key method that is used to make the Prototype pattern work.

3. Name the three methods that all elements of the Composite pattern must implement.

4. The Subject pattern-class is used in a pattern along with the _____.

5. Patterns are used in applications to provide a well-known framework for software designers and implementers to work within. Give a number of reasons why this is important.

11.6 Practical exercise: Using the Observer pattern

We have already seen and used a number of the patterns discussed in this chapter in the practical exercises in previous chapters. In this exercise, we will work through a simple implementation of a Subject–Observer pattern that will allow us to create a variety of different clock faces to act as the display of a single clock model.

A computer clock

All modern personal computers know what time it is, provided their real-time-clock (RTC) has been set occasionally and the built-in battery is working to keep the time in the periods when the computer is off. In Visual Basic, it is a trivial matter to display the time on a form to which a **Timer** control has been added (Figure 11.4).

Figure 11.4 *Form design to display the time.*

The form design in Figure 11.4 has a single Label control, **lblTime**, and a Timer control, **Tim**, whose **Interval** property has been set to 500 (approximately 500 milliseconds). The **Timer** event-handler to make this form into a real-time clock is:

```
Private Sub Tim_Timer()
   lblTime.Caption = Format(Time, "hh:mm:ss")
End Sub
```

With a little extra work, we can develop various clock faces, and if we use the **Subject–Observer** pattern, we can ensure that as many of these as we wish will stay in synchronization by providing only one real-time clock engine. The main form will have a timer on it, and become the **Subject** of the pattern. All of the time display forms will be developed as observers.

> Create a new project, and set its Name property to **Clock**.
>
> Add a new form to the project and name it **frmMain**. Add command buttons and a timer control to it as shown in Figure 11.5.

Figure 11.5   *The controller form for a multi-view clock.*

 Set the main form's properties and those of its various objects as shown in Table 11.1.

Table 11.1   *Properties of the main form and its objects.*

Control type	Property name	Property setting
Form	Name	frmMain
	BorderStyle	1 – fixed single
	Caption	Clock controller
CommandButton	Name	cmdDigital
	Caption	Digital clock
CommandButton	Name	cmdAnalog
	Caption	Analogue clock
CommandButton	Name	cmdBar
	Caption	Bar clock
CommandButton	Name	cmdExit
	Caption	Exit
Timer	Name	Tim
	Interval	500

Add event-handler code to the form.

This form is the *Subject* of the pattern. As such, it needs to implement the two required methods, **AddObserver** and **Update**. In addition, we will add code to each command button event-handler for creating new observers and closing down the clock program, and to the timer's event-handler to make the subject perform a periodic call to **Update**.

```
Option Explicit

Private Observers As Collection  ' Keeps track of all observers.

Private Sub cmdAnalog_Click()
Dim f As frmAnalog
' Create a new analogue display form and make it an observer..
  Set f = New frmAnalog
  f.Show
  AddObserver f
End Sub

Private Sub cmdBar_Click()
Dim f As frmBar
' Create a new Bar display form, and make it an observer..
  Set f = New frmBar
  f.Show
  AddObserver f
End Sub

Private Sub cmdDigital_Click()
Dim f As frmDigital
' Create a new digital display form, and make it an observer..
  Set f = New frmDigital
  f.Show
  AddObserver f
End Sub

Private Sub cmdExit_Click()
Dim f As Form
  ' Unload all of the observer forms..
  For Each f In Observers
    Unload f
  Next
  ' and destroy the collection
  Set Observers = Nothing
  ' This is the last form, so unloading it will cause an exit..
  Unload Me
End Sub
```

```
Private Sub Form_Load()
  Set Observers = New Collection
End Sub

Private Sub Tim_Timer()
  Caption = Time
  Update
End Sub

Private Sub Update()
Dim f As Form
  For Each f In Observers
    ' Send the Notify message to each..
    f.Notify Hour(Time), Minute(Time), Second(Time)
  Next
End Sub

Private Sub AddObserver(f As Form)
  Observers.Add f
End Sub
```

Create a new form to act as an analogue clock display (Figure 11.6).

The property settings required for this form are minimal, as shown in Table 11.2.

The code on the form will need to take care of all of the display update functionality. This will involve drawing the clock hands and reacting to changes in the size of the form.

Figure 11.6 *A face for an analogue clock.*

Table 11.2 *Properties of the analogue clock form.*

Control type	Property name	Property setting
Form	Name	`frmAnalog`
	Caption	Analogue clock
	MaxButton	False
	MinButton	False

Add code to the form.

```
Option Explicit

Private Const PI = 3.1415927
Private mvarHours As Integer
Private mvarMinutes As Integer
Private mvarSeconds As Integer

' The Notify message causes the clock face to be redrawn..
Public Sub Notify(hh As Integer, mm As Integer, ss As Integer)
  mvarHours = hh
  mvarMinutes = mm
  mvarSeconds = ss
  UpdateFace
End Sub

' This is called in response to a Notify message..
Private Sub UpdateFace()
Dim hAngle As Single, mAngle As Single, sAngle As Single
Dim hX As Single, hY As Single
Dim mX As Single, mY As Single
Dim sX As Single, sY As Single
Dim cX As Single, cY As Single
Dim hLength As Single, mLength As Single, sLength As Single
  ' Calculate the lengths of the hands..
  hLength = ScaleHeight * 0.4
  mLength = ScaleHeight * 0.5
  sLength = ScaleHeight * 0.45

  ' Work out the angle for each hand..
  hAngle = (PI / 2) - (mvarHours / 6) * PI
```

```
  mAngle = (PI / 2) - (mvarMinutes / 30) * PI
  sAngle = (PI / 2) - (mvarSeconds / 30) * PI

  ' Work out the end-points of the hands..
  sX = sLength * Cos(sAngle)
  sY = -sLength * Sin(sAngle)
  mX = mLength * Cos(mAngle)
  mY = -mLength * Sin(mAngle)
  hX = hLength * Cos(hAngle)
  hY = -hLength * Sin(hAngle)

  ' Get the form centre..
  cX = ScaleWidth / 2
  cY = ScaleHeight / 2

  ' Draw the hour hand..
  Cls
  DrawWidth = 4
  Line (cX, cY)-Step(hX, hY)

  ' Draw the minute hand..
  DrawWidth = 2
  Line (cX, cY)-Step(mX, mY)

  ' Draw the second hand..
  DrawWidth = 1
  Line (cX, cY)-Step(sX, sY)
End Sub

' Necessary to ensure the clock face stays square..
Private Sub Form_Resize()
  ' Need to keep a square aspect..
  If ScaleWidth > ScaleHeight Then
    Height = Width
  Else
    Width = Height
  End If
End Sub
```

 Test the analogue clock form.

It is an easy matter to determine if the analogue clock display works as expected, using the Immediate window. First adjust the position and size of the Visual Basic IDE so that you can fit the analogue clock form beside it, then close the analogue form's designer window and enter the following commands:

```
frmAnalog.Show
frmAnalog.Notify 6, 30, 45      ' Should show half past six and 30
                                ' seconds.
```

We can also create a digital clock display.

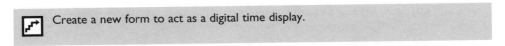

Create a new form to act as a digital time display.

This form is simple, having just a single **Caption** control on it. Design the form to appear as shown in Figure 11.7 and set the properties as shown in Table 11.3.

Figure 11.7 *A face for a digital clock.*

Table 11.3 *Properties of the digital clock form.*

Control type	Property name	Property setting
Form	Name	frmDigital
	Caption	Digital clock
	BorderStyle	1 – fixed single
Label	Name	LblTime
	Caption	00:00:00
	Alignment	2 – center
	BorderStyle	1 – fixed single
	BackColor	White
	BackStyle	Opaque
	Font	MSSansSerif, bold, 16 point

Code the Notify message for the digital form.

```
Public Sub Notify(hh As Integer, mm As Integer, ss As Integer)
Dim tString As String
   tString = Format(hh, "00") & ":" & _
             Format(mm, "00") & ":" & _
             Format(ss, "00")
   lblTime.Caption = tString
End Sub
```

Just for fun, we can provide a novel clock display that shows a series of bars whose height is proportional to the hour, minute or second of the time.

 Add a new form to act as a bar display of the time (Figure 11.8).

The clock display shown in Figure 11.8 uses three Shape controls to display the time. The first displays hours as a proportion of the total available form height, the second minutes and the third seconds. Add the controls and apply properties as shown in Table 11.4

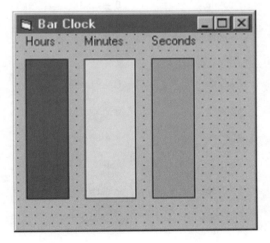

Figure 11.8 *A face for a bar clock.*

Table 11.4 *Properties of the bar clock form.*

Control type	Property name	Property setting
Form	Name	frmBar
	Caption	Bar clock
Label	Name	lblHours
	Caption	Hours
	AutoSize	True
Label	Name	lblMinutes
	Caption	Minutes
	AutoSize	True
Label	Name	lblSeconds
	Caption	Seconds
	AutoSize	True
Shape	Name	shpHours
	Top	360
	FillColor	(select one)
	FillStyle	0 – solid
Shape	Name	shpMinutes
	Top	360
	FillColor	(select one)
	FillStyle	0 – solid
Shape	Name	shpSeconds
	Top	360
	FillColor	(select one)
	FillStyle	0 – solid

This form also must respond to the **Notify** message, and react appropriately to being resized:

```
Option Explicit

' Variables to mark the horizontal positions of bars and labels..
Private hPos As Single
Private mPos As Single
Private sPos As Single

' When the form is resized, we must resize all of the shape controls
' and distribute the shapes and labels across it appropriately..
Private Sub Form_Resize()
Dim LabelSpace As Single
    ' How much space per shape and label?..
    LabelSpace = ScaleWidth / 3
    ' Now work out positions for everything..
    hPos = LabelSpace / 2
    mPos = LabelSpace + LabelSpace / 2
    sPos = ScaleWidth - LabelSpace / 2
    ' Position the labels..
    lblHours.Left = hPos - lblHours.Width / 2
    lblMinutes.Left = mPos - lblMinutes.Width / 2
    lblSeconds.Left = sPos - lblMinutes.Width / 2
    ' And re-size and position the shapes..
    shpHours.Width = LabelSpace
    shpHours.Left = 0
    shpMinutes.Width = LabelSpace
    shpMinutes.Left = LabelSpace
    shpSeconds.Width = LabelSpace
    shpSeconds.Left = LabelSpace + LabelSpace
End Sub

Public Sub Notify(hh As Integer, mm As Integer, ss As Integer)
Dim hHeight As Single, mHeight As Single, sHeight As Single
Dim maxHeight As Single
    ' Work out the available height on the form surface..
    maxHeight = ScaleHeight - lblHours.Height - 100
    ' And work out the height of each shape..
    hHeight = maxHeight * hh / 12
    mHeight = maxHeight * mm / 60
    sHeight = maxHeight * ss / 60
    ' Now set the heights..
    shpHours.Height = hHeight
    shpMinutes.Height = mHeight
    shpSeconds.Height = sHeight
End Sub
```

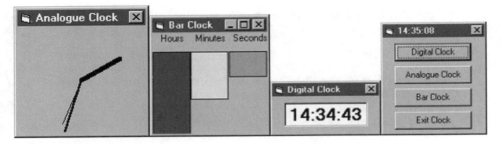

Figure 11.9   *A variety of clock faces displaying a single clock object.*

Now that we have coded the **Subject** and a range of **Observers**, we can test the program.

 Run the program, and press the buttons to create a range of time observers. You can resize instances of the analogue and bar forms as you wish, and can create as many of each as you wish: see Figure 11.9.

Conclusions

In this chapter, we have looked at software patterns and the way that they can influence program design to enable reuse and simplify structure. There are a number of good texts on the subject of software patterns, and as you gain expertise in object oriented programming, you would be well advised to look to these to maximize the benefits of your object oriented programming.

11.7   Answers to questions

QUESTION 11.1

Structure exists at a number of levels in software. Lines of code are controlled by simple structures such as `If..Then..Else` selection and `For..Next` loops. Objects can be interconnected in regular structures such as collections, queues, stacks and trees. Software patterns are a structural form that relates to the design of well-known and well-defined solutions to common problems. They are not specifically data (or object) structures, nor are they purely ways of organizing lines of code, but instead they are predefined elements of application design. The distinction between a pattern and a data structure such as a collection is subtle, but essentially the simple data structure is a single solution that can be applied unchanged to many situations, while a pattern is a more general solution that can be applied in many forms in many different circumstances.

QUESTION 11.2

(a) A creational pattern will centralize the code that is responsible for creating new objects at run time, thereby making full use of polymorphism and removing the need for an application programmer to consider the class of objects that the application will work with.

(b) A Factory Method is a function that creates objects on demand from a menu of available classes. The Prototype pattern is a method of creating new objects that are direct copies or clones of existing objects in the application.

QUESTION 11.3

(a) The Composite pattern differs in that it ensures that every item in a group is compatible over a range of operations, and that each item is potentially composed of several items, which in turn are compatible over the same range of operations. This composition can continue recursively.

(b) The Adapter pattern enables existing classes to be reused, unchanged, in applications that they were not designed to be compatible with.

QUESTION 11.4

Behavioural patterns differ from subroutines and functions in that they define operations purely in terms of the interfaces and interconnections needed to support them. Algorithms are therefore replaceable elements of a behavioural pattern.

11.8 Answers to review questions

1. (a) *Software patterns that are used to assist in the generation of new objects in an application are called* creational patterns.

    (b) *Software patterns that are used to assist in interconnecting objects in an application are called* structural patterns.

    (c) *Software patterns that are used to assist in the design of algorithms in an application are called* behavioural patterns.

2. *Name the key method that is used to make the Prototype pattern work.* The Clone method.

3. *Name the three methods that all elements of the Composite pattern must implement.* `Add`, `Remove` and `GetChild`.

4. *The Subject pattern-class is used in a pattern along with the* Observer.

5. *Patterns are used in applications to provide a well-known framework for software designers and implementers to work within. Give a number of reasons why this is important.* By using a tried and tested framework within an application, a designer can be confident that (a) it works, (b) any problems in its use will not be structural, (c) it has been tested over a range of applications, and (d) it is efficient in terms of design and development time.

CHAPTER 12

Creating and using
ActiveX objects

Programs do not run in a vacuum. Any piece of software, no matter how simple, will have been designed with certain expectations of the environment it runs in: some form of user input, a display, a system for handling data storage. Visual Basic programs are very demanding, in that they expect to run within a very feature-rich environment. Part of the reason why Windows provides so many facilities for the software that runs in it is due to the way that applications and components can be interconnected. The Windows operating system builds on an underlying object model known as the Component Object Model (COM), or more recently COM+. COM acts as a *software bus*, providing mechanisms for different applications to inter-communicate, sending and receiving data, requesting services and enabling specially developed functionality to be put to general use.

By the end of this chapter, you should be able to:

- embed objects in your programs that are the product of other programs,

- use services provided by other software in your programs,

- create programs that can be used to provide services to other software.

12.1 Component object technologies

Object oriented programming gives us the ability to create programs in which we can reuse code in the form of classes. If we have already developed a program in which one or more classes do something that we could apply in a new program, we can include these classes in our new program by simply adding the `.cls` files to the project. However, sometimes it would be useful to add classes from software written by someone else to a project. We must always rely on the generosity of other programmers if we wish to use their work, but even if a programmer is perfectly happy to allow you to reuse the fruits of their labour, he or she is unlikely to distribute class files along with an application program.

A number of programming technologies are available, across a range of operating systems, to allow work that has already been compiled and is therefore not available in source-code format to be used in programs. Microsoft have provided for this since the early days of Windows, when it was necessary to ensure the minimum of duplication of program code just to enable Windows programs to fit into the small amount of memory that was common on PCs in those days.

Current software technology allows the use of precompiled software components, which can be installed on the local PC or on a network server. The two main competing technologies are ActiveX (a Microsoft technology that is hosted by the Windows operating systems) and CORBA (Common Object Request Broker Architecture), which is a more generic technology, supported by Unix, OS2 and Windows operating systems. In both cases, the aim is to provide a mechanism for creating programs that use components that are available to any program on a computer or a network.

In this chapter we will look at the use of ActiveX components. Visual Basic gives us the ability to create and use ActiveX components in programs, allowing us to:

- use the services of another program or library in our programs,

- provide services to other programs by creating an ActiveX program or object library.

12.2 ActiveX

ActiveX is a title Microsoft has now applied to a range of software technologies previously called *OLE*. OLE is Object Linking and Embedding, a mechanism by which programs can provide services to each other. It is a Microsoft technology that has been available for several years and has gone through a number of different incarnations.

The first version of OLE, now referred to as OLE 1, allowed programs to provide display or print services to other programs. Using OLE, a drawing program, for example, could be used from within a word processor so that drawings created from it would appear in a document. Services provided were simple. The drawing program takes responsibility for the display or print of a drawing in a document (during which it acts invisibly). At any time it can be called up (by double-clicking on the displayed drawing) to allow the drawing to be edited. When in edit mode, the drawing program appears in front of the *client* program it serves. When editing is complete, closing the drawing program causes the embedded drawing object to be updated.

Version 2 of OLE made the transition between client and server program more seamless. When an OLE object is edited in OLE 2, the server program does not appear as a separate program, but instead takes over the menus and tool bars of the client program, allowing an object to be edited *in-place*. This gives the user the illusion that the services provided are simply another part of the functionality of the client software and so makes the facility appear less complex to the user.

In developing OLE, Microsoft were creating an environment in which software modules could be interchanged in a similar way to objects in object oriented programs. This would allow a user to work with software components that fitted their specific needs, by buying a fundamental component, such as a word processor, of a simple design and then adding modules (OLE servers) to provide for the non-core functionality such as tables, equation editors, indexing programs, etc.

It was a short step from the provision of OLE servers (and the required interfaces built into client software) to allowing programmers to access their software functionality directly using a style of object oriented interface. **OLE Automation** is based on the exposure of selected methods and properties to third party programmers. Using this facility, a programmer can instantiate objects of a supported class from an OLE server in their own programs, and make use of these properties and methods to perform processing, control the server program or provide some other service to their own program.

The move to make these facilities available over a wider arena (i.e. the Internet) led to Microsoft having to create tighter and yet more flexible specifications. **COM**, the **Component Object Model**, defines how one component can access the services provided by another, and introduces a framework that goes beyond the realms of the Microsoft operating systems (COM is also supported by CORBA, a non-proprietary object interaction framework). Further, **DCOM** (Distributed COM) extends this definition to encompass objects in a networked environment.

The title **ActiveX** has now been applied to cover all of these technologies plus a few others (ActiveX Controls, ActiveX Documents). Using Visual Basic, a programmer can make use of ActiveX servers in a program, or can create their own ActiveX classes, controls or document servers.

QUESTION 12.1

(a) Briefly describe the advantages of a component technology that allows classes defined within one program or library to be accessed from another.

(b) What might the disadvantages of this type of technology be compared to plain object oriented programming?

12.3 The OLE control

Among the Visual Basic controls available, the OLE control is an oddity. Its only functionality is to allow access to the functions and views provided by OLE server modules. Using an OLE control (and therefore an OLE server) in a Visual Basic program is very easy. Place an OLE control on a form (it is very like a PictureBox control in appearance) and the dialog box shown in Figure 12.1 appears immediately.

This dialog box prompts the programmer to select either a class of objects to create a new one from, or a file which will be a specific object. If an object type is selected, the server program will run inside the OLE control, displaying its own menus and/or tool bars in place of or alongside the client's menus/tool bars to allow the content to be edited.

For example, if an OLE control is added to a form in a new project, and **PowerPoint Presentation** is chosen as the server when the Insert Object dialog appears, the client area of the PowerPoint program will take over the inside of the OLE control. This occurs at *design time*, allowing you to add some initial content to the presentation. If you run the program, the slide content will appear inside the OLE control, as shown in Figure 12.2.

As it stands, the OLE control apparently provides little control over the presentation content in this state. However, a right-click on the OLE control will pop-up a *context menu*, which provides a list of available commands for the OLE content – in this case **Show**, **Edit** and **Open**. Choosing **Edit** will add PowerPoint menus to the form, allowing the content to be edited and reformatted: see Figure 12.3.

The overall effect is that the functionality of PowerPoint has been added to a program without need of a single line of code. In Figure 12.3 you can see that the PowerPoint menu system has been added to the Visual Basic form, allowing complete access to PowerPoint's editing facilities.

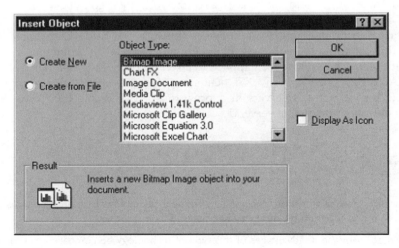

Figure 12.1 *The OLE control's Insert Object dialog.*

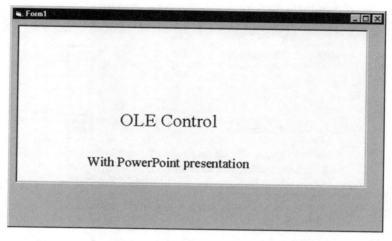

Figure 12.2   *An OLE control on a Visual Basic form displaying a PowerPoint presentation.*

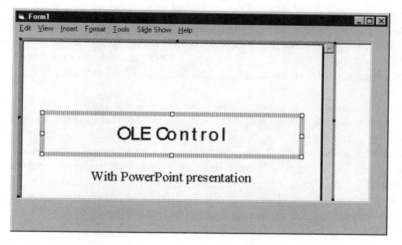

Figure 12.3   *The OLE application with the* **Edit** *method activated.*

12.4   OLE Automation

OLE Automation is a mechanism for controlling other software from within a program. As suggested by the name (*Object* Linking and Embedding), OLE Automation provides control of software via an object oriented interface; classes of objects *expose* a layer of properties and methods to other software. For this to work, the interface is mediated by the operating system, so OLE Automation relies on services provided by Windows.

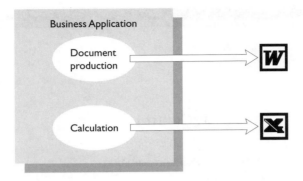

Figure 12.4 *Using ActiveX servers in an application.*

As an example of the use of OLE Automation, imagine the situation where a business system is being used to manage a database of customer records and sales. There is a requirement to print out a variety of professionally formatted invoices and letters to customers, as well as to perform calculations such as cash flow, income projections, etc. Writing all of this functionality in Visual Basic could involve a large programming effort, extending the development time from days to months. However, all of this functionality exists already on most systems in the form of a word processor (for creating nicely formatted documents) and a spreadsheet (for performing complex calculations).

Using OLE Automation, a *programmer* can control Word and Excel, for example, passing information to these programs and using them as servers to perform the required functions. The class model of the program being used as a server is added to the class model of the Visual Basic programmer's own program. Because of this, it is possible to write statements in Visual Basic code that manipulate the server's object model, sending messages to objects defined in the server but created in the client. The resulting *compound applications* are often perfect for automating the day-to-day business processes that are often required in offices (Figure 12.4).

QUESTION 12.2

How do OLE and OLE Automation differ?

12.5 Using an ActiveX server

Since OLE servers are based on an object model, client programs must interact with them by calling on the services of the objects within the server, i.e. *properties* and *methods.* For example, to use Microsoft Word as a server program, it is first necessary to create an instance of a Word object whose services are required in the client program. Assume, for example, that as part of an office automation system, you were to use Word to compose standard letters to customers, inserting the customer name and address into the Word document and then printing it from a Visual Basic program. The steps involved in this process would be:

1. Create a **Word.Application** object, this being the top-level object in any Word OLE service, as an object variable in a Visual Basic sub.

2. Use the **Word.Application** object to create a new document (using the **Add** method of the **Documents** collection, which is a property of **Word.Application**).

3. Move the insertion point in the new document to the required position to insert the customer data, using the **Selection** property.

4. Insert the information into the document.

5. Print the document, using the **PrintOut** method.

6. Destroy the **Word.Application** object.

The equivalent Visual Basic code to perform this task is:

```
Sub CreateCustomerDocument(CustDetails As String)
Dim WOLE As Word.Application
  ' Create an instance of a Word server..
  Set WOLE = CreateObject("Word.Application")
  ' Add a new document (using the named document template)..
  WOLE.Documents.Add "ATemplate", 0
  ' Move the insertion point to the 'Customer' bookmark..
  WOLE.Selection.Goto wdGotoBookmark, wdGotoAbsolute, _
                    1, "Customer"
  ' Now insert the required customer details..
  WOLE.Selection.InsertAfter CustDetails
  ' Print the document..
  WOLE.Printout
  ' And shut down the server..
  Set WOLE = Nothing
End Sub
```

Of course, to write code to control an OLE server, it is necessary to know what objects, properties and methods are available in the server that you make use of. To get this information, Visual Basic provides an Object Browser.

12.6 Using the Object Browser

A perennial problem – where to get information? Visual Basic comes along with a confusing enough set of objects (information in help files), but once you start working with OLE objects, a whole new universe of unknowns suddenly appears. Fortunately, Microsoft have provided an Object Browser (*View/Object Browser...* from the menus) to allow you to look up help information, object hierarchies, method and property names, etc., for all of the objects registered for your system.

For example, if you want to use OLE to control a Microsoft *PowerPoint* presentation, you can get information on how to do this as follows:

1. Go to *Project/References...* and ensure that *Microsoft PowerPoint 8.0 Object Library* is checked (a different version may be installed – this should not be a problem).

2. Go to *View/Object Browser...*, and then select *PowerPoint* from the combobox at the top of the browser; see Figure 12.5.

Once you have access to the list of objects, you can choose a class or module that belongs to the specified set (e.g. `Presentations`, right), and look up help on it, or any of its methods or properties (use the button marked **?**). This will bring up a help page on the selected item, with the usual cross-indexing to get directly to related items.

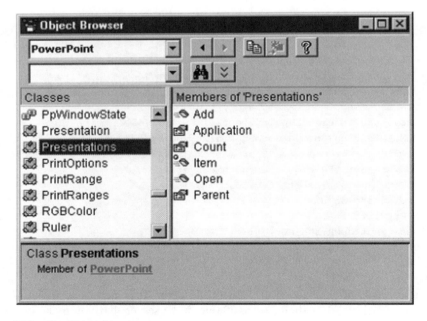

Figure 12.5 *The Object Browser.*

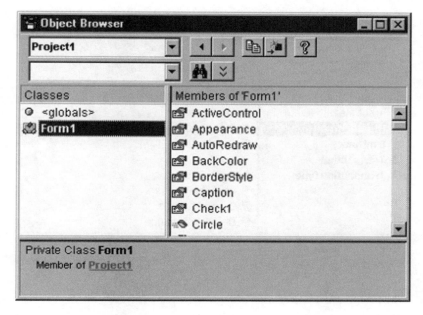

Figure 12.6 *Using the Object Browser to examine your own programs.*

Note that in some cases, the search can proceed through a number of levels. For example, selecting the **Presentations** class (as shown above) will lead to a list of methods and properties. Some of the listed properties will also be objects (e.g. **Application**, in the list of methods/properties above), and so you would then need to search the left-hand list for the **Application** object for a list of its methods and properties. Once you have found a combination of object and method or property whose name suggests that it might perform a function you require, simply press the '**?**' button to see detailed help on it.

The Object Browser is also used to display information on the classes that you create in your own programs, including the forms in programs. For example, from the browser select **Project1** (the default name for a new project – if you have given your project a name, select this instead) and the browser will appear as shown in Figure 12.6.

Note that the list of classes shown in the left-hand pane contains only the default form (**Form1**) and **<globals>**. Since this is a new project with no global variables defined, the **<globals>** list is currently empty.

If you load an existing project, for example the **BankSimulation** project developed earlier, and select **BankAccount** from the classes list, you will see the properties and methods defined for this class as in Figure 12.7 in the right-hand pane.

Object scope

Note that although you can view the properties and methods of the classes in your own projects in the Object Browser, you can only view this information for the classes

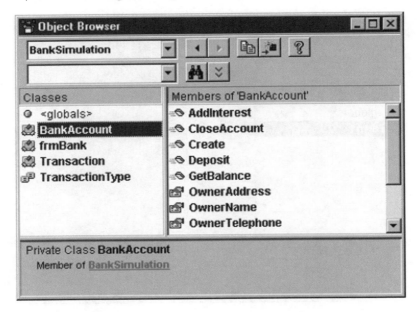

Figure 12.7   *Classes, properties and methods in the Object Browser.*

in the current project if this is a standard Visual Basic executable. To make classes that can be viewed in the browser from within another project, you will have to create an ActiveX server project.

QUESTION 12.3

(a) Why is the availability of an object browser so important to a programmer using component technology?

(b) What would be the alternative to an object browser if one were not available?

12.7   Creating ActiveX servers

An ActiveX server is a special purpose project that has been designed to be controlled by other programs. To make this possible, the program must *expose* an object interface to other programs (and the Object Browser), in the same way that Word, PowerPoint, Excel, etc., expose their own object interfaces. Obviously, such programs must contain classes, which define the object interfaces to be exposed.

For example, let us assume we wish to make information about a range of products available to a number of different programs through a simple and robust interface. The requirement for a simple and robust interface rules out the possibility of just making a database available to all of the programs, since any of the programs which access it could alter the database's contents and consequently upset its integrity. Instead, we can use an ActiveX server (or an OLE server) to provide the necessary information through a number of interface classes. We would create a new class called, for example, `ProductFinder` and provide this with an interface of properties and methods to make it externally accessible. A suitable interface description for the server might be:

```
' ProductFinder class file
' Public Methods...
Public Function FindProduct(ProductID As String) As Boolean
Public Property Get Name() As String
Public Property Get Price() As Currency
Public Property Get NumberInStock() As Integer
```

Note that we can define a server's interface by simply listing the first line of each property and method; each property and method still needs to be coded, and private data and methods will be needed to actually implement this functionality. However, this is a good way of describing the interface, since it is explicit about how an external program might access the server but states nothing about how the actual server class(es) are implemented. Note also that in this case all of the class properties are *read only*, i.e. we have created only `Get` properties. It will therefore not be possible to make any changes to the underlying database using this OLE interface – a good security feature, unless there is a specific requirement to allow the data to be updated from a client application.

Instancing

You may have noticed that so far there is no difference between the class we have just defined for an ActiveX server and any class we might create within a program. The significant difference between these is a property of the type of Visual Basic application we create. So far, we have created only *Standard EXE* Visual Basic projects. These are projects that we intend to run as programs. If we instead create an *ActiveX EXE* project, any included class modules will have an extra standard property, called an `Instancing` property. The `Instancing` property is used to control the scope of objects of a class, and has the possible settings listed in Table 12.1.

In many cases, `MultiUse` is an appropriate setting for a server application, since a number of programs might wish to make use of the server simultaneously, and might need to create several objects of the server class. If the project is `SingleUse`, then only one instance of each class in the project can be created. This is most appropriate for applications in which data is retrieved from a server program or library. If several programs were then to access the object, some form of access control would have to be provided within the class to prevent contention between client applications.

Table 12.1 *The* **Instancing** *property of an ActiveX class.*

Instancing property setting	How it affects objects of the class
Private	Other applications cannot access properties or methods (a typical class in a VB Project)
PublicNotCreatable	Other applications can access properties and methods of objects, but objects have to be created within your server application (other applications cannot use **New** or **CreateObject** for these objects)
SingleUse	Allows other applications to create objects from the class, but every object of this class that a client creates starts a new instance of your component. Not allowed in ActiveX DLL projects
GlobalSingleUse	Similar to **SingleUse**, except that properties and methods of the class can be invoked as if they were simply global functions. Not allowed in ActiveX DLL projects
MultiUse	Allows other applications to create objects from the class. One instance of your component can provide any number of objects created in this fashion
GlobalMultiUse	Similar to **MultiUse**, with one addition: properties and methods of the class can be invoked as if they were simply global functions. It is not necessary to explicitly create an instance of the class first, because one will automatically be created

ActiveX EXE or DLL

A further decision that must be taken is how to build a project that contains server classes. It might be that we are building an application that just happens to contain classes that will be useful to other programs; Word and Excel, for example, come into this category. In that case, we would build an *ActiveX EXE* project that could run in its own right, but that would also contain class definitions that would be made accessible to other programs.

However, we may just wish to create classes of objects to be used by other programs; the project may need no 'life of its own'. In that case, an *ActiveX DLL* (Dynamic Link Library) would be built. An ActiveX Exe project is a separate process that runs within its own memory allocation, while an ActiveX DLL is known as an *in-process server*, since it runs in the memory space of the client application. An in-process server is a more efficient form of ActiveX component, since there is no need to pass data across process boundaries, which would require the involvement of the operating system. Since an in-process server has no life of its own, it would contain only class definitions and forms, subs and functions to support these classes.

Building the ActiveX project

We would create our server by starting a new *ActiveX EXE* or *DLL* project and changing the name of the default class supplied by the server to `ProductList`. To complete the server application, we would complete the properties and methods, adding and referring to private data members where necessary. If the project was an *ActiveX EXE*, we would also have to create the forms and/or modules required, providing it with its own behaviour. Finally we would compile the server application. If we had built an *ActiveX EXE*, our server would be complete but Windows would be ignorant of it. To *register* the server classes with Windows, we would have to run the program once. This last step is not necessary for an **ActiveX DLL**.

Testing an ActiveX project

Visual Basic provides a number of ways to test an ActiveX project. The most obvious, that of building the projects and then creating a separate, new project to test it, is not always the most efficient method. There are three methods available:

1. Build and compile the ActiveX project and then create a new project to test it from. Declare instances of the object(s) to be tested and use these in the new project, using `InputBox()` and `MsgBox()` calls to pass and retrieve parameters.

2. Use the Immediate window to create and test objects.

3. Add a new project *without closing the ActiveX project*, thereby creating a *project group*. This has the advantage that you can work on both the ActiveX project and the project that tests it without having to close and reopen workspaces. Since a project group can be saved and reinstated, it also allows a lengthy build and test cycle to continue over a number of sessions with the minimum of housekeeping.

Brief examples of each of these test methodologies will be based on the `ProductFinder` class described earlier. This is organized as a new project, `ProductServer`, that contains the class definition and nothing else. The class code is shown below:

```
Option Explicit

Private Conn As ADODB.Connection
Private R As ADODB.Recordset
Private GotProduct As Boolean
```

```
Private Sub Class_Initialize()
Dim DbName As String
  ' Create a database connection for our Products database..
  DbName = App.Path & "\Product Guide.mdb"
  Set Conn = New ADODB.Connection
  Conn.Open "Provider=Microsoft.Jet.OLEDB.4.0;" & _
            "Data Source=" & DBName & ";"
  ' Create a recordset to access the Products table..
  Set R = New ADODB.Recordset
  With R
    .CursorType = adOpenForwardOnly
    .LockType = adLockReadOnly
    .Open "Products", Conn
  End With
End Sub

Public Function FindProduct(ID As String) As Boolean
  ' Use the primary index for this recordset..
  R.Index = "Primary"
  ' Do a database search for the product ID..
  R.Seek ">=", ID
  If R.NoMatch Then
    FindProduct = False
    GotProduct = False
  Else
    FindProduct = True
    GotProduct = True
  End If
End Function

Public Property Get Name() As String
  If GotProduct Then
    Name = R!Name
  Else
    Name = ""
  End If
End Property

Public Property Get Description() As String
  If GotProduct Then
    Description = R!Description
  Else
    Description = ""
  End If
End Property
```

```
Public Property Get Price() As Currency
  If GotProduct Then
    Price = R!Price
  Else
    Price = 0
  End If
End Property

Private Sub Class_Terminate()
  R.Close
  Set R = Nothing
  Set Conn = Nothing
End Sub
```

Note that the class makes use of a database of product descriptions (**Product Guide.mdb**), and simply returns database information to the client. When an instance of the class is created, the database is opened (in the **Class_Initialize()** event) using ActiveX Data Objects to provide the connectivity (see Chapter 9 for more information on using ADO). The extra parameters in the call to **OpenDatabase()** specify that the database should be opened in **Shared** and **Read-Only** mode, since this provides the most efficient access without restricting other programs. When the object is disposed of, the **Class_Terminate()** event is used to close the database.

A single member function, **FindProduct()**, is used to look up a product given an ID string, returning True if the find has been successful and False otherwise. This function also sets a flag, **GotProduct**, which is used internally when requests for other information are made. Three 'get' properties, **Name, Description** and **Price**, are used to get information about a selected product. The names of these properties corres- pond to the names of columns in the **Products** table in the database (this is not strictly necessary, but makes programming more convenient).

To build the server, this class is defined in an ActiveX DLL project and its **Instancing** property is set to **MultiUse**. The project is then built as normal, using *File/Make ProductServer.dll*. The three options for testing the server classes are described below.

Option 1: Creating a separate test project

In this case, we need to start a new project of type *Standard EXE*, which will of course close the existing ActiveX project. Before we can access objects of the **ProductFinder** class, a reference to it needs to be built into the project. This is done using *Project/References...* and checking the **ProductServer** entry. If this entry does not exist for some reason, the browse button can be used to locate the *ProductServer.DLL* file.

To test the class, we would create an instance of it and use this look-up product information. The easiest way to do this is to use a TextBox control to collect the product ID to be looked up and then display returned information in **MsgBox** calls. The form shown in Figure 12.8 would do the job.

Figure 12.8 *A simple user-interface for the ProductServer's client program.*

Given that the TextBox control is named **txtProductID**, the following event-handler for the click event of the command button would perform a test of the class:

```
Private Sub cmdFind_Click()
Dim P As ProductServer.ProductFinder
  If txtProductID.Text <> "" Then
    Set P = CreateObject("ProductServer.ProductFinder")
    If P.FindProduct(txtProductID.Text) Then
      MsgBox P.Name & " " & P.Description & " " & P.Price
    End If
    Set P = Nothing
  End If
End Sub
```

In the event-handler, we have simply instantiated an object of class **ProductFinder**, used it to look up a product as specified by the **txtProductID** TextBox, and then displayed specific product information as provided by the class properties in message boxes.

As a testing process goes, this is perfectly straightforward. However, there are some significant drawbacks:

- We need to create a new, separate project for the test. This involves closing down the server project and therefore losing immediate access to the server code.

- If an error in the server surfaces, we will have to close down the test project to reload the server.

- It is not convenient to build up the server interactively, e.g. add a new method or property and then add test code to see whether it behaves properly or not. In some cases and for some developers, this can hinder the development process.

Ideally, we would wish to be able to work on the server and test it interactively. This is, after all, one area where Visual Basic is significantly better than other Windows development systems.

Option 2: Using the Immediate window

Using this method, we need never leave the **ProductServer** project to test it. To make this style of testing possible, it is necessary to provide a variable of the server class for use in the Immediate window. To use the Immediate window as a test bed, it is useful to create a variable of the correct type, since this will then assist us in the test by providing pop-up lists of properties and methods. To create the variable, add a module to the project (if one does not already exist in it) and add a single `Public` variable declaration for a reference variable of the correct type. In this case, we would add the line:

```
Public S As ProductFinder
```

to the module. If we have added the code module just for the purpose of testing the class, it would be wise to remove it once the tests are complete.

To test the `ProductFinder` class, simply click on the Immediate window and proceed to issue commands. Since we are testing a class, the first command should be to create a new object of the class:

```
Set S = New ProductFinder
```

Once a member of the class is available (`s`), we can issue commands to it, in the form of method calls and property accesses. Because the `ProductFinder` reference variable is defined as `Public`, typing `S.` will result in a pop-up list of the available properties and methods:

```
? S.FindProduct("MEMO0001")
True
```

The above statement calls the `FindProduct` function seeking a product with `ID` `"MEMO0001"`. Because a matching product exists in the database, the result of the find is `True`. Note that we use the `?` (shorthand for `Print`) statement as part of the function call, resulting in the function result being printed on the next line. Property accesses are treated similarly:

```
? S.Name
8 Mb Memory Module
```

We can continue to test the remaining properties and methods. The final action should be to destroy the object by setting it to nothing. The entire transaction sequence is shown in Figure 12.9.

Note that a single test would seldom be considered sufficient to demonstrate that a class was error free. It would be sensible to proceed with other tests, passing both valid and invalid parameters to examine how objects behave in correct and erroneous situations.

Option 3: Using a project group

A project group is a set of related projects. The most usual situation is where one project in a group provides a test bed for the other project(s). We can create a project group by using *Add Project...* from the *File* menu to add a new project when there is an existing project in the IDE. In this case, the *Project* window becomes a *Project*

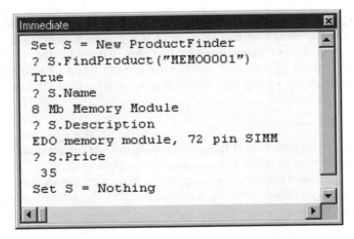

Figure 12.9   *Testing a server in the Immediate window.*

Group window, showing an entire structure tree for each project in the group: see Figure 12.10.

To test the `ProductFinder` class by this method, we would start by building the `ProductServer` ActiveX DLL as before. Once we had enough of it to test, selecting ***File/Add Project...*** from the menus allows a second project to be opened simultaneously. Moving between the projects is no more difficult than selecting the appropriate window (i.e. the `ProductFinder` class window or the form or code window of the new test project). The test project can be exactly the same as the test project described in Option 1 above.

If at any point you wish to end the build and test session for your ActiveX server, closing the system down will cause you to be prompted for file names to save the test

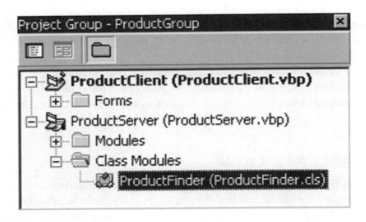

Figure 12.10   *A project group.*

project, and also a project group name (the default file extension is .**vbg**). In future, by opening this group file instead of opening an individual project, all of the projects in the group will be opened simultaneously.

QUESTION 12.4

(a) Why is it necessary to have a variety of different **Instancing** properties for ActiveX server classes?

(b) Explain the advantage of using a project group when developing an ActiveX server.

12.8   Review questions

1. How does a component differ from an object in a program?

2. Describe the role of the operating system in an OLE transaction.

3. How should the **Instancing** property for a server that provides for creating structured diagrams with an application be set?

4. Describe how the Immediate window could be used to test a new ActiveX server.

12.9   Practical exercise: A sound server

Music and sound files are frequently used on current computer systems. Microsoft provides a multimedia control for use with Visual Basic, and this can be used to load and play a variety of media types. However, as a control, the device has a visible presence on the screen and presents the user with controls (start, stop, forward, rewind, pause, etc.). In many cases, we would like sound to be an incidental part of a program and provide the user with no control over it. To meet this requirement, we will develop a simple ActiveX DLL server that allows us to include sound in our programs with little effort.

Note that the operation of this project depends on the existence of a sound adapter in the computer.

Server specifications

Playing a sound file in Visual Basic program code is not difficult, but does involve a number of steps to ensure that errors are properly dealt with. We will build our server so that it will maintain a list of sound files (all of the *.**wav** files in a given directory), any of which can be played simply by passing its number. Since sound files are stored by name, a list of these file names will be stored internally in the server, so we can also provide a method to determine the name of a file in the list. Finally, any errors that occur should be reported, descriptively if possible, to the programmer.

Our server will provide three main functions:

1. Build and maintain a list of sound files given a file location and type, in the form of a standard file mask (e.g. `c:\Windows\*.wav`).

2. Play a file, given its position in the list.

3. Return the name of a file, given its position in the list.

By creating these methods as functions, we can pass back any error messages. To make sure the specification is usable, we should convert it into a program style, as follows:

```
Function GetSoundFileList(Pattern As String) As Integer
Function PlaySoundFile(Index As Integer) As String
Function GetSoundFileName(Index As Integer) As String
```

The first of these returns an integer, which indicates the number of files found. The other functions take an integer parameter to specify the specific file required. `PlaySoundFile()` will actually play the file or return a string error message. `GetSoundFileName()` will return either the name of the file or an error message.

 Create an ActiveX DLL project.

The first step is to create the project for the ActiveX server. Select *File/New Project...* and choose *ActiveX Server* from the list of options. When the new project appears in the IDE, it will be called `Project1` and will contain a new class module called `Class1`. The class's `Instancing` property will already be set to `MultiUse`, which is exactly what we need it to be.

Change the project name to `SoundServer` and the class name to `SoundPlayer`. Now save the project (*File/Save Project*).

 Create declarations for multimedia API files.

To use multimedia devices such as a sound adapter without making use of Visual Basic's multimedia control, it is necessary to make use of the standard Windows Application Programmers Interface (API) for multimedia. This is a Dynamic Link Library (DLL) named *winmm.dll*, installed in every Windows system. Unfortunately, it is an old-style DLL that does not act as an ActiveX server, so we will need to build a proper server that accesses it for us.

The Windows operating system (any version) is made up of a number of system-level functions that reside in DLLs. Any program that knows how to communicate with it can use an API function in a DLL. Visual Basic provides for the use of API functions in a program, but requires that these are first declared, so that VB is made aware of the name and location of valid functions, and of the types of parameters to be passed to them. Declarations for these functions are only allowed in Basic modules (not class or form files).

The functions we will need to access to gain control of the computer's sound interface are **mciSendString()** and **mciGetErrorString()**. The first of these is a catch-all function that allows commands to be send to a multimedia device in the form of a string, for example:

```
"Play c:\Windows\DrumRoll.wav"
```

Using this function, sound files (i.e. **wav** files) can be opened, played, tested to see if they have finished playing, stopped and closed.

The second function is used to retrieve a description of an error condition from the multimedia device's driver software. **mciSendString()** will always return an error code when it is called, but since a multimedia device is not necessarily a standard piece of hardware, programmers and users cannot be expected to understand these. By calling **mciGetErrorString()**, passing it an error code, an English error message can be returned. The functions are to be found in the *winmm.dll* library file, which is normally installed in the Windows system directory.

Suitable declarations for these functions can be typed into a module. Provided the declarations typed are character-perfect, they will serve to inform Visual Basic how to treat calls to the functions. The actual declarations are listed below:

```
Declare Function mciSendString Lib "winmm.dll" Alias _
                "mciSendStringA" (ByVal lpstrCommand As String, _
                ByVal lpstrReturnString As String, _
                ByVal uReturnLength As Long, _
                ByVal hwndCallback As Long) As Long
Declare Function mciGetErrorString Lib "winmm.dll" _
                Alias "mciGetErrorStringA" (ByVal dwError As Long, _
                ByVal lpstrBuffer As String, _
                ByVal uLength As Long) As Long
```

Since these are long and unwieldy, even for program statements, it would not be unusual for a programmer to add some typographical errors by mistake when typing them into the appropriate code module. Because of this possibility, and because there are thousands of such functions housed in the Windows API, a programmer's utility is provided with Visual Basic so that such function declarations can be simply copied from a library file. This utility program is housed in the WinAPI directory of your Visual Basic installation:

c:\Program Files\Visual Basic\WinAPI\ApiLoad.exe

or

c:\Program Files\DevStudio\VB\WinAPI\ApiLoad.exe)

or

c:\Program Files\Microsoft Visual Studio\Common\Tools\WinAPI\ApiLoad.exe

It may be that this utility program has been provided as a Visual Basic add-in, available from the add-ins menu, or you may have to run it from Windows Explorer. Once you have started up the API viewer, use it to insert the required declarations into your project:

1. Add a Basic module to your project (*Project/Add Module*) and change its name to `MCIDeclares`.

2. Run the *ApiLoad* utility, and when it appears, select *File/Load Text File* from the menus. Select the file *Win32API.txt* from the same directory that the APILoad utility was run from.

3. With the *API Type* combo-box displaying *Declares*, indicating that the list shown contains function declarations, scroll down to the group of functions whose name begins with `mci..`, or use the *Search* button to locate the `mciGetErrorString` function.

4. Click on the function `mciGetErrorString` in the **Available Items** box and click the **Add** button.

5. Click on the function `mciSendString` in the **Available Items** box and click the **Add** button again.

6. Press the **Copy** button (note the message All entries in Selected Items List copied to the clipboard ...).

7. Return to the Visual Basic IDE (click anywhere on it, or press the appropriate button on the task bar) and place the cursor in the new module window.

8. Select *Edit/Paste* from the menus to paste the function declarations directly into the project. The following declarations should be pasted into the code module:

```
Public Declare Function mciGetErrorString Lib "winmm.dll" _
    Alias "mciGetErrorStringA" (ByVal dwError As Long, _
    ByVal lpstrBuffer As String, ByVal uLength As Long) As Long
Public Declare Function mciSendString Lib "winmm.dll" _
    Alias "mciSendStringA" (ByVal lpstrCommand As String, _
    ByVal lpstrReturnString As String, ByVal uReturnLength _
    As Long, ByVal hwndCallback As Long) As Long
```

With these declarations, it is now possible to call either of the declared functions in a Visual Basic program.

Code the **SoundServer** class.

The sound-server class requires two member variables. One will be a reference to a collection, which will store the name of every sound file in a given folder. The second will be a string specifying the path to the folder the current collection of sound files occupies.

```
Option Explicit

Private FileList As New Collection
Private FileDir As String
```

 A method to build a collection of sound file names.

The **SoundServer** will work by building a collection of all of the **.wav** files for a nominated folder. To do this, we can define a function to build the collection, taking a string that defines the path to the folder as a parameter:

```
Public Function GetSoundFileList(ByVal Pattern As String) As Integer
Dim FileCount As Integer
Dim F As String, P As Integer
  ' Make sure the list is cleared..
  Set FileList = Nothing
  ' Build a list of all of the matching files in this
  ' directory..
  FileCount = 0
  F = Dir(Pattern)
  While F <> ""
    FileList.Add F
    FileCount = FileCount + 1
    F = Dir
  Wend
  ' Store the directory path given in Pattern..
  P = Len(Pattern)
  While Mid(Pattern, P, 1) <> "\"
    P = P - 1
  Wend
  FileDir = Left(Pattern, P)
  ' Return the number of files found..
  GetSoundFileList = FileCount
End Function
```

Getting a name from the collection.

Now that we have a collection of sound files, we can create a simple function to return a name from the collection, given an index number:

```
Public Function GetSoundFileName(ByVal Index As Integer) As String
   If FileList Is Nothing Then
     GetSoundFileName = ""
   ElseIf Index > 0 And Index <= FileList.Count Then
     GetSoundFileName = FileList(Index)
   Else
     GetSoundFileName = ""
   End If
End Function
```

 Playing a `wav` file.

The technical part of the server is the function that actually plays a **wav** file. This will use the **mciSendString** API function that we created a declaration for earlier. The required format of the **mciSendString** function call is awkward due to its origins in the C language, so it would be best to hide this from the user. In fact, the raw function call is wrapped up in a private method, so the user does not need to know the exact mechanism for playing a multimedia file.

```
Private Function DoMMCommand(ByVal MMCmd As String) As String
Dim res As Long
Dim cmdString As String, errString As String * 128
   ' Try to send the command..
   res = mciSendString(MMCmd, 0&, 0, 0)
   ' Check result for error..
   If res > 0 Then
     ' Uh-oh, some error. Must identify it..
     res = mciGetErrorString(res, errString, _
                          Len(errString) - 1)
     If res <> 0 Then
       ' return the error message..
       DoMMCommand = errString
     Else
       ' No message for this error condition..
       DoMMCommand = "Unknown Error Condition"
     End If
```

```
      Else
        ' Success..
        DoMMCommand = ""
      End If
    End Function
```

 Getting a sound file played.

The final method of the server is the one that does the useful work of playing a sound file. The parameter to this is an integer that indicates which file from the collection of **.wav** file names is to be played.

```
    Public Function PlaySoundFile(ByVal I As Integer) As String
    Dim Result As String
      If I > 0 And I <= FileList.Count Then
        Result = DoMMCommand("Open " & FileDir & _
                              FileList(I))
        If Result <> "" Then
          ' An error message - report it..
          PlaySoundFile = Result
        Else
          ' File is open - must play it then close it..
          Result = DoMMCommand("Play " & FileDir & _
                                FileList(I) & " wait")
          PlaySoundFile = Result & DoMMCommand("Close " & _
                                        FileDir & FileList(I))
        End If
      Else
        PlaySoundFile = "Index out of range."
      End If
    End Function
```

Overall, the class has three **Public** functions and one **Private** one. A collection of sound file names and a string containing the path to the directory the files are in are stored as private data. To use the class, a programmer simply sets it up by calling **GetSoundFileList()**, passing a pattern mask such as *c:\Windows*.wav* (meaning all of the files with a **wav** name extension in the *c:\Windows* directory). Once the list has been set up, calling **PlaySoundFile()** with a number between 1 and the number of files (returned from the **GetSoundFileList()** function) will play a file from the list. The **GetSoundFileName()** function can be used to retrieve the names of the sound files in the list (pass the number, receive the name in return).

The private function **DoMMCommand()** is used to issue a command string and, if necessary, collect an error message resulting from it.

```
Immediate                                                    ×
 Set S = New SoundPlayer
 ? S.GetSoundFileList ("c:\winnt\media\*.wav")
  16
 ? S.PlaySoundFile(9)

 ? S.PlaySoundFile(17)
 Index out of range.
 Set S = Nothing
 |
```

Figure 12.11 *Testing the sound server in the Immediate window.*

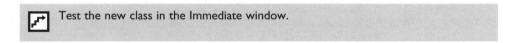

Test the new class in the Immediate window.

We can quickly check out the new class by issuing commands from the Immediate window. Changing the directory parameter in the `GetSoundFileList()` call to match the location of sound files on your PC, issue the sequence of Immediate statements shown in Figure 12.11 (note that the function results printed will very probably be different on your system).

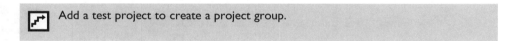

Add a test project to create a project group.

As described previously, it is possible to create a project group so that work on ActiveX components can be tested without continually opening and closing projects. Before setting up this group, make sure you save the existing project.

1. Select ***File/Add Project*** from the menus, and choose ***Standard EXE*** as the type of project to add. Note that the project window now shows an additional branch, entitled `Project1`. Select this branch in the project window, and change the name in the properties box to `SoundClient`.

2. Name the form in the new project `frmSounds`, and set its caption to `"Sound Server Test"`.

3. Add a list box and a command button to `frmSounds` to make it appear as shown in Figure 12.12.

4. Name the list box `lstSounds` and the command button `cmdPlay`.

5. Add declarations and event-handlers as shown in the following listing.

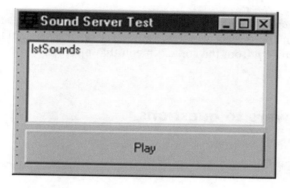

Figure 12.12   *Form design for a sound client application.*

```
Option Explicit

Const SndMask = "c:\winnt\media\*.wav" ' Change this to match
                                       ' the location of
Dim SndDrv As SoundPlayer              ' ".wav" files on
                                       ' your system.
Private Sub cmdPlay_Click()
Dim Msg As String
  If lstSounds.ListIndex > -1 Then
    Msg = SndPlay.PlaySoundFile(lstSounds.ListIndex + 1)
    If Msg <> "" Then
      MsgBox Msg
    End If
  Else
    MsgBox "You must select a file to play."
  End If
End Sub

Private Sub Form_Load()
Dim F As String, N As Integer, I As Integer
  ' Create a sound-driver object..
  Set SndPlay = New SoundPlayer
  ' Fill up the list box with the names of sound files..
  N = SndPlay.GetSoundFileList(SndMask)
  lstSounds.Clear
  For I = 1 To N
    lstSounds.AddItem SndPlay.GetSoundFileName(I)
  Next
End Sub

Private Sub Form_Unload(Cancel As Integer)
  Set SndPlay = Nothing
End Sub
```

One final requirement to make the project group operational is to set the test project as the start-up. In the project window, right-click on the **SoundClient** project and choose *Set As Start-Up* from the context menu that appears.

12.10 Answers to questions

QUESTION 12.1

(a) There are several advantages of such a component technology:
1. Maximize the reuse potential of software
2. Provide operating system-wide services for any application
3. Allow a range of software to reuse data structures and types
4. Minimize the potential for errors – errors are often introduced while copying program code between projects
5. Facilitate sharing of data between programs.

(b) The major disadvantage of this type of technology is performance – using classes across program boundaries involves the operating system. Since this must take a very general approach to connecting applications together, it is likely that a large amount of memory will be used in the interconnection, and that the movement of information between applications will be much slower than moving a similar amount of information around a single program.

QUESTION 12.2

OLE is a generalized method for applications to share services and works entirely from standard options within supporting applications – it is user-oriented. OLE Automation involves the use of program code to allow one application to access the services of another, and so is more difficult to deal with.

QUESTION 12.3

(a) Before it is possible to use an existing class in a program, it is necessary to become familiar with the range of properties and methods it can provide (at the very least – usually, some training or access to examples of use is desirable). An object browser provides this core information, and operates in the absence of other documentation.

(b) The alternative to an object browser if one were not available would be good documentation.

QUESTION 12.4

(a) It is necessary to have a variety of different `Instancing` properties for ActiveX server classes for reasons of efficiency and integrity. For some classes of object, it would be wasteful of memory and processor power to create several instances when a single one could be used simultaneously by a number of clients. In this case, `PublicNotCreatable` could be used to provide a single-instance-multi-use server, which would be sensible. For others, multiple clients of a single server could cause problems with data integrity, since several clients could access a server that allowed them to update information simultaneously, with the result that information could get out of synchronization between the various clients' accesses to it. In this case, a `SingleUse` server would be crucial.

(b) A project group allows two or more projects to be loaded simultaneously into Visual Basic. This is useful when, for example, one project is for a server application or component and another is a client to that server. In cases like this, the Visual Basic IDE will deal with registering the server on a temporary basis so that it can be tested and amended as necessary.

12.11 Answers to review questions

1. *How does a component differ from an object in a program?* A component is a type of object that can be used across application boundaries without including any source code.

2. *Describe the role of the operating system in an OLE transaction.* The Windows operating system is central to OLE transactions. An OLE connection is created by the operating system, which then mediates between the client and server application, transporting data in an efficient way and managing the creation and destruction of objects.

3. *How should the `Instancing` property for a server that provides for creating structured diagrams with an application be set?* Since each application that uses the server might expect to contain several diagrams, `GlobalMulti-Use` would seem to be the best form of instancing.

4. *Describe how the Immediate window could be used to test a new ActiveX server.* The Immediate window can be used as a client to an ActiveX server. Immediate window statements can create instances of server classes, execute their methods and access their properties to ensure that they perform as expected.

APPENDIX 1

Visual Basic style guide

Style may seem like a bizarre word to apply to the coding of a computer program, but one of the key factors that makes the work of one programmer unintelligible and that of another readable is the style in which the program code is written. Most software houses require a set of stylistic conventions from their programmers: naming conventions for variables and components, standard forms for the layout of program code, and specifications for in-program comments. By imposing the use of these conventions, companies are making sure that all the programmers in a team can read each other's code. This makes it easier to change or debug software, even in the absence of the original programmer. It also makes it easier to introduce new programmers to the projects a team is working on.

Rigorous use of a well-thought-out programming style has other benefits. In many projects, particularly in subcontracting work, customers may well look through the code to get a feel for its quality. Consistent code looks professional and looks as though it has been the product of a mature and stable life-cycle. Code that is written to a well-defined style can also be easier to construct analysis tools for, often a key component of a quality assurance programme. Finally, well-written program code tends to be self-documenting, requiring less in the way of additional explanatory text to expose its algorithms, assumptions and limitations.

In this appendix, I will describe a small number of conventions that can be applied to the creation of program code. One point that will hit you in the eye a number of times as you read it through is that I am not very diligent at following my own style guide. From this you can conclude that I am either a bad author or a hypocrite, or, I hope, that programming in a professional environment must be different from the work of creating small example programs for educational purposes. While writing this book, I did frequently agonize over the way that code was being laid out. The main requirement was to demonstrate programming techniques in a way that would encourage new programmers. While I have used several of the techniques described here in the program examples in the book, I shied away from several of them simply because they might make the code look more technical and therefore less clear to non-programmers. Maybe as an exercise you could go through the book 'marking' my code examples.

General principles

Several things you should always aim for when writing program code:

- Apply your chosen formatting rules as you go along – writing code with the intention of going back over it to make it look nice later is never satisfactory because in general you are unlikely to back over it immediately, and when (if) you do get around to it, you may already need the extra help the nicely formatted code gives you to be able to read it.

- Try to get it right first time – an adage we would all like to adhere to always, though this might seem a tall order. However, code that you lash up to do a quick fix or experimental code may just end up becoming the core of the final version. If you skimp at the point where you create code, that code will be harder to convert into 'well-formed' code later. If the code you write does not end up in a final version, nothing has been lost, and you might thank yourself for making it easy to read when you go back to borrow from it later.

- Develop a coding style that you are comfortable with. If you have to struggle to remember how to apply a naming convention or look up a manual to see how you are supposed to format the heading comments for a procedure, you are more likely not to do it.

Elements of program style

There are three major elements that make up style in program code:

1. The way the code is laid out

2. The choice of identifiers for constants, variables, subs, functions, objects and classes, and the way they are typed

3. The use of comments as in-code documentation.

None of these elements will make any difference to the way that the code works. If you choose to enter all statements at the left-hand margin, give all variables a single-letter name and never add any comments, the program will in theory work exactly the same. In practice, humans write program code, and less than perfect humans (i.e. all of us) need to be able to read what they write before adding to it, changing it or using it in another context.

Laying out program code

There are several aspects to this:

- Indenting – making the structure of your code visible by varying the left margin of passages of it

- Including extra spaces – blank lines make code more readable by making logically separate groups of statements distinct

- Breaking up long lines – apart from saving the reader from having to scroll a code window to the right to read long statements, this also has the benefit of preparing code for hard copy, since code that goes beyond the right-hand margin of a printed page will automatically wrap to the start of the next line, making a mess of any other formatting you have carefully applied.

Indenting

The general principle here is to show which lines of code are enclosed or governed by which others by offsetting their left margin. Indent one extra level for each level of enclosure. Indentation should take place in several constructs, as follows.

Subs and functions

Every *executable* statement in a sub or function should be indented. Declarative statements (variable declarations and labels for error handlers) should appear at the left margin.

```
Public Sub SomeSub()
Dim someVariable As Integer
   ...
   ...
End Sub

Private Function MyFunction() As Integer
   On Error Goto errHandler
   ...
   ...
errHandler:
   ...
End Function
```

Note that while the **onError** statement is treated as an executable statement (it switches an error handler on at run time), the **errHandler:** label is a declarative statement.

`If..Then` *and* `If..Then..Else` *blocks*

Indent the statements controlled by an `If..Then` or `If..Then..Else` block.

```
If x = 0 Then
  ...
End If

If name = "" Then
  ...
Else
  ...
End If
```

`Select Case` *blocks*

There are two schools of thought here and I think both work well. You can indent everything between `Select` and `End Select`, so that all of the lines that begin with the `Case` keyword are indented and their contents are indented one more level, or you can line up all of the `Select`, `Case` and `End Select` lines and indent their contents one level. My personal preference is for the first, since long lines will have a bit more space before they get beyond the right-hand margin.

```
' Either...
Select Case customerCreditLevel
Case 0
  ...
Case 200
  ...
Case 1000
  ...
Case Else
  ...
End Select
' Or...
Select Case customerCreditLevel
  Case 0
    ...
  Case 200
    ...
  Case 1000
    ...
  Case Else
    ...
End Select
```

Loops

For, **While** and **Do** loops can be treated the same as **If..Then..Else** blocks.

```
For count = min To max
   ...
Next

While someCondition
   ...
Wend

Do
   ...
Loop Until someCondition
```

Multiple level indenting

Indentation should be hierarchical. Where one enclosing structure appears within another (a **For** loop inside a sub, for example), its contents should be indented to two levels, and so on. This can lead to heavily indented lines of code where structures are nested to several levels deep. However, it is a good idea to try to break up code into sub-procedures and before you get to too many levels of structure, so very heavily indented lines might just be an indication of over-complex code that should be redesigned.

You can control the amount of indenting that pressing the Tab key introduces in Visual Basic by changing the **Tab Width** setting on the **Tools/Options/Editor** menu selection. The standard setting is 4, where a single tab press moves in four spaces, but I have found 2 to be adequate, 3 to be optimal.

Introducing extra space in code

White space is a very valuable commodity in program code. It can be used to visually indicate the logical sub-divisions of an algorithm or to highlight certain sections, as well as simply to make the code look neater. Visual Basic will automatically introduce extra spaces in lines of code (for example, on either side of an '=' sign), and will also resist any attempt you make to add or remove any of the spaces within a syntactically correct line of code. It has its own opinion of how space characters in code should be used, and in this, it knows best. However, when it comes to the number of spaces at the start of a line (already covered in the previous section on indentation) and the amount of space *between* lines, you are in control.

I have generally skimped on blank lines in the exercises in the book, since every blank line is a bit of a page that could be used to add explanatory text. In production code, I am lavish with extra blank lines.

It is sensible to leave at least one blank line between each sub or function in a code module (oddly, the Visual Basic editor does not enforce this automatically), but extra blank lines within subs should be used to indicate logical groupings.

Use blank lines to separate:

■ The declarative statements at the beginning of a procedure and the executable statements in it:

```
Public Sub MySub()
Dim myInteger As Integer

  myInteger = GetInteger()

    ...
  Print myInteger

End Sub
```

■ Logical sections of a procedure:

```
Public Function OpenAndReadFile(ByVal fileName As String) As
String
Dim fileHandle As Integer
Dim fileLine As String
Dim fileText As String

  fileHandle = FreeFile                  ' This section to open
  Open fileName For Input As #fileHandle ' the file.

  Do                                     ' This section to read
    Line Input# fileHandle, fileLine     ' its contents.
    fileText = fileText & fileLine
  Loop Until EOF(fileHandle)

  Close #fileHandle             ' This to close the file.

  OpenAndReadFile = fileText   ' This section returns the result.
End Function
```

■ Logical groups of variable declarations in the General Declarations section of a module:

```
Option Explicit

Private dataFileName As String     ' Variables for file handling
Private dataFileHandle As Integer
Private dataPath As String

Private dataElements() As Double    ' Data variables
Private dataCount As Integer
Private dataMin As Double
Private dataMax As Double

Private lastDataError As ErrObject ' Error reporting
Private errorCount As Integer
```

■ Any sections of code that you wish to distinguish from others.

Breaking up long lines

Long lines are almost inevitable in program code. Definitions of and calls to subs and functions that take a number of parameters will often go beyond the width of a code window, even when it is maximized. Statements that combine a number of logical sub-expressions using **And** and **Or** tend to get lengthy, as do statements containing complex arithmetic. Very long lines are an annoyance because they cannot be viewed without scrolling on a screen, and they do not print properly. Apart from this, it is often difficult to follow the logic of a single line that is made up of a number of terms, while one that has been broken down into logical units can be perfectly clear in its intentions.

For these reasons, Visual Basic code windows allow the use of the line continuation sequence: a space followed by an underscore, ' _ ', to allow a line of code to be broken and continued on the next screen line. As diligent coders, it is up to us to make sure that lines are broken at an appropriate point and that subsequent lines are indented to best indicate the logical flow.

Breaking up lines that define a procedure and its parameters

The most effective format for this is easy to deal with.

```
Public Sub myProcedure(intParameter As Integer, _
                       strParameter As String, _
                       dateParameter As Date, _
                       numParameter As Double, _
                       curParameter As Currency)
```

Breaking up this type of line as shown above brings the advantage that all of the parameters and their types appear as columns in a table – an immediate boon to readability. This format also makes it possible to add end-of-line comments to indicate the purpose of the parameters:

```
Public Function LoanPayments(capital As Currency, _   'Amount borrowed
                             term as Integer, _       'No of months
                             interest As Single, _     'Rate of loan
                             frequency As Integer, _   'Payment interval
                             ) As Currency
```

A function definition line written in this way is its own documentation. By aligning the left of each 'column', we again produce a tabular and easy-to-read structure.

Breaking up lines that contain long combinations of numbers or strings

This type of line breaks up naturally.

```
errorMessage = "Error: " & Err.Number & vbCrLf & _
               "Description: " & Err.Description & vbCrLf & _
               "Location: " & Err.Line & vbCrLf & _
               "Do you want to try to recover?"
```

```
diagonal = Sqr((right - left) * (right - left) + _
                (top - bottom) * (top - bottom))
```

Breaking up lines containing a long procedure call

Some of the Visual Basic graphics methods (for PictureBoxes and forms) can get quite long due to the large number of potential parameters:

```
With PieChartPictureBox
    .Circle((.Width / 2), (.Height/2)), _        ' Centre of box.
            .Width / 2, _                        ' Size of pie
            segmentColour, _                     ' Colour of slice
            segmentStartAngle, segmentEndAngle)  ' How big a slice
```

By combining these techniques for adding readable space to programs, it is very possible to write code that is both easy to read and professional in appearance.

Choosing identifiers

All truly professional programming teams use naming conventions. They clarify program code in a way that no other formatting measure can, turning lines that are intended to be followed by a dumb machine into expressive statements of the intention of programming code. Read the following block of code:

```
If (a < 65) Then
   Y = 65 - a
Else
   Y = 0
End If
```

To know what is happening here, you need to be aware of what the identifier 'a' represents, the relevance of the number **65** and the purpose of the identifier 'y'. It is so much easier to interpret:

```
If (age < RETIREMENT_AGE) Then
   yearsStillToWork = RETIREMENT_AGE - age
Else
   yearsStillToWork = 0
End If
```

Basically, you should not use a single-letter variable or an obscure combination of letters and numbers in place of a meaningful term. The only time an exception should be allowed is when a single letter or abbreviated variable name is used frequently enough that it will not be misunderstood, for example using the letter '**i**' as a counter in a **For** loop, or the identifier **msg** to hold a message string. Keep to a well-defined set of these 'standard' identifiers and no-one will be surprised by them. The rule should be that, if anyone who needs to read the code has to have it explained, it should not be used.

Beyond this obvious simple rule, several equally obvious conventions can be applied.

Use the names that are used in the application domain

If you are writing code for a user who refers to his customers as 'Clients', use `Client` instead of `Customer`. Years ago I had to write a database application for a driving school proprietor who referred to his clients as 'pupils'. I decided this sounded silly and used the term 'Student' in the database. At a later date the driving school proprietor introduced me to a new requirement – he was introducing a student discount scheme to encourage new young drivers. This caused so many misunderstandings as we discussed the new requirements that eventually I had to give up and replace all instances of the word 'Student' with the word 'Pupil'. In situations like this, the customer is always right and his or her terminology is the best terminology to use.

Avoid abbreviations

Some programmers and designers still advocate the use of whole words with all of the vowels removed as variable names. I was even party to a book that made this suggestion in the early 1990s – although it was for C++ programmers who never use three keystrokes when two will do. Even so, I am now ashamed of the suggestion and my association with it. It is generally a bad idea, since code written in this way is difficult to read out loud and can lead to an ambiguous situation if two such abbreviations clash. Write your code so that if you need to, you can read it to a colleague over the phone. Remember that on today's hard disks, extra space taken up by additional characters is virtually free.

Break up words with capitals

Using more than one word squashed together to form a variable, sub or function name is almost essential to get meaning into the identifiers you use. Unaided, this can result in identifiers that need to be decrypted laboriously by the reader. For example:

```
Private datatablename As String
Public customeridentitynumber As Long
Public customercreditlimit As Currency

Public Sub Enrolnewcustomer()
    ...
```

These long and tortuous sequences of characters can easily be made readable by the strategic introduction of capitals at the start of each new word:

```
Private dataTableName As String
Public customerIdentityNumber As Long
Public customerCreditLimit As Currency

Public Sub EnrolNewCustomer()
    ...
```

It's not that it is very difficult to read the first version; just that it is so much easier to read the second. Note that I use a starting capital for a procedure name, but start variable names with a lower-case letter. This can be a matter of choice, since it does not affect the way that capitals break up the words within an identifier. However, more and more programmers are using this convention so it probably makes sense to conform. One very persuasive reason for using this convention in Visual Basic is that the editor will make sure, once you have introduced an identifier for the first time, that every subsequent time you use it, the case will automatically be made to match the first use. Essentially, type it right the first time and ignore the shift key from then on.

Use plurals

Arrays and collections exist to keep several things of a similar type together, for example:

```
Private Cards(1 To 52) Of CCard
Public Players As Collection
```

You should always use the plural form for these, and for any classes or types that you create that manage more than one of anything. For example, the user-defined type

```
Type InvoicePrintSettings
    LeftMargin As Single
    RightMargin As Single
    TopMargin As Single
    BottomMargin As Single
    LinePitch As Single
End Type
```

contains not an array, but a number of related items that will be dealt with in the plural, so it makes sense to make the type name a plural.

Use UPPERCASE to define constants

C programmers have used this convention successfully for many years. It pays to be able to pick out constants from other identifiers, since otherwise you might be tempted to try to assign values to them. Refer back to the **RETIREMENT_AGE** code fragment for an example.

Documentation

Program code is the culmination of the development life-cycle, of which the only other evidence that exists is the documentation – specifications, diagrams, etc. As you will probably have noticed throughout this book, program code can be expressive, but still tells only part of the story. While a subroutine can be written in a style that spells out quite clearly what is happening, there are other aspects that go beyond the code: the assumptions that have been made, the conditions under which the code can be expected to run (and fail), the place a piece of code has in the grand scheme of things.

To make a piece of code tell the whole story, extra documentation is necessary. Within a program, this comes in the form of comments.

What comments are used for

Comments in program code play several distinct roles:

1. To state the purpose of a class or routine in plain words

2. To describe the conditions required for a routine to run properly

3. To indicate the effects that a procedure will have on variables and objects within its scope

4. To state any known limitations of a piece of code

5. To describe significant changes that have been made to program code

6. To indicate who has written a module or procedure and when.

Styles of comment

I tend to use three forms of comment in test and production code. These are:

- In-line comments, placed at the end of statements to further describe their purpose

- Single-line comments, normally placed immediately before a statement or block of code I wish to clarify

- Block comments, normally placed at the start of a module, before blocks of variable declarations, at the start of a procedure (sub, function or property) and in front of any passage of code that I think needs significant clarification.

Examples of each of these are taken from the `CordList` collection class and example in Chapter 8 on Objects as Building Blocks.

In-line comments

```
If Key > colData(midPos).Key Then
   startPos = midPos + 1                    ' Look in 2nd half
ElseIf Key < colData(midPos).Key Then
   endPos = midPos - 1                      ' Look in 1st half
Else
   Exit Do
End If
```

Single-line comments

```
' Use a binary search to locate position within list..
Do While startPos <> midPos And endPos <> midPos
   ' Bisect the list..
   midPos = (endPos + startPos) \ 2
   ...
```

Block comments

```
' This event-handler does its work when the Enter key is pressed.
' (i.e. KeyAscii = 13)
' It assumes a pair of words have been typed into txtAnimal, an
' animal's name and the noise it makes. A suitable object is
' created and added to the ordered list..
Private Sub txtAnimal_KeyPress(KeyAscii As Integer)
Dim A As CAnimal
   ...
```

Commenting out blocks of code

You can temporarily remove a block of Visual Basic code from a program by commenting it out – preceding each statement with a comment character (apostrophe). You can either do this laboriously a line at a time, or use the Comment Block command, available only from the Edit toolbar (select View/Toolbars and check the Edit toolbar on). Select the text you want to temporarily disable and press the Comment Block button (hover the mouse pointer over buttons to see their names). All of the selected lines will be preceded with a comment character. To remove the comments and restore the code, select the commented out lines and press the Uncomment Block button.

General commenting principles

Use comments to spell out your intentions

Describe your intentions for a procedure in comments, and then fill in the program code, leaving the comments in place. For example:

```
Private Sub CreateDataFile(ByVal dataFileName As String)

   ' Open the data file for output
   ' Write the number of items
   ' Send the collection of objects to it
   ' Close the data file

End Sub
```

Now that the required process has been adequately described, it is a simple matter to 'fill in the blanks' and create the sub, either immediately or at a later date:

```
Private Sub CreateDataFile(ByVal dataFileName As String)

Dim fileHandle As Integer
Dim dataItem As CdataObject

   ' Prepare the data file for output
   fileHandle = FreeFile
   Open dataFileName For Output As #fileHandle
   ' Write the number of data items
   Write#fileHandle, dataCollection.Count
   ' Send the collection of objects to it
   For Each dataItem In dataCollection
      dataItem.SaveToStream fileHandle
   Next
   ' Close the data file
   Close# fileHandle

End Sub
```

Do not simply repeat the code in comments

If comments do not add something to the expressiveness of your code, there is no point in having them. Avoid comments such as:

```
' Add 1 to x...
x = x + 1

' Get the first character of customers(x)...
ch = Left(customers(x), 1)
```

Instead, try to use comments to describe what you are actually doing:

```
' Move to the next customer and get the initial...
x = x + 1
ch = Left(customers(x), 1)
```

Write comments in the active voice

Program code is an active medium – as a programmer, you do not have things done to your variables; *you* do things to them.

Keep comments and code in synchronization

Finally, the most heinous crime imaginable is to change program code without updating the comments that describe it. This looks shoddy when it is obvious, and can cause a lot of wasted effort when it is not.

APPENDIX 2

Application checklist

If you are writing a program for a customer, it pays to apply a little Quality Assurance to the job before you finally deliver it. The code will look better, you will find it easier to change and fix, and if the customer does look at it, you will be making a much better impression. You can apply the following checklist to almost any program to produce an objective measure of how well written it is, both stylistically and technically. Each *No* answer indicates a shortfall in quality.

Routines (subs and functions)

- Does each routine's name describe exactly what it does?

- Does each routine perform a single, well-defined task?

- Have all parts of each routine that would benefit from being put into their own routines been put into their own routines?

- Is each routine's interface obvious and clear?

- Have functions been used when a routine has a useful result?

- Do the routines in a module perform related tasks?

Data names

- Are type names descriptive enough to help document data declarations?

- Are variables meaningfully named?

- Are variables used only for the purpose for which they're named?

- Are loop counters given informative names (e.g. *not* i, j, n)?

- Are well-named enumerated types used?

- Are named constants used instead of *magic numbers*? (e.g. 3.1415926 is a magic number – `PI` is a good identifier).

Classes

- Have classes been used to model real-world objects in the application domain?

- Have the relationships between real-world objects in the application domain been modelled in the program?

- Are class interfaces defined to expose only necessary interface properties and methods?

- Are method names action words?

- Do property names describe attributes of the class?

- Do parameters have descriptive names and appropriate types?

Data organization

- Are extra variables used for clarity when needed?

- Are references to variables close together and near the variable definitions?

- Are data structures simple so that they minimize complexity?

- Is complex data accessed through abstract access routines (abstract data types or classes)?

Control

- Is the nominal path through the code clear?

- Are related statements grouped together?

- Have relatively independent groups of statements been packaged into their own routines?

- Does the normal case follow the `If` rather than the `Else` in an `If..Then..Else` structure?

- Are control structures simple so that they minimize complexity?

- Does each loop perform one and only one function?

- Is nesting minimized?

- Have variable expressions been simplified by using additional Boolean variables, Boolean functions and decision tables?

Layout

- Does the program's layout show its logical structure?

- Are blank lines used to indicate logically distinct segments of code?

- Are long lines broken in suitable places so that they can be read easily on-screen and in hard copy?

Design

- Is the code straightforward and does it avoid cleverness?

- Are implementation details within a routine or class hidden as much as possible from statements that use the routine or class?

- Is the program written in terms of the problem domain (e.g. finance) as much as possible rather than in terms of computer-science or programming language structures?

Documentation

- Does each module have a headline comment block that describes its overall purpose?

- Does each sub and function have a heading comment to describe its purpose?

- Are necessarily complex algorithms adequately described in comments?

- Are comments used to describe the purpose of all significant Public, Private and Local variables?

- Are all comments up to date with the program code?

INDEX